Understanding Religious Life

The Religious Life of Man Series
FREDERICK J. STRENG, SERIES EDITOR

Texts

Understanding Religious Life, Third Edition
 Frederick J. Streng

The House of Islam, Second Edition
 Kenneth Cragg

Japanese Religion: Unity and Diversity, Third Edition
 H. Byron Earhart

Chinese Religion: An Introduction, Third Edition
 Laurence G. Thompson

The Christian Religious Tradition
 Stephen Reynolds

The Buddhist Religion: A Historical Introduction, Third Edition
 Richard H. Robinson and Willard L. Johnson

The Way of Torah: An Introduction to Judaism, Third Edition
 Jacob Neusner

The Hindu Religious Tradition
 Thomas J. Hopkins

Native American Religions: An Introduction
 Sam D. Gill

Anthologies

The Chinese Way in Religion
 Laurence G. Thompson

Religion in the Japanese Experience: Sources and Interpretations
 H. Byron Earhart

The Buddhist Experience: Sources and Interpretations
 Stephan Beyer

The Life of Torah: Readings in the Jewish Religious Experience
 Jacob Neusner

Islam from Within: Anthology of a Religion
 Kenneth Cragg and R. Marston Speight

Native American Traditions: Sources and Interpretations
 Sam D. Gill

Understanding Religious Life
Third Edition

Frederick J. Streng
Southern Methodist University

Wadsworth Publishing Company
Belmont, California
A Division of Wadsworth, Inc.

For Elizabeth and Mark
who eventually will be confronted by some
of the issues suggested in these pages

Religion Editor: Sheryl Fullerton
Production Editors: Vicki Friedberg and Deborah M. Oren
Managing and Cover Designer: Andrew H. Ogus
Copy Editor: Elaine Linden
Illustrator: Philip Li
Technical and Cover Illustrator: Joan Carol

Printed in the United States of America

1 2 3 4 5 6 7 8 9 10 — 89 88 87 86 85

ISBN 0-534-03699-6

Library of Congress Cataloging in Publication Data

Streng, Frederick J.
    Understanding religious life.

    (The Religious life of man series)
    Includes bibliographical references and index.
    1. Religion.   I. Title.   II. Series.
BL48.S77   1985   200   84-7503

ISBN 0-534-03699-6

Contents

Foreword   ix
Preface   x

1   The Nature and Study of Religion   1
What Is Religion?   1
Why Study Religion?   9
How Can We Study Religion?   12
Summary   Selected Readings   15

PART ONE. Four Traditional Ways of Being Religious   20

2   Personal Apprehension of a Holy Presence   25
The Problematic in the Human Condition: Sin,
    Inherent Weakness, Separation from the Holy One   27
The Ultimate Reality: The Holy Presence   29
Means to Ultimate Transformation: A Personal
    Relationship with the Holy One   32
Personal Expression: The Life of Worship and Faith   35
Social Expression: Witness, the Holy Spirit, Visual
    Images   38
Summary   Selected Readings   40

3   Creation of Community Through Sacred Symbols   43
The Problematic in the Human Condition:
    Meaninglessness, Impurity, and Disorder   45
The Ultimate Reality: The Sacred Realm   46
Means to Ultimate Transformation: Conforming to
    Sacred Symbols   48
Personal Expression: Blessings, Joy, and Wisdom   55
Social Expression: Puberty Rites, Sacred People,
    Places, and Time   56
Summary   Selected Readings   59

4 Living in Harmony with Cosmic Law   63
  The Problematic in the Human Condition: Chaos
      Due to Selfishness   66
  Ultimate Reality: The Cosmic Law   67
  Means to Ultimate Transformation: Living in
      Harmony with Cosmic Law   73
  Personal Expression: Relationships and
      Self-Fulfillment   78
  Social Expression: Right Social Action, Tradition,
      Texts, and Teachers   80
  Summary   Selected Readings   82

5 Attaining Freedom Through Spiritual Discipline   84
  The Problematic in the Human Condition:
      Bondage to Things and Ideas   88
  Ultimate Reality: Unconditional Freedom in Pure
      Consciousness   90
  Means to Ultimate Transformation: Freedom
      Through Spiritual Discipline   92
  Personal Expression: Union, Illumination, and
      Freedom   97
  Social Expression: The Art of Spontaneous Living   99
  Summary   Selected Readings   101

**PART TWO. Modes Of Human Awareness Used to
Express Religious Meaning**   104

**6 The Religious Significance of Fulfilling
Human Relationships**   109
  Human Relationships Within Traditional Religion   111
  Fulfilling Human Relationships as a Means to
      Ultimate Transformation   114
  Summary   Selected Readings   121

7 The Religious Significance of Social Responsibility   124
  Ethics as a Mode of Becoming Human   125
  Ethics as an Implementation of Divine Will   127
  Ethics as a Reflection of the Natural Good   130
  Social-Political Revolution as a Means to Ultimate
      Transformation   132
  Summary   Selected Readings   138

8 The Power of Rationality   141
  The Power of Defining Experience with Words   142
  Reason in Traditional Religious Thought   145

Reason as a Means to Ultimate Transformation 149
Personal Expression: Intellectual Exercise 154
Social Expression: Education 155
Summary   Selected Readings 155

9   The Power of Artistic Creativity 159
The Religious Importance of Art 159
Liturgical Art as Visual Theology 160
Music as Benediction 164
Art as a Means to Ultimate Transformation 166
Summary   Selected Readings 170

10   The Religious Response to Physical Existence 174
Cosmologies at Work in the World 174
The World as God's Creation and Time as Revelation of
   God's Purpose 176
The World as the Eternal Rhythm of Primal Energy 177
The Everyday World and the Reality Beyond 178
The Power of Cosmologies 180
Science and Technology as a Means to Ultimate
   Transformation 182
Summary   Selected Readings 186

**PART THREE. Approaches to an Objective Study
of Religion** 190

11   The Origins of Religious Life 193
Religion as a Product of Faulty Thinking 195
Religion as a Product of Awe 197
Religion as a Product of Social Identity 198
Religion as a Product of Primitive Mentality 198
The Relation of Religion to Magic 199
Religion as an Expression of High Being 200
The Coexistence of Multiple Religious Forms:
   Expressions of a Symbolic World 201
The Archaeological Record 202
Can the First Religious Expression Be Found? 202
Summary   Selected Readings 203

12   Psychological and Social Functions of Religion 207
Religion as the Subject of Psychology 208
Religion as the Subject of Sociology 213
Religion as the Subject of Cultural Anthropology 216
Summary   Selected Readings 218

13 The Comparative Study of Religion   222
    The Historical Method   223
    The Phenomenological Method   226
    The Relation of Religiousness to Cultural Situations   229
    Summary   Selected Readings   232

14 Understanding Through Interreligious Dialogue   235
    The Process of Dialogue   236
    Dialogue as Reconciliation of Religious Plurality
        and Ultimate Reality   237
    Dialogue as a Discovery of Personal Values   244
    Dialogue as a Way of Making Choices and
        Resolving Conflict   245
    Summary   Selected Readings   247

15 Consequences of Understanding Religious Life   250
    The Significance of Religious Pluralism   251
    The Relevance of Contemporary Religious Processes   254
    Subjectivity and Objectivity in Religious
        Commitment   256
    Three Approaches to Understanding Religion   257
    Can the Alternative Approaches Be Reconciled?   263
    Selected Readings   263

Notes   266

Index   274

Foreword

THE RELIGIOUS LIFE OF MAN series is intended as an introduction to a large, complex field of inquiry—religious experience. It seeks to present the depth and richness of religious concepts, forms of worship, spiritual practices, and social institutions found in the major religious traditions throughout the world.

As a specialist in the languages and cultures in which a religion is found, each author is able to illuminate the meanings of a religious perspective and practice as other human beings have experienced it. To communicate this meaning to readers who have had no special training in these cultures and religions, the authors have attempted to provide clear, nontechnical descriptions and interpretations of religious life.

Different approaches have been used, depending upon the nature of the religious data; some religious expressions, for instance, lend themselves to developmental, others to topical studies. The lack of a single interpretation may itself be instructive, for the experiences and practices regarded as religious in one culture may not be as important in another.

THE RELIGIOUS LIFE OF MAN series is concerned with, on the one hand, the variety of religious expressions found in different traditions and, on the other, similarities in the structures of religious life. The various forms are interpreted in terms of their cultural context and historical continuity, demonstrating both the diverse expressions and commonalities of religious traditions. Besides individual volumes on different religions, the series offers a core book on the study of religious meaning, which describes several modes and structures of religious awareness and examines different study approaches. In addition, each book presents a list of materials for further reading, including translations of religious texts and detailed examinations of specific topics.

During a decade of use the series has experienced a wide readership. A continuing effort has been made to update the scholarship, simplify the organization of material, and clarify concepts through the publication of revised editions. The authors have been gratified with the response to their efforts to introduce people to various forms of religious life. We hope readers will also find these volumes "introductory" in the most significant sense: an introduction to a new perspective for understanding themselves and others.

Frederick J. Streng
Series Editor

Preface

UNDERSTANDING RELIGIOUS LIFE, THIRD EDITION, like the first and second editions, is intended for a first course in religion—for students with no background or experience in the subject. It continues the basic approach of the earlier editions in helping students to understand and examine the differences and similarities of religious life. This approach interprets past and present religious experience as a dynamic process of ultimate transformation, that is, it focuses on the power of religious feelings, ideas, and behavior to evoke people's deepest sensitivities and highest values.

This volume in THE RELIGIOUS LIFE OF MAN series seeks to provide an interpretive framework in which the significance and purpose of religious life as understood by its advocates can be put in a global context without oversimplifying different religious claims or reducing them all to a single religious content. The result is a phenomenological typology that can be a useful framework for locating and interpreting basic religious questions and answers. It also provides an orientation in which readers can raise personal religious questions for themselves.

The third edition of UNDERSTANDING RELIGIOUS LIFE differs from the first and second in that it simplifies the basic material in those earlier versions. The three parts have been reorganized so that the chapters on traditional ways of being religious (which were previously Part Two) and nontraditional expressions of religious meaning (formerly Part Three) precede the discussion of methods for understanding religious life. Basic ideas throughout the book have been elaborated, and the organization of all the chapters has been simplified. More examples have been given, and charts or diagrams have been added to make key concepts and explanations clearer and more accessible for students.

The third edition also includes in Part Three, on methods for the study of religion, a new chapter (Chapter 14) on religious dialogue, which has become prominent during the last decade. In this chapter we will explore another approach for solving the difficult problem concerning the relation of subjective and objective elements in understanding religious life. We will cover not only the exchange of experiences and ideas between members of different religious communities, but also the discussion of world problems by philosophers, scientists, and jurists who do not claim traditional religious affiliation, as well as reflect on the significance of having many ultimate claims for personal religious commitment.

Since all comparative analyses, including typologies, require abstractions from concrete phenomena, they expose the conceptual lenses of the investigator as well as the content of whatever is being investigated. At best, comparative studies of religion draw attention to significant aspects of human experience without gross distortion of the purpose, procedures, and assumptions of religious participants. Any cross-cultural comparison requires the translation of the particular terms used by participants into general terms. Such terms refer to concrete expressions which have important similarities, but also some differences. The general term *religion* itself—as well as the phrase *means to ultimate transformation*—carries implied and designated meanings that sometimes help and sometimes hinder understanding. Whatever general terms one uses, they need continually to be checked and redefined by concrete religious expressions. The other volumes in this series provide basic information. If the interpretive concepts used in this book serve to open readers' perceptions to the significance, similarities, and differences of the wide variety of religious life, they will have fulfilled their purpose.

I want to express my thanks publicly to the students and teachers who have found earlier editions of this book useful and who have discussed with me the problems as well as the pedagogical potential in the approach. I would particularly like to thank the following reviewers for their valuable suggestions: James Breckenridge, Baylor University; Spencer Lavan, Tufts University; Richard B. Pilgrim, Syracuse University; Mary L. Schneider, Michigan State University; and Gerald L. Smith, University of the South.

I also want to thank Elaine Linden, diligent and insightful copy editor; Vicki Friedberg and Debbie Oren, production editors; and Sheryl Fullerton, religion editor. I am indebted to Sally Snow and Terry Smith for their help in typing the manuscript. To Jane Albritton especially, I extend my gratitude for her contribution to the rewriting of this edition, in particular Parts Two and Three, and for her ideas in preparing the preliminary forms of the various figures found throughout the book.

Frederick J. Streng

"My third theory," the bishop went on hurriedly . . . "is this: there is some Eternity even in our ephemeral lives, only it is very difficult for us to discover it alone. Our daily cares lead us astray. A few people only, the flower of humanity, manage to live an eternity even in their transitory lives on his earth. Since all the others would therefore be lost, God had mercy on them and sent them religion—thus the crowd is able to live in eternity, too."

—From Nikos Kazantzakis, *Zorba the Greek*

CHAPTER 1

The Nature and Study of Religion

The terms *religion, religious, religious studies,* and *religious experience* are all familiar to us, and most people have general definitions for each of them. Sometimes these terms seem to overlap so that it is hard to distinguish the meaning of one from the meaning of another. However, many people today find significant differences between them. Some feel that what is generally called religion is not really a religious experience. Others feel that what they do with their sense of religious commitment does not fit into an accepted definition of a religion. Still others who reflect on religious life suggest that studying religion should be distinguished from a religious activity, or that religious studies go beyond the study of religious traditions.

Where do these various ideas come from, and what are we to make of their differences? In part, the variety is caused by the fact that different people have diverse yet sometimes overlapping notions of *religion, a religion, religious,* and *religious studies.* Furthermore, people often have different interpretations of what it means to understand religious life. Faced with such a variety of religious understandings, the student of religion may feel lost in a mass of conflicting definitions and attitudes. Like so much of human life, religion is an interaction of subjective and objective experiences. But, whereas there may be large differences among the answers to religious questions, there are important similarities in the questions themselves.

To clarify some basic concerns in the study of religion, we respond in this first chapter to three questions that are often asked: What is religion? Why study religion? How can we study religion?

WHAT IS RELIGION?

Any individual may sit down and, upon reasonable reflection, write his or her own definition of religion. Although the definitions will vary from person to person, they are likely to vary along predictable lines: according to one's deepest personal feelings, according to one's culture, and according to one's highest values in life.

Scholars who study religion are likely to arrive at their definitions of religion in much the same way that other people do. They look at religion as it affects individuals, as it operates in a culture, and as it expresses the highest life values. And, like others, scholars come to different conclusions. So, how is it possible to know what religion really means if scholarly definitions can vary as much as those of ordinary people? This chapter does not attempt to formulate a final definition of religion. What it does is offer a working definition that will serve as the basis for the discussion in the rest of the book. We begin with a working definition of *religion*, or *religious life*, and then turn to a discussion of its three dimensions: personal, cultural, and ultimate.

A Working Definition of Religion

The definition of religion in this book focuses on the role of various *processes of change* through which people bring into their lives what they consider life's highest values. In this analysis of religious life, our formal definition is as follows: Religion is a *means to ultimate transformation*. What does "ultimate transformation" mean? An ultimate transformation is a fundamental change from being caught up in the troubles of common existence (sin, ignorance) to living in such a way that one can cope at the deepest level with those troubles. That capacity for living allows one to experience the most authentic or deepest reality—the ultimate. Although the ultimate reality is defined differently in various religious traditions, the adherents of those traditions define their lives in terms of that ultimate context and try to live in such a way that deficiencies are transformed into fulfillment.

Our definition of religion incorporates two basic elements: ultimacy and effective power. In the context of religious awareness, ultimacy means the most comprehensive resource and deepest necessity of which a person can be aware. It is one's sense of superlative value that motivates and structures one's life. A common assumption of religious people is that the fullest life calls on the highest sensitivities to be put into the service of the most comprehensive reality, such as God's will, the Buddha-nature, or the Tao. A religious awareness incites one to act from a view of life that transcends cultural habits or mere short-term gain. When people are sensitive to living in the ultimate context of existence, they seek the deepest comprehension of life. Then they feel compelled to try to live in the framework of that awareness.

Religion expresses its *effective power* in a variety of ways. For example, this power may involve expressing a deep feeling, gaining self-identity through participation in a sacred rite, performing an ethical act that confirms a cosmic order or that expresses a divine will, or experiencing a transcendent state of consciousness. In all these cases, the believer experiences and expresses ultimate reality as a power that transforms him or her to the core. Religious participants realize that their very being is grounded in this ultimate resource for their lives. In realizing the nature of his or her being, a person becomes spiritually whole.

Religion is a personal and social experience of an ultimate, dynamic process. The process of transformation may be activated by symbols, social relationships, feelings, and states of consciousness. For people participating in the transforming process, these symbols or states of consciousness are regarded not simply as forms of biological needs or social pressure but expressions of an ultimate dimension of existence. When the sense of living in an ultimate dimension motivates human self-awareness, it starts a total process in which a person or a community extends and grows beyond former limitations.

The idea of religion as effective power, then, stresses the recognition by religious adherents that their symbols, techniques, and social expressions are not wishes, hopes, or fantasies; rather, these are practical means of transforming life from unreality to reality, from inauthentic existence to authentic existence. Believers may feel that such ultimate power comes from outside human existence or from within it. In either case, the believer is not destroyed by the problems and frustrations of daily existence; for a person participating in a religious process of transformation senses a lifesaving and freeing reality that cures life's troubles. The final justification for the power of transformation is not an appeal to a particular institution or cultural identity; nor is it a specific practice or discipline, as such. Rather, the validation is found in its total experience-affirming character. Anywhere and in any circumstance, whether for a family person or a solitary recluse, the entire surroundings confirm and are confirmed by the power of what is felt to be ultimate reality.

In summary, religion as we discuss it in this book is a process whereby people reach beyond themselves to connect with the true and ultimate reality that will save them from the destructive forces of everyday existence. These processes of religion have the power to change lives at the deepest level of being. If we portray the religious process graphically, it looks like figure 1. Here we see that the ultimate reality stands in opposition to the pervading troubles of common existence. Through various means, which we discuss in the course of this book, an individual can participate in, or with, the ultimate reality, become free of life's troubles, and find both social and personal ways to express the experience of the ultimate. Each chapter in Parts One and Two offers variations on this theme. The introduction to Part One explains further the elements of the process of ultimate transformation.

The Personal Dimension

For the individual, the process of interpreting religious life involves internal reactions, decisions, and meaning. For example, someone might ask: How should I respond to the religious claims and practices of my neighbors? Does my religion pertain only to special (sacred) activities like going to the synagogue or church, bowing before the image of the Buddha, or praying in the direction of Mecca? Can my neighbor's passion for football or my friend's concern to provide justice for all be called "religious"? Does religion also have to do with the way I relate to other people, integrate new experiences with old, or generally feel and think about life? Should I pray to Jesus? Should I chant "Hare Krishna"? Should I reserve certain times each day for

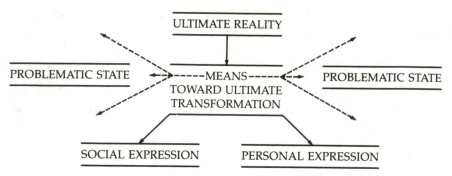

FIGURE 1.   *Process of Ultimate Transformation*

solitary meditation? In a large measure, the way of interpreting religious life depends on an individual's experience with what he or she labels religion.

When people participate in a particular means to ultimate transformation, they partially express the transforming power in highly personal and emotionally toned statements. In each of the types of ultimate transformation that are discussed in Parts One and Two, we note such typical personal expressions of inner attitudes, feelings, sensitivities, and convictions. They often reflect one's deepest awareness that religious experience is not easily expressed in objective terms.

Deeply personal expression makes many people uneasy. They feel perhaps a certain anxiety or irritation when confronted by someone whose religious beliefs differ from their own. Some people feel that, because of the emotional character of religious life, there can be no fruitful discussion about the most significant aspects of a personal commitment. One might ask, for example: Can two deeply committed adherents from different traditions, say, a Southern Baptist and an American devotee of Krishna Consciousness, reach a consensus? Or do they simply try to convert one another? Could an exchange of personal experiences of divine presence lead both individuals to a deepened awareness? Are all deeply felt experiences of the same value? Can two people with different kinds of religious awareness even perceive the ultimate quality within each other's religious affirmation? These differing personal perspectives and commitments are an important aspect of a general notion of religion, however difficult they make a deeper understanding of other devotees' views.

A person who tries to understand the personal character of someone else's religious life is immediately involved in a dilemma, for the observer and the believer rarely perceive and evaluate the believer's religious commitment in the same way. The devotee lives within a religious symbol system and social structure, and the resulting beliefs and moral decisions confirm and reinforce personal experiences of ultimate (divine or most enhancing) reality. This pattern of meaning not only explains for the devotee such extraordinary events as birth and death and prescribes behavior toward friends and enemies but it also suggests how to overcome suffering and tragedy and how to become complete, whole, and spiritually free. That reality, however, is considered to be, at best, a *possible* (not a necessary) value by the observer; thus, it often does not have the convincing power for the observer that it does for the believer.

Those who can find value only in their own patterns of meaning are sometimes insensitive to the deepest commitments of others. Religious piety itself is the rationalization that some devotees use for failing to investigate different interpretations of scriptures or ethical and philosophical claims within their own tradition—to say nothing of exploring the meaning of other traditions. Those who wish to explore the personal character of others' religious lives must be open to new possibilities. They must also become aware of their own patterns of experience if they are to avoid projecting their personal experiences on others.

A similar dilemma in awareness and understanding confronts the scholar who tries to interpret a variety of religious data. A scholar must not only try to feel what it is like to see the world from the standpoint of a devotee but must also try to put his or her observations into a wider—even a universal—interpretive scheme. In an attempt to avoid judgmental statements, the scholarly observer often uses abstract and impersonal language. He or she talks about what is observed and avoids proclaiming the validity of direct personal experiences or convictions. But the scholar is also a person who is tempted to ask: Can I learn anything new that will change my assumptions—for example, about the inner dynamics of religion? Should I allow the claims that I am studying to challenge my present convictions about the ability of religious life to probe the deepest aspects of life? Do the questions that I am asking in the name of objectivity reflect merely personal or cultural bias?

In summary, the personal character of religious life shows up in at least three ways: (1) It affects the life stance of the devotee as expressed in the statements about his or her attitudes, feelings, and sensitivities; (2) it plays a role in the devotee's attempt to learn about other people who have different deep commitments; and (3) it concerns a scholar (both as observer and devotee) who formulates questions about religion and tries to interpret it.

The Cultural Dimension

To the extent that religion is expressed in institutional and cultural forms, it can be understood as a social expression of particular hopes, problems, and models for living. Many religious people and scholars recognize that religion, like any other human expression, is conditioned by historical, social, economic, and political forces. They also realize that the social expression of religious life is a complementary and reciprocal force in conditioning personal religious experience. As we describe basic personal expressions of each type of ultimate transformation in Parts One and Two, we also describe some typical social expressions of each type of transformation. These include general ethical obligations, social educational processes, public preaching, and communal rituals. To grasp something of the power of social expressions, however, we should note that they are an aspect of the cultural dimension found in all human experience. The cultural dimension includes both (1) historical conditions, that is, the particular time and place in which people and communities exist, and (2) the general communal, organizational, and institutional character of human societies.

The cultural dimension gives a religious expression its particular historical and social form. Diverse cultures give religious life many forms. The combined experiences of an individual or of a community create a history and affect (or condition) the values, concepts, and models for religious self-awareness that are available in any given time and place. Thus, a person living in a Navaho community, in what is now the southwestern United States, during the sixteenth century C.E. (common era) would have a different cultural exposure than one living in first-century Rome; seventh-century Lo-yang, China; or second-century Benaras, India. Language, in these different cultural settings, has provided different options for expressing the ultimate reality as various spiritual-natural forces (sun, moon) of life, God, Tao, or Brahman. Moreover, religious expression has been affected by historical change. Many assumptions about life expectancy, production of food, and social relationships that were common in preliterate archaic societies were revised in classical traditional societies and have again changed in modern, technological societies.

In our analysis of different means to ultimate transformation, we do not try to show how one religious form developed historically into a new form. We do, however, describe some of the basic social expressions that each type of ultimate transformation takes to indicate their dynamic character as part of the transforming process in religious life.

Culture, then, is an expression of, and a conditioning force for, attitudes about religious life. On the one hand, such conditioning limits understanding, and on the other, it provides the learning processes that make it possible to go beyond that limited understanding. For example, those whose experience with religion has been strongly moralistic (Don't do this! Don't do that!) might regard religion as a restrictive force that limits their ability to make personal decisions for right and wrong. On the other hand, those who have been trained to follow a strict set of rules of behavior may find they have been given a sense of security that allows them to be daring in other areas, such as difficult missionary work.

Another prominent example of how a culture may affect religious views is the widely held assumption that religion is a special institutional activity. A religious person is thus expected to be a member of a special organization and of only one religious institution at a time. For these religious people, revelation is expressed in a sacred book (or collection of writings), which is protected from profanity by special authorities, such as priests or theologians, and preserved by a community of like-minded people. This perspective has led many to divide the world into sacred and secular spheres and has been the basis for much tension in the Western world since the 1700s. Many people who believe that science and the use of reason are valid techniques for self-understanding place themselves in the secular—and non-religious—category. From the standpoint of science, traditional religion may be, at best, only one authoritative cultural element that contributes to self-awareness, and at worst, a superstition that is no longer useful as a controlling social authority. Here we can see how a major cultural change (such as the one caused by advanced technology) can lead to changes in religious attitudes. Part Two of this book examines various modes of human awareness and activity—such as psychotherapy, art, social revolution, and technology—that are often seen as secular but that function for some people as their means to ultimate transformation.

Today, those living in a modern society can decide whether to participate in the religious forms of their culture. They have greater possibilities open to them for the expression of ultimate values. Likewise, interpreters of religion today are redefining religion in order to ask new questions about its nature and to discover new forms that express the expansive character of people's ultimate hope, trust, and love.

In summary, the cultural dimension of religious life is important because it structures religious experience along different communal, linguistic, and economic lines; more particularly, it organizes the manner in which a particular person and community express their ultimate values. A powerful example of cultural forces is the common assumption among Western peoples that at the core of religion is sacred reality, which is radically different from profane existence. This assumption has contributed to the tension between religious claims of truth and the claims of science.

The Ultimate Dimension

The ultimate dimension is what distinguishes religious expression from nonreligious personal and cultural expression. To understand this distinction, consider the following analogy. There are various answers to the question: Why read this book? One response, "It is assigned reading for a class," would answer the question within the context of an educational system, with a value placed on an academic degree. Another response, "I am curious to see how someone in the last two decades of the twentieth century makes sense out of the world characterized by religious pluralism," would answer in the context of Western intellectual history. A third reply, "I am trying to understand how to go about learning the secret of living fully," would raise a religious or ultimate question. A religious answer relates to the most profound meaning of one's existence and may be found inside or outside the traditional religious life. This kind of answer responds to the question of whether ultimate truth can even be expressed or ultimate reality known through words, reflections, and symbolic images.

The ultimate dimension is the sensitivity for that to which one gives one's loyalty as the true character of life. At the deepest level of human experience, religious sensitivities and behavior express more than the subjective and cultural forms we discussed previously. Ideally, religious life expresses a commitment to the reality or value that an individual or group recognizes as the source of happiness and the fullest possible expression of reality. This ultimate dimension is the limit that confronts human sensitivity and the limitless power that makes it possible to rise above a former limitation. As the all-filling or pervading character of life, the ultimate reality is recognized by adherents as existing prior to any particular sensitivity or knowledge of it, while, at the same time, it is the fullest possible expression of joy, goodness, balance, or power. In short, it is what is most fully real. The ultimate dimension differs from both the personal and cultural dimensions, though it is expressed through them.

One practical expression of the ultimate dimension is its force in establishing values, including the ultimate value or overarching family of values according to which people live. The impact of an evaluating process is seen in the common experience of deciding what is real and what is significant. Not everything people experience is equally real. For example, holding a silver dollar in your hand is not the same as remembering that you held one yesterday, dreaming that you hold one, or mistaking a piece of aluminum foil on the ground for a silver dollar. Likewise, there are important differences in the ways people evaluate similar experiences or the values they place on objects like food, clothing, status symbols, and art. Everyone's personal history has moments that are more "real" than others—moments that define a person, such as a birthday party, a first date, graduation, or some unusual state of consciousness. Thus, individuals make judgments consciously or unconsciously about their experiences, forming them into patterns that together make up existence. The fact that human beings can and must make choices is both exciting and troublesome. There is something awesome about the power to choose; for people's choices—saying "yes" to some things and "no" to others—shape their character and give them a sense of direction. The world provides no automatic sense of identity; each individual must forge his or her own within the context of a particular society. Nor are the reasons for individual behavior self-evident. Life is filled with confusion, decision, and possibility.

Those who confidently live according to their deepest sense of ultimate reality experience themselves to be free from confusion and are able to make decisions or choose among possibilities with assurance. A person who lives in an ultimate frame of reference claims the power and insight to distinguish what is real or true from what is secondary, derivative, or even false. This insight, which has been called "revelation" or "wisdom," opens new horizons for self-realization. As individuals realize who they really are, they are able to grow beyond both habits and fantasies. Living in an ultimate context not only relieves the destructive tension, limitations, and biases that prevent joyful living but also transforms ordinary human existence and gives it new purpose.

We can also consider the ultimate context by looking at the kinds of questions that may lead a person to religious or ultimate truth. To express a religious concern is to be conscious of the question: How am I to be real— rather than fake or phony or less than what I could be? In general, to have a sense that one is real means to know what is true and right, to translate this knowledge into aims (or decisions for action), and then to have the means to accomplish these aims. From the standpoint of "conditionedness"—living within the limitations of time and place—the ultimate reality is what appears as the ideal. Thus, questions about the nature of freedom or a right action in a particular situation are vital questions in the effort to make sense out of existence. Some practical ultimate questions might be: How can I experience ultimate happiness when I can't even do simple things that others seem to do easily? How do I know when I am living in truth and not in illusion? Is there any way to test the assertions of others who claim to know what life is all about? When does my personal experience give a true picture of reality? If I admit that I can make a single mistake in judging life, how do I know that the "correction" is not also a mistake? Maybe my experience is only a facade; perhaps there is something greater or more profound that is escaping my view? With such questions, people "lift off" from everyday life into the less familiar atmosphere of religious awareness. The ultimate dimension of religious expression, then, is the reality that emerges or appears when a person lives within an extraordinarily deep sensitivity to life (ultimacy) and possesses a profound strategy for action (effective power).

Summary: Personal, Cultural, and Ultimate Contexts

Religious life involves a personal subjective element, takes specific cultural forms (for example, in ideas, art, and institutions) and expresses an ultimate, supreme, or comprehensive reality. The interaction of these three dimensions of religious phenomena makes the study of religious life a complex effort, because it requires the interpretation of a variety of *particular* cultural expressions in relation to a *general* notion of ultimate value. This effort is necessary whenever investigators of religion seek to understand those aspects of religious meaning and intention that include, but go beyond, the functions of social and physical existence.

WHY STUDY RELIGION?

The notions with which people begin their investigation of religion become a part of their interpretation of religious life. Some people are merely curious to explore some idea or experience that seems different from their own. Based on a personal religious commitment, others study unfamiliar religious expressions to find their weaknesses. In both cases, the notion of religion is often a direct extension of a person's cultural experience. A Western person usually identifies religion with beliefs about God, tries to find the sacred writings, or scriptures, of a community, and looks for sacred rituals and symbols. Although beliefs, scriptures, rituals, and symbols are indeed important elements in some religious traditions, they need not be the most important aspects of all religious life. At least, students of religion will find it useful to examine whether all people regard them as equally important.

To Gain Information

The first object of studying religion, then, is to gain some specific information about other people's religious activities and about the variety found in one's own religious-cultural tradition. The data for a cross-cultural study of religion are in the acts, feelings, and attitudes about the ultimate meaning of life that are recorded in painting, poetry, social-economic systems, holidays, philosophy, and architecture throughout the world. Therefore, to understand religious life means to comprehend the feelings, activities, ideas, and social forms of people as they express the ultimate dimension of their lives.

To Examine Religion in Its Cultural Context

A second reason for studying religion is to examine its relation to other cultural forms. Many scholars analyze the various parts of religious beliefs, institutions, and ethical expressions in the hope of finding answers to questions about cultural life. Do certain beliefs lead to economically discriminatory practices, for example, or does a doctrine about nature promote or hinder the development of technology? Other scholars may want to investigate the social, psychological, political, economic, or linguistic factors of particular religious forms. Thus, a historian might ask about the impact of political forces on the development of the Christian church in the third century C.E., or a sociologist might study the relationship between family life and religious affiliation in post-World War II Japan. Such scholars examine historical changes in religious claims or institutional forms to identify constant elements, differences in content or function, and repeated patterns of change.

To Achieve a Universal Perspective

A third reason for studying religion is to place one's own religious life within a universal perspective. A study of religious experience throughout history offers insights into the temper of one's age, which is all too often taken for granted as the only possible, or even the best, form of existence. Information about religious life in other times and societies may stimulate sensitivities to hidden or latent aspects of one's religious heritage. It may also provoke one to reinterpret some accepted doctrine or symbol in a more comprehensive and revitalized way. To understand religious life, then, means to go beyond acquiring bits of information; it means acquiring the skills and sensitivities that can organize concrete data into a larger understanding of humanity. A knowledge of the history and culture of other traditions, as well as one's own, provides an understanding of oneself in relation to others that is superior to an interpretation of life based primarily on a narrow, timebound perspective or on mere wishes and hopes.

To Gain a New Religious Self-Awareness

Finally, a fourth reason for studying religion is to gain a new awareness of oneself as a religious person. Although not every academic study of religion is intended to transform the researcher, many investigators indicate that learning about different religious options and gaining a cross-cultural perspective of humanity can lead to a new self-understanding. To listen with an open mind to another means to engage in a meaningful dialogue with another and with the person's "otherness," thereby helping to define one's own self-awareness. In considering the religious self-awareness of other people, the investigator must reflect on his or her own assumptions about humanity, existence, and the nature of truth. Unless people are conscious of the attitudes they take for granted—especially in regard to religious transformation—they are unknowingly bound by them.

The Effects of Religious Dialogue

A dialogue with another person about ultimate values has all the possibilities and dangers that are a part of any real communication. It can extend and deepen a person's religious sensitivities, helping him or her to become more fully human and more aware of a wider range of possibilities for realizing the meaning of human life. On the other hand, learning about another value system may produce great discomfort by causing a person to judge past attitudes and ideas as irrelevant and to develop a new orientation toward what it means to be human. Understanding another orientation makes it possible to compare and eventually to integrate or decide between two or more value orientations. A person may be forced to ask: Which elements in my orientation are so basic to my being that to lose them means spiritual death? A real encounter with another life orientation may make a person judge that, though the death of a particular orientation may be painful, it is good to grow beyond it. One meaning orientation may have to disintegrate so that a new one can emerge.

These processes of change—maturing, death, and rebirth—are not separate segments of a step-by-step process. The thrust toward maturity is simultaneous with release from the old and building of the new. In discovering the variety of possibilities for becoming human, people can discover and rediscover who they are. Unconscious urges, as well as conscious images of life, influence one's basic decisions every day. What a person does in relation to other people either individually (for example, "my mother") or collectively ("the Chinese") depends on what he or she imagines these people are like. Images are derived in part from personal and intellectual experiences. To engage another person fully means, in part, to achieve release from some limitations by which one previously defined existence. Such release means that individuals are more free because they are more self-conscious and can choose from a wider range of possibilities. In this way, some students of religion seek to become more fully human by transcending their individual culturally bound selves.

In summary, although there may be others, four reasons for studying religion are addressed in this book. These are as follows: (1) to gain some specific information about other people's religious activities and about the variety found in one's own religious-cultural tradition; (2) to examine the relation of religion to other cultural forms; (3) to place one's own religious life within a universal perspective; and (4) to gain a new awareness of oneself as a religious person. A student of religious life should also recognize that real understanding of different religious positions can lead to the expansion of one's intellectual, emotional, and social horizons.

HOW CAN WE STUDY RELIGION?

Religion is not merely some external thing to be found and then analyzed. There is nothing that is purely religious as such. On the other hand, anything may serve as a source of religious information for the person who knows how to use the evidence. To recognize what is religious, a person must ask about the religious meaning of some human expression. Of course, some human expressions, such as prayers, religious rituals, or mystical experiences, have been used to expose the ultimate dimension of life more often than others, such as economic theories or a parts description of an electrical appliance. However, prayers and rituals may be interpreted purely from a psychological or a sociological perspective, which does not expose their religious significance. At the same time, economic theories or mechanical drawings can express the creative spirit in life. The evidence gives answers only when the questions proper to religious meaning are asked, and many questions that would reveal the meaning of religion for contemporary people have not yet been asked.

So, how are we to approach religion—that transforming power in the recesses of consciousness that draws people beyond what they can measure with their senses? What methods can be used to describe and display the nature and forms of ultimate value and meaning?

Objective Data and Subjective Experience

The central problem in understanding religious phenomena is how to balance the competing claims of objective data and subjective awareness. Whereas social scientists attempt to collect facts from observation (empirical data) and historians seek to base their interpretations on documents, artifacts, or other observable data, the worshipper or mystic maintains that an objective observer can only scrape the outer surface of human religious expression. Similarly, the more the psychologists speak of the "psyche" or the "unconscious," the more they are regarded as moving out of the scientific realm. The philosopher and the theologian are also aware that certain personal attitudes influence their understanding and limit their interpretations. The concepts we use and the self-imposed limitations of empirical methods are the barriers, as well as the vehicles, for understanding. Since we cannot stand outside this conditioned situation, the best we can do is to become self-conscious about our personal and cultural presuppositions.

Limitations of the Believer's and the Scientist's Assumptions. Let us first consider the question of personal religious belief. Can a Christian really understand a Buddhist? Some people hold that religions are closed systems of dogma, which a person either accepts or rejects. But there is a difference between "understanding" and "believing"; a person can understand another religious form without believing it and thus entering it. "To understand" means to appreciate how it is possible for others to believe what they do, given the presuppositions they hold. "To believe" means to accept certain presuppositions about life and to live according to them. To understand a religious claim or act calls for the same sort of effort necessary to understand any other human claim or act. It may not be easy to listen to another person explain a religious view different from one's own. Understanding requires a conscious attempt to identify with the thought patterns and emotional tone of another person's convictions. Because it is often more difficult to identify with the emotional tone than with the thought patterns, two religious people of different faiths may be able to communicate better with each other than with a person who has not grown up in a religious tradition. The attempt to empathize, however, is filled with problems. The danger of projecting one's own symbol system or type of religious awareness onto the beliefs and sensitivities of the other person is always present.

In seeking to avoid a sectarian (limited) or a dogmatic interpretation of religion, we must also beware of reducing human events to mechanical changes or universal principles. This danger arises with any assumption that one single, universal, scientific method can be applied in the same way to every phenomenon. Different objects of study require varying kinds of analysis, because they have different basic characteristics or qualities. For example, both human beings and stones have physical properties, but to reduce human beings to physical properties is to miss a large part of what it means to be human. Similarly, historical events and philosophical principles have a different relevance for human beings. The human past, which is the object of historical study, is different from both laws of physics and rational deduction. Knowledge of the meaning of human life, especially as it is expressed in ultimate hopes and fears, desires, and wisdom, is often indirect and inferred. Such knowledge is always founded on an interpretation.

Understanding That Includes Empathy, Integration, and Openness. The person who develops a sensitivity for the dimension of religious meaning will learn to think and feel—to empathize—with those people in the past and present whose intellectual exploration, artistic commitment, and social behavior reveal the ultimate dimension of life. The person who does not develop this sensitivity will never understand the hopes, frustrations, and perseverance of people who yearn for what is true.

Understanding requires one to examine specific, concrete data, such as ideas in literature and descriptions of rituals, social institutions, historical developments, lives of great personalities, and political and social conditions. But this examination does not involve merely memorizing unrelated facts. To understand means to integrate data within a context that does not give equal weight to every element in an experience but that provides the concepts and questions permitting one to understand the data in a certain way. The basic interpretive principle of this book is the identification of elements in processes of ultimate transformation.

Finally, understanding requires that one remain open to the development of further possibilities and resist the temptation to close one's mind to other value orientations. It means to examine seriously all aspects of the data, however unfamiliar some may be. It also means to rise above the conflict sometimes generated by the differences between religious belief and objective study. Understanding requires an awareness that the presuppositions of both positions are important for people who affirm them.

Religious Intention and Cultural Forms

Only rarely in recorded human experience has the religious dimension in a particular life been developed to a high point. Although many people are partially aware of ultimate truth in their lives, seldom does their awareness of religious reality become an example or model for future generations and a dramatic force in social awareness. Among the exceptional cases are the founders and leaders of institutionalized mass religions, such as Christianity, Buddhism, or Confucianism. The forms that these religions have taken furnish the clearest data for studying human experience that is self-consciously religious. However, many religious people do not identify the form of religions with the ultimate reality that the forms intend to convey. For them, religious experience and expression differ from, and go beyond, religion's physical, historical, cultural, or institutional elements.

The power of religion, say intensely involved religious advocates, is an awareness of what is true or real that transcends the institutional forms while being expressed through them. Thus, students of religion must be aware not only of the concrete data, the forms of religious expression, but also of the *intention* of these forms, which is to point beyond themselves. The religious intention of a Buddhist monk in practicing meditation is to be free from the self-imposed attachments to the ego and objects of desire; it is not just to have an unusual experience or a feeling of peace, which also takes place. Or the religious intention of the Christian participating in the Eucharist is to allow symbolically the infusion of the spiritual body of Christ—a sacred reality—into one's life; it is not just the formation of a group of like-minded people nor the reinforcement of social values, though it is this too.

A person who is aware that religion is not simply an idea, ritual, or a social form recognizes religion as a force that establishes a person's very being and opens consciousness to insight. This person will see that such a one lives with a deepened awareness in which an enriched dimension of living gives strength of character, courage, insight, and serenity. This dimension of human experience is the power people wrestle with when they are self-consciously religious. The conceptual formulations, ethical practices, and social institutions that are generally labeled religious data are not in themselves the sum of religious reality. However, the historical forms and patterns are regarded as crucial by those who, transformed by the power embodied in them, thereby fulfill their life and purpose. These forms are therefore important in any consideration of religious experience that seeks to go beyond the personal.

So, religion encompasses both the power of transformation and the cultural forms that express and release this power—like the gold whose malleability gives it millions of forms or the electrical current that takes the forms of light, heat, and mechanical movement. To speak of the former without the latter is impossible; to speak of the latter without the former is to ignore the very mode of being, the ultimate quality, the depth perspective of religious life. These two aspects mean that religious life is not simply some petrified shape of past human experience, an interesting but irrelevant impression left in culture by prescientific society. Rather, religion is the ultimate transforming power derived from the most comprehensive sense of universal necessity and the deepest need to evaluate existence, which emerges in particular cultural forms.

Assumptions of Religious Understanding

This book examines some different ways in which human beings have answered religious questions but does not judge the rightness or wrongness of the answers. The effort to study religion objectively follows a century-long tradition of scholarship dedicated to examining the nature, forms, and meaning of religious life. The goal of an objective study of religion is quite different from the goal of religious practice or belief. The methods used in seeking to understand the meaning of religious symbols and institutions are comparable to those used in any other academic study of human life.

Any attempt to understand human expression starts from an assumption about what constitutes human life. The basic assumption here is that people are symbolizing, feeling, and reflecting makers of things. We express ourselves in, and are limited by, emotions, behavior, and patterns of thought. This assumption has two direct implications.

First, the perceptions of all interpreters are limited by the assumptions and terms of their analysis. It is entirely possible that the analyst's perceptions may be inappropriate to another person's concerns and sensitivities. Likewise, investigators of religion must consider whether their ideas correspond to the actual dynamics and internal characteristics of religious life. The questions asked about religion determine, in part, the answers received.

A second implication, which balances the limitations of the first, is that every human expression tells something about humanity. The symbols and social patterns we use to express ourselves are part of the reality we find. Our sensitivity to the limitations of every analysis should not lead to the conclusion that cultural forms are superficial expressions of some untouched inner reality. Rather, they are part of the dynamics, the changing and living character, of human self-awareness. Thus, the ultimate symbols, ethical actions, transcendental experiences, and perfection of insight examined in this study are not mere exterior forms behind which there is a more "real" religious reality. Instead, concrete religious expressions are forces through which individuals know themselves, relate to other people, and leave impressions for posterity. The things people do and make, their laughter and tears, their feelings of ecstasy and depression—all are threads woven into the fabric of existence.

SUMMARY

Before beginning the study of the religious life in both its traditional and nontraditional forms, let us review the major assumptions and concerns of the discussion to follow. As you read the following chapters, try to keep these five points in mind.

First, the religious life is a complex *process* that includes at least three dimensions: personal, cultural, and ultimate. Any person attempting to understand and interpret religious experiences is also participating in them as a human being. Thus, it is important to become self-conscious about one's assumptions and attitudes about religion.

Second, religion is defined in this book as a means to ultimate transformation. This definition focuses on the dynamic process of change in religious life: a change from a disharmonious, illusory, evil, or destructive state of existence to ultimate harmony, enlightenment, purity, or creative power.

Third, the reasons for studying religion are varied and depend on the investigator's attitude and definition of religion. One reason is to collect data on religious life in order to explain changes that occur over time and to account for variations in form. Another is to understand an individual's particular religious expression through a transcultural perspective. This is a way to understand comparable and distinctive elements within diverse cultural forms. A third is to examine the relation of religion to other cultural forms. Finally, a purpose not accepted by all students of religion, but which is affirmed in this book, is to develop a new self-awareness whereby the investigator continually examines his or her ultimate stance. Different religious dynamics permit people to rediscover latent resources for meaning, to probe their basic presuppositions and sensitivities of ultimate value, and to gain perspective on the options for religious commitment in a time of rapid social change.

The general purpose, then, of understanding religious life is neither to judge whether one or another religious answer is right or wrong nor to convince the reader of the ultimate truth of any one religious expression. Rather, it is to point out various possibilities for religious living, each of which is recognized by its adherents as having the power to transform a person ultimately.

Fourth, the differences among religious expressions are as important as the similarities. The traditional religious data examined in Part One are organized under headings that express different types of religious processes. The differences among these processes help account for the sometimes basically different orientations of religious life within any one tradition or between different historical traditions. Part Two of this book describes how processes of human awareness can also be used as nontraditional means to ultimate transformation.

Fifth, some basic methodological assumptions contribute to the analysis in this book. One is that a wide range of objective data is necessary for gaining a general view of religion. A complementary assumption is that empathy is required to understand the subjective aspects of other people's religious experiences and to describe accurately the objective factors of an ultimately transforming process—religion. Another methodological assumption is that all human beings are self-conscious, symbolizing, and value-forming beings who are, on the one hand, limited by their culture, and on the other hand, capable of using culture as a means to ultimate transformation. Thus, religious data express dynamic forces in the lives of human beings and reveal not only the historical-cultural conditioning of any human form but also the religious intention of the dynamic forces that make transformation possible.

SELECTED READINGS

Paperback editions in this and subsequent sections are marked with an asterisk.

*W. H. Capps, *Ways of Understanding Religion* (New York: Macmillan, 1972). This book of readings covering seven basic problem areas in the Western study of religion organizes the systematic understanding of religion in a fresh way.

*M. Eliade, *The Sacred and the Profane: The Nature of Religion* (New York: Harcourt, 1959). Focusing on myth, ritual, and symbolism, this well-known religious historian explores the nature of religion as the manifestation of a wholly different reality—the sacred.

J. Ellul, *The New Demons* (New York: Seabury Press, 1975). A French Reformed Church layman passionately argues for the religious—although often demonic—character of such contemporary secular expressions as politics and technology.

*M. Friedman, *The Human Way* (Chambersburg, PA: Anima Books, 1982). This book presents the study of religion as an interpersonal dialogue in which the touchstones of religious reality are exposed by the character of each participant.

*A. H. Maslow, *Toward a Psychology of Being*, 2nd ed. (Princeton, NJ: Van Nostrand, 1962). Basing his views on psychological inquiries, this famous psychologist calls for an understanding of the human awareness of being, which is traditionally called religious, is known in peak experiences, and leads to self-actualization.

H. Nakamura, *Ways of Thinking of Eastern Peoples: India-China-Tibet-Japan*, rev. ed. (Honolulu: East-West Center Press, 1964). An analysis of the ways that different cultures in Asia interpret key Buddhist values and ideas.

K. Nishitani, *Religion and Nothingness* (Berkeley: University of California Press, 1982). A Buddhist philosopher of religion explores the depth of the awareness of "nothingness" to describe the heart of religion as an encompassing viewpoint that breaks apart the conventional field of consciousness to provide a new perspective.

N. Smart, *The Phenomenon of Religion* (New York: Herder and Herder, 1973). In Chapter 2, "Religion as a Phenomenon," this British philosopher of religion presents an incisive discussion of the basic elements in a descriptive phenomenology of particular religious expressions.

N. Smart, *Worldviews: Crosscultural Explorations of Human Beliefs* (New York: Charles Scribner's, 1983). A brief introduction to the study of religion that is not only cross-cultural but also cross-disciplinary, achieved through analyzing six dimensions of traditional religious forms and contemporary ideologies.

H. Smith, *Forgotten Truth: The Primordial Tradition* (New York: Harper & Row, 1976). This book is a clear articulation of the position that the deepest awareness of every major religious tradition is that of a hierarchical universe and the goal is absorption of the self into the infinite.

*W. C. Smith, *The Meaning and End of Religion* (New York: Macmillan, 1962). A noted scholar argues that man's religious life can be properly understood only if the abstract concept of "religion" is replaced by the two separate concepts of "a cumulative tradition" and "a personal faith."

*P. Tillich, "Religion as a Dimension in Man's Spiritual Life," in *Theology of Culture,* edited by R. C. Kimball (Oxford: Oxford University Press, 1959). In a short essay, this well-known Protestant theologian argues that religion is not limited to a special kind of human expression, but provides the dimension of depth in all human life.

Two provocative books of essays on the contemporary consciousness of the religious dimension of life as it reflects both the religious traditions that set up the conceptual and social patterns of religion and the modern consciousness that continually breaks and reforms these patterns are J. Needleman, *Consciousness and Tradition* (New York: Crossroad, 1982) and R. J. Zwi Werblowsky, *Beyond Tradition and Modernity* (London: Athlone Press, 1976).

Three books that focus on the transformative power of the depth experience of life are *J. Campbell, ed., *Man and Transformation*, Bollingen Series XXX.5 (Princeton, NJ: Princeton University Press, 1964), a book of essays by specialists of different religious traditions; *J. A. Argüelles, *The Transformative Vision* (Berkeley, CA: Shambhala, 1975), an exploration of the deepening and transforming character of perception as one begins to see beyond appearances; and J. A. Taber, *Transformative Philosophy: A Study of Sankara, Fichte and Heidegger* (Honolulu: University of Hawaii Press, 1983), a comparative study of three philosophical positions whose purpose is to bring about an awakening that restructures one's experience of life.

For an analysis of deepest religious spirit as "sageliness," which permits a person to find his or her proper place within a moral-cosmic network throughout the universe, see Chün-i T'ang, "Religious Beliefs and Modern Chinese Culture—Part II: The Religious Spirit of Confucianism," *Chinese Studies in Philosophy*, 5/1 (1973), pp. 48–85, and his "My Option Between Philosophy and Religion," *Chinese Studies in Philosophy*, 5/4 (1974), pp. 4–38.

Two recent philosophical analyses of the nature of religion that seek to include religious forms from the major religious traditions are J. Barnhart, *The Study of Religion and Its Meaning* (The Hague: Mouton, 1977), and D. Crosby, *Interpretive Theories of Religion* The Hague: Mouton, 1981).

PART ONE

Four Traditional Ways of Being Religious

When adherents of different religions discuss a religious question, why do they so often speak past each other and then end in violent emotional disagreement? What is happening when an unconscious personal bias influences the perceptions of an "objective" observer? Why do a researcher's findings so often interest only like-minded people? One reason for these problems is that everyone tends unconsciously to understand and evaluate religious acts and claims according to preconceived notions. Therefore, those people who wish to investigate different kinds of religious life must become aware of their own emotional responses and conceptual patterns.

When many Westerners think of religion, they think of an institution, a faith, a set of doctrines. They often look down on the religious life of people in cultures that are not technologically advanced, such as the tribal peoples in Brazil, Africa, or Australia. Sometimes they criticize the mingling of religious and secular aspects of life in some of these cultures, or their lack of documents and commentaries. Ignorance may also encourage feelings of superiority of one's own tradition over others or even rejection of them as insignificant and meaningless. Moreover, members of a traditional religious community—for example, Christians, Buddhists, or Jews—may assume that people who are not members of such a community have no inner spiritual life. This assumption raises the question of the meaning of religion.

Can we really understand the vitality of another person's religious claim when it seems natural—perhaps necessary—to interpret it in terms of our own experience? The hope in this book is that we can expand our horizons of interpretation even if we may never see exactly how the world appears through another person's eyes. At least we can become conscious of how we give focus to what is meaningful and significant for us. This is a first step in avoiding misunderstanding. Even when we must decide the truth or value of different religious positions, we then will not be as confined to unconscious assumptions about reality, familiar vocabulary, and emotional reactions to our past experience.

To help extend the range of our interpretive focus, this book is organized to show different ways in which religious life can be, and is, a transforming power in people's lives. To do this we describe different structures of religious consciousness, thought, and behavior that create the deepest values by which people live. This approach requires going beyond a comparison of different ideas of God, rituals, or ethical norms. It focuses on different processes of ultimate transformation to account for the importance some people give to experience, others to symbols and rituals, and still others to ethical social actions.

The most significant comparisons of religious life, then, are of the processes through which the advocates claim they are ultimately transformed. If one advocate (a Christian) claims that salvation is only through belief that Jesus Christ is Lord, and that the New Testament is the ultimate norm for joy now and hereafter, and another (a Muslim) holds that Muhammad is the culmination of the prophets, and that the Qur'an (Koran) is the final revelation of God, this is an important difference—and indeed it has been the ground for contention, hostility, and even war. However, other religious advocates assert that the deepest sense of reality cannot be found in words at all—even those writings that some communities hold as revelation from God. Theravada Buddhist monks and Zen masters, for example, hold that the deepest insight into the nature of things cannot be found in teachings, even though doctrines, correct views, and ethical rules are useful spiritual tools for beginning the path to ultimate release from suffering. By focusing on the different dynamics or means to ultimate transformation, we hope to highlight some of the basic elements in the different processes through which people make their ultimate commitments.

CONTENT

The four chapters of Part One (Chapters 2–5) describe and comment on the basic elements of four traditional kinds of religious processes. These processes are (1) personal apprehension of a Holy Presence, (2) creation of community through sacred symbols, (3) living in harmony with the cosmic law, and (4) attaining freedom through spiritual discipline.

Although these religious processes are found in the major world religions, no one way of being religious equals any particular religious tradition. Within any given tradition, different processes dominate its different parts, and intermingling occurs with many structural variations. In our discussion, the references to particular traditions are merely illustrative. We make no attempt to explore the full range of any historical tradition. Furthermore, the order of the chapters does not suggest historical development or a movement from less to more sophisticated forms. The general historical development of religion and the evaluation of different religious processes does not concern us here. What we are trying to do is to describe each process from the point of view of its adherents in order to reveal the inner religious dynamic of their process of ultimate transformation.

We should also keep in mind that the elements in one process sometimes overlap with those of other processes. For example, both the personal apprehension of the Holy Presence and creation of community through sacred symbols can have a transcendent, personal creator of existence as the ultimate reality. Likewise, in the former, where personal experience is emphasized, symbols are used to communicate the experience; and in the latter, where special sacred symbols (myths and rituals) are emphasized, deep feelings can be aroused. Thus, the different processes of transformation are not to be seen as separate, self-contained mechanisms. Rather, they are interpretive models of how people create, locate, and express their ultimate values. The descriptions of these models in the next four chapters are like maps drawn to highlight features of the landscape, oversimplified organizational charts of a social institution, or a musical score written down after skilled musicians have performed.

Consider this last analogy. Imagine the different ways of being religious as musicians in a jazz quartet. At any given time, one instrument or another may take the lead and the melody or even, on occasion, "take a ride" (play solo). But even then the sax player, the piano player, the bass player, and the trombone player never play in isolation. It takes the vibration of the bass to hold the saxophone true even when the sound of the bass is barely audible. The different religious modes behave similarly. The lead expression at any time may be personal devotion, symbolic expression, moral behavior, or mystical insight. Nevertheless, the vibration of one or more of the others holds the leader true, adds resonance, and adds wholeness to the performance.

ORGANIZATION

One of the major assumptions of this book is that the religious life is a life in process. Therefore, each of the chapters in Part One follows a five-part organization of the religious process itself. These are as follows:

1. *The problematic in the human condition* as one major element of the religious process defines the source of human suffering. Different religious processes locate this source in different places; for example, as separation from God, disobedience to God's will, inappropriate (unethical) action within a universal order of life, or ignorant attachment to any mental, emotional, or physical thing.

2. *The ultimate reality* is the ideal state for living free from human suffering. The ultimate reality is the cure for the problematic state and will shift as the understanding of the deepest source of suffering shifts. Religious transformation is the transformation of existence as it is perceived at the deepest level, whether that reality is called "God," "Tao," "Brahman," or "nirvana."

3. *The means to ultimate transformation* answers the question of *how* one experiences and expresses ultimate reality. Just as the nature of the ideal state changes from one process of ultimate transformation to another, so do the means for achieving that state. The term *means* is used in two senses. First, it expresses a practical process for achieving the most comprehensive transformation of life. The process is both the model and the effective action for transforming the individual, society, and all existence from the problematic state to the

ideal. It eliminates or reforms the problematic character of life so that the ultimate reality is evident. Second, the process is not just a means to some end external to it but the consummation as well. This is because, from the religious advocate's perspective, the activity of salvation, enlightenment, and harmonious living has its deepest resource in, and thus expresses, the ultimate reality. Religious truth and action are by definition expressions of the very source of existence.

4. *The personal expression* expresses the internal experience of the individual as she or he is or becomes related to the ultimate reality. It attempts to communicate how it feels to overcome or dissipate the basic problematic state. Often this is expressed as joy, serenity, courage, compassion, and humility.

5. *The social expression* describes the effect of transformation in relation to others in groups, communities, and social institutions. It is self-evident that the personal and social expressions are related, so that, for example, the feeling of courage will often show itself in overcoming social evils or serenity will contribute to peace within institutions or nations. However, it is useful to distinguish personal and social expressions, since different processes of ultimate transformation emphasize one or another as central in that process.

As you read the chapters that follow, remember that each process represents an interaction of all five elements, each receiving energy from the others. Also remember that each process holds the deepest meaning of reality for those who accept its power.

CHAPTER 2

Personal Apprehension of a Holy Presence

St. Theresa, a Spanish Roman Catholic nun of the sixteenth century, described thus the rapture she experienced in prayer:

> When I tried to resist these raptures, it seemed that I was being lifted up by a force beneath my feet so powerful that I know nothing to which I can compare it, for it came with a much greater vehemence than any other spiritual experience and I felt as if I were being ground to powder. It is a terrible struggle, and to continue it against the Lord's will avails very little, for no power can do anything against His.[1]

Three centuries later, Joseph Smith, the founder of the Mormon church, after trying to find out which of the contesting Christian denominations in America expressed true Christianity, experienced a vision that revolutionized his thinking:

> I had actually seen a light, and in the midst of that light I saw two Personages, and they did in reality speak to me, and though I was hated and persecuted for saying that I had seen a vision, yet, it was true; and while they were persecuting me, reviling me, and speaking all manner of evil against me falsely for so saying, I was let to say in my heart: Why persecute me for telling the truth? I had actually seen a vision, and who am I that I can understand God, or why does the world think to make me deny what I have actually seen?[2]

During the same century in India, the Hindu teacher, Sri Ramakrishna, had extraordinary visions while performing his priestly duties in a temple of the Kali, the Divine Mother. He later described one of his early experiences:

> No sooner had I sat down to meditate . . . than I heard clattering sounds in the joints of my body and limbs. They began in my legs. It was as if someone inside me had keys and was locking me up, joint by joint, turning the keys. I had no

power to move my body or change my posture, even slightly. . . . When I sat and meditated, I had at first the vision of particles of light like swarms of fireflies. Sometimes I saw masses of light covering everything on all sides like a mist; at other times I saw how everything was pervaded by bright waves of light like molten silver. I didn't understand what I saw, nor did I know if it was good or bad to be having such visions. So I prayed anxiously to [the Divine] Mother: "I don't understand what's happening to me. Please, teach me yourself how to know you. Mother, if *you* won't teach me, who will?"[3]

In Japan, in 1837, a housewife by the name of Miki was acting as a medium during a healing ritual for her eldest son when she was possessed by a powerful deity, called the "heavenly General," who is reported to have said: "I am the True and Original God. I have a predestination to the Residence. Now I have descended from Heaven to save all human beings. I want to take Miki as *Tsuki-Hi's yashiro,* Shrine of God and mediatrix between God the Parent, and men."[4] After several occasions in which Miki and her family resisted this power, she became the mouthpiece of this "Heavenly Ruler" and the founder of Tenrikyo (the Religion of Divine Wisdom).

How are we to understand the religious significance of these experiences from the four corners of the world? They all seem so dramatic and different from what the ordinary person expects of religion. They are overwhelming experiences that break into conventional everyday expectations and fill the devotee with feelings of ecstasy and effervescence, exploding any previous sense of him- or herself. Such spontaneous and extraordinary encounters are not the only forms of personal awareness of a Holy Presence. This religious awareness is also found in the quiet piety of personal devotion to God, in the sense of a comforting presence in times of illness or suffering, or in the serene strength brought about through trust (faith) in the Eternal Thou.

The most common expressions of the awareness of the Holy Presence are perhaps found in the spontaneous celebration of thanksgiving to God for life or in the impassioned call for help in the time of need. In either case, the devotee expresses joy or wonder and makes an appeal for help in the realization that he or she is wholly dependent on an extraordinarily different reality. Having such a personal relationship with the all-powerful supreme and infinite force is one of the four traditional religious processes that appeared in the ancient world and which are still active in the modern one.

Before beginning this chapter, look at the following figure, which indicates how contact with the Holy Presence completely changes a person's sense of reality. At the moment of contact with the Infinite One, the beholder is suddenly blown free from weakness, sinfulness, uselessness, and purposelessness. Devotees say that this contact with holiness is the most amazing and profound human experience possible. It can crack accepted religious practices and doctrines wide open, as it did for the participants quoted in the preceding examples, or it can offer an unsurpassable sense of comfort, as we shall see later in this chapter. But the apprehension of the Holy Presence involves not only the initial event of contact with the holy but also the living out of this newly found reality.

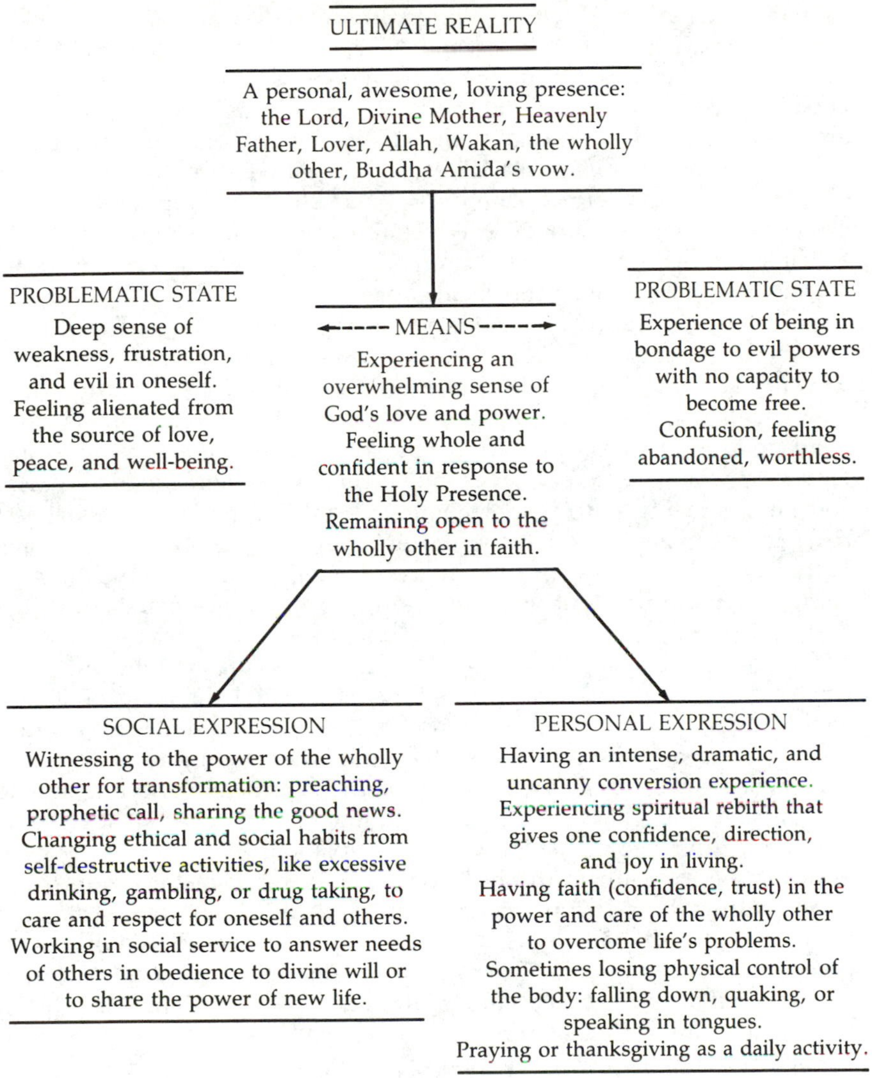

ULTIMATE REALITY

A personal, awesome, loving presence:
the Lord, Divine Mother, Heavenly
Father, Lover, Allah, Wakan, the wholly
other, Buddha Amida's vow.

PROBLEMATIC STATE

Deep sense of
weakness, frustration,
and evil in oneself.
Feeling alienated from
the source of love,
peace, and well-being.

◄---- MEANS ----►

Experiencing an
overwhelming sense of
God's love and power.
Feeling whole and
confident in response to
the Holy Presence.
Remaining open to the
wholly other in faith.

PROBLEMATIC STATE

Experience of being in
bondage to evil powers
with no capacity to
become free.
Confusion, feeling
abandoned, worthless.

SOCIAL EXPRESSION

Witnessing to the power of the wholly
other for transformation: preaching,
prophetic call, sharing the good news.
Changing ethical and social habits from
self-destructive activities, like excessive
drinking, gambling, or drug taking, to
care and respect for oneself and others.
Working in social service to answer needs
of others in obedience to divine will or
to share the power of new life.

PERSONAL EXPRESSION

Having an intense, dramatic, and
uncanny conversion experience.
Experiencing spiritual rebirth that
gives one confidence, direction,
and joy in living.
Having faith (confidence, trust) in the
power and care of the wholly other
to overcome life's problems.
Sometimes losing physical control of
the body: falling down, quaking, or
speaking in tongues.
Praying or thanksgiving as a daily activity.

FIGURE 1.   *Personal Apprehension of a Holy Presence*

THE PROBLEMATIC IN THE HUMAN CONDITION: SIN, INHERENT WEAKNESS, SEPARATION FROM THE HOLY ONE

Given that the apprehension of the Holy Presence may be a terrifying experience, why do some people from every major religious tradition seek it as
a means to ultimate transformation? As devotees see it, the unhappy human
condition is caused by alienation from the creative and illuminating force (or
forces) of the universe who is the source of all goodness, peace, well-being,
and truth. In a world locked up in weakness, sinfulness, and disharmony,

human effort is insufficient. Philosophical reflection, efforts at self-improvement, even culturally accepted religious doctrines and rituals lack the power to overcome this basic human weakness. The noblest effort to do good, to discover truth, and to experience fulfillment are pervaded by greed, illusion, and weakness. A release from the troubles of life requires an intense, personal connection with a radically different resource: the Holy One (or the Fully Perfect One). Ask yourself this: Suppose you were chained by the leg in a dark cave. Which resource would be the most useful? A manual on chain making, a program of physical fitness, or a big, powerful friend who comes to snap the chains apart with a touch?

In the theistic traditions—those expressing a belief in a god or gods—weakness and corruption are believed to result from people's failure to respond passionately to God's initiating love; instead, they tend to center their attention on themselves. Expressed theologically, human beings are in bondage to evil powers that are vastly stronger than they are, and they require transhuman power to overcome them. Only when human weakness and life-destroying powers are removed can one experience the deepest relief and happiness. Because the powers of evil are themselves a personal but uncanny force, only an intimate relationship with the very source of being provides sufficient creative energy to overcome evil or the life-destroying force.

The inability of people to cope by themselves with the inherent problematic character of existence is seen, for example, in the writings of literary geniuses from two different religious traditions. The seventeenth-century English Christian "dissenter" preacher and writer, John Bunyan, warned readers of his allegory *Pilgrim's Progress* that the present world is a strange and difficult land; those who know the promises of God are just pilgrims who are returning home to him. Various temptations try to draw the pilgrim from the narrow path to the heavenly city. To make matters worse, the pilgrim carries a great burden upon his back; this is his guilt, which is removed eventually only by God's grace. This world is a place full of danger, despair, and temptation from which one should flee as quickly as possible. At about the same time in India, the Hindu poet Tukaram (1607–1649), who wrote nearly a thousand hymns, portrayed his sense of deep need for God's (Vishnu's) help when he prays:

> I am a mass of sin; / Thou are all purity;
> Yet thou must take me as I am / and bear my load for me.
> Me, Death has all consumed; / In thee all power resides.
> All else forsaking, at thy feet / Thy servant Tuka hides.[5]

Similarly, in the Japanese Pure Land Buddhism, there is a deep sense of the difficulty in pursuing spiritual exercises as long as one is in a predominantly evil world imbued at the deepest level with ignorance. In the degenerate age we live in now, a person must rely on the gracious power of Amida Buddha. One must trust in Amida's vow to save (that is, enlighten) all beings and hope to be reborn in Amida's Pure Land after this life, when one will attain perfect enlightenment. The single-mindedness of faith necessary to escape the world's evil is seen in the following admonition given by

Honen Shonin (1133–1212 C.E.), the founder of Pure Land Buddhism as an independent Japanese Buddhist sect:

> When a deer is being pursued by the hunters, it does not stop even to look around for its fellows or look back at its pursuers, but with all eagerness, hastens straight forward, and no matter how many may be following, it escapes in safety. It is with the same determination that a man fully entrusts himself to the Buddha's power, and without regard to anything else, steadfastly sets his mind upon being born into the Pure Land.[6]

In each of these examples we note the deep sense of one's incapacity, worthlessness, and drivenness. These qualities are inherent in everyday existence, which is controlled by evil powers that cannot be defeated through mere human effort.

THE ULTIMATE REALITY: THE HOLY PRESENCE

Whether the one who experiences a vision of the Holy Presence expects that encounter or is taken completely by surprise, the experience is clearly different from any normal physical encounter. Recall that in the experiences described at the beginning of this chapter, the Holy Presence confronted St. Theresa, Joseph Smith, Shree Ramakrishna, and Miki in an overpowering way and terrified them. But, at the same time, this presence reassured them so that they could recognize the positive power that relieves all worldly fears. So, we see that the Holy Presence possesses two major and opposite (bipolar) characteristics: awesomeness and compassion.

The sense of awe in the devotee is a response to the basic nature of the ultimate reality perceived in this process of ultimate transformation. The basic nature of the ultimate reality is that it is "wholly other" than what people normally experience in their daily lives. This wholly other character is expressed in the claim that this kind of ultimate reality is infinite, complete, and an incomprehensible power while, at the same time, the source of the most intimate, personal, caring relationship possible. It/she/he is the supreme mystery of unthinkable possibilities, which evokes terror and awe, while also the ever-present, loving, generous, compassionate source of all security, joy, serenity, and justice. In this religious process the ultimate reality is transrational—though not irrational—requiring a personal mode of response that must transcend mental calculation, common-knowledge facts, and cultural conventions. At a deep level, the devotee is aware that he or she cannot even take the initiative in knowing or relating to this kind of reality. The Holy Presence is not just an infinite extension of oneself. As one contemporary writer describes it:

> When man takes the initiative, his discourse on God becomes a discourse on himself; therefore, a meeting with God cannot be serious unless it is God who takes the initiative. . . . God is an irruption, an unanticipated occurrence in man's life. All anticipations are in reality only anticipations of oneself.[7]

Those who want to know and properly respond to such reality try to keep attuned to the wholly other, but know that it is completely beyond their control.

Several examples of the awesome and caring characteristics of the Holy One will demonstrate the basic nature of the ultimate reality in this type of religious transformation. In the biblical book of Isaiah, God's action is portrayed as bipolar (terrifying and gracious) and as breaking into the natural world. The word of the Lord thunders a devastating warning:

O sinful nation, people loaded with iniquity,
race of evildoers, wanton destructive children
    who have deserted the Lord,
    spurned the Holy One of Israel
    and turned your back on him.
Where can you still be struck
    if you will be disloyal still?
    Your head is covered with sores,
    your body diseased;
from heat to foot there is not a sound spot in you—
nothing but bruises and weals and raw wounds . . .
Your country is desolate, your cities lie in ashes.
Strangers devour your land before your eyes; . . .[8]

The Holy Presence does not always reveal power in such gruesome descriptions, but the potential for destruction is implicit in any of its expressions.

This terror-provoking character of the holy is only half of the bipolar force field that holds a person in awe. The other impact of the power is the glory, which is living, generous, compassionate, and forgiving. The passage from Isaiah continues, and God offers the reassurance:

Though your sins are scarlet,
they may become white as snow;
though they are dyed crimson,
they may yet be like wool.
Obey with a will,
and you shall eat the best that earth yields . . .[9]

By balancing terror with reassurance, God prevents despair. The people know who will ultimately judge their action and who can grant blessing.

Similarly, in Islam we find that the one and only God, who is beyond comprehension and yet gracious, is the only hope for the Muslim. One of the obligatory prayers, said by pious Muslims five times a day, reflects total dependence on God to overcome the power of the Evil One, Satan:

Glory to Thee, O God, Thine is the praise and blessed is thy name and exalted is Thy majesty, and there is none to be served beside Thee. . . . I betake me for refuge to God against the accursed satan.[10]

This all-powerful and compassionate nature of the Holy One is found in Asian traditions, as well. Consider the experience of the nobleman Arjuna, described in the Hindu religious classic, the Bhagavad-Gita. Arjuna is the finest warrior in the land, but on the eve of an important battle, he finds himself depressed and unable to enter the fight. Fortunately, his chariot is guided by the great Lord Krishna, who has instructed Arjuna in matters of wisdom, action, renunciation, self-control, and life in general. The god and the mortal are friends: charioteer and warrior. However, in the midst of their discussion, Arjuna asks Krishna if he can see Krishna's divine form. Krishna complies, giving Arjuna "divine sight" with which to behold all of Krishna's supreme grandeur. This is the supreme form that Arjuna sees:

> Of many mouths and eyes, of many marvelous visions, of many divine orna-ments, of many uplifted weapons;
> Wearing divine garlands and garments with divine perfumes and ointments, full of all wonders, radiant, infinite, His face turned everywhere.
> If the light of a thousand suns were to spring forth simultaneously in the sky, it would be like the light of that great Being.

Arjuna, overcome with awe, exclaims:

> I behold Thee without beginning, middle or end, of infinite power, of innumer-able arms, the moon and sun as Thine eyes, Thy face as a shining fire, burning this universe with Thy radiance . . .
> Seeing Thy mouths, terrible with tusks, like time's devouring fire, I know not the directions of the sky and I find no security. Have mercy, O Lord of gods, Abode of the world!

The Blessed Lord, Krishna, then comforts and reassures Arjuna with the words:

> By My grace, O Arjuna, and through My great power, was shown to thee this highest form, full of splendor, universal, infinite, primal, which no one but thee has seen before. . . .
> Be not afraid nor bewildered in seeing this terrible form of Mine. Without fear and of satisfied mind, behold again My other form.[11]

Krishna continues to explain that the knowledge Arjuna has gained through his vision could not have been achieved through the study of the Vedic scriptures, the practice of austerities, or offering sacrifice. Arjuna has connected himself with the source of life through devotion to the Holy One. Here we again note that although the Holy Presence is completely different from anything in common reality, he is gracious and kind to those who seek his help. In the Bhagavad-Gita, the Supreme Lord, Krishna—the source of the universe—is the friend and charioteer of Arjuna. No spouse, child, or teacher could have been closer to Arjuna than was Krishna, the wholly other.

In summary, the Holy Presence is terrifying and loving, most different and most intimate. The Holy Presence is the great mystery and the loving lord or goddess.

There are a number of variations in people's experience of the Holy Presence. It is perhaps easiest for the Western mind to imagine the Holy Presence as having at least a human voice and possibly a human shape. When a North Carolina tenant farmer talks about the Holy Presence, he speaks as if the presence were a person:

I come out of [the church] and I'm taller. I feel God has taken me to him. He put His hand on my shoulder and said, "Brother John Wilson, the reason that I want you praying to Me is so you won't be looking at yourself and feeling so low."[12]

Brother John Wilson feels that he knows exactly what he is talking about when he takes God to be a personal comforter and source of strength. It is likely that he would understand the Bhagavad-Gita's portrayal of Arjuna's feelings of amazement and relief in the return to the human presence of Krishna. Arjuna and Brother John Wilson see divinity with a human face.

A more impersonal experience, which nevertheless maintains a clear faith in the glory and power of an extraordinary presence, is expressed in a Pure Land Buddhist text of the thirteenth century, *Tanni Sho (Notes Lamenting Differences)*. Here the author describes what he regards as true faith. The compassionate vow of the Buddha Amida to bring all beings to enlightenment is depicted as the power unto salvation:

> At the moment when one thought (of Faith) arises in us, due to Amida's Light shining upon us, we are endowed with the Diamond Faith and received into the Rightly Established State [that is, the Pure Land]; and when life ends, all passions and evil hindrances are turned (into Bodhi) and we are enlightened to the Truth of Birthlessness. Without the Compassionate Vow, how can we, paltry sinners, ever be freed from Birth-and-Death?[13]

A still different form of the Holy Presence may be found in the Hindu hymns of the Rig Veda. In these songs, the seers of ancient India expressed their awareness that a sacred power dwelled in, and was manifested by, such natural phenomena as the sun, wind, fire, and juice of the *soma* plant. The hymn to Agni (fire), for example, expresses the awesome wonder of the worshipper:

> 1. Thy auspicious face, O mighty Agni, shines in the neighborhood of the sun. Brilliant to see, it is seen even by night. Soft to behold is the food in thy (beautiful) body.
> 2. O Agni, disclose (wise) thoughts for him who praises thee; (disclose) the opening, when thou, O strong-born, hast been praised with trembling. Grant unto us, O very great one, such a rich prayer as thou with all the gods wilt hold dear, O brilliant one.[14]

Here, fire, seen in the sacrificial flame, the sun, and the moon, is not just an everyday natural phenomenon. It is regarded as the effective force to which an individual may appeal for physical and spiritual benefits. Similarly, the sun's energy, the fertilizing rains, the psychedelic experience derived from drinking *soma* juice—all these expose the presence of holiness experienced by the Vedic hymn writers.

MEANS TO ULTIMATE TRANSFORMATION: A PERSONAL RELATIONSHIP WITH THE HOLY ONE

The personal apprehension of the Holy Presence is among the major modes of being religious; however, not all of those who believe will have experiences as dramatic as those of St. Theresa or Shree Ramakrishna, and indeed there are other ways to achieve a reconnection with the source of reality. Still, the means whereby one is rescued from a painful and sinful existence is the experience of living in an intimate relationship with the holy and caring savior. For participants in this religious process, the intimate relationship is felt deeply within one's consciousness and manifested in daily devotional life and service to others. The relationship, nevertheless, is not of equals. The vastness of the Holy Presence reveals the smallness of the individual, who paradoxically receives tremendous power through the experience. In dramatic divine surprises or in the daily prayer and quiet contentment in living in God's presence, or in the power of the Buddha Amida's vow, comes the recognition of possibilities far beyond what one thought one could do. The devotee ideally responds to all of life as an act of worship, and experiences faith, or trust, that all experiences work toward an ultimate, if incomprehensible, good. One's eyes are opened to the smallest things in life as gifts; the world is seen with amazement and responded to with care.

The quality of a personal awareness of the Holy Presence rests on the sense of weakness and evil that is the inherent problematic state of existence and the recognition that the wholly other is the true comprehensive resource of life. Although the Holy Presence emerges from unknown depths of existence and appears foreign, no human being—according to this means to ultimate transformation—can disregard it. All people need a personal experience with this power to deal with the fundamental nature of existence. To avoid this devastating-exalting encounter is to forego the one possibility of actualizing one's fullest potential. While neglecting or even avoiding the Holy Presence, people, at the same time, want this relationship with the source of everything. The advocates of this way proclaim that all people sense something of their dependence on the infinite Holy One and yearn for him, because existence depends on this ultimate reality. The personal awareness of the Holy Presence, then, is the insight into the way things really are.

Knowing the Holy One personally has given rise to powerful symbols used to express an awareness of the intimate nature of the relationship. This intimacy may be symbolized in the relationships that exist between lovers, parents and children, deliverer and delivered. The "Gita Govinda," a twelfth-century Hindu devotional poem, describes the yearning of the cow-maid Radha—who symbolizes all devotees—for her Lord:

> She secretly sees you everywhere, drinking the
> sweet honey of her lips.
> Lord Hari [Krishna], Radha pines in the lover's bower.
> As she hastens in her eagerness to go to meet you,
>   she moves a few steps, and falls in a swoon.
> Lord Hari, Radha pines in the lover's bower.[15]

Similarly, in the Muslim tradition, the mystic poet Halal al-Din Rumi (1207–1273) uses love imagery to express the notion that true devotion to God is an overwhelming passion. He writes:

The lovers who dwell within the sanctuary are moths
   burnt with the torch of the Beloved's face.
How long wilt thou dwell with words and superficial
   things?
A burning heart is what God seeks.
Consort with burning.
Kindle in thy heart the flame of love . . .[16]

Perhaps more familiar to a Western audience is the symbol of God's love expressed as that which a father has for his obedient children. Here, God is seen as the provider, protector, and source of life who cares for his children. A stanza of a Christian hymn conveys the intermingling of warmth, trust, and commitment found in this personal relationship:

Dear Lord and Father of mankind, forgive our feverish ways;
Reclothe us in a rightful mind, in purer life thy service find,
In deeper reverence praise.

Not only is the symbol of the divine father celebrated in theistic traditions, but also in many cultures we find appeals from devotees to the divine mother. The mother goddess often has the characteristics of power, love, and mercy—an awesome being who protects and nourishes the universe. For example, the following invocation to the goddess Durga is found in the Hindu tradition:

O Goddess who removes the suffering of your supplicants,
   Have mercy!
O mother of the whole world, be gracious!
O mistress of the universe, protect the world!
   Have mercy!
You are the mistress of all that moves and moves not!
You alone are the foundation of the world, residing in the form of earth.
O you whose prowess is unsurpassed, you nourish the world in the form
   of the waters.[17]

Another symbol used to describe the personal relationship between human beings and the Holy Presence is friendship. This can be the friendship between the spiritual Master and his disciples as depicted in the Christian Gospels (Christ and his disciples) or the Buddhist *suttas* (Buddha and his disciples), or it can be the kind of friendship recognized in the intimacy of Muslim Sufi awareness of God's closeness to his devotee.

One of the most common symbols of God's personal relationship to human beings is carried through the word *savior* (or *deliverer* or *refuge*). The savior is one who overcomes powers that are hostile to life; thus, God is a great and victorious conqueror. The savior (in Christianity, Islam, and Judaism) is victorious over sin and spiritual death (damnation). In Buddhism and Hinduism, the savior triumphs over the pain of continual rebirth in the cycle of death and rebirth. The human response to symbols of savior, father, lover, or friend emphasizes the human need for personal fulfillment through the power and grace of the divine reality.

Two words, *worship* and *faith*, are central to understanding how the apprehension of the Holy Presence expresses itself on a personal level. Both are needed to keep the lines of communication open between the devotee and the source of fulfillment and truth. The personal expression attempts to communicate a deep inner experience that is often intense, dramatic, and uncanny. The extraordinary experiences of the wholly other are described—as we saw earlier—first in terms of fear and awe and then of comfort and security. In Christian religious conversion experiences, the relationship with the Holy One is described as being "born anew" after having died to the old self. The expression of the experience of holiness is always a transcending of the conventionally perceived self.

Commonly, people who give witness to such experiences warn others that no words can do justice to their deepest sensitivities and that these sensitivities are not just uncontrollable emotions. Sometimes the encounter is so overpowering that the expression is not controlled by conventional symbols and metaphors and is manifested in unusual activities such as "speaking in tongues" (glossolalia), trembling, loud shouting and repetitive singing, or swooning in apparent unconsciousness. More commonly in theistic traditions, the deep emotions give rise to hymns of praise, spontaneous and joyful singing, psalms, or devotional poetry. However expressed, the emphasis is on the personal direct experience of spiritual power.

The urgency and intensity of a personal apprehension of the Holy Presence is the dominant characteristic of devotionalism or pietism found in the major historical religious traditions. Despite other contrasting features, the intense personal awareness of God is characteristic of such Christian leaders as St. Francis of Assisi and the Methodist leader, John Wesley. It is seen in the Roman Catholic movement of the Sacred Heart of Jesus, the pietists of the German Reformation, and in American Protestant revivalism, such as is found in the Pentecostal churches or the Four-Square Gospel Movement. In African Christianity today, the Aladura churches emphasize the use of personal visions during ecstatic prayer, and spiritual healing. In Hinduism, ecstatic fervor dominates the medieval devotional movements, as typified by the Baul sect of Bengal, and is prominent in the Hari Krishna practice in the United States today. It is also a prominent feature of Japan's "new religions," of which Miki's experience presented earlier is an example.

Worship

In the context of this type of ultimate transformation, worship means the inner sense of praise, honor, and love felt toward the Eternal Holy One. Such worship is a special and necessary activity for those who want to enjoy the presence of God. The American evangelist Rufus Jones, in *The World Within*, expresses his sense of the need for worship and describes its core in the following way:

By worship, I mean the act of rising to a personal, experiential consciousness of the real presence of God which floods the soul with joy and bathes the whole inward spirit with refreshing streams of life. Never to have experienced the joy of personal fellowship with God, is surely to have missed the richest privilege and the highest beatitude of religion.[18]

The late Protestant theologian Nels Ferre expresses a similar sentiment when he describes prayer as the definitive expression of all religious life.

Prayer is the main highway to making religion real. Unless we meet God in prayer, we never meet Him, for prayer is meeting God. Unless we meet Him, He can never become real to us. A person can be fully real to us only as we get to know him personally . . . To be sure, God is always and everywhere present as the one who creates, sustains, and controls the world. But as such He is not *personally* present. We can meet God personally only in communion with Him and *such communion is prayer.*[19]

The worship experiences that both Jones and Ferre describe express the special character of the Holy Presence, as well as the deeply personal means of responding.

The attitude of thanksgiving is an element in both personal experience of the Holy Presence and communal worship services. For example, when people are aware of how the best that is found in life depends on a power wholly other than themselves, they want to express this in praise and honor. An example of cultivation of a sensitivity to live in a thankful attitude for God's gifts is found in the popular handbook used by German reformation pietists in the eighteenth century. Its author, J. F. Starck, admonishes believers as follows:

All our life is nothing but prayer and thanksgiving, that is to say, we should cry to God every day in our prayers for His blessing, assistance, comfort, and grace, and when these are obtained, we should give thanks unto Him with all our hearts. Therefore, O believer, when thou dost awake in the morning from thy slumbers, let it be thy first care to raise thine eyes to Heaven; think not immediately for thy business and thy toils, plunge not at once into the search for gain, but fall upon thy knees, thank God, and command thyself to His gracious protection.[20]

Here is a joyful sense that all goodness in life comes as a gift from God.

Similarly, the common folk in other traditions often see the best of life coming as a gift from the holy and infinite source of life and truth—whether that is defined as God the Almighty, many different divinities, the original ancestors and their most noble descendents, or embodiments of true insight, as found in some Mahayana celebrations of the Buddhas. Gratitude characterizes all major religious traditions to some degree.

Faith

The second key word in the description of personal expression is *faith.* When the awareness of a Holy Presence becomes the center of personal life, then, ideally, all human functions, abilities, and decisions are affected by the special impact of this experience. Yet, except for a few short, ecstatic experiences of the Holy Presence, a person's response to this presence is often unclear. People most often become aware of holiness in an ambiguous context of fear, skepticism, enthusiasm, and through a feeling of power derived from the Holy One. Their reaction is often called "faith."

The ambiguity of the awesome-loving experience, however, does not reduce the urgency that the advocates feel in calling others to experience the dependence on the wholly other power for salvation. It is faith (trust) in that power that provides the confidence to live as a new being. In the following two statements from religous traditions that have different understandings about the nature of existence, note that faith is the central spiritual attitude required to overcome the basic problematic state of existence. The sixteenth-century German leader of the Protestant Reformation, Martin Luther, claims:

> If you believe that only God can take away your sins, you have the right faith, but from here you must go on to believe, and *you yourself must believe* (and it is not you that can do this but the Holy Spirit must enable you to believe) that through him you really have the forgiveness of your sins.[21]

Shinran Shonin (1173–1262), a preacher and teacher of Japanese True Pure Land (Shin) Buddhism, says in his collection of verses on true faith (*Shoshin Ge*):

> When one receives Faith, sees and reveres the
> Vow and greatly rejoices,
> He instantly transcends the Five Evil Realms
> crosswise.
> All common men, whether they be good or evil,
> If they hear and believe the Tathagata's [that is,
> the Buddha Amida's] Universal Vow,
> The Buddha praises them as "men of great and
> superior understanding";
> They are also named "Pundarikas" ["pure white lotus"
> or perfect beings].[22]

As a religious term, faith does *not* mean what it has come to mean in common speech in the West: an intellectual and emotional acceptance of something a person does not know with precision and cannot prove. Such a definition emphasizes a secondary character of the life of faith. It shifts the focus from the transcendent *source* of faith to a concern with rules of logic and methods of empirical verification. These are only secondary considerations, say the advocates of faith, when wrestling with the most profound elements of human experience. Faith is a way of living, not merely a way of thinking, that places everyday existence in the context of eternal reality. Such an act of faith gives one an exuberance in living and confidence that one can achieve the deepest kind of fulfillment because of the Perfect One's unlimited power; one turns his or her life over to the highest (the Lord's, Allah's, Krishna's, Buddha Amida's) spiritual purpose. Whatever circumstances in life prevail, a person will be provided with the strength, insight, and serenity to serve others with joy.

Eternal reality, as pointed out before, is not without its ambiguity. The strangeness of the Holy Presence results in both certainty and uncertainty for people of faith. This ambiguity cannot be removed if the Holy Presence is really regarded as the other. The faithful person is always in a learning open situation. On the one hand, faith includes an immediate, direct awareness of reality; on the other, the object of awareness (God, Buddha-nature) is not the usual object of human knowledge, but it becomes the expanding, demanding force that breaks open the old, convenient, and seemingly sure ideas. Deeply pious people often find it difficult to bring together their conventional self-identity with this paradoxical experience in which the object of love and awe requires a transformed and risky sense of who one really is. In addition, because the source of one's life is the wholly other, such people are often unsure if their most profound insights are demonic compulsions or if their gravest doubts and anxieties are divine revelation. Thus, faith is not a cheap solution to ignorance of the ultimate nature of things. It is the self-conscious, affirmative response to the Holy One—in all his mystery, revelation, terrible power, and creative possibilities.

SOCIAL EXPRESSION: WITNESS, THE HOLY SPIRIT, VISUAL IMAGES

The discussion so far has described parts of a process: the apprehension of the Holy Presence as the only way to overcome the deepest sense of alienation and helplessness that comes from feeling alone and weak in the world. Once an individual recognizes the need for this connection and opens him- or herself to its possibilities for freedom, the way is clear to apprehend or grasp the reality revealed by this mysterious and loving force. The advocates are clear in expressing that a deep experience of the Holy Presence is not an end in itself but a growing sensitivity to a transcendent power that can change a world still bound by sin and weakness—the human problematic situation.

Witnessing

The basic social expression of this type of religious transformation is to witness to the spiritual power that has broken into one's life. This can take the specific form of proclamation in public preaching, especially with an appeal to others to live in the same awareness that has moved the preacher. The lives and proclamations of the ancient Hebrew prophets, such as Isaiah or Jeremiah, are prime examples of people moved by a sense of the Holy One to call their contemporaries to repentence. In the Christian tradition, St. Paul, and in the Muslim tradition, Muhammad, are dramatic examples of men who felt compelled to witness to extraordinary personal experiences of God's will for all humanity. In all these examples, the prophetic preachers claimed they were obedient to an authority far higher than the currently prominent political or religious institutional authority, with whom they were often in conflict. The tension between the prophet who calls for a change in attitudes and behavior and the political-economic-religious establishment is a typical result of a commitment to transcendent ideals, and is found throughout history down to the present. For example, the Mormon leader Joseph Smith had a hard time convincing the religious community that what he had experienced was divinely inspired. He and his followers were condemned by their neighbors and eventually he had to leave. His witness became a public statement and the test of faith. Following his example, each generation of Morman males accepts house-to-house witnessing as part of its devotion to the Lord.

Expressions of the Holy Spirit

In twentieth-century United States, perhaps the most significant example of the power of personal witness is found in the Pentecostal churches. Pentecostal believers hold that true Christian lives are spirit-filled lives. Baptism in the Holy Spirit, rather than ritual baptism, is the means to ultimate transformation, while such spiritual baptism is marked by extraordinary experiences, especially speaking in tongues. Ideally, these experiences must lead to changed lives. Some of the converted contrast their previous sordid lives of sexual promiscuity, drunkenness, and drug addiction with their new lives, characterized by happiness, self-control, and service to others. Even where conversion does not require such a contrast in behavior, many "cultural Christians" have been moved to give witness to a renewal in their lives in recent years. For many young people in a generation left out of the great social rights enthusiasm of the 1960s and confronted with prediction of nuclear war and economic bleakness, having a friend in Jesus is a very reassuring reality. The times seem to call for something more personal than learning what religious authorities said or repeating ancient ritual. Obedience and love are thought to be the answers.

Another social expression of the practice of God's presence in the everyday affairs of many Pentecostal businessmen is the Full Gospel Business Men's Fellowship International. The participants in this fellowship are committed to giving their time and money to promote Jesus Christ, whose power, they claim, will change society. A third form of social witness found in Pentecostal churches is found in healing services. Claiming that the Holy Spirit heals people in the twentieth century, as well as in the early church, some popular Christian preachers who give a Pentecostal witness, such as the Oklahoma-based Oral Roberts, stress that the healing ministry is a natural, if inexplicable, effect of being attuned to the Holy Spirit.

Visual Images

People who have a personal experience of the holy are faced with a real dilemma: How do they talk about it? When they personally experience the Holy Presence, people are filled with awe in response to the strange and sometimes extrahuman qualities that confront them. However, the experience can only be communicated to others through human symbols, actions, or ideas. Believers face an unresolvable tension in trying to express the inexpressible in a particular visual symbol. In fact, some religious leaders have strenuously opposed the use of any symbols or cultic acts. They argue that true faith must avoid putting the Holy Presence into any objective form. Thus, within such religious traditions as Judaism and Islam, the pious refrain from pictorial symbols of God. Islamic Saudi Arabia goes so far as to forbid the import of any representational art whatsoever, even by foreigners. Islamic art, rather, expresses the otherness of the Holy One through the continuous flow of unbounded geometric arabesque patterns.

The dilemma of communicating the reality of the wholly other is a dilemma of extremes. Whereas some argue that no depiction is the best depiction, others claim that only a multitude of depictions can do justice to the nature of the divine. Such a congregation of shapes and sizes, for example, is found in the great variety of Hindu images. Gods or goddesses may have multiple heads or arms; they may be white, blue, black, or gold. They may be draped in skulls or garlands, have heads like elephants, or look like boars and birds. Yet, whether the mysteriousness of the holy reality is shown in the absence of depiction or the multiplicity of it, believers are always aware of human dependence on the ultimate reality and the difference of human reality from it.

SUMMARY

Being religious through a personal apprehension of the Holy Presence is not limited to any culture. Whether the persons who are reconnected with the source of life in this way live in the United States, Spain, India, Saudi Arabia, or Japan, their experiences share the following common elements:

1. *Problematic existence:* Life without a deep reverence for the Holy Presence is seen as evil, full of pain, and without reward or meaning.
2. *Ultimate reality:* The source for all blessing, goodness, and truth is the uncontrollable and unconditioned wholly other, whose presence often provokes terror and awe, but who, at the same time, is compassionate, generous, and loving.
3. *Means to transformation:* Evil, selfishness, pain, and meaninglessness are overcome when a person is deeply moved by the power of the Holy Presence in an emotionally charged experience that transforms his or her life at the deepest possible level.
4. *Personal expression:* A person spiritually reborn or renewed in the unlimited power of the wholly other has an inner experience of peace, well-being, joy, and truth that is expressed in an emotional outpouring of worship and faith.
5. *Social expression:* The social forms of expressing this inner change is giving witness to this awesome and loving resource, changing evil habits, and showing care and compassion to others. People may also express their experience of the holy through visual symbols.

A classic exposition of personal awareness of the Holy Presence is found in *R. Otto, *The Idea of the Holy* (Oxford: Oxford University Press, 1958; first published in 1923). Here the core of all religious experience is discussed as the transrational awareness of the numinous.

Short excerpts from advocates for the experience of the Divine Presence, plus sympathetic interpretations and critiques of these claims, are found in F. J. Streng, C. L. Loyd, Jr., and J. T. Allen, eds., *Ways of Being Religious* (Englewood Cliffs, NJ: Prentice-Hall, 1973), Chapter 1, "Rebirth Through Personal Encounter with the Holy." Descriptions of personal religious awareness and an interpretation that emphasizes transcendent power is found in *G. van der Leeuw, *Religion in Essence and Manifestation: A Study in Phenomenology* (New York: Harper, 1963; first published in 1933), especially Part I and Part III, Section B, "Inward Action." For documents depicting the object of the personal apprehension of the holy, see *M. Eliade, ed., *From Primitives to Zen* (New York: Harper, 1967), Chapter 1, "Gods, Goddesses, and Supernatural Beings."

General overviews of devotion and extraordinary religious experience are found in:

W. King, *Introduction to Religion* (New York: Harper & Row, 1968), Chapter 14, "The Discipline of Devotion." A useful summary statement on the structure of devotion.

*R. S. Ellwood, Jr., *Introducing Religion from Inside and Outside* (Englewood Cliffs, NJ: Prentice-Hall, 1978), Chapter 3, "Oases of the Mind: The Psychology of Religion." This analysis of personal religious awareness is placed within a psychological framework of altered states of consciousness.

*N. Soederblom, *The Living God: Basic Forms of Personal Religion* (Boston: Beacon Press, 1962; first published in 1933), Chapters 4 and 5. A somewhat dated but still useful comparative study of a variety of religious forms.

A classic study of prayer is *F. Heiler, *Prayer: A Study in the History and Psychology of Religion*, translated and edited by S. McComb (New York: Oxford University Press, 1958; first published in 1932). Chapters 5, 6, 9, and 10 deal with personal prayer as found in a variety of religious traditions. An extraordinary exposure to the act of prayer is A. Menashe, *The Face of Prayer* (New York: Alfred A. Knopf, 1983). It captures prayer as a deeply personal act through fifty black and white photographs of devotees who belong to several religious traditions.

Five volumes from the Classics of Western Spirituality series (New York: Paulist Press), which provide resources for the study of personal religious experience and devotional piety in Christianity, are:

*P. C. Erb, ed., *Pietists: Selected Writings*, 1983.

*P. C. Erb, trans., *Johann Arndt: True Christianity*, 1979.

*E. Colledge and J. Walsh, trans., *Julian of Norwich: Showings*, 1978.

*K. Kavanaugh and O. Rodriguez, *Teresa of Avila: The Interior Castle*, 1979.

*S. Noffke, trans., *Catherine of Siena: The Dialogue*, 1980.

Resources for understanding Hindu devotional life *(bhakti)* are found in *A. K. Datta, *Bhaktiyoga* (Bombay: Bharatiya Vidya Bhavan, 1959); essays by different scholars in H. Bhattacharyya, ed., *The Cultural Heritage of India*, Vol. 4: The Religions; Part II, "The Saints and Their Teachings"; A. T. Embree, *The Hindu Tradition* (New York: Random House, 1966), Part IV, "The Tradition and the People's Faith"; and portions of *L. Renou, ed., *Hinduism* (New York: Washington Square Press, 1963).

Studies of faith in Pure Land Buddhism are found in A. Bloom, *Shinran's Gospel of Pure Grace* (Tucson: University of Arizona Press, 1965); *P. O. Ingram, *The Dharma of Faith: An Introduction to Classical Pure Land Buddhism* (Washington, D.C.: University Press of America, 1977); and *D. T. Suzuki, *Shin Buddhism* (New York: Harper & Row, 1970), a personal statement by a scholar better known in the West for his expositions of Zen.

Two classical psychological analyses of personal religious experience that focus on the function of extraordinary experience in personality development are *G. W. Allport, *The Individual and His Religion* (New York: Macmillan, 1950) and *A. Maslow, *Religions, Values, and Peak-Experiences* (New York: Viking Press, 1964).

Two Christian contemporary reflections on, and appeals to affirm, the importance of prayer as a deep act of faith in response to an awareness of God's self-disclosure are J. Ellul, *Prayer and Modern Man*, translated by C. Hopkin (New York: Seabury Press, 1970) and L. Howe, *Prayer in a Secular World* (Philadelphia: United Church Press, 1973).

CHAPTER 3

Creation of Community Through Sacred Symbols

In the beginning, say the Hopi people, the Creator, Taiowa, formed Sotuknang. At Taiowa's command, Sotuknang gathered together from endless space that which became solids, winds, and water. Then Sotuknang made Kokyangwuti, Spider Woman, who was to be his helper in creating all the living beings on earth. First she made the twins, the great beings who keep the world in order, who formed sound, and who, even now, are at the north and south poles stabilizing the ordered movement and changes of the earth. Then she covered the earth with trees, grass, birds, and all kinds of animals. When Taiowa saw it, he was joyful; it was ready for human life. Then, say the Hopi seers:

> Spider Woman gathered earth, this time of four colors, yellow, red, white, and black; mixed with *tuchvala*, the liquid of her mouth; molded them; and covered them with her white-substance cape which was the creative wisdom itself. As before, she sang over them the Creation Song, and when she uncovered them, these forms were human beings in the image of Sotuknang. Then she created four other beings after her own form. They were *wuti*, female partners, for the first four male beings.
>
> When Spider Woman uncovered them, the forms came to life. This was the time of the dark purple life, Qoyangnuptu, the first phase of the dawn of Creation, which first reveals the mystery of man's creation.
>
> They soon awakened and began to move, but there was still a dampness on their foreheads and a soft spot on their heads. This was the time of the yellow light, Sikangnuga, the second phase of the dawn of Creation, when the breath of life entered man.
>
> In a short time, the sun appeared above the horizon, drying the dampness on their foreheads and hardening the soft spot on their heads. This was the time of the red light, Talawva, the third phase of the dawn of Creation, when man, fully formed and firmed, proudly faced his Creator.
>
> "That is the Sun," said Spider Woman. "You are meeting your Father the Creator for the first time. You must always remember and observe these three phases of your Creation. . . ."[1]

What is myth and why is it so powerful? Myth is more than a story about supernatural beings. It is a story whose symbolic creative force orders a person's existence into a meaningful world. It is a perspective that has ultimate value for those who live in its ordering power.

Traditional religious communities use myths and sacraments to express the nature of things as *sacred* reality. This process of ultimate transformation differs from the one discussed in Chapter 2, as it emphasizes the transforming power of symbols, myths, and rituals instead of personal experience. Although the elements of each of the four processes of ultimate transformation are the same, their expression varies. The process on which we focus in this chapter centers on the sacred symbol. Here the fundamental assumption is that it is symbols such as those declaring the sacred name of God, telling the story of the founders or divine heroes of the human race, or offering accounts of the creation that crystallize a person's deepest sensitivities for living. In this type of religious life, the use of words, symbolic gestures, and physical objects channel sacred power and thus are central to spiritual transformation.

The basic elements of ultimate transformation through sacred symbols and their expression are outlined in the following diagram. These are:

1. *The problematic in the human situation:* Human life that does not duplicate the eternal structure of meaning and order as found in the Sacred Realm is merely profane existence, characterized by weakness, ignorance, impurity, and meaninglessness.

2. *The ultimate reality:* The original and eternal resource for happiness and order is the Sacred Realm (Being), which sets limits for the profane existence and provides creative power for all long-lasting success in existence.

3. *Means to ultimate transformation:* Sacred power is released in existence (creation) through sacred words and actions, which are to be duplicated at special times and places by a sacred order of people (priests, priestesses) and which provide the models for daily living.

4. *Personal expression:* People recognize their inherent confusion and celebrate the power available from the Sacred Realm to provide meaning; people learn meaningfulness, joy, and hope through special manifestations of the true order of life known in sacred books, rituals, and contemplation of power-giving images and words.

5. *Social expression:* One's life is integrated with others into a community that express the core of its members' existence by regular repetition of solemn and awesome sacred words and gestures and by daily living in conformity with the ideal sacred order as preserved in the sacred stories and moral teachings.

This chapter, then, discusses the importance of myths, rituals, and sacred language, which creates communities and gives them power to ward off the constant creeping disorder that appears as fear, unconcern for the original and deepest resource, and meaninglessness.

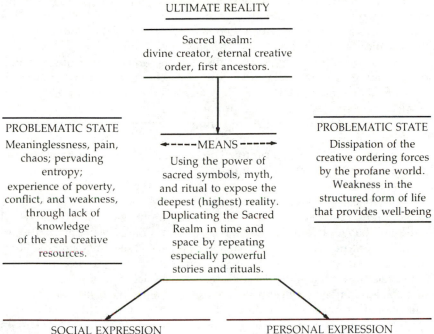

ULTIMATE REALITY

Sacred Realm:
divine creator, eternal creative
order, first ancestors.

PROBLEMATIC STATE

Meaninglessness, pain,
chaos; pervading
entropy;
experience of poverty,
conflict, and weakness,
through lack of
knowledge
of the real creative
resources.

◄----MEANS-----►

Using the power of
sacred symbols, myth,
and ritual to expose the
deepest (highest) reality.
Duplicating the Sacred
Realm in time and
space by repeating
especially powerful
stories and rituals.

PROBLEMATIC STATE

Dissipation of the
creative ordering forces
by the profane world.
Weakness in the
structured form of life
that provides well-being

SOCIAL EXPRESSION

Developing public rituals, initiation.
Using sacraments, sacred scripture, holy
words, sacred stories, holy places
(church, temple, holy mountain,
river, grotto).
Celebrating the sacred calendar
(holy days).
Acknowledging special persons: for
example, priests and holy persons.

PERSONAL EXPRESSION

Participating in public rituals, initiation.
Learning the deepest truths about life
from sacred writings, storytellers,
and official interpreters.
Cultivating one's conscience by
conforming to the sacred norm.
Gaining a sense of personal security, joy,
meaning, and sometimes physical healing
from sacred places, objects, and names.

FIGURE 1.   *Creation of Community Through Sacred Symbols*

THE PROBLEMATIC IN THE HUMAN CONDITION: MEANINGLESSNESS, IMPURITY, AND DISORDER

What is the problematic in the human condition that is cured by an appeal to myth and ritual? It is a world of meaninglessness, chaos, selfishness, and impurity. Adherents to this point of view believe there are two kinds of world: sacred and profane. In this case, *profane* simply means a world of human experience that is untouched or uninformed by the sacred eternal order. Basically, the profane world is troubled with boredom, waste, and disorder; it is a "dog eat dog" world. Indeed, it takes no special insight to see that the experience of many people is full of pain, tedium, and disappointment. The pain of the profane world affects both individuals and communities, whether Christian, Hopi, or Muslim, and leads to frustration with oneself and one's physical and social environment.

The profane world is any experience of the common world that is uninformed by wonder and ultimate significance. It is tedium experienced in a monotonous routine from which there is no escape. It is the forgetfulness of the sacrifices of one's ancestors, the viewing of heroic exploits as mere responses to mechanically conditioning factors, and the fear of imagining the (seemingly) impossible. The common, conventional experiences in which festivity and fantasy have disappeared jeopardize one's ability to see beyond the expected. Thus, the profane world is a way that life appears when its vitality is gone and there is no substance to mold aspirations.

A fundamental aspect in some expressions of the sacred-profane dichotomy is the notion of pure-impure. The sacred reality is pure, whereas the profane world is impure. The impure state is known wherever there is illness, misfortune, weakness, and death—all these experiences show a reduced or absent power. The impurity of the profane world is not primarily moral, though this is an element. Rather, the impurity of the profane world indicates that it is contaminated, mixed with strange elements, substandard, and untrue to its deepest character. As we will see, the sacred reality is the origin and deepest resource for all things including the profane world. However, through a series of mistakes, a removal from the pure source, through ignorance or willful decision, human beings have allowed the pure source of life to become contaminated so that most of human experience is a mixture of good and bad, joy and sorrow, sickness and health. Only certain forms of existence (discussed later) offer access to the original, pure source of everything.

A final aspect of the problematic character of human existence is the tendency toward disorder. Profane existence robs humanity of its true, essential nature. In this state human beings are deformed, by contrast to their original state, and those without access to the sacred reality hidden within the conventional forms of existence take the distorted forms, that is, the deformed images, of human life as the normative way for people to live together. However, because the deformed images are only partial expressions of the true reality, they lead people astray. What appears to work for human benefit in the short term often turns out to lead to self-destruction in the long run. What appears to give one security, happiness, and understanding turns out later to result in fear, suffering, and delusion. Thus, say some contemporary spokespersons, the hope of the world is not found in planned economies, military superiority, and technological discovery. These false solutions simply lead to social unrest, greater fear of war (or maybe despair), and technological control of people's lives.

THE ULTIMATE REALITY: THE SACRED REALM

If the profane world were the only world available for human habitation, humanity might despair. However, there is another world, the Sacred Realm, which can provide protection and happiness. This realm is eternal, pure (perfect), transcendent, mysterious, and all-powerful. We will call this a sacred "realm" to indicate a general notion of an incomprehensible, unchanging state of being, an original order before all worlds, and a transcendent source of all power and knowledge. This notion includes a single personal God or godhead and several powerful and complementary divinities.

The term *sacred* comes from the Latin word *sacer*, which means "set off," "restricted." It originally designated something out of the ordinary or off-limits to most people. For the ancient Romans, it could be thought of as analogous to the restricted area of an electrical or nuclear power plant because of the danger for the person coming close to it or of its destructive power for the community if the power were misused. Whatever was sacred was awesomely powerful. Similarly, Sacred Being is basically an irresistible power that moves everything—that either energizes or removes it. It is the original: the first and the most basic reality and thus also the final, last reality. Many sacred myths describe what happened "in the beginning" because to know this and to retell that kind of story reconnects one with the pure, original power. Just as important, the images of the final culmination, the end of the age (the Final Judgment) reveal the nature of things.

Like the understanding of the ultimate reality in all four traditional means to ultimate transformation, the Sacred Realm is an eternal, perfect, completed kind of reality. Like the Holy Presence, the Divine Being is often a personal ultimate reality. However, whereas the Holy Presence is infinite and awesome, and sometimes engages reality through a spontaneous symbol wrecking and institution breaking, the Sacred Realm, or Being, is also infinite and awesome, but expresses a structure or reveals *inherent characteristics* that are reflected in everyday existing forms. The eternal structure becomes incarnate, or visible, in particular gestures (sacred rituals, sacraments), physical forms (human incarnations, saints, priests), and words (names of God, scriptures, mantras). The sacred reality is, like the Holy Presence, the awesome mystery; but, unlike the Holy Presence, the sacred reality manifests an eternal, universal structure known either through the interaction of the gods with each other and human beings, as known by inspired seers or oracles or visions, or through special revelation in words and actions. The proper response to this ultimate reality is to duplicate the divine actions through repetitious chants, retold stories, careful performance of symbolic activities, and everyday actions that comply with the divine model.

Because the Sacred Realm is so powerful, it is contrasted in human awareness with the inherent weakness and impurity of the human condition. In relation to human action, the Sacred Realm also has another important function: It sets the limits of human behavior, marking the boundaries beyond which human effort should not go. When human behavior is contrary to the eternal universal structure known from divine actions or divine words, human beings are destroyed. The Sacred Realm, then, is a limit on human desire, which people have recognized throughout history by respect, humility, and fear of punishment.

Nevertheless, the Sacred Realm is also the source of life and the power to establish order and meaning to which human beings respond with trust, honor, and hope. The absolute demands of Sacred Being are combined with another prominent aspect of this ultimate reality: For the creatures who worship the Sacred Being, there is only one pattern—the sacred pattern established by God or the gods—that people must follow if they will be blessed. People are called upon to fulfill a strong either-or demand and also to recognize that there is an inherent structure manifested in a perfect or ideal *form* (name, word, image).

Such ultimate reality requires a commitment to the deepest resource of life, or God, who is revealed in specific natural or historical forms. Thus, the Sacred Being is near to everything—not identical with it, because of the contrast between the nature of the sacred and of the profane—and is the source of all natural life and social order and meaning. However, people tend to turn away from the Divine Source and find themselves in the problematic human condition. For them, the Sacred Being is hidden and even hostile. In contrast, say the advocates of God's way to live in the world, those individuals and communities that have discovered the secret power of the divine world by hearing or seeing the divine in everyday life have more power and more success than those who have not found it. From the point of view of those who observe rituals and respond to the images and teachings of sacred beings, the best way to make sense out of the profane world is to duplicate mythically prescribed patterns of behavior (sacred symbols) that will open the gate to a usually invisible, but nearby, sacred power.

MEANS TO ULTIMATE TRANSFORMATION: CONFORMING TO SACRED SYMBOLS

Symbolic images convey the deepest sensitivity to the inherent structure of the Sacred Realm, say the proponents of this religious type. All of life is imbued with symbolic structures that organize and evaluate the billions of sensory inputs into our minds. From the time we are very small children, our senses, emotions, and mental images are structured into patterns. No one can avoid the symbolizing process, which organizes and evaluates life's experiences into a meaningful awareness. From this perspective, nobody can avoid giving ultimate value to, that is, worshipping, something; such activity is inherent in the human process of building a meaningful world. Human beings have no choice of whether they will construct a symbolic order; they must decide, however, if that symbolic order accurately reflects the Sacred Realm (Being). The basic religious question, then, is whether that which one worships is indeed the true Sacred Being.

From the standpoint of the participant in this process of ultimate transformation, myth is more than a possible interpretation of life and more than a literary technique to express personal hopes and fears. Similarly, religious ritual is more than a way to reinforce a community's collective self-identity—as some social scientists suggest (see Chapter 12). Within a traditional religious context, myth and ritual are more than expressions *of* something else; they are the power for salvation, the dynamic power embodied in language and gesture that expresses the most profound, wholly encompassing, eternal (divine) reality in everyday existence. Certainly, myth and ritual are not identical with the sacred reality they reveal; however, there is a basic relationship between divine power and its symbolic image. Sacred symbols embody the Sacred Realm.

Examples of Myths and Rituals

In portraying the means to ultimate transformation through sacred symbols, we focus on both myths (sacred stories, heroic legends) and rituals (sacraments, initiation, repeated symbolic physical activity). Without trying to solve the much-debated problem of whether myths or rituals came first, we regard rituals as the dramatically acted-out representations of myths and myths as the verbal expression of the power, order, and comfort that is also found in repetitious communal symbolic action. In this way, we view such sacred activities as the Jewish Passover, Christian Holy Communion, Hindu Upanāyana, Creek Indian purification, and American Thanksgiving as reciprocally reinforcing aspects of the Jewish, Christian, Hindu, Creek, and American myths.

Keep in mind that when myth is the central means of spiritual transformation, it seeks to reveal things that are ultimately true, not things that are only vaguely known or not verified by common experience. We are not using the term *myth* in the sense of a popular superstition; for example, "It is just a myth that you get warts from picking up toads." Myths, as we discuss them here, are always true within their communal boundaries. They are the real models of what human life should and could be—and once was, according to some myths.

Before looking at the particular rituals, it might be helpful to have some idea of what rituals do for those who participate in them. A ritual provides the participant with some information about his or her community, and, more important, it reorders ordinary experience. Once the participant has been put in touch with the sacred reality, the profane world is transformed, if even for a short time. Also, the ritual offers the participant a sense of purification and rebirth. Finally, ritual offers the additional benefit of being repeatable. If the reordering of the universe becomes vague or the purification somehow wears off, one may return to the ritual for renewal.

Passover. This Jewish springtime celebration, with its unleavened bread and sanctified wine, is not simply an education for the children in the family or a reinforcement of social solidarity. This ritual is an expression of thanksgiving to God and a re-presentation of God's redeeming activity. Briefly, the first Passover (described in Chapter 12 of the biblical book of Exodus) was announced by God to Moses and Aaron, leaders of the community of Israel enslaved in Egypt. Having given instruction for the selection, slaughter, and preparation of a lamb or kid, God said the following words:

This is the way in which you must eat it [the roast lamb, unleavened bread and bitter herbs]: you shall have your belt fastened, your sandals on your feet and your staff in your hand, and you must eat in urgent haste. It is the Lord's Passover. On that night I shall pass through the land of Egypt and kill every firstborn of man and beast. Thus will I execute judgment, I the Lord, against all the gods of Egypt. And as for you, the blood [from the lambs] will be a sign on the houses in which you are: when I see the blood I will pass over you: the mortal blow shall not touch you, when I strike the land of Egypt.[2]

In writing about the major Jewish festival of Passover, Jacob Neusner, professor of Jewish studies at Brown University, points to the ultimate significance of the Exodus from Egypt:

To be a Jew means to be a slave who has been liberated by God. To be Israel means to give eternal thanks for God's deliverance. And that deliverance is not at a single moment in historical time. It comes in every generation and is always celebrated. . . . Jews think of themselves as having gone forth from Egypt, and Scripture so instructs them. God did not redeem the dead generation of the Exodus alone, but the living too—especially the living.[3]

Thus, the Passover, for a practicing Jew, is the symbolic re-presentation and celebration of Jewish self-identity, a liberation from bondage to any emotional, social, historical, or political situation. To be free to live life fully, responsibly, and with love of others is possible in everyday life when life is experienced as the extension of God's action.

Holy Communion. Although we may realize that myth and ritual reveal divine activity, or sacred power, we must be careful not to reduce myth to an information service, even if the information is sacred. Viewed from the perspective of the believer, myth and ritual transform existence and connect the Sacred Realm and profane world. In the mid-1960s, the Christian Ecumenical Council in Rome reaffirmed the ultimate significance of the sacred ritual of the Eucharist (Holy Communion) with the following words:

The renewal in the Eucharist of the covenant between the Lord and man draws the faithful into the compelling love of Christ and sets them afire. From the liturgy, therefore, and especially from the Eucharist, as from a fountain, grace is channeled into us, and the sanctification [that is, making holy] of men in Christ and the glorification of God, to which all the activities of the Church are directed as toward their goal, are most powerfully achieved.[4]

You may notice that some of the language in this statement sounds as if it could describe the apprehension of the Holy Presence. However, in this case, the emphasis is on the ritual, rather than on a personal, symbol-breaking, overwhelming experience, and on liturgical words and actions, which serve as a channel of power from the sacred reality.

In Holy Communion, the participants not only learn that it is possible to be born anew but also that they may regard themselves as new creatures. The Roman Catholic priest breaks the wafer and places a small piece in the wine, praying, "May this mingling of the body and blood of our Lord Jesus Christ bring eternal life to us who receive it."[5] By these acts, the priest is not simply remembering the Last Supper of Jesus or expressing his personal good wishes. Rather, he is symbolically repeating an action that began with God's action by which people will be transformed. In the Mass, the participant becomes a part of Christ's sacrifice. While the priest is saying the prayer just quoted, the participants chant three times, "Lamb of God, you take away the sins of the world; have mercy on us."

Roman Catholics understand that the self-sacrifice of the individual is the transformation of a human act into participation in God's act.[6] They regard the change as more than an improvement of existing nature; it is a shift from the profane life to the Sacred Realm. When the sacred power manifests itself, people learn something—but they also become something new. Thus, the myth as acted out in the ritual is more than an ideal; it is more than an explanation of life. It is an open channel to the ultimate reality.

Upanāyana. There is perhaps no other culture on earth that offers its people more opportunities for ritual practice than the Hindu culture of India. The symbolic acts of orthodox Hinduism are considered vitally important for daily living. Indeed, special rituals covering conception to funeral rites at cremation have marked the lives of many males above the lowest class for the last two thousand years. These rituals, or sacraments, are called *samskaras*. One of the most important *samskaras* is the initiation of a young boy when he first goes to a teacher for his education. It is called *upanāyana*. In this ceremony, the boy receives a sacred, unbroken thread, which he loops over his body from his left shoulder to his right hip and which he wears for the rest of his life. Regarding the significance of this rite, R. B. Pandey, formerly principal of Benares Hindu University, writes:

> The sacrament of *upanāyana*, performed at the beginning of study, marks the dawn of a new life. The student is now an *upanita*—one who is introduced to a life of perfect discipline. The sacrament symbolizes the student's entering the boundless realm of knowledge, it marks for him his destination, it asks him to be vigilant and steadfast in his path, and it reminds him of the need of complete harmony between him and his teacher. In his venture, the student is assured of the help of society, of all living creatures, and of the invisible powers. Brhaspati (the lord of knowledge), Indra (the lord of power), and Agni (the source of brilliance and energy) are held before him as his ideals.[7]

This ritual, including chanting from the Veda (the earliest Hindu sacred texts) by Brahmin priests and a ritual bath and change of clothes, symbolizes that the young boy is in a new state of purity.

Native American Purification. So far, the rituals we have discussed imply a need for purification but do not focus on that particular act. For instance, before Roman Catholics take Holy Communion, they are expected to have confessed their sins and show repentence. Through confession and absolution, a person comes to communion in a pure state. Some rituals, however, make the process of purification the focus. Through the religious ritual of purification, the finite and impure activities of people are placed in the sacred sphere where they become clean. In everyday, profane existence, life powers become choked with tensions and lose their force. Life loses its freshness and its vitality. It becomes chaotic. To correct this, the religious ritual revives the energy of life according to the divine pattern of reality.

Purification rites characterize the religious practices of some native Americans. The Oklahoma Creeks, for example, go to sacred places called "stomp grounds," where they swallow plant extracts, perhaps jimson weed and redroot, and alternate days of fasting with all-night dancing around the sacred fire. There the oldest men sing traditional songs, and the women and girls keep time with tortoise-shell rattles attached to their legs. Ingestion of the plants is supposed to purge the Indians of impurities due to wrong deeds. Pure Indians do not get sick, whereas others experience nausea and vomiting, a sign that toxins are being purged. The fasting and dancing continue the process of cleansing and renewal, until finally, at dawn, all the people wash their bodies, particularly hands, face, and feet, in the juice of the plant extracts. The Creeks must come to the stomp grounds and take "the medicine" four times a year for four years. In this way, they regain their original state of purity.

American Thanksgiving Day. Although the rituals associated with Thanksgiving Day are probably not considered by most contemporary Americans to manifest ultimate reality, they demonstrate at least two additional points about myth and ritual: (1) myth-ritual says something about where people came from and where they are going, and (2) myth-ritual requires that people personally accept the stories and rituals as part of their own basic orientation to life.

In one variation or another, American schoolchildren learn to recite the story of the pilgrims. Even though the biological ancestors of most Americans were not these people, the pilgrims have become spiritual ancestors for many. After coming as strangers to the northeastern shores of what is now the United States of America, they struggled through a harsh winter, and many died. Some were helped by friendly Native Americans who taught them how to plant corn and survive in this new world. When the first harvest was celebrated, thanks was given to God for the bounty. This story, this American myth, continues to tell Americans that courage, perseverance, and the helping hand of the Lord will grant them a bountiful life. These days, the harvest may be computer chips or cash, but the means to getting it are the same.

To relive the myth of American perseverance, schoolchildren present Thanksgiving plays and many American families sit down on the fourth Thursday in November to eat the ritual turkey and pumpkin pie. By eating as the pilgrims ate, the American family identifies itself with an ideal past and the promise of a bountiful future. A visitor from Japan might ask: "Why no prime rib of beef and cherry pie?" The answer is that Americans commemorate what their mythic forefathers did at the beginning. The myths and rituals repeat specific acts of the cultural heroes—those who had special power and insight.

Although for many Americans, the transcendent power of Thanksgiving rituals does not compare with that provided by the feast of the Passover or Holy Communion or by the sacrament of *upanāyana* for a traditional Hindu family, it is clear that communal symbols and rituals are powerful forces in structuring one's world of meaning and value. Likewise, it is important to realize that a sacred string would be meaningless to a Catholic boy, just as a communion wafer would hardly reveal the sacred to the Hindu. This failure of particular myths and rituals to translate into another community's understanding of the Sacred Realm brings up the question of whether the mystics are right when they say that all religious forms are in the final analysis just illusion.

The Power of Words

So far in this discussion of sacred action as a means to ultimate reality, we have discussed ritual as it is acted out in a kind of ceremony. These rituals are commonly formal, orderly, and solemn. Part of the power that a person derives through them comes from the action involved: taking the wine and wafer, putting on the string, eating the Passover meal. There is, however, another component of ritual that is equally powerful: the power of language. As an example, the Muslim holy book, the Qur'an, is the recitation of Allah's (God's) words as spoken to Muhammad through the angel Gabriel.[8] For centuries, this holy book was not translated from the original Arabic because orthodox Muslims felt that the power was in the words, as they were expressed in the language of Muhammad, which presumably was the language of Allah, as well.

What is it about words that makes them powerful? From daily experience we know that words have power, even if we cannot exactly explain how or why they do. Calling someone a name can lead to violence. On the other hand, speaking words can calm the frightened and quiet the angry. We know, then, that words have a psychological power; they establish a personal relationship between the speaker and the hearer. In daily use, words rarely have any more than psychological power. However, a benediction (blessing), a curse, the words used in a sacrament, and to some extent, the proclamation of the Christian gospel or the Jewish sacred history of God's salvation are felt by the participants to have power because they manifest the Sacred Realm. Such religious acts are uncommon uses of words. They still establish a relationship between the speaker and the hearer, but religious use seeks to express the ultimate, *inexpressible* reality.

When words are perceived to have creative power, they must be used carefully. In some cultures, people have secret names that outsiders do not know. If enemies should happen to learn a person's name, they would have power over him or her forever. Similarly, to use God's name "in vain" is to forget that using the name of God generates power. A priest, for example, can heal or destroy life since he knows the divine name. The names and myths of supreme beings—within the context of mythical thought—are gates of power that open ordinary experience to the awesome Sacred Realm.

Just as musical sounds can be made louder through amplification, so can the power of a word be increased in various ways. The potency of an oath can be intensified by repetition, or the manner of taking an oath can heighten its power. In the United States, an oath is taken with the right hand up, palm forward, and the left hand on another sacred word, the Bible. Likewise, raising the voice or using rhythm or rhyme can heighten the power of utterances. If the Hindu holy men saying public prayers for the pilgrims who come to bathe in the holy river Ganges were to speak in a conversational tone, the effect of the prayers would be greatly diminished. Instead, the prayers are sung to a clipped and regular rhythm. Finally, some special words possess intensified power: *Hallelujah* and *Amen* in the Christian West, *Om* in Hinduism, and the chant, *Namo Myoho Renge-Kyo* in Nichiren Buddhism of Japan.

When a devotee uses a chant, blessing, curse, or myth in a ritual way, the power that arises—according to advocates of this way—does not come from personal desire or hope, but from its sacredness. In turn, the sacred word has the power to structure existence, organize human life, and recreate everyday events in terms of the eternal, divine model. When speech is used as a ritual act and possesses transcendent force, the words the devotee uses become extremely important. To unlock divine power, the devotee must use a specific invocation, benediction, or name for God. Only the exact combination will work. For example the orthodox Hindu Brahmin priest believes that the Sanskrit verses of the ancient Veda are themselves powerful.[9] However, the power depends on repeating the verses exactly as they were spoken originally—the sounds may not be changed. Therefore, to translate the verse into another language would make it useless in the religious ritual. The sounds would be lost and so would the power in them.

Mantras (ritual verses) are also part of ritual Buddhism, reaching their most elaborate form in Tibetan Buddhism. Although meditation was the central means of transformation among serious followers of the Buddhist way, ritual practice was often combined with it to control the mind and emotions. In an Indian Mahayana Buddhist manual called *The Lamp for Beginners*, for example, is the following instruction for a disciple who worships the Buddha image and thereby invokes the power of Buddhahood (the Sacred Power) through the mantras *Om* and *svaha*.

> He calls down the deity, saying: OM delight in the Law SVAHA!
> He established him therein, saying: OM well-founded diamond SVAHA!
> He consecrates it, saying: OM womb of the realm of reality, come, take away! SVAHA!
> And he asks for forbearance toward errors in the ritual he has performed, saying: OM womb of the realm of space SVAHA![10]

In Judaism, Christianity, and Islam, the power of the word is recognized in the unique quality ascribed to sacred scriptures: the Torah, the New Testament, and the Qur'an. These books describe God's creative acts and give accounts of God's law, as well as portray special divine actions in history. Central to each of these religions is the belief that human beings have access to divine power through God's disclosure of himself at particular times and places. By following God's will as expressed in these writings, human beings can live to some degree in sacred reality.

In summary, from the perspective of those who take sacred (ritual) action to be the true means to ultimate transformation, the profane world is filled with pain, disappointment, and lack of personal or communal control of happiness. There is, however, a cure for the profane world that is hidden in it: the sacred reality. This sacred power may be an impersonal one, a personal lord or goddess, or a collection of forces. However the sacred is known, it is the source of all life, the source of renewal, and the source of complete happiness.

To get in touch with this power that will cure the profane world, the devotee depends on sacred symbolism, rather than on a personal experience of God, ethical behavior, or mystical insight. Only myth and ritual bear enough power for salvation. Ritual language and action may initiate, purify, or transform life altogether. How then does the individual, both personally and socially, demonstrate his trust in sacredness as a means to the ultimate?

PERSONAL EXPRESSION: BLESSINGS, JOY, AND WISDOM

The individual who discovers the ultimate reality through sacred symbols holds the conviction that, without the special power that comes from myth and ritual, a person is sinful, weak, and self-destructive. Therefore, the devotee regularly practices the recurring rites of his or her religious tradition. For example, daily Bible study and frequent attendance at Holy Communion deepen the meaning of Christ's life, teaching, sacrifice, and resurrection for the Christian; the repetition of prayer *(Salat)* five times a day beginning early in the morning and ending when one goes to bed or the pilgrimage to Mecca keeps the devout Muslim in the attitude of self-surrender to, and praise of, God; and the Hopi who reflects on the meaning of the monthly sacred dances year in and year out becomes sensitive to the unseen forces of life symbolized in the special masks, corn, spruce branches, and other ritual objects.

Similarly, the devotee maintains that the sacred stories and sacraments are necessary processes for transformation. For the development of conscience and the ethical skills of acting from pure motives, a person will look to sacred authority for direction. The model of the sacred world as found in scripture or oral tradition serves to guide one's personal life. The truth about life is eternal and has been revealed to the ancient seers.

Although the significance of the particular symbolic forms and central myths of a religious tradition is continually reinterpreted throughout history, the power of ultimate transformation is seen to reside in the sacred word and actions (for example, sacraments, initiations, and sacred dances). People from all religious traditions who affirm the centrality of symbolic power therefore often regard personal extraordinary experiences of a holy presence (discussed in Chapter 2) as secondary expressions of sacred power; or sometimes they judge individual religious experiences to be the work of evil spirits, especially when the experience departs radically from the myths and symbols preserved by the priests. For such religious adherents, only the sacred knowledge found in sacred scriptures or ancient oral tradition can give direction for distinguishing truth from self-deception.

From this standpoint the goal of sacred rituals is to open the gates of the sacred world to let blessings, joy, and wisdom flow into life. The blessings that people experience are matched by a sense of contamination and turmoil, which result from breaking the sacred law; the blessings set things straight. Likewise, there is a sense of celebrating life or of serenity despite everyday problems and a hope of an abundant life derived from the sacred power. By using the sacred models as a basis for self-examination, a person will know how to experience the true riches of life. Since the awareness of the sacred world is the purest and most enjoyable experience of life possible, life modeled by myth and ritual expresses the deepest sense of vitality and wholeness.

SOCIAL EXPRESSION: PUBERTY RITES, SACRED PEOPLE, PLACES, AND TIME

The most obvious social forms of sacred action are religious celebrations, such as the Passover, the Mass, and *upanāyana*. By joining in the celebration, the individual confirms his or her association with the community and affirms the sacred source of life. There are, however, other social expressions that are equally important. Among them are participation in puberty or initiation rites, accepting the authority of priests and teachers, recognizing the power of holy places, and following the observances of a sacred calendar.

Puberty and Initiation Rites

In general, the purpose of puberty and initiation rites is to change ceremonially an unconnected, ignorant child into a new adult—one who is connected to the sacred reality as known by the community. The change gives the person who is being initiated the knowledge and spiritual power he or she needs to live in the context of ultimate reality. Looking at secular initiation processes might help clarify what happens in the religious context.

When a new army recruit enters basic training, he begins a kind of initiation. He is ignorant, despised, and unconnected. His head is shaved and his civilian clothes are taken away from him to be replaced with army issue. In the weeks that follow, he endures physical and mental hardship, lives separated from his previous friends and family, and shares the experience only with his fellow recruits. At the end of the designated period, the recruit achieves the rank of private and is no longer a child but a man. He acts as part of a community of soldiers, putting his old responsibilities behind him. In a similar fashion, college fraternities strip their pledges of their previous lives and through various ordeals transform them into "frat men." The initiation process gives these new men the experience of being a nobody until a new self-identity is symbolically created through secret names, ritual ceremonies, and a new network of obligations.

When we turn to traditional religious initiation rites, such as those found among the aborigines in Australia or the Masai in Kenya, Africa, we find that the symbolic learning processes are similar to those in military and fraternal initiations but different in degree and value. The Masai boys (ages twelve to sixteen) prepare for the ceremony by spending two months in the countryside without weapons. After that two months, the ceremony takes place:

On the day before the ceremony, the boys wash themselves in cold water. When their foreskin is cut off, the blood is collected in an oxhide and put on each boy's head. For four days the boys are kept in seclusion, after which they emerge dressed like women and having their faces painted with white clay and heads adorned with ostrich feathers. A few weeks later, when their sex organs have healed, the heads are shaved and the boys grow new hair and can become warriors.[11]

Although it is not as elaborate as the ceremony for the boys, the girls have their own ceremony, which includes cutting or piercing the sex organ. After the wounds have healed, the girls can get married.[12]

Aside from making them a real part of the community, Masai initiation turns the individual candidates into a single unit. This unity extends into every part of daily living. J. Mbiti, professor of religious studies at Makerere University in Uganda, Africa, describes the connection as follows:

The young people who have been initiated together become mystically and ritually bound to each other for the rest of their lives: they are in effect one body, one group, one community, one people. They help one another in all kinds of ways. The wife of one man is equally the wife of other men in the same [initiation] group; and if one member visits another he is entitled to sleep with the latter's wife, whether or not the husband is at home. This is a deep level of asserting the group solidarity, and one at which the individual really feels that "I am because we are; and, since we are, therefore I am."[13]

Although not all initiation rites are as dramatic as those practiced by the Masai, initiation rites in any religious context expresses to the community the power of the symbolic means to transformation and, by repeating the ceremonies of ages past, offers the community a sense of continuity.

Sacred People

In addition to participating in specific rituals for initiation into adulthood, people may acknowledge the value of ritual in various other ways. In theistic traditions, a person conforms his or her life to God's word, will, and purpose as preserved in a sacred calendar or in holy places. Furthermore, special persons such as priests, teachers, and masters are recognized as embodying the sacred, at least during the sacred ritual. In the ritual, the priest, the sacred objects used in the ritual, and the sacred (consecrated) place are the point of contact between the sacred and profane worlds.

During the religious ritual, the priest loses his individual identity as a person and speaks in the name of God. The masks used by the officiants in some African religious ceremonies, the ceremonial robes used by Christian priests, the purification rites performed by priests of Hinduism or Shinto are necessary to separate the person of the priest in his everyday existence from his personification of sacred power during the ritual activity. Similarly, the painted bodies of the Native Americans in ceremonial dances symbolize the nature of things. For example, Black Elk, a holy man of the Oglala Sioux, recounts the vision of an old man who explained the sacred meaning of body markings in the Sun Dance:

> The bodies were to be painted red from the waist up; the face, too, must be painted red, for red represents all that is sacred, especially the earth, for we should remember that it is from the earth that our bodies come, and it is to her that they return. A black circle should be painted around the face, for the circle helps us to remember WAKAN-TANKA [the Great Spirit], who, like the circle, has no end. There is much power in the circle, as I have often said; the birds know this for they fly in a circle, and build their homes in the form of a circle; this the coyotes know also, for they live in round holes in the ground. Then a black line should be drawn from the forehead to a point between the eyes; and a line should be drawn on each cheek and on the chin, for these four lines represent the Powers of the four directions.[14]

Such devices convert the frail human person into the manifestation of sacred power in concrete form.

Whenever a priest performs his sacred role, he re-presents the sacred: He manifests anew the divine patter or acts of God. In theistic religion, the priest becomes the representative and servant of God, mediating divine power to the world. In the ancient Vedic religion of India, however, where the impersonal divine power (Brahman) was regarded as the source of existence, the sacred ritual gained even more significance. The ritual became the machinery for transforming the hidden divine power into the everyday biological and social processes. Through his ritual activity, the Brahmin priest, in fact, had the responsibility to maintain the cosmic order. In both the theistic and nontheistic interpretations of the sacred, the priest, under the special circumstances of officiating at the sacrifice or sacrament, becomes the vehicle or channel for exposing the ultimate creative force of the universe.

Sacred Places

A sacred place is a gateway between the two worlds of the sacred and the profane. A pious person visiting a place that is sacred to his or her religious tradition, such as a shrine or a sacred city (Mecca, Jerusalem, or Benares), is touching the cosmic boundary shared by both worlds. To be at a sacred place means to participate in the power of the eternal. Even though most existence is seen as chaotic, dead, or meaningless, at a sacred place new life can come forth. Because the place serves as the point of contact with God or with infinite power, it takes on the quality of holiness or sacredness. But, although a sacred place may be beautiful, fascinating, or difficult to get to, its sacredness does not come from any of its physical qualities. It is the specific actions of the ritual celebrating the unusual (sacred) power of truth and reality that appeared in the location that gives its power.

For instance, there is a sacred hill in South India called Tirukkalikkundram. There are 800 steps leading to the top of the hill where there is a small temple dedicated to Shiva, the god of creation and destruction. According to tradition, two sacred birds (kites, or eagles) fly to the temple each day to be fed by Shiva's priests. This hill has become a place of pilgrimage for the devout. They give alms to the beggars who have gathered there, make the hard climb to the top of the hill, and wait for the birds to arrive. Whether the birds come (and they often do not) is almost irrelevant. The place has been invested with spiritual value by the devotee's recognition of the great god Shiva. A trip there brings renewal for the pilgrim and confirms the sacredness of the location.

A temple, like some geographic locations, is a specific place where divine power reveals itself. Since the temple is the point of contact between earth and heaven, it is only natural that the temple reveal symbolically the character of the Divine Realm. The Hopi Indian kivas (underground ceremonial chambers) of the American Southwest were placed in a central location in a pueblo. Inside is a fire pit and a small hole—the *sipapu*—which symbolizes the place where human beings emerged from previous levels of other worlds. Similarly, the effort to build according to the divine plan, rather than according to human imagination, is seen in the detailed instructions for temple building in the writings of the ancient Hebrews, of classical India, and of China. Indeed, the architect's lack of personal freedom to design a temple was an indication of the sacredness or divine power in his work.

Sacred Time

Just as the profane world runs on a civil calendar, so does the sacred world run on a holy one. However, instead of being marked by days, months, and years, the sacred calendar marks time in the important festivals of life: Christmas (Christian), Yom Kippur (Jewish), Diwali (Hindu). A religious calendar is a repetition of the divine life, and those who follow it renew their lives. Thus, New Year festivals (which do not all occur on December 31) are preceded by events of disorderliness. Even the popular American celebration often demonstrates that, before the beginning of new, pure life, represented by the new year, there is a return to chaos, represented by the New Year's Eve party.

SUMMARY

All religious communities and societies use symbols, including myths and rituals, to structure a comprehensive world of experience. The power to construct meaning through symbols is not regarded by all religious people as the only, or even central, means whereby people know the ultimate context of life or bring it most significantly into daily living. However, for some the use of symbols is the central mode of religious life. This is so despite the fact that the advocates of this mode of ultimate transformation in different communities have quite different symbol systems. The differences and sometimes conflicts between these advocates are not over questions of whether sacred symbols are important or whether there is a Sacred Realm but over where and when the Sacred Realm has most completely been manifested. What is the true sacred word? Which sacred ritual or sacrament truly transforms—eliminates ignorance, washes away guilt, connects the weak and immature with the source of all life? The elements that are common to all expressions of this way of being religious are as follows:

1. Life in the everyday, profane world that is unconnected with a hidden, sacred, transcendent world is full of weakness, ignorance, impurity, evil, and meaninglessness.

2. The source of the most complete happiness, of continual renewal, of all blessing is a personal or impersonal sacred force or set of forces that transcends all creation and destruction and, at the same time, manifests itself in specific cultural and natural forms.

3. Weakness, evil, and ignorance in the profane world is transformed into power, goodness, and knowledge through a community's participation in sacred words, gestures, and rituals, which reveal and release sacred power.

4. Personal expression focuses on conformity with the sacred models found in sacred scriptures and rituals, self-examination based on religious heroes and ancestral models, and celebration of the well-being provided by the sacred power.

5. Social expression focuses on public repetition and social conformity to the sacred order of life, which is manifested through sacred places, times, persons, and objects.

SELECTED READINGS

M. Eliade, primarily using data from nonliterate cultures, elaborates the significance of this religious form in *Cosmos and History* (New York: Harper, 1954), especially Chapters 1 and 2; *Myth and Reality* (New York: Harper, 1963), Chapters 1, 3, and 6; *The Sacred and the Profane*, Chapters 1–3; and *Rites and Symbols of Initiation* (New York: Harper, 1965). See also M. Eliade, ed., *From Primitives to Zen* (New York: Harper & Row, 1967), Chapters 2 and 3 for examples of myths of creation, and descriptions of sacred place and time, sacrifice, rituals, and initiations.

Two other important explanations of establishing the sacred through myth and sacrament are found in *G. van der Leeuw, *Religion in Essence and Manifestation* (New York: Harper, 1963; first published in 1933), Part I, "The Object of Religion," and Part III, Section A, "Outward Action"; and in W. B. Kristensen, *The Meaning of Religion*, Part III, "Cultus."

F. J. Streng, C. L. Lloyd, Jr., J. T. Allen, eds., *Ways of Being Religious* (Englewood Cliffs, NJ: Prentice-Hall, 1973), Chapter 2, "Creation of Community Through Myth and Ritual," provides excerpts, sympathetic descriptions, and critiques of a mythic-ritual religious process.

An important anthropological analysis of ritual as symbolic action is found in the work of Victor Turner. In *The Forest of Symbols* (Ithaca: Cornell University Press, 1967) and *The Ritual Process: Structure and Anti-Structure* (Chicago, Aldine, 1969), he shows that a major function of ritual is to give form to personal and social transitions; in *The Drums of Affliction* (Ithaca: Cornell University Press, 1981; originally published in 1968) and *Dramas, Fields and Metaphors: Symbolic Action in Human Society* (Ithaca: Cornell University Press, 1974), he continues his analysis of ritual, emphasizing that symbols are not only bearers of sacred information, but also creators of social values.

Various anthropological studies of myth and ritual from different parts of the world are collected in two books of readings edited by J. Middleton: *Myth and Cosmos* (Garden City, NY: Natural History Press, 1967) and *Gods and Rituals* (Garden City, NY: natural History Press, 1967).

A psychoanalytic approach to myths and symbols from different cultures is found in the works of C. G. Jung and J. Campbell. One volume from the *Collected Works of C. G. Jung* where readers can get an orientation to Jung's understanding of the central role of symbols in the formation of human personality is *Symbols of Transformation,* 2nd ed. (Princeton, NJ: Princeton University Press, 1967). In J. Campbell's four-volume work *The Masks of God* (New York: Viking Press, 1959–1968), the first three analyze symbols from primitive, Eastern, and Western cultures, and the fourth volume, subtitled *Creative Mythology,* analyzes literature, secular philosophy, and the arts to expose living myth in contemporary Western life. A single-volume introduction to Campbell's approach to symbols in human experience is *The Hero with a Thousand Faces* (Cleveland: World, 1956).

Two classic studies of myths and ritual in archaic and ancient societies, which deal with the reality experienced in psychosocial change, are:

*A. van Gennep, *The Rites of Passage* (Chicago: University of Chicago Press, 1960; first published 1908). While much anthropological information has been collected since this book was first published, it still makes an important contribution to the interpretation of sacred action in describing the magico-religious aspect of crossing personal, social, and geographic boundaries.

T. Gaster, *Thespis: Ritual, Myth and Drama in the Ancient Near East* (New York: Henry Schuman, 1950). This study focuses on seasonal rituals that combine concrete and ideal forms to cleanse and to give power to those who participate in them.

Two philosophical analyses of religious symbols are:

*S. K. Langer, *Philosophy in a New Key* (Cambridge, MA: Harvard University Press, 1942). A study of the processes involved in forming symbols that are used in reason, sacrament, myth, and art.

J. E. Smith, *The Analogy of Experience* (New York: Harper & Row, 1973). The author places the Christian claims of truth in the context of religious intention and communal transforming power.

A still useful comparative exposition of the meaning found in ritual forms is E. O. James, *Sacrifice and Sacrament* (London: Thames & Hudson, 1962), a study of sacramental forms in the religions of the Near East and Vedic India. Chapters 1 and 9 present James's understanding of the principles of religious meaning in sacraments.

Studies of particular sacred places created through living in the symbolic world of myth and rituals are found in *S. D. Gill, *Native American Religions* (Belmont, CA: Wadsworth, 1982), Chapter 1, "The Place to Begin"; and D. L. Eck, *Banaras: City of Light* (New York: Alfred A. Knopf, 1982). For a general introduction to religious landscapes in various cultures, see *D. E. Sopher, *Geography of Religions* (Englewood Cliffs, NJ: Prentice-Hall, 1967).

CHAPTER 4

Living in Harmony with Cosmic Law

The traditional means to ultimate transformation discussed in the last two chapters are probably familiar to most readers. People in the West are accustomed to thinking about religion in terms of God, holiness, religious visions, personal faith, prayer, sacraments, religious symbols, and mythology. Religion is often defined as a belief system or an organized community, such as a church or synagogue. Nevertheless, for many people throughout the world, the means to ultimate transformation is not essentially a personal apprehension of a Holy Presence nor a manifestation of the sacred through symbolic forms. For example, the late Indian philosopher, S. Radhakrishnan, writes:

> Hinduism is more a way of life than a form of thought. While it gives absolute liberty in the world of thought, it enjoins a strict code of practice. The theist and the atheist, the skeptic and the agnostic, may all be Hindus if they accept the Hindu system of culture and life. Hinduism insists not on religious conformity but on a spiritual and ethical outlook in life. "The performer of the good—and not the believer in this or that view—can never get into an evil state." In a very real sense, practice precedes theory. Only by doing the will does one know the doctrine. Whatever our theological beliefs and metaphysical opinions may be, we are all agreed that we should be kind and honest, grateful to our benefactors and sympathetic to the unfortunate.[1]

In this excerpt, Radhakrishnan uses the term *religious* in the restricted sense of a belief system or doctrine and indicates that for him, "a spiritual and ethical outlook" is even more basic. In this chapter, we will see that for some people there is nothing more important than social morality and ethical principles.

Another recent statement, this one from a Chinese philosopher and advocate of Confucianism, Chün-i T'ang, affirms that learning one's proper "place," or set of relationships, within the social order is the very nature of being human. He writes:

> To talk about the Confucianist religion we have to discuss first of all the Confucianist learning . . . The more important part of his learning lies in this: how to be filial as a son, to be benevolent as a father, to be a friendly companion as the elder brother to a younger brother, to be respectful as a younger brother—learning to practice the ethical principle in all kinds of human relationships. The extension of it calls for learning to run the government properly, to bring about peace and harmony to the world, and to set up political, economic, social, and legal systems for people far and near. But, still more important is that the Confucianist learning progresses from full utilization of one's intelligence to complete actualization of the principles in human relations, in all systems and to the complete actualization of his "human heart" and "human nature" so as to make himself a "real" man. This is what is called "learning to make one *the* man."[2]

Here we see that the highest human attainment is moral conduct, which expresses the deepest reality of life.

Before outlining the five basic elements in this process of ultimate transformation, let us compare them with some of the elements in the religious processes discussed earlier. In Chapters 2 and 3, the central dynamics of the transforming processes were inner personal experiences or verbal and ritual symbols; here the focus is on harmonious social relationships that reflect a concept of a natural universal order of life. As we mentioned before, different religious processes include some of the same elements. A deep awareness of the Holy Presence or participation in the symbolic power of sacredness is usually accompanied by ethical concerns. Moveover, individuals with an ethical outlook, like Radhakrishnan and T'ang, are also likely to use specific symbols or rituals and may even have a personal sense of awesome presence in life. The differences in the processes, however, lie in the importance assigned to personal experience, sacred symbols, or ethical actions. Awareness of a Holy Presence includes an ethical concern, but it emerges from the overwhelming experience of personal confrontation with God. Symbolic transformation often includes a sense of awe before the sacred, as well as a concern to live a righteous life in conformity with God's will, but these feelings develop from the ultimately transforming power in the symbols. Some forms of theistic religion do, nevertheless, emphasize social ethics more than others, for example, the Jewish effort to live the life of Torah (God's law) and the orthodox Muslim's focus on submission to God's will as revealed in the Qur'an and in orthodox tradition.

To distinguish the third type of traditional religious process, we use the nontheistic expressions from China and India as the prime models. They demonstrate that one religious option is the recognition of a transcendent law of life that provides a universal moral order without a divine lawgiver. In this chapter, then, the central dynamics of ultimate transformation will be daily living in harmony with the cosmic, universal, ultimate law.

The basic elements in the religious process of transformation centered on living in harmony with cosmic law, outlined in Figure 1, are as follows:

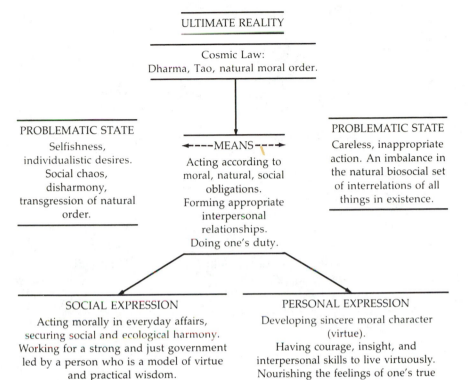

ULTIMATE REALITY

Cosmic Law:
Dharma, Tao, natural moral order.

PROBLEMATIC STATE

Selfishness,
individualistic desires.
Social chaos,
disharmony,
transgression of natural
order.

←---MEANS---→

Acting according to
moral, natural, social
obligations.
Forming appropriate
interpersonal
relationships.
Doing one's duty.

PROBLEMATIC STATE

Careless, inappropriate
action. An imbalance in
the natural biosocial set
of interrelations of all
things in existence.

SOCIAL EXPRESSION

Acting morally in everyday affairs,
securing social and ecological harmony.
Working for a strong and just government
led by a person who is a model of virtue
and practical wisdom.
Instituting ancient tradition wisely
interpreted for present conditions.
Legal and social norms based on educating
in appropriate action, duties, and
understanding the self.

PERSONAL EXPRESSION

Developing sincere moral character
(virtue).
Having courage, insight, and
interpersonal skills to live virtuously.
Nourishing the feelings of one's true
place so social obligations are
spontaneously expressed.
Cultivating practical wisdom.

FIGURE 1.   *Living in Harmony with Cosmic Law*

1. *The problematic in human existence:* Disharmony, and even chaos, in
   the natural world is seen in disasters and illness; and in the social
   world, in hate, immorality, conflict, war, or inappropriate social activity that does not reflect one's place in the natural order. It is
   caused by a selfish misuse of the potential inherent in life.
2. *Ultimate reality:* The Cosmic Law is eternal and implicit in all existing
   forms. This natural and pervasive principle is expressed by both
   physical nature and social life, demonstrating the interrelated organic nature of existence.
3. *Means to ultimate transformation:* By living according to the natural
   organic rhythm of the physical world and the ancestral tradition in
   one's social relationships, a person can express her or his proper
   nature and function properly (that is, morally) within the Cosmic
   Law.

4. *Personal expression:* The inner experiences sought in this religious process are a sense of security, peace with oneself and the world, affection for, and loyalty to, one's primary social group, and a personal sense of responsibility to live a productive and orderly life.
5. *Social expression:* Proper (moral) social relationships that are lived out in everyday life are a necessary element. The norms for the proper relationships are found in natural distinctions, tested traditions of many generations, revered writings of the ancients, and noble and just leaders of a society.

THE PROBLEMATIC IN THE HUMAN CONDITION: CHAOS DUE TO SELFISHNESS

The basic difficulty with life is the disharmony and trouble—chaos—that results from individual desires and selfishness. When individuals do not recognize that they are part of the eternal order of things, they bring discord to natural harmony and interrupt the flow of life. Those who are ignorant of the natural balance and interaction of everything tend to make inappropriate choices in relation to other people, nature, and even the natural development of their own lives. Such inappropriate decisions lead to psychological, social, and even biological imbalances known conventionally as hate, fear, international conflict, and destruction of land, water, and air. In sum, selfishness destroys true self-identity and leads to disharmony, which is in unnatural opposition to the eternal order.

In one of the basic Confucian books, *Central Harmony* (about 400 B.C.E.), the character of one who creates disharmony (called the vulgar person) is compared with that of the moral (ideal) person:

> The life of the moral man is an exemplification of the universal moral order [*chung yung,* usually translated as "the Mean"]. The life of the vulgar person, on the other hand, is a contradiction of the universal moral order.
>
> The moral man's life is an exemplification of the universal order, because he is a moral person who unceasingly cultivates his true self or moral being. The vulgar person's life is a contradiction of the universal order, because he is a vulgar person who, in his heart, has no regard for, or fear of, the moral law.[3]

The vulgar man is a wretched creature who, at every misdirected turn, sends ripples of discord, however slight, into the natural organic flow of the universe.

From the Hindu tradition, we can see from some verses in the Bhagavad-Gita the problematic state of chaos that civil war causes. The warrior Arjuna laments the destruction of a war in which one must kill one's kinsmen just to get control of an empire:

> Even if they, whose minds are destroyed by greed, do not see the sin caused by the destruction of a family and the crime incurred in the injury to a friend;
>
> Why should we not have the wisdom to turn back from this sin, we who see the evil in the destruction of the family, O Janardana (Krishna)?

In the ruin of a family, its immemorial laws perish; and when the laws perish, the whole family is overcome by lawlessness.

And when lawlessness prevails, O Krishna, the women of the family are corrupted, and when women are corrupted, O Varshneya, a mixture of caste arises.

And this confusion brings the family itself to hell and those who have destroyed it; for their ancestors fall, deprived of their offerings of rice and water.

By the sins of those who destroy a family and create a mixture of caste, the eternal laws of the caste and the family are destroyed.

The men of the families whose laws are destroyed, O Janardana, assuredly will dwell in hell; so we have heard.

Alas, what a great sin we resolved to commit in undertaking to kill our own people through our greed for the pleasures of kingdom.[4]

Those who destroy a family, provoke lawlessness, and disregard the immemorial laws (dharma) because of greed surely work their own destruction. Krishna eventually admonishes Arjuna that his duty (also dharma) as a warrior is to fight to establish righteousness, and thus he appeals to a deeper sense of law; but here we can see that greed causes suffering and destruction.

As we will see later, there are significant differences in the particular social expressions of what it means to follow the immemorial and natural law in China, India, the ancient Roman Empire, and the modern West. However, here we want to point out some general similarities in this type of religious life, where disorder (chaos) results from upsetting the natural organic relationships that are assumed to pervade the whole of human experience. A person who abuses his or her position in the social order destroys the natural social harmony. If one has no sense of obligation, duty, and responsibility to others, one does not really perceive what it means to be human at the most fundamental level. Personal happiness requires a relationship with one's physical and social environment. Exploitation of natural resources and of other people upsets the organic flow of existence. Aggressive behavior motivated by individual, selfish interests leads to self-destruction, as well as competition and conflict in society. If people forget that they owe a debt for life to their ancestors, family members, the producers of food, educators, responsible government officials, or anyone working for the social welfare, they do not understand the delicate nature of life. Such lack of awareness leads to a confused attachment to the self and to behavior that is detrimental in the long run to the whole network of life.

ULTIMATE REALITY: THE COSMIC LAW

Simple observation confirms that both vulgarity and discord are at work in the world today. What, then, is the nature of the ultimate reality that transforms that discord and shows the way to the moral human being? What is the ultimate context of all existence that restores harmony and provides for a moral existence? It is the Cosmic Law. This universal principle in the ancient Chinese way of life is called the Tao; in Hinduism it is the dharma; in Western thought it is sometimes referred to as the universal moral nature.

Before we look at these particular cultural expressions, let us examine three general characteristics of the Cosmic Law: (1) natural distinctions are intrinsic to the ultimate reality; (2) all existing phenomena, which are in an orderly relationship to each other, are parts of an organic whole; and (3) there is an intrinsic continuity between the universal principle and concrete events and things.

General Characteristics

The ultimate reality in this religious process is expressed in natural distinctions between the forms of existence. Some of these natural distinctions are social and others are physical; many are commonly accepted in different societies: the distinctions between men and women, plants and animals, infants and adults, heat and cold, wetness and dryness, and hardness and softness. Some of these distinctions reflect a social, as well as a physical or biological, difference. Similarly, the eternal social or moral order is an extension of a natural universal order in all existence.

These distinctions are natural because they are given with one's birth. They not only vary in form but also imply a ranking of higher and lower, primary and secondary, better and worse. Contemporary expressions like "He is a natural comedian," or "She has a gift for playing the piano" reflect this kind of distinction. A person is born with an intrinsic advantage or disadvantage in any situation. Natural distinction is also at the basis of the contemporary issue of the proper roles of men and women. Few doubt the biological differences between men and women; however, at issue is whether men and women have equal capacities for the same roles in society. The Cosmic Law orientation assumes that the biological difference extends into the very order of social relationships because social relationships are an extension of biological distinctions. (In Chapter 7, on the religious nature of social responsibility, we will see that there is no such assumption.)

The second characteristic of the Cosmic Law is that any expression of life in the universal natural order is a part of the organic whole. Thus, the growth of every seed, the flow of every river, the development of every person—all perceptions, feelings, decisions to behave appropriately or inappropriately—are part of a larger whole and ultimately part of a universal, cosmic process. If people are not aware of this, they will behave in a distorted way. Thus, it is necessary to know what the ultimate Cosmic Law is if one wants to live fully and function smoothly in that universal natural process. Although this may seem to suggest that the part—what one had for lunch, what one is thinking at any moment, how one behaves when meeting another person—is unimportant by comparison to the larger set of relationships, such as one's ongoing habits or general life style, this is not the case. Each part is important for the functioning of the whole. A person's thoughts, attitudes, feelings, or perceptions in any given moment contribute to his or her whole personality. Similarly, every individual's particular behavior affects the behavior of any social group, and any subgroup's behavior contributes to the working of a larger group and of the extended environment. So, every moment of a person's life is important for the harmonious—or disharmonious—working of the cosmic process.

Related to the first two characteristics is the third, which is the intrinsic continuity between the eternal Cosmic Law and the changing concrete phenomena of life. This means that the Cosmic Law is not some different kind of reality from the forms and flow of ordered existence. In contrast to the sense of radical difference in the ultimate reality experienced by the advocates of the first two types of religion, Cosmic Law adherents see no break between the Holy Presence and the secular world or between the Sacred Realm and profane existence. Indeed, the Cosmic Law is eternal, whereas life forms are seen as temporal; the Cosmic Law is by nature harmonious, whereas existence can include disharmony, as well as harmony; and the Cosmic Law is infinitely comprehensive—that is, incomprehensible in its totality—whereas parts of the cosmic process can be understood and used as models for harmonious action. However, the Cosmic Law expresses itself through specific physical forms and each person's thought and actions. Thus, the term for the ultimate reality in this type of religious life may be the same as for the concrete moral action, as we see in the Hindu term *dharma* (law, duty, reality); or the ultimate reality, the life principle, may be designated by different terms in different contexts, as Chün-i T'ang explains:

> [The] life principle is the foundation of the formation and development of every event. Therefore, it is the most general principle in the universe. It is also a basic principle underlying the rise of any event. Since it is the principle followed and shared by all things, it is the Tao of myriad things or the Tao of nature. It is also what the *I Ching* [a Chinese classic text containing some of the most ancient Chinese cosmology] called the principle of *ch'ien* and *k'un* through which all existences are evolved and completed. It is also the principle of jen ["human-heartedness," or human nature] in the universe. This principle of life, or principle of jen, being imminent in everything, makes the rise and growth of every natural object or event possible and necessary. This is also the principle which makes the natural world continue to exist.[5]

All phenomena that manifest the natural order—every event, individual, life process, or action—are naturally bipolar. This means it is natural for everything to be weak and strong, below and above, part and whole, depending on the shifting contexts of existence. Likewise, life processes naturally put one into advantageous and disadvantageous positions, dangerous and secure situations, beginnings and endings, ritually polluted and ritually pure conditions. Even death at old age, although a radical change, is natural. In sum, the Cosmic Law mandates the inherent distinctions in life and the organic interrelatedness of everything, and it pervades concrete everyday life. To act out one's place in this Cosmic Law, as it is manifest in every changing form, is the goal in this process of ultimate transformation.

The Tao in Confucianism

The term *Tao* means "path," "road," or "way." It is *the* way of natural life, the principle of the way things really are. This kind of ultimate reality is immediately present in one's experience. So, we are not surprised to find a statement credited to Confucius that reads:

> The Master said, *Tao* is not far from man. If what one takes to be *Tao* is far from man, it cannot be considered [the true] *Tao*.[6]

As a principle, however, the Tao should not be considered a static, absolute structure that implants itself in forms. Rather, it is the ordering process that makes possible the changing movement of the world. The overarching universal way of life is as much a product of the particular movement of things, human decisions, and individual experiences as it is the condition for making order—instead of chaos—possible.

A basic set of concepts used by the Chinese to show the inherent capacity for change and development in the Tao are the concepts of yin and yang (Figure 2). These are the bipolar opposites that are aspects of everything, dramatically experienced as darkness-light, cold-hot, down-up, wet-dry, female-male. Yin is expressed in the former, yang in the latter of these bipolarities. These essential qualities continually interact, and the dominance of one is naturally replaced by the dominance of the other in every situation.

The shifting nature of life is also seen in the five basic qualities (*hsing*, sometimes translated as "elements") of existence: earth, water, fire, metal, and wood. Each possesses fundamental (natural) characteristics that distinguish it from the others. At the same time, each is related to the others and is continually being "overcome" by another. Lawrence G. Thompson, a specialist in Chinese religion, reminds us that the term *hsing* is a verb that means "to walk, to go, to act." He suggests:

> Thinking of *hsing* as verbal will help us to keep in mind their active nature (water overcoming fire, fire buring wood, and so forth); while thinking of *hsing* as adjectival will help us to understand their elemental nature (that is, all things may be categorized as either "watery," i.e., liquid; "fiery," i.e., gaseous; and so forth).[7]

The Tao, as manifested in the everyday physical and social world, then, is an interrelated and continually changing process. It is seen in the change of the four seasons, day and night, waxing and waning of the moon, birth and death, growth and decay, the rise of an individual into prominence and his or her fall into obscurity, and the development of power and its dissipation.

The Tao is also seen in social relationships among, for example, mother, father, ruler, son, daughter-in-law, farmer, and scholar. By nature, the Cosmic Law arranges people (and things) in their proper order from the lowest to the highest. However, where a person fits changes continually in relation to his or her environment. Take, for example, the man who chooses to become a minister for his sovereign as described by the late Chinese scholar Fung Yu-lan:

> Traditionally, when a man joined the official ranks, he was in a sense "married" to the sovereign. He transferred himself from his own family to the royal family, which, in this sense, was but one of the many families. Before this transference he was the son of his parents, but after it, he became the minister of the sovereign. With this transformation he had new duties and new obligations, and, above all, he had to be absolutely loyal to the sovereign. This loyalty was called *chung*, and was considered the most important virtue of a minister.[8]

FIGURE 2   *Yin and Yang*

As this passage illustrates, an individual's place in the cosmic order is not fixed in one location. Daughters become wives, sons become fathers, husbands become public servants. In each case, there are rituals, sages (teachers), and ancient wisdom available to help an individual understand his or her various and shifting relationships within the universal order. We discuss the sources of this guiding wisdom later in the chapter.

The Dharma in Hinduism

Hinduism, like Confucianism, recognizes that a deep relation exists between how one does something and who one is. Every group of people in society—in fact, every form of life—has its dharma, its way of being. Thus, religiousness is seen as an attempt to properly express one's relationship to all other people and things, or to follow one's dharma.

The root form of the term *dharma* is a verb meaning "to secure or uphold." Dharma is the law of life that holds the pulsating, flowing, dissolving impressions of our experiences long enough for us to distinguish one thing from another and thereby define what is. Dharma designates the correct order and arrangement of everything in life. Everything and everybody fits into the universe in a unique and positive way. Although dharma is an impersonal power, it is a power on which the individual may depend to see him or her through the difficulties of life.

The notion of dharma has had different and sometimes conflicting meanings among Hindus. In early India, it referred primarily to what one ought to do to perform the Vedic sacrifices correctly. Every ritual action corresponded symbolically to aspects of nature and classes of society. Gradually, its meaning expanded to interrelate the ritual order, the cosmic order, and the order of society. Therefore, dharma partakes equally of the following qualities: (1) It is an eternal law, order, or natural law that is constant through existence; (2) it is the expression of duty in particular virtuous or appropriate actions of social and biological organisms (including humans); and (3) it is the formulation in rules of behavior recorded in law books.

In the orthodox Brahmin tradition of Hinduism, the meaning of life depended on a person's birth into a certain class (*varna*), a person's sex, and his or her stage (*asrama*) of maturity in life. The moral duties of a farmer and king, student and teacher, husband and wife were different. One's possibilities and limitations at any time in life depended on the responsibilities and potentials of one's dharma. To live contrary to that dharma would rupture the ordered flow of energy in the universe—affecting organic and social life and personal psychological structure—and cause chaos.

The Universal Moral Nature in the West

Although the prime examples of the moral, Cosmic Law, process of transformation are found in Hinduism and Confucianism, the process is present also in Western and Middle Eastern religious expressions. It found mythical expression in early Greek religion and continued in the thought and life of various Greek and Roman philosophers. Emperor Marcus Antonius of the Roman Empire, for example, gives the following advice in one of his meditations. As you read, keep in mind that Antonius uses "Universal Nature" and "Zeus" interchangeably.

> Let the performance and completion of the pleasure of the Universal Nature seem to you to be your pleasure, precisely as the conduct of your health is seen to be, and so welcome all that comes to pass, even though it appear rather cruel, because it leads to that end, to the health of the universe, that is, to the welfare and well-being of Zeus. . . . Thus, there are two reasons why you must be content with what happens to you: first, because it was for you it came to pass, for you it was ordered and to you it was related, a thread of destiny stretching back to the most ancient causes; secondly, because that which has come to each individually is a cause of the welfare and the completion and, in truth, of the actual continuance of that which governs the Whole. For the perfect Whole is mutilated if you sever the least part of the contact and continuity alike of its causes as of its members; and you do this so far as in you lies, whenever you are disaffected, and in a measure you are destroying it.[9]

Note here how everything that a person does or that happens is part of an interrelated network of life and that the actions of individuals affect "the perfect whole."

The focus on the moral order as the prime reality in life has continued in Western thought, but only rarely has it taken the form of an organized social institution. In the Near East and European West, moral concern has been derived predominantly from the processes of personal religious experiences or sacramental-symbolic formation (or both). However, in the twentieth century, the humanist Ethical Culture movement has clearly affirmed a universal moral law without appealing to any notion of God and God's revelation. In *Ethics as a Religion*, D. S. Muzzey describes the first two basic principles of ethical religion:

> The first postulate of ethical religion is the existence of a moral law in the universe, as permeating and indefeasible as the physical laws of nature. Belief in this moral law far antedates the rise of Christianity. Thousands of years ago the Egyptian sages recognized the binding force of this law. . . .
>
> A second postulate of ethical religion is the existence of a spiritual element in man's nature which makes him capable of seeking the fulfillment of the moral law in his daily conduct. It is on the ground of that capability that we attribute worth to him. And it is to that capability that the appeal of every worthy religion has been made.[10]

Here we see that the cultivation of moral excellence assumes a universal moral law to be realized in every human action; there is no mysterious power demanding personal devotion or manifesting itself in uniquely significant symbols. Indian and Chinese writings also affirm that human beings have both the capacity and the prime duty to attain moral excellence.

MEANS TO ULTIMATE TRANSFORMATION: LIVING IN HARMONY WITH COSMIC LAW

Because of the selfishness shown by most people, maintain the advocates of this means to ultimate transformation, the world would soon be in total chaos if individuals or societies were free to pursue only their own desires. However, since the ultimate reality is a Cosmic Law that is naturally expressed in physical and social life when it is not distorted, there is a means directly available to all beings to express the central harmony of life. In this type of religious life it is important to see that everyday social life is itself a religious power to transform potential chaos into harmonious order.

Although this means of transformation may not be as emotionally overwhelming as a conversion experience in response to the Holy Presence, nor as dramatic and colorful as the use of sacred symbols, it is—say its advocates—the most fundamental. As the popular proverb claims: Actions speak louder than words! Where moral actions and appropriate relationships express the very nature of things, any human activity is religiously significant. The everyday, secular affairs of existence are the medium for conveying concretely the eternal power and order of life. From this perspective, then, correct social behavior is a basic way to express this order. When rules of proper behavior are systematized into codes and laws, their authority does not ultimately derive from a group of people or from personal desire. It comes from the awareness that the written form, or letter of the law, always reflects greater spiritual laws, which have the power either to create or to destroy existence.

In this section we again focus on expressing the Tao through appropriate action *(li)* in Confucianism and on living according to the dharma in Hinduism. Then we comment on the importance of social relationships in other societies: tabu among Polynesian societies and ethical obligations in theistic Western communities.

Appropriate Action in Confucianism

To live in the Tao, say the Confucianists, requires a sensitivity to the natural order, which is both inherent in existence and needs to be cultivated. All people can use their natural capacity to be good—that is, live according to their proper role and status in society—but many people do not do it. Two statements from classical Confucian sources express this paradox:

> Confucius remarked: "To find the central clue to our moral being which unites us to the universal order, that indeed is the highest human attainment. For a long time, people have seldom been capable of it."[11]

The other statement comes from Mencius, one of Confucius's key spokesmen, that human beings have the innate ability to act properly because of natural (rather than learned) feelings:

> Man's innate ability is the ability possessed by him that is not acquired through learning. Man's innate knowledge is the knowledge possessed by him that is not the result of reflective thinking. Every child knows enough to love his parents, and when he is grown up he knows enough to respect his elder brothers. The love for one's parents is really humanity and the respect for one's elders is really righteousness—all that is necessary is to have these natural feelings applied to all men.[12]

Thus, living as a moral being requires a sensitivity to one's natural relationships and an effort to express those as perfectly as possible. The natural relations between father and son, sovereign and subject, husband and wife are to be expressed by proper actions in symbolic gestures, such as bowing, formal or less formal modes of speech, and many forms of etiquette. Such appropriate actions showing proper relationships are called *li*, and the central action of *li* is filial piety. This act of care, reverence, and honor shown by children to their parents has been called the basis of traditional Chinese society. In the Confucian classic *Book of Propriety (Li Chi)*, the importance of filial piety is stated as follows:

> The fundamental lesson for all is filial piety. . . . True love is the love of this; true propriety is the doing of this; true righteousness is the rightness of this; true sincerity is the being sincere in this; true strength is being strong in this. Music springs from conformity to this; punishments come from violation of this. . . . Set up filial piety, and it will fill the space from heaven to earth. Spread it out, and it will extend over all the ground to the four seas. Hand it down to future ages, and it will be forever observed. Push it on to the eastern sea, the western sea, the southern sea, and the northern sea, and it will be everywhere the law of men, and their obedience to it will be uniform.[13]

In a brief dialogue between Confucius and a student from the same classic, we find also that all expressions of propriety *(li)* are central concerns for a moral person:

> "Is *li* so very important as all that?" asked Tseyu again. "This *li*," replied Confucius, "is the principle by which the ancient kings embodied the laws of heaven and regulated the expressions of human nature. Therefore he who has attained *li* lives, and he who has lost it, dies."[14]

In conforming to the *li*, the moral (ideal) person participates in the universal moral-organic order. This participation, suggests the Confucian ideal, is a higher attainment than loving God or learning to repeat sacred ritual action.

Confucianism has been called the "religion of li" (ritual propriety, good manners). Sometimes *li* is simply translated as "religion" to indicate both its practical and ultimate qualities. The character (禮) contains two elements: that of a sacrificial bowl (豐), and "to manifest" (示). The combination suggests an omen expressed through a sacrifice. To behave properly in society, therefore, is not just social convention but also a social expression of the hidden deep order of all life. For the Confucian scholars, social rituals such as public worship, funeral rites, and agricultural festivals provided the outward symbols of the cosmic order, and these symbols helped to instruct all levels of society how to live in the natural order.

To use funeral ritual as a pattern for religious instruction may seem peculiar to a Westerner; however, the mourning system at death is a good example of how individual relationships and responsibilities work themselves out in an orderly fashion according to natural law. Fung Yu-lan, a twentieth-century Chinese philosopher, summarizes the system in the following manner:

> A man, at the death of his parents, must wear mourning dress for three years (actually twenty-five months); this is called mourning of the first degree. At the death of his grandparents, he is to wear mourning dress for one year; this is called mourning of the second degree. Theoretically a man would not wear mourning dress at the death of his great-great-great-grandparents, even though they lived long enough to see their great-great-great-grandchildren.[15]

Fung Yu-lan's description extends to children and their offspring as well as brothers and their offspring. In each case, the ritual of mourning not only assigns appropriate behavior to each family member but it also defines the limits of the responsibility. By observing the funeral ritual, the young Chinese could learn something about their place in the family order.

This example illustrates the concept that lies at the heart of Confucianism: There are natural distinctions among things, and those distinctions should be expressed in social observances.

Doing One's Duty (Dharma) in Hinduism

In the orthodox Hindu tradition, the meaning of life depended on an ethical code of action. As we noted, this code is for everyone, but the specific acts associated with the code are determined by a person's birth into a certain class (*varna*) and the stage (*asrama*) of maturity in life. One's possibilities and limitations at any given time in life depend on one's obligation, or dharma, at that station of life. To live contrary to that dharma would rupture the ordered flow of energy in the universe and cause chaos.

Because most individuals are unable to arrive at an intuitive sense of the class to which they will naturally belong in Hinduism, class has become a function of birth. On being born into a class, a Hindu receives as a birthright certain rights and responsibilities. According to the law books called *Dharma Shastras*, four ideal classes compose the Hindu community. Those classes are as follows: Brahmins—the priestly class; Kshatrias—the warrior class (Arjuna, as portrayed in the Bhagavad Gita, was a member of this class); Vaishyas—the farmers and manufacturer class (producers); and Shudras—the laboring class. Besides these people were others who were not ritually a part of the Hindu community—outcastes and foreigners.

The notion of a hierarchy of classes (varna), according to the ancient writings, extends to the recognition of many different actual social groups called "castes" (jati). There are thousands of castes and sub-castes in India today. They are distinguished by such things as occupation, guild membership, family lineage, rules of ritual purity, cult practices, and food taboos. Different social expectations, privileges and obligations (dharma) pertain to different castes. These castes are related to each other in a hierarchical manner much as we have described the classes but in a much more complex way. Caste distinctions are not insurmountable; it is possible for a person to move to a higher or lower caste under special conditions, or even for the whole caste to move up or down relative to other castes.

In the total cosmic plan, the different classes and castes complemented one another to provide a harmonious society. By following their dharma, people exercised their capabilities—whether as rulers, farmers, teachers, or sweepers—and thus manifested truth, or reality. Just as most people assume there is a natural biological distinction between men and women, between adults and children, and between rocks and trees, so from this perspective there is a natural distinction between duties of different people. For a person to do the duty of someone of another class or stage of life is as incongruous as a rock growing like a tree or a fish chanting Vedic hymns. In this context, the passage in the Bhagavad-Gita, "Better one's own duty [though] imperfect, than another's duty well performed" (III.35) does not sound so strange.

Although the biological fact of birth is significant as it does determine one's sex, class, and general duties, the details of how one reaches an understanding of the ultimate reality are far from fixed. Dharma provides the rules of the game, but the hand that one is dealt and how one plays that hand depend on another force. This force is called *karma*.

According to the law of karma, there is an orderly expansion of cosmic energy that complies with universal law (dharma). Every person continually molds his or her character simply because life requires a person to *do* something or to *act* in one way rather than another. Every action has a consequence, which one must live out immediately or at some future time, either in this life or in some other. No energy is lost. When people's actions comply with the eternal order of the universe, they grow and experience life according to their inherent character, which is determined by their place in the total cosmic plan.

Here it is important to understand that a person's existence is not wholly determined by some fixed universal pattern. To regard human destiny in this fashion would deny the dynamic power and capabilities of individual actions. People develop their future capacities through present actions; and present actions either accord with or oppose the roles individuals have constructed through previous actions. Recall Arjuna from the Bhagavad-Gita. All his previous actions had brought him to the position of being a great warrior. When we meet him, he is faced with the choice of fulfilling his dharma by going into battle or of denying his true self by declining to fight. Arjuna finally behaved (karma) in the ideal manner and fulfilled his present role as the greatest bowsman in the land. Thus, in the orthodox Hindu tradition in India, a person accepts birth into a class (or caste) and sex role without question, recognizing that actions performed in this life span within a particular station will determine whether one will be born into a higher state in the next life. In this way, a person's karma (action and its result) can be an expression of the eternal dharma.

In summary, then, for the orthodox Hindu to live in the deepest sense of personal value, he or she must be sensitive to two major related forces of life: dharma and karma. Dharma, as one's essential duty, lays out the potential and the boundaries for living, while karma is the action that expresses the interaction of past, present, and future. Ideally, a person's action complies with his or her natural capacity and boundaries. In extraordinary cases, some individuals step outside the boundaries by renouncing the world altogether. (This is discussed in the following chapter.) When achieved at the right stage of life, their special enlightenment, however, in no way disrupts the order of nature.

Social Interaction in Other Traditions

In all major religious traditions, there is a concern to make spiritual life effective in everyday social existence. Nevertheless, in some religious orientations more than in others, common daily tasks are self-consciously used to expose the deepest religious quality.

A different, but related, expression of infinite power through social behavior is seen in the power of tabu among Polynesian peoples. A tabu is not simply a restriction placed on some thing or person due to a reasoned argument or as a social convenience. A plant, animal, food, or person can be declared tabu by a person who has power (*mana*). Such an object is tabu because of its peculiar relationship with the transcendent power of *mana*. The term *tabu* suggests two qualities: (1) sacred, or holy, and (2) impure, or polluted. People who live according to tabus are defined by them in relation to other people and the natural world. In a religious sense, tabus prevent the Polynesians from destroying themselves with extraordinary power and provide order and proper relationships among members of society who have different grades and kinds of power. To place a tabu on something means to fix it in place for a particular purpose—a purpose that cannot be defied without self-destruction.

Among Polynesians, individuals had power to the extent they were able to effect tabus. A person's claim to power in Polynesian society had to be manifested in concrete demonstrations. The chief of a tribe, for example, was acknowledged as possessing *mana* when he extended his administration, when he was successful in battle, and when his people had all the physical necessities of life. Any conflict of authority was settled decisively by one person's demonstration of his physical or social power over another person. Whoever was successful had *mana*. Similarly, a person's political authority was measured by the tabus he could impose. One person's tabus were regarded invalid when they were overruled by the tabu of a more powerful person. The different kinds and number of tabus reflected power in concrete situations.

The concern to show true spirituality by living morally has sometimes been dominant in the major Western theistic traditions. One of the most dramatic recent expressions of moral concern in the Christian tradition, is the American "social gospel" movement of the late nineteenth century, which developed a program of social improvement by trying to imitate Christ's life of self-sacrifice. Similarly, in traditional Judaism, the effort to live in the covenant with God requires a definite course of conduct. God promises peace and blessing in return for obedience to his divine commands. This law of the Lord is a delight to the Jew—it is his and her means for salvation and joy. When people live in "the light of the face of God," they are open to God's love and power, which overcome all evil.

Islam also emphasizes worshipping God through social actions. The Muslim community's fasting during the month of Ramadan and the annual alms tax are concrete forms of submission to God. According to Muslim orthodoxy, the true community can exist only where God's law can be infused into the total way of life, both socially and politically. Despite the variety of political forms the Muslim community has taken, especially in the twentieth century, its ultimate goal is to provide conditions under which the will of God can be done.

PERSONAL EXPRESSION: RELATIONSHIPS AND SELF-FULFILLMENT

Because the Cosmic Law places so much emphasis on appropriate (ethical) action in relation to others, its personal expression requires the cultivation of the attitudes, knowledge, and psychological qualities that encourage proper interpersonal relationships. A person cultivates these inner qualities in her or his private life in the context of social regulation and obligations, beginning with the extended family of aunts and uncles and ancestors and proceeding to other subgroups in the society (such as the caste in India), to the whole society, and eventually to all people. As we have noted, from this religious perspective, the actions of the very lowest person in the social structure or the most intimate personal sensitivity can create ripples that spread throughout the entire network of relationships that make up life.

At the same time, we should not think that external actions are the only important aspects of this structure; such a misconception fails to take seriously the all-pervading character of the Cosmic Law. External actions should be the genuine expressions of the heart, will, and mind. Similarly, the ideal expression of the Cosmic Law does not simply mean to act in socially approved ways, simply out of fear of punishment or pragmatic obedience to social authority. Right action (righteousness, justice, care for others) should be the means for personal, as well as social, authentic existence. Adherents of this type of religious life are deeply concerned to cultivate the authentic sense of relationship to others, to nourish the feelings of proper obligations, to structure the natural harmony in every moment, and to perfect their sensitivity to the truth by learning from tradition and conscientious leaders.

The effort to live according to one's true nature is seen in the Confucian ideal of humanity, *jen. Jen* (true humanity or human-heartedness) is self-fulfillment through proper relationships with others. The natural order of things requires people to perceive themselves in a context of relationships. A few excerpts from the Confucian classic, *The Doctrine of the Mean (Chung Yung)*, highlight some personal attitudes, such as discrimination, moral

strength, loyalty (or conscientiousness), and a sense of reciprocal relationships with others.

[Confucius remarked:] "The man with the true force of moral character *(chün-tzu)*
is one who is easy and accommodating and, yet, without weakness or indiscri-
mination. How unflinchingly firm he is in his strength! He is independent without bias. . . .

"When a man carries out the principles of conscientiousness *(chung)* and reci-
procity *(shu)*, he is not far from the moral law. What you do not wish others
should do unto you, do not do unto them. . . .

"There is only one way for a man to be true to himself. If he does not know
what is good, a man cannot be true to himself. Truth is the Law of Heaven *(t'ien
chih tao)*. Acquired truth is the law of man *(jen chih tao)*. He who intuitively
apprehends truth is one who, without effort, hits what is right, and, without
thinking, understands what he wants to know; whose life is easily and naturally
in harmony with the moral law. Such a one is what we call a saint or a man of
divine nature. He who acquires truth is one who finds out what is good and holds
fast to it."[16]

Similarly, living according to one's dharma in Hinduism is also the
means for fulfilling one's potentiality. To the degree that a person identifies
with the tasks and possibilities of his or her social role in the hierarchy of
things, he or she is "real." Ideally, people sacrifice their egotistic desires
where they conflict with the duties and requirements of social expression.
The loss of egocentricity makes it possible to present a perfect and un-
clouded image of one's role or station within the cosmic order. The ideal is
not to struggle for some abstract, "highest" goal for all people but to behave
properly according to one's individual inherent nature, defined by one's
sex, age, and birth.

A contemporary Hindu philosopher, M. Hiriyanna, summarizes the personal virtues that are cultivated in the expression of a person's station, or
place, in the social and cosmic fabric. He uses as his textual basis a commentary *(Smriti)* by a famous interpreter of the law (dharma), Yajnavalkya:

Yajnavalkya, in the Smriti which goes by his name, reckons [the virtues] as nine—
noninjury, sincerity, honesty, cleanliness, control of the senses, charity, self-
restraint, love, and forbearance. It will be seen that some of these, like noninjury
and charity, have a reference to the good of others or are altruistic, while others,
like sincerity and self-restraint, serve to develop one's own character and will. It
should not, however, be thought that this division into self-regarding and other-
regarding virtues is a hard and fast one; for, as an individual has no life of his own
independently of society, the former has a bearing on the latter, as surely as the
latter has on the former.[17]

Ideally, then, one cultivates such inner feelings as sincerity, self-restraint, and forbearance as the way to express authentic moral outward
behavior. To do one's duty in a genuine manner requires the inner desire to
show proper respect to authority, to do the appropriate work of one's station well, and to manifest the natural distinctions that are expressed by
one's social role. The outward expressions of love, charity, noninjury, and
cleanliness should be natural extensions of comparable inner attitudes and
intentions.

SOCIAL EXPRESSION: RIGHT SOCIAL ACTION, TRADITION, TEXTS, AND TEACHERS

The means to ultimate transformation centered on living in harmony with the Cosmic Law emphasizes right (moral) action in one's everyday life. Specific examples of the social order have already been given, the primary models being the Hindu dharma and the Confucian *li*. Here we briefly repeat the general principle of using right social action as a spiritual technique and then focus on the importance of tradition, revered texts that preserve moral values, and specialized teachers of the law (priests, scholars) as the prime resources for social expression.

By living according to the dharma, *li*, or universal moral order (and also by following the tabus in Polynesian society and the Divine Law in Western theistic traditions), people express their deepest sense of what is true and real. Every thought or action manifests either a harmony or disharmony with the way things really are. A judge handing down a verdict, a son speaking to his father, a man and a woman making love, warriors in combat—each of these situations, even combat, could be an expression of *either* harmony *or* disharmony in the cosmic order. In each, harmony is expressed when the actions expose such virtues as honesty, kindness, courage, and wisdom. To be an immoral person means being egotistical or making an arbitrary decision. To be a moral human being means to practice the appropriate action in a given situation so as to bring out the central harmony of the universe. All people can develop themselves in whatever station or role they find themselves if they have guidance from those who know the nature of the world and if they set themselves diligently to express the truth. From this perspective, spiritual perfection is meaningless unless it manifests itself in, and grows out of, actual human relations.

One of the basic social resources for knowing the right way to live is tradition. Whereas advocates for religious transformation through knowing the Holy One or spokespersons for some of the nontraditional means to ultimate transformation (discussed in Part Two) regard tradition as insufficient or even detrimental for their ultimate fulfillment, Cosmic Law advocates look upon tradition as a proven spiritual resource. For them, a living tradition is something that is preserved, treasured, and guarded because it is a practical long-term solution to the problem of how people can live together in the most creative way. Tradition's claim to truth is that it reveals the way things are. Often, the beginning of a tradition is credited to ancient seers who were also sages—people who acted wisely because they knew the truth.

A living tradition is so precious that it is placed in the custody of priests or scholars whose formal learning is required to keep it pure. These specialists preserve the tradition, ideally, by passing on the ancient teaching exactly as they learned it. At the same time, they are called on to interpret the eternal pattern of living to make it relevant to people of different circumstances. In this way, a body of assumptions about life is passed on from generation to generation. Later generations preserve the tradition by approaching life in terms of these assumptions, although they may be interpreted differently at different times. The body of often *unarticulated assump-tions in a life orientation* constitutes the most lasting and pervasive quality of a tradition.

In China, for two millennia before the twentieth century, a major seg-ment of traditional Chinese wisdom was derived from Confucius and his followers. Their advice for living has furnished the dominant guiding princi-ples in traditional Chinese life. According to Laurence G. Thompson, "The Confucian Canon (codes) occupies a position in Chinese culture comparable to that occupied in the West by the Bible, plus the major works of Greek and Roman Literature."[18] There was no aspect of traditional Chinese life that could not receive guidance from Confucius.

Among other matters, the Confucian Canon provided the guiding princi-ples of philosophy, statecraft, personal and social ethics, and religion. After the death of Confucius, the tradition was preserved by the scholars who followed him. They read and studied the ancient texts of history and rites to learn what ancient sages had said and done. They wrote commentary upon commentary explaining the meaning of ancient sayings. They often tried to apply Confucian norms to the political decisions of their day. Although it is clear that throughout Chinese history Confucian political philosophy was not the only policy, government officials were expected to study the Confu-cian classics.

In India, for the past two millennia, Brahmin priests and other scholars who had studied the ancient Sanskrit texts have preserved and interpreted the orthodox tradition. The Brahmins were called "lovers of dharma." Often they were jealous of their sacred heritage, and they directly exposed only the three upper classes to their sacrificial power and learning. Nevertheless, they regulated social relations among all members of society. The ancient law books, compiled by the Brahmins, reflect the concern to regulate every detail in the daily life of the individual.

Many Hindus regard the Rig Veda as the earliest source of Indian law. However, it was the later law books and commentaries on the Vedas that formulated explicit rules and regulations for various classes of people. One of the law books, *The Laws of Manu*, about 200 B.C.E.–200 C.E., stresses the importance of dharma and suggests sources where people can learn what their duties are:

> The whole Veda is the (first) source of the sacred law; next, the tradition and the virtuous conduct of those who know the (Veda further); also the customs of holy men, and (finally) self-satisfaction.
>
> Whatever law has been ordained for any (person) by Manu, that has been fully declared in the Veda: for, that (sage was) omniscient.
>
> But a learned man, after fully scrutinizing all this with the eye of knowledge, should, in accordance with the authority of the revealed texts, be intent on (the performance of) his duties.
>
> For, that man who obeys the law prescribed in the revealed texts and in the sacred tradition gains fame in this (world) and, after death, unsurpassable bliss.[19]

The principles for right living in India, as in China, are preserved in ancient revered writings and interpreted by scholars to maintain a social order that is presumed to comply with a natural, moral, and all-pervasive Cosmic Law.

SUMMARY

Whereas a knowledge of the natural order is of secondary importance in the theistic traditions (Chapters 1 and 2), it becomes primary in a major part of Hinduism and in Confucianism. In these traditions, the person who possesses the knowledge of his or her proper place in the social and natural order contributes to cosmic harmony. This knowledge, although deep, is not beyond comprehension; it is available to all who seek it from books of ancient wisdom, the sayings of sages, and living traditions. For those who seek out the knowledge and live by it, there is a life of balance, harmony, and order, here and now.

The process of transformation that centers in living in harmony with the Cosmic Law is based on the following ideas:

1. The fundamental problematic state in common experience is the selfish concern to fulfill personal desire without regard to one's place in the total harmony of life, leading to social chaos and destruction of life.
2. Ultimate reality is a universal moral order, or Cosmic Law, which pervades all existence and is manifest in the natural distinctions in everyday life.
3. Social morality and personal virtue are religious powers that express the natural harmony of all existence.
4. All people have the capacity to learn right action, to cultivate a deep sense of obligation to, and affection for, others; to develop honesty and sincerity, and to engender an inner strength of character.
5. People learn their social obligations best when they follow ancient tradition as preserved and interpreted by wise teachers and when they follow leaders who are models of virtue.

SELECTED READINGS

Two useful general introductions to the expression of religion through right social action are *J. Wach, *The Comparative Study of Religions* (New York: Columbia University Press, 1958), Chapters 4 and 5; and W. L. King, *Introduction to Religion*, revised edition (New York: Harper, 1968), Chapters 3 and 13. Both studies include some cultic expression as part of their explanation of religion in social activity.

*J. Wach, *Sociology of Religion* (Chicago: University of Chicago Press, 1944). Chapters 4 and 5 of this well-known study deal with the importance of social relationships in religious life.

F. J. Streng, C. L. Lloyd, Jr., and J. T. Allen, eds., *Ways of Being Religious*, Chapter 3, "Living Harmoniously through Conformity to the Cosmic Law." A collection of readings expressing advocacy, sympathetic interpretation, and critiques of this way of being religious.

Two introductory explanations of Hindu dharma are found in *S. Radhakrishnan, *The Hindu View of Life* (London: George Allen & Unwin,

1927), Chapters 3 and 4; and *T. J. Hopkins, *The Hindu Religious Tradition* (Encino, CA: Dickenson, 1971, pp. 73–86. More detailed studies can be found in *The Cultural Heritage of India*, 2nd ed. (Calcutta: Ramakrishna Mission, 1962), Vol. 2, Part IV, "The Dharmasastras." For a detailed study of the caste system in India today, including its relation to the *varna* (class) structure, see *L. Dumont, *Homo Hierarchicus*, rev. ed. (Chicago: University of Chicago Press, 1980).

For an introduction to Confucianism as part of the whole Chinese religious tradition, see *L. G. Thompson, *Chinese Religion*, 3rd ed. (Belmont, CA: Wadsworth, 1979). See especially Chapter 3, "The Family: Kindred and Ancestors," which introduces the reader to the importance of communal relations within the cosmic order, and Chapter 7, "Literati and Laypersons." For an anthology of readings, see *L. G. Thompson, *The Chinese Way in Religion* (Encino, CA: Dickenson, 1973); for material on Confucius and *li*, Chapters 2, 4, 18, 19, 20, and 21 are especially important. A classic statement on the social structure in Chinese religion is C. K. Yang, *Religion in Chinese Society* (Berkeley: University of California Press, 1961). A brief, but suggestive, study of the cultivation of Confucian ideals for forming a truly human person as a deeply religious act is *H. Fingarette, *Confucius—the Secular as Sacred* (New York: Harper & Row, 1972).

Japanese society traditionally has been deeply influenced by Confucian ideals and strong family ties. An introduction to this aspect of Japanese religion is found in *H. B. Earhart, *Japanese Religion*, 3rd ed. (Belmont, CA: Wadsworth, 1982), especially in Chapters 3, 4, 6, 14, and 19. A useful anthology of materials on this subject is *H. B. Earhart, *Religion in the Japanese Experience* (Encino, CA: Dickenson, 1974), especially Part 4: Confucianism, and Part 10: Religious Significance of the Family, Living and Dead.

A provocative sociological study of natural social differentiation, pollution, and tabu, drawn from a variety of cultures is *M. Douglas, *Purity and Danger* (Baltimore, MD: Penguin Books, 1966).

Introductions to the social expression of religious life in the Western religious traditions are available in the following:

For Judaism, see *J. Neusner, *The Way of Torah*, 3rd ed. (Belmont, CA: Wadsworth, 1979), Part III, The Way of Torah: A Way of Living; and *J. Neusner, *The Life of Torah: Readings in the Jewish Religious Experience* (Encino, CA: Dickenson, 1974).

For Islam, see *K. Cragg, *The House of Islam* (Encino, CA: Dickenson, 1975), Chapter 4, "Law"; and *K. Cragg and M. Speight, *Islam from Within: Anthology of a Religion* (Belmont, CA: Wadsworth, 1980), Chapters 3, "Tradition," and 4, "Law."

For Christianity, see S. Reynolds, *The Christian Religious Tradition* (Encino, CA: Dickenson, 1977).

Two books that describe effectively the concern with social action in American religious life are *C. L. Albanese, *America: Religions and Religion* (Belmont, CA: Wadsworth, 1981), especially subsections on the moral law, ethics, and morality, and Chapters 6, "Visions of Paradise Planted," and 11, "Civil Religion"; and H. W. Schneider, *Religion in Twentieth Century America* (Cambridge, MA: Harvard University Press, 1952), Chapter 3, "Moral Reconstruction."

CHAPTER 5

Attaining Freedom Through Spiritual Discipline

A fourth way of being religious is attaining a deep sense of freedom through insight or spiritual wisdom. This awareness, say its advocates, makes living in an authentic manner possible. Through it, one lives a life of inner freedom set securely in a comprehensive intuition of unconditional reality. This way contrasts profound sensitivity to the core of life with a superficial, conventional perception of the world, which is being unconscious of true consciousness. The need for a radical shift in one's mode of cognition to gain true consciousness (wisdom) is suggested by the following twentieth-century advocates of this way.

The Japanese Zen master *(roshi)*, Abbot Zenkei Shibayama, dramatically stated this need:

> The aim of Zen training is to die while alive, that is, to actually become the self of no-mind, and no-form, and then to revive as the True Self of no-mind and no-form. In Zen training, therefore, what is most important is for one to revive from the abyss of unconsciousness. Zen training is *not* the emotional process of just being in the state of oneness, nor is it just to have the "feeling" of no-mind. *Prajna* wisdom (true wisdom) has to shine out after breaking through the extremity of the Great Doubt, and then still further training is needed so that one can freely live the Zen life and work in the world as a new man.[1]

Thus, although sitting meditation and the experience of awakening *(kensho)* are important aspects of Zen practice, the kind of transformation for which Shibayama Roshi is calling is one in which every moment of a person's life is affected in a radical way.

In India, one of the most renowned Hindu mystics of the twentieth century is Sri Aurobindo, who advocates an "integral yoga" whereby the transcendent immortal reality emerges in a pure or clear manner in every-day experience. The yogic practice is the realization of a divine supramental consciousness (supermind) that pervades every feeling, decision, and action. He writes in his book, *The Synthesis of Yoga*:

> The transition from mind to supermind is not only the substitution of a greater instrument of thought and knowledge, but a change and conversion of the whole consciousness. There is evolved not only a supramental thought, but a supramental will, sense, feeling, a supramental substitute for all the activities that are now accomplished by the mind. All these higher activities are first manifested in the mind itself as descents, irruptions, messages or revelations of a superior power. . . . The final stage of the change will come when the supermind occupies and supramentalizes the whole being and turns even the vital and physical sheaths into moulds of itself, responsive, subtle and instinct with its powers. Man then becomes wholly the superman. This is at least the natural and integral process.[2]

Here we see that, whereas special divine revelations or "irruptions" found in extraordinary visions are beginning sensitivities of the supramental consciousness, they are to be perfected by transforming the vital and instinctual forces of life. Awe and worship of the Holy One may be the beginning of wisdom, but it needs to be perfected in the yogic discipline through which a person realizes that he or she *is* the supreme reality.

Similarly, in China, the followers of the Way of the Tao (Taoism) seek to know and actualize the deepest flow of reality in their every experience. The scholar Chang Chung-yuan, while commenting on the classical Taoist texts of the masters Lao Tzu and Chuang Tzu, points out the importance of awakening pure consciousness:

> According to the Taoists, breathing exercises may facilitate the attainment of spiritual wisdom, but its actual realization is the spontaneous awakening of the pure consciousness, from the center of one's innermost being. This pure inner consciousness is not esoteric, available only to a few, but is universal, innate in all. However, not every one of us is conscious of possessing it. As for its general characterization, it is not inferential or rationalistic, but immediate and primordial. It leaves no trace, but indicates the significance of the absolute moment, disregarding space and time. The experience of it comes only from the highest level of one's own nature. To achieve it is to free oneself from the bondage of the limitations of the finite mind and to gain an insight into one's innermost being.[3]

Pure consciousness is seen here as transrational and beyond empirical verification because it is the source and inner power of reason and normal perception. It is an illumination of the nature of things, rather than the description of the externalities evident to any aware person.

In all these statements affirming freedom through spiritual discipline, there is the expectation that probing the depth of one's experience frees one from conventional, self-imposed feelings, self-images, and social expectations. Exploring this depth of experience includes the practice of meditation or contemplation, knowledge and reflection of what the ancient masters have said, and daily application of the insights in everyday affairs. The process that leads to illumination and to the art of living fully is just as important as the mystical experience itself. To gain spiritual insight, people learn to explore their inner selves. Religious seers (wise persons) who have already had the experience serve as guides to help seekers find a new consciousness. Ideally, this depth experience will free the seeker from bondage to the world and its material values.

The five basic elements of this way of being religious are summarized here and illustrated in Figure 1.

1. *The problematic in human existence:* Self-deception and blind desire are the problematic state. Human beings have forgotten or are ignorant of the fact that they already *are* the ultimate reality. According to the seers of this way of disciplined insight (wisdom), people are blindly attached to conditioned forms (ideas, wealth, self-images) and seek false security and joy in transient things. Living with false expectations leads to suffering, disappointment, hate, and self-deception.

2. *Ultimate reality:* This reality consists of unconditional freedom in pure consciousness. Similar to ultimate reality in the other types, it is described as transcendent, immortal, unconditioned, the Original, and the Absolute; and as in Cosmic Law reality, it is all-pervasive and immanent in the world. However, it is not reflected in the distinction of forms. It is known in the depth of human consciousness when one realizes who, or what, one really is. It is not an object of knowledge, because it is fundamentally *within* all beings.

3. *Means to ultimate transformation:* Spiritual discipline is the keystone. Because the ultimate reality is freedom from self-imposed bondage, the way to overcome self-deception is to disassemble the illusion that is caused by attachment to limited images and goals. Elimination of illusion is insight into the way things really are; its result is enlightenment, unified consciousness *(samadhi)*, and direct awareness of the nondiscriminatory, ultimately undifferentiated unity of everything.

4. *Personal expression:* The focus of this way is an inner realization of the deep relatedness of all things beyond past and future, living and dying. This requires a basic shift in a person's understanding of what is most valuable in life, and is expressed in metaphors of union with ultimate reality, illumination, and freedom. It leads a person to experience serenity and inner strength and spontaneously express compassion.

5. *Social expression:* The concern to avoid attachment to conventional physical and social facts often leads practitioners to join a community in which the spiritual discipline is practiced under the guidance of a master. Abstinence from conventional social roles and life-styles, such as found in monastic communities, is meant to re-educate the followers of this way so that whether they stay in a cloistered environment or return to the life of the marketplace, they will live their everyday lives within a higher consciousness. Such people teach others the art of living by precepts and daily action.

This process of ultimate transformation shares certain characteristics with the elements of other processes. For example, freedom through spiritual discipline shares with personal awareness of a Holy Presence a focus on

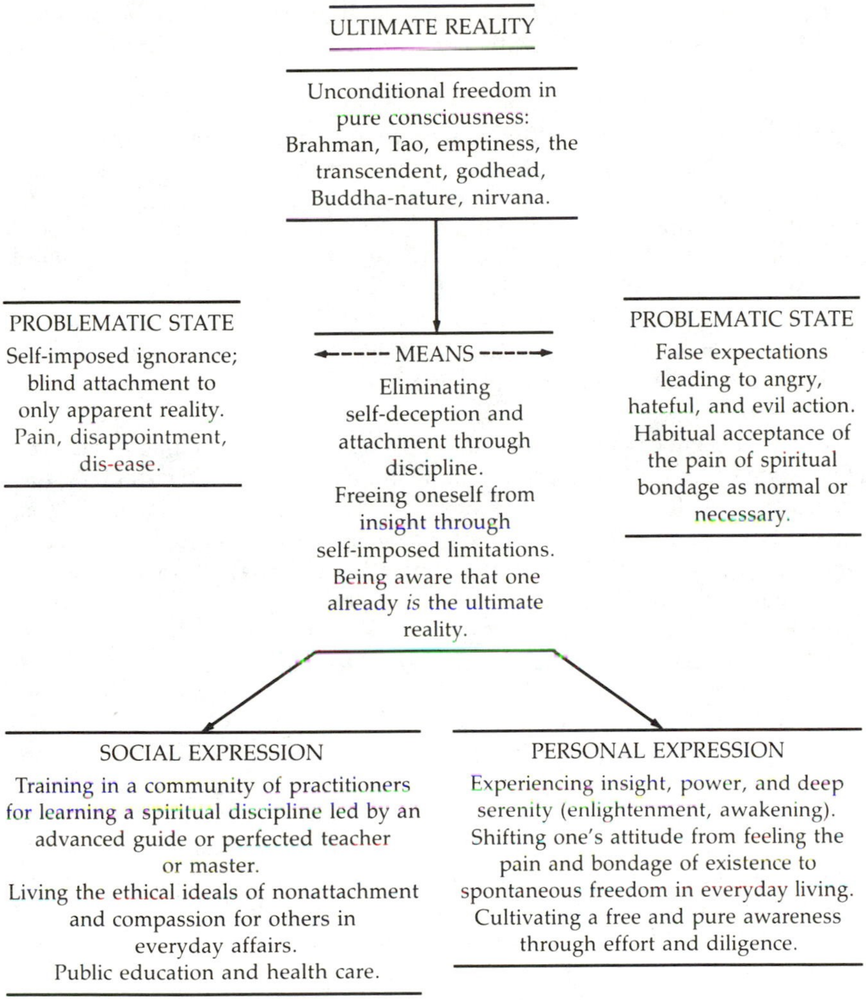

ULTIMATE REALITY

Unconditional freedom in
pure consciousness:
Brahman, Tao, emptiness, the
transcendent, godhead,
Buddha-nature, nirvana.

PROBLEMATIC STATE

Self-imposed ignorance;
blind attachment to
only apparent reality.
Pain, disappointment,
dis-ease.

◄----- MEANS -----►

Eliminating
self-deception and
attachment through
discipline.
Freeing oneself from
insight through
self-imposed limitations.
Being aware that one
already *is* the ultimate
reality.

PROBLEMATIC STATE

False expectations
leading to angry,
hateful, and evil action.
Habitual acceptance of
the pain of spiritual
bondage as normal or
necessary.

SOCIAL EXPRESSION

Training in a community of practitioners
for learning a spiritual discipline led by an
advanced guide or perfected teacher
or master.
Living the ethical ideals of nonattachment
and compassion for others in
everyday affairs.
Public education and health care.

PERSONAL EXPRESSION

Experiencing insight, power, and deep
serenity (enlightenment, awakening).
Shifting one's attitude from feeling the
pain and bondage of existence to
spontaneous freedom in everyday living.
Cultivating a free and pure awareness
through effort and diligence.

FIGURE 1. *Attaining Freedom Through Spiritual Discipline*

individual, inner experience of transcendent truth; a perception that people
are responsible for their own spiritual darkness; the belief that spiritual
forces lie beyond normal rational understanding and conventional social
expectation; and often, a rejection of the clerical, ritual, and intellectual
expectations of a culturally acceptable religious institution.

At the same time, these two processes differ, as in the process of spiritual
discipline the person is not seen as essentially weak and sinful, without the
capability of spiritual perfection. Here each person is responsible for overcoming his or her basic illusion without help from a wholly other holy
power. The ultimate reality is already the very nature of one's deepest
consciousness. The contrast between the understandings of the ultimate
reality results in different spiritual practice, described in several traditions as
the difference between self-help and other-help.

The process of attaining freedom through spiritual discipline also has some elements in common with the process of living in harmony with Cosmic Law: the recognition of continuity between the eternal and the temporal aspects of life; the belief that people have distorted the eternal ultimate reality, the most natural reality, by pursuing short-lived pleasures; and the view that faith, discipline, and determination can reveal this natural source of joy for all living beings. However, the process of spiritual discipline differs significantly from that of living in Cosmic Law in that the social distinctions and rules for moral behavior seen as natural expressions of the eternal order of life by advocates of the latter process are seen by the meditation masters as social fabrications. At best, these distinctions and rules of behavior are meant for beginners in this spiritual path; at worst, they are external objects of attachment that prevent one from realizing the pure, undifferentiated source of everything.

The discussion of this type of religious life draws its primary models from Hindu yoga, Buddhist meditation, and Chinese Taoism. Nevertheless, this process is also found in aspects of the Christian and Muslim traditions, especially in the activities of religious specialists, such as monks and nuns, who follow a spiritual discipline to purify their awareness of God and to seek union with him. In general discussions of these traditions, the religious specialists have been called mystics. Many of their practices, like eliminating attachment to one's self-image, purifying all thought and action, and reinterpreting conventional doctrines and symbols to find a deeper meaning, have parallels in the practice and sometimes even in the assertions of the meditation masters discussed here. We should, however, keep in mind that in the theistic traditions the primary focus is on God, who is fundamentally different from his creatures. As we have noted, the difference in traditions is not basically one of different doctrines and rituals; it is a difference in the process of transformation, leading to the centrality of faith as a personal experience, symbolic actualization of the Sacred Realm, self-fulfillment through Cosmic Law, or complete freedom from self-imposed limitations through spiritual discipline.

THE PROBLEMATIC IN THE HUMAN CONDITION: BONDAGE TO THINGS AND IDEAS

Spiritual discipline is a technique or process for overcoming human limitations. It is a method for releasing a person's spiritual potential. But what is this bondage, this limitation, from which people are to be released? In part, it consists of everyday thought processes and common emotional responses, such as sorrow or frustration. Most people take these feelings for granted as natural or inevitable—and that is the heart of the problem. Human beings simply accept that they will become attached to certain things and that if they lose those things the loss will hurt. Take, for instance, the pilot for airline B. In a time of plenty for the airlines, the pilot enjoys social status, a comfortable house in the suburbs, a boat, maybe a small private plane, and a lot of leisure time. However, if the industry slumps and airline

B goes bankrupt, all of the "good" things for the pilot go too. If the pilot has become really attached to all those things, the pain of being separated from them could be almost unbearable.

Just as the pilot did, people tend to attach themselves to things (power, people, intellect, money) that cannot fulfill their ultimate needs. Only what is beyond change is truly perfect and ultimately real. Being attached to what is changing will only bring pain. But most people learn to feel at home with their own aches and pains. They feel that it is easier to put up with human discomforts than to risk a revolution in their consciousness. People learn to keep a stiff upper lip or to rationalize their lack of success. They escape through laughter and imagination or drugs and alcohol. They begin to calculate every risk very carefully to avoid unnecessary pain. In these ways, people attempt to cope with life; but those who follow spiritual discipline would say that they are only adding more chains to their bondage.

To recognize the psychological bondage of attachment to wealth, status, self-image, and false expectations is important; but if we define the basic problem only in terms of material versus spiritual goals, we will have missed a crucial aspect of the problem. It is not simply that people yearn for limited and ephemeral values; the problem is that to make evaluations at all, people must separate one thing from another—self and other, good and bad, now and then—and they tend to attach ultimate significance to this process. People, then, define their lives by attachments to what they like and fears of what they dislike. To respond to the neutral, everyday processes of sensation and cognition in this manner without being aware of their self-limiting character is to act in a dualistic way. The problematic state is the failure to be aware that the conventional way one perceives oneself and the world is limiting. To see the depth of the problem, let us look at two examples of teachers who warn their students about carrying over dualistic thinking into their spiritual practice.

In the first, the late Zen master Shunryu Suzuki asks his students to return to their "original mind," or "beginner's mind," so they do not carry over the dualism of attainment-nonattainment into their practice:

> For Zen students, the most important thing is not to be dualistic. Our "original mind" includes everything within itself. It is always rich and sufficient within itself. You should not lose your sufficient state of mind. This does not mean a closed mind, but actually an empty mind and a ready mind. If your mind is empty, it is always ready for anything; it is open to everything. In the beginner's mind there are many possibilities; in the expert's mind there are few. If you discriminate too much, you limit yourself. If you are too demanding or too greedy, your mind is not rich and self-sufficient. . . .
>
> In the beginner's mind there is no thought, "I have attained something." All self-centered thoughts limit our vast mind. When we have no thought of achievement, no thought of self, we are true beginners. Then we can really learn something. The beginner's mind is the mind of compassion. When our mind is compassionate, it is boundless.[4]

The second example is taken from the Taoist classic, *The Way and Its Power (Tao Te Ching)*. In it, the sage Lao Tzu criticizes the Confucians for their effort to teach filial piety, righteousness, and human-heartedness (translated as "humanity" in this excerpt) as a moral rule (see Chapter 3). For Lao Tzu, the best advice for government officials is no advice. All talk of goodness and duty are based on dualistic thinking and thus is destructive of spontaneous expression of the Tao. He claims:

It was when the Great Tao declined,
   That there appeared humanity and righteousness.
It was when knowledge and intelligence arose,
   That there appeared much hypocrisy. . . .
Banish sageliness, discard wisdom,
   And the people will be benefited a hundredfold.
Banish humanity, discard righteousness,
   And the people will return to filial piety and paternal affection.
Banish skill, discard profit,
   And thieves and robbers will disappear.
These three are the ill-provided adornments of life,
   And must be subordinated to something higher:
See the simple, embrace primitivity;
   Reduce the self, lessen the desires.[5]

Here, we see that the means to ultimate transformation for Cosmic Law advocates—and this is true also for sacred rituals and special revelations—are also part of the basic problematic in human existence for advocates of spiritual discipline. All claims to moral rules based on eternal natural distinctions, sacred symbols, revealed truths, and ecstatic visions are conditioned human forms, which must be transcended to know the ultimate core of one's being.

ULTIMATE REALITY: UNCONDITIONAL FREEDOM IN PURE CONSCIOUSNESS

When the masters of spiritual discipline look at the world, they too see the human frustrations and suffering, but they do not see those conditions as inevitable. For them—and finally, for all people—there is an alternative to living attached to illusion (fame, wealth, power). The Buddhist meditator finds this release in knowing the "emptiness" of all things or realizing "empty mind"; the Hindu mystic finds it in recognizing that all earthly forms are Brahman, which is also the transcendent self; the Islamic Sufi finds it in the "extinction" of all self that is not Allah, so that the only true reality, God, is manifest. Because terms like *emptiness, nonattachment,* or *extinction* do not sound particularly positive to Western ears, it is important to understand that this ultimate reality is not desolate or without warmth. The true reality offers enlightenment, release from pain and suffering, and a way to live that takes the devotee beyond selfishness, greed, and illusion.

This insight often involves forming a new image of life or destroying old images of life in an illuminating moment of transcendent consciousness, or "supermind." In such a moment, the ultimate reality is simultaneously known by, realized in, and manifested through, the practitioner. This means that the pure manifestation of ultimate reality is, at the same time, a mode of knowing and a mode of being. Contrary to the clear distinction between knowing and being made by practitioners of Western philosophy (see Chapter 8) and science (see Chapter 10) down through the mid-twentieth century, the advocates of this type claim that (1) subjective awareness and objects of perception are mutually dependent on each other; (2) there are different realms or dimensions of reality, which correlate with specific states of consciousness or modes of knowing; and (3) the most profound and important awareness of reality is the open-ended awareness of nondualistic reality, or transcendent (pure) consciousness. Such awareness-reality is beyond any description or designation; but to avoid the imputation that it is simply a blank unconsciousness or a nihilistic void, we indicate something of its character by calling it "unconditional freedom."

The nature of ultimate reality is paradoxical. It is the basis for everything—without it, even the illusion is not possible. At the same time, the awareness of the true nature of things is totally different from conventional greed-based experience. This ultimate reality is called the uncreated, the unconditioned, the center (around which all things revolve), the transcendent, the void. It is the hidden self in all beings, the one in the many forms, the pure consciousness within—but not falsely identified with—conventional moments of consciousness, and God behind all gods. This reality requires a wholly different order of awareness than that which most people commonly experience with their senses, reason, feelings, imagination, or dreams, because it is a pure, direct, and unobscured mode of manifesting the only reality there is. The Tao for the Taoist, the Brahman or transcendent self for the Hindu, "thusness" (*tathata*) or emptiness for the Buddhist is the ultimate reality that accounts for all existence and is the perfect reality that is beyond all dualistic experience.

The first verse of the *Tao Te Ching* is a famous statement of this paradox. There it is written:

> The Tao [Way] that can be told of
>   Is not the eternal Tao;
> The name that can be named
>   Is not the eternal name.
> Nameless, it is the origin of Heaven and earth;
> Namable, it is the mother of all things.[6]

In the ancient Hindu spiritual texts called the Upanishads, the religious seer contrasts conditioned phenomena with the eternal self (*atman*) and warns the seeker of truth to search for a depth of the self that is beyond conventional pleasures and expectations:

> The Self is not to be sought through the senses. The Self-caused pierced the openings (of the senses) outward; therefore, one looks outward and not within oneself. Some wise man, however, seeking life eternal, with his eyes turned inward, saw the self.
>   The small-minded go after outward pleasures. They walk into the snare of widespread death. The wise, however, recognizing life eternal, do not seek the stable among things which are unstable here.

That by which one perceives both dream states and waking states, having known (that as) the great, omnipresent Self, the wise man does not grieve.

He who knows this Self, the experiencer, as the living spirit close at hand as the lord of the past and the future—one does not shrink away from Him. This, verily, is that.[7]

One difficulty, of course, is that the seeker after spiritual perfection must abandon the assumptions that most people feel are necessary for existence and meaning. To eliminate such assumptions is extremely difficult, but to use logic or everyday experience to see the dynamics, the brilliance, the perpetual explosion of life, say the accomplished meditators, is like trying to catch one's shadow. With the aid of regular spiritual practice under the guidance of a master who has perceived the truth, it is possible to attain a superconscious awareness.

To expect that any descriptive proposition can accurately answer the question "What is the true nature of things?" is to miss the point of practicing a spiritual discipline and attaining insight. The instruction at the beginning of the meditation process includes metaphysical statements on which the practice of spiritual life is based, but at the end, these statements must be recognized as only relatively true. The different conceptual formulations found, for example, in early Buddhism, Jainism, Yoga, or Advaita Vedanta can be learned and analyzed as philosophical systems, but the accomplished saints claim that these are only props to be used at first and then discarded.

MEANS TO ULTIMATE TRANSFORMATION: FREEDOM THROUGH SPIRITUAL DISCIPLINE

Since conventional experience inevitably results in pain, frustration, guilt, and meaninglessness, the pursuer after liberating truth—say the advocates of this process of ultimate transformation—must unlearn the habits of conventional experience. A person must probe beyond his or her own selfish hopes and expectations to know the self within and to gain a release from the bondage created by an attachment to illusion. The means to release is a spiritual discipline that focuses on disassembling the illusion based on self-centeredness. This process is not primarily a struggle for attaining higher knowledge, a vision of the holy, or life everlasting. Rather, spiritual discipline focuses on letting go of false value. When the mystic reaches insight, bliss, or enlightenment, he or she will let go of the discipline itself.

Hindu Yoga

Classical Hindu yoga offers one of the most explicit ways to set aside the illusions of everyday life. The specific exercises include external methods of eliminating agitation: restraint, attention to good habits, practice of yoga positions, controlled breathing, and detachment of the senses from external objects. There are also three internal aids for attaining complete peace: holding the mind steady, meditation, and concentration (samadhi).

Of external methods, detachment of the senses from external objects is probably the most unusual, particularly for those who feel they know things because of their sense awareness. However, say the spiritual masters, conventional resources for knowledge are limited and perverted in comparison with spiritual insight. Therefore, one must break the habit of trusting the senses and learn how to restrain them.

Of the three internal aids for attaining complete peace, holding the mind steady is the first requirement. Until this occurs, neither meditation nor concentration is possible. Except during the mature practice of yoga, pure consciousness gets confused with shifting mental and emotional attachment to physical objects, ideas, and emotions. According to the Yoga Sutras of Patanjali (perhaps second-century B.C.E.), there are five kinds of shifting consciousness that can become confused with unchanging pure consciousness through self-deception: generally valid sources of knowledge—perception, inference, and authoritative assertions; misconceptions; imagination; sleep; and memory. These mental states may be useful for acquiring information in conventional experience, but none of them expresses a pure, unchanging consciousness. In fact, these habits of thought can cause spiritual problems. The Hindu mystic Shree Aurobindo described the importance of holding the mind steady by eliminating the confusion of pure consciousness with shifting consciousness in the following way:

> Man is shut up at present in his surface individual consciousness and knows the world only through his outward mind and senses, and by interpreting their contacts with the world. By Yoga there can open in him a consciousness which becomes one with that of the world: he becomes directly aware of a universal Being, universal states, universal Force and Power, universal Mind, Life (and) Matter, and lives in conscious relations with these things. He is then said to have cosmic consciousness.[8]

Exercises in Nonattachment

Advocates of spiritual discipline stress sensual restraints and austerity as techniques to free people from social habits and personal desires. Although sensual restraint is not the primary or central power of ultimate transformation in this process, it is of great importance at the beginning stages of spiritual practice. The assumption is that every human action either benefits or harms a person. Therefore, the devotee must be morally pure to achieve true spiritual insight.

Because disciplined morality has the power to cleanse, extraordinary and severe mental and physical practices may be used to nip out attachments to old behaviors. These practices release the spiritual person from seemingly harmless, but actually deep-rooted, attachments to worldly pleasures. An excerpt from the early Indian Buddhist literature describes the monk's practice as follows:

> When his eyes see a visible object, [the monk] does not label it, nor grasp at its details: but rather, he sets himself to restrain what might be an occasion for evil and impure states, for desire and regret to attack his sight, were it not restrained; and thus, he guards his sight and restrains his eyes.

And when his ear hears sounds, or his nose smells odors, or his tongue tastes flavors, or his body touches a tangible object, or his mind perceives a mental event, he does not label it, nor grasp at its details; but rather, he sets himself to restrain what might be an occasion for evil and impure states, for desire and regret to attack his mind, were it not restrained: and thus, he guards his perceptions and restrains his mind.

And, as he practices this noble restraint of his senses, he experiences an untainted happiness within himself; and thus, the monk guards the gates of his senses.[9]

Some practitioners endure severe physical punishment, and a few even fast until death. The effort toward purification through extreme physical discipline is, for instance, a characteristic of Jainism, a sect that became institutionalized in India during the sixth century B.C.E. The following passage describes the trials of Mahavira, who founded the historical tradition of Jainism after engaging in severe asceticism:

[For] more than four months many sorts of living beings gathered on his body, crawled about it, and caused pain there.

For a year and a month he did not leave off his robe. Since that time, the Venerable One, giving up his robe, was a naked, world-relinquishing, houseless [sage].

Then, he meditated [walking] with his eye fixed on a square space before him of the length of a man. Many people assembled, shocked at the sight; they struck him and cried.

Knowing [and renouncing] the female sex in mixed gathering places, he meditated, finding his way himself: I do not lead a worldly life.

Giving up the company of all householders whomsoever, he meditated. Asked, he gave no answer; he went, and did not transgress the right path.[10]

Although householders (laity) follow ethical rules and adepts like Mahavira practice austerities, these efforts are only adjuncts to the central dynamics of this process of ultimate transformation. The goal of freedom through spiritual discipline is not conformity to society's moral expectations or to biological and social patterns derived from nature, as it is in the process of living in harmony with Cosmic Law. Instead, the goal is to manifest ultimate truth, which may be attained through knowledge of the deepest self and the practice of spiritual disciplines.

Advancement as Nonattachment

The notion of using discipline to advance one's spiritual insight and then to ultimately dissolve the need for that discipline may be understood by considering the following analogy.

Suppose it were possible for a person (in this case, a woman) to fly unaided in space, drifting around in the stars. First, however, we would have to blast her up there in a spaceship. The first rocket stage is very big and complicated, but when the big rockets have done their work, they fall away. Then the smaller rockets fire and fall away as well. Finally, only the spaceship and the flier are left. At just the right moment, the flier leaves the spaceship, strips off her suit, and flies into the galaxy free from all of the equipment that got her there in the first place. At last she realizes that conditions of gravity, air, physical pressure and all so-called needs are an illusion. For the seeker of transcendence through spiritual discipline, the discipline is like the rockets and the spaceship—they will get the seeker where she wants to go, but once she is there they become unnecessary.

In Muslim Sufism and Christian mysticism, as well as in the methods of Hindu yoga and Buddhist meditation, stages of advancement lead from the first steps of a new awareness through further steps of purification and rebirth in a new dimension of reality. In the beginning stages, the disciplinary process is especially exacting and clearly defined. However, the more accomplished a person becomes, the more he or she must become unattached to—that is, avoid pride or disappointment in—disciplinary techniques. This need to disengage may sound strange at first, but no thought, perception, or activity can contain in itself the nature of truth. Ultimate truth must be experienced by the individual as a release even from the techniques of knowing any thing. The disciplinary process must be regarded, at best, as a vehicle that removes a person's apparent needs and wants. But it, too, can become a chain of illusion that binds, and so must be discarded. Until then, people will not be free to fulfill the possibilities of their ultimate nature.

In most cases, then, spiritual insight comes in steps. In the Hindu movement called Advaita Vedanta (from about the eighth century C.E.), for example, discipline helps a person remove the illusion that the world consists of separate and independent physical or mental entities. In fact, there are no natural or essential divisions at all. However, to attain true freedom *(moksha)*, a person must see that even the act of removing illusion requires a construction that, by definition, is an illusion too. (Actually, the individual was free all along. Only due to illusion did one think he or she was bound.) The purpose of discipline, especially as a means of purification, is to bring the individual to this point of awareness. Discipline is not an end in itself.

The idea of a discipline that gives a devotee freedom that he or she always had may be difficult to grasp for anyone who assumes that ideas and sensations refer to independent things outside oneself. Explaining the process has never been easy—even for those who practice it. The difficulty of prescribing a spiritual discipline that must be transcended led the Indian Mahayana Buddhists two thousand years ago to say that the training for the highest wisdom, that is, the path of the bodhisattva (an enlightened being), was a teaching in which nothing was taught, a position that "stood" nowhere, and a training that made no distinction between nirvana and the shifting world of forms. One should not be attached even to the training in nonattachment. The text called *The Perfection of Wisdom in Eight Thousand Lines* credits the following statement to the Buddha's accomplished disciple, Subhuti:

> Even so, should a Bodhisattva stand and train himself. He should decide that "as the Tathagata [the Buddha] does not stand anywhere, nor not stand, nor stand apart, nor not stand apart, so will I stand." Just so should he train himself "as the Tathagata is stationed, so will I stand, and train myself." Just so should he train himself. "As the Tathagata is stationed, so will I stand, well-placed because *with-*

out a place to stand on." Even so, should a Bodhisattva stand and train himself. When he trains thus, he adjusts himself to perfect wisdom, and will never cease from taking it to heart.[11]

This way of striving to the point of letting go, even of the path and the projected goal of spirituality, is emphasized in the Zen Buddhist use of koans. Koans are the riddles a Zen master asks to help a student break away from intellectual conventions and see directly and spontaneously. One of the most famous of these is: What is the sound of one hand clapping? In the Buddhist tradition, some of the most famous koans were expressed and commented on in poetic verse, as in the following:

> Wu Tsu said: When you meet an enlightened man on
> the road, do not greet him with words and do not
> greet him with silence. Tell me: how do you greet him?
> *Comment:* If you can greet him deep and sharp, nothing can hinder your
> happiness. But if you can't, you had better start looking at everything.
> An enlightened man met on the road:
> do not greet him with words or silence
> punch his jaw and split his face
> he'll get the message.[12]

Among the Chinese Taoists there is also a clear expression of the need to let go, to relax, to realize that ultimate reality is not attained by striving but is already available. Some comments in the ancient Taoist text, the *Tao Te Ching*, indicate the importance of quieting agitation, struggle, and achievement if one wants to manifest the all-embracing selflessness, or absolute emptiness, of the Tao:

> Devote yourself to the Absolute Emptiness;
> Contemplate earnestly in Quiescence.
> All things are together in Action,
> But I look into their Non-action,
> For things are continuously moving, restless,
> Yet each is proceeding back to its origin.
> Proceeding back to the origin means Quiescence.
> To be in Quiescence is to see "Being-for-itself."
> "Being-for-itself" is the all-changing-changeless."
> To understand the all-changing-changeless is to be enlightened.
> Not to know that, but to act blindly, leads to disaster.
> The all-changing-changeless is all-embracing.
> To embrace all is to be selfless.
> To be selfless is to be all-pervading.
> To be all-pervading is to be transcendent.[13]

So, in the course of training in the Taoist brotherhood, meditation is a growing relaxation from artificial conventions of thought and action. Growth and understanding do not mean intellectual comprehension of the forces within a person, nor living according to prescribed rules, but opening oneself to spontaneous living. The goal is "actionless activity" *(wu wei)*. A sage is one who does not interfere with the natural flow of the Tao.

Like the type of religious life we have called personal experience of the Holy Presence, this type emphasizes personal transformation within the practitioner. Nevertheless, spiritual discipline has a different structure of transformation for the following reasons: (1) the problematic in the human condition is a correctable ignorance (rather than inherent weakness and sinfulness); (2) the ultimate reality is already pervading all existence and only awaits human realization (rather than conceived as a wholly other personal divine force who saves the lost); and (3) the means is a spiritual discipline of nonattachment to conventional things, ideas, and experiences (rather than an overwhelming experience that releases power to reform the world).

Because the illuminating moment may be dramatic—as when the meditator experiences intense light or loses a sense of individuality—such moments attract the interest of curiosity seekers and are thus the best known aspect of religious mysticism. However, for the meditator, the religious significance of the transcendent moment of insight does not lie in the form of the experience: rather, the significance *is* the release into a universe of spiritual, psychic, intellectual, and physical power that is no longer attached to form.

Such power is inexpressible in conventional language. In fact, to even talk about transcendent consciousness as "something" appears to contradict an ultimate reality of emptiness or extinction. Nevertheless, to express the inner transformation that is the goal of discipline, people have used metaphors and symbols. They describe their inner feelings as peace, serenity, joy, and bliss, as well as in the negative terminology of lack of suffering, anxiety, and struggle. Three terms commonly used to describe the realized unconditional consciousness are *union, illumination,* and *freedom.* We briefly elaborate these three terms here.

Union

Union, or reunion, is an especially appropriate description of the illusion-smashing experience that occurs when people overcome the spiritual poverty caused by their separation from the source of life. In this metaphor, the spiritual goal is to return to the original identity found in the single source of all things. For example, the Christian mystic Meister Eckhart (around 1260–1327 C.E.) spoke of God's being as a part of all things. Even more forcefully, Eckhart said that the Divine Father begets (generates) his Son in the individual's soul. Thus, the nature of the Father is born in the person's soul, unifying the two forever. Similarly, the Advaita Vedanta (Hindu) seer Shankara claimed that all things are, in essence, the eternal Brahman (pure being-consciousness-bliss). For him, the most profound spiritual truth was that "I" *(atman)* and Brahman are identical.

Both Meister Eckhart and Shankara insisted that all existing things are derived from one source and find their ultimate fulfillment in a reunification with this source. However, there are important differences in their views. Whereas Shankara claimed that unity can be realized in this life, Eckhart felt that human beings can never entirely escape their limitations as creatures. There was, said Eckhart, a "little point" in the process of the soul's reunion with God at which the creature recognized his or her "creatureliness" and therefore could not sink completely into the "divine void."

In addition to the specific differences between the Christian and the Hindu, there is also a general distinction between a theistic and an impersonal form of mysticism. The theistic form emphasizes the absolutely different nature of God before whom the devotee surrenders his or her ego. The most significant religious act is to respond as fully as possible to the love and grace of God. In the impersonal form, ultimate reality exists beyond any image of divine personality. According to the advocates of Advaita Vedanta Hinduism or Zen Buddhism, those who cannot give up the image of a personal God are missing the point of ultimate reality. Only insight can dispel this ignorance by revealing the original identity in which there is no ultimate distinction between the godhead and humanity.

Illumination

Illumination, or enlightenment, is another basic image used to describe the nature of mystic consciousness. Enlightenment removes the blinders that have prevented people from seeing themselves and the world as they really are. This image is particularly meaningful where ignorance or spiritual blindness is the basic spiritual illness. The name *Buddha*, for example, means "the enlightened one." In the moment of enlightenment, a person awakes as if out of unconsciousness or a coma. The enlightened person, however, not only sees the light but also is the light. In manifesting light, the enlightened one reveals the truth. The illumination is said to be like that of the sun, which brings forth new life and with each dawn causes a new world to appear.

The process of illumination can be described in several ways. One image is the uncovering of reality behind existence. In this image, reality is hidden by daily existence. Illumination occurs when the obstacle that was blocking the view is removed. Related to this image is the notion of the "third eye of illumination." This eye is symbolically located at a point between the eyebrows and sees with a clarity not possible for the two physical eyes.

Whether one is given true sight because a barrier has been removed or because the "third eye" gains its vision, the illumination releases a power for ultimate transformation of the individual.

Freedom

Freedom is a basic religious image used to express the new reality experienced through spiritual insight. This image is especially meaningful where the basic image of the human spiritual problem is bondage. As used in Hindu yoga and in Buddhist meditation, spiritual insight is the power to *liberate* one from attachment to the self. The "I" or "me," as experienced in everyday life, is constructed with mental and emotional patterns that cause fear, greed, and anxiety. Spiritual insight allows people to see the mental and emotional prisons they have constructed. In turn, this new knowledge gives people the power to free themselves from their own bondage.

To be free means to have the capacity to use one's creative potential in love, judgment, and understanding. People often cannot make use of their potential because they are attached to their anxieties; and they are attached to their anxieties because they are bound by superficial goals, values, and self-images. Where there is unconditional freedom, there is the capacity for faith—and also for doubt. Human beings have the capacity to make mistakes freely and thus to act correctly spontaneously. To live spontaneously in an open, noncompulsive relationship with all existing things is to be unconditionally free.

SOCIAL EXPRESSION: THE ART OF SPONTANEOUS LIVING

The moment of insight changes the religious practitioner's perspective on the meaning of existence. The subsequent way of life, however, depends on whether the person finds the real only on a completely transcendent plane or also in the everyday events of the world. There are some expressions, in Hindu and Christian devotional mysticism, for example, in which the ecstatic experience, the beatific vision, is regarded as the highest attainment. In this case, life in the world is considered a burden to be dropped as soon as possible. Also, in such religious traditions as classical Hindu yoga or Jainism, the eternal self (*purusha* or *jiva*) within people is regarded as bound by worldly fabrication and the highest goal is to release the eternal self from this bondage. In such cases, any return to "normal" experience is regressive.

In contrast to this withdrawal orientation, some mystics recognize that avoidance of life can leave a person as much in bondage as participation in it. For example, in the meditative schools of Chinese Taoism and in some schools of Mahayana Buddhism, such as the Tibetan Kargyüpa Order or Japanese Zen, the goal is a *new way of life*. The *sheng jen* (holy sage, "man with a calling") or the *siddha* (spiritually perfected saint) holds that spiritual discipline is a guide to maturity. At the point of transcendent consciousness, such a spiritual adept realizes the nature of truth and from that point on seeks to express spontaneously what he or she is. New sensitivities and relationships with the environment develop when a person applies the new knowledge of self to everyday experience. Living becomes an art rather than a task. When the spiritual master manifests truth in daily living, he or she becomes the truth.

For such religious models as the Zen master Hiu-neng of the seventh to eighth century C.E. and the twentieth-century Hindu *yogin* Shree Aurobindo, mystical insight leads to a fuller, more spontaneous participation in life. According to them, a person's personality and everyday experiences are not bad in themselves. They, too, can be used as means for expressing the truth in particular and concrete situations. In fact, reality requires living life out fully and completely, since life is as real as anything can be. When people lower their self-imposed psychological and intellectual barriers, the divine activity or "suchness" takes form within their lives spontaneously. A person who lives free from bondage to the world is one who lives free to enjoy all facets of worldly experience. The spiritually perfected person is indeed aware of the deception in the conventions, fads, and styles of life to which the ignorant look for meaning. At the same time, such a person can use these conventions to communicate with other people and yet remain free from their binding power because he or she knows their relative character. In being free, one is exposing the true nature of things.

The spiritual adept, then, uses everyday language and eats and sleeps as a normal person, but his or her living is a self-conscious art. Perfected beings are not limited in the experience of joy or in the depth of their sensitivity, because they are no longer deceived by the limitations of the world; they accept their limitations as a part of full existence. The conventional absolutes that govern preenlightenment human experience and divide the world into opposite things, such as you or me and right or wrong, no longer tug at them and close off possibilities for life and action. Faith and doubt are parts of the same process and are necessarily reciprocal for those who are fully aware that their lives are part of the dynamic process of change. The world is not a thing to be observed; it is a dynamic power to be participated in by creating every moment spontaneously out of the depths of one's being.

Some readers might question the extent of the social impact in the spiritual discipline way of being religious. A common attitude is that this way is all right for a few spiritually inclined people, but most individuals live in a world full of competition, external controls, misunderstandings, and wrong (if sincere) judgments that cannot be corrected by meditation and insight. However, advocates maintain that it is only a deep shift in consciousness from attachment to freedom, from dualistic thinking to unitive thinking, and from self-deprecation to self-affirmation for living a different kind of life that is a true solution to the common world ills of hunger, war, and fear. Such is the claim of a Buddhist revered master from Sri Lanka, Nyanaponika Thera, who says:

> To this sick and truly demented world of ours, there comes an ancient teaching of eternal wisdom and unfailing guidance, the Buddha-Dhamma, the Doctrine of the Enlightened One, with its message and power of healing. It comes with the earnest and compassionate, but quiet and unobtrusive question whether, this time, the peoples of the world will be prepared to grasp the helping hand that the Enlightened One has extended to suffering humanity through his timeless Teaching. . . .
>
> The nations of the world seem unthinkingly to assume that their reserves of strength are inexhaustible. Against such an unwarranted belief stands the Universal Law of Impermanence, the fact of incessant Change, that has been emphasized so strongly by the Buddha. This Law of Impermanence includes the fact shown by history and by daily experience, that the external opportunities for material and spiritual regeneration, and the vital strength and inner readiness required for it, are never without limits, either for individuals or for nations. . . .
>
> The Message of the Buddha comes to the world as an effective way of help in present-day afflictions and problems, and as the radical cure for ever-present Ill. [14]

101
*Attaining
Freedom
Through
Spiritual
Discipline*

For him, it is only the way of mindfulness, of pure awareness, that has sufficient power to transform self-delusion and suffering into truth and well-being. It is the necessary and radical cure.

SUMMARY

Some of the key points held by the advocates for attaining freedom through spiritual discipline are as follows:

1. The simplest and most profound problems are self-made and can be solved if one's spiritual blindness does not obscure ultimate reality.
2. People have ultimate reality within themselves (such as the Tao, Buddha-nature or Brahman).
3. Discipline, though difficult for most people, releases them from the conventions and compulsions that produce suffering and illusion.
4. Although several religious traditions use various techniques for spiritual discipline and describe transcendent states of consciousness differently, the goal of all people using this process of transformation is release from the attachment to physical and social conditions.
5. This release from self-made bondage transforms the short-term tasks in everyday life into an art of living. Such shifts in personal attitudes provide the bases for overcoming the radical ills of society.

SELECTED READINGS

*D. K. Swearer, ed., *Secrets of the Lotus: Studies in Buddhist Meditation* (New York: Macmillan, 1971). An introduction to Theravada meditation and Zen practice based on lectures to American students given by noted practitioners from those traditions.

An excellent introduction to Theravada Buddhist meditation is *Nyanaponika Thera, *The Heart of Buddhist Meditation* (New York: Samuel Weiser, 1962). It is a manual for mental training *(Satipatthana)* by a venerable teacher from Sri Lanka.

Two useful explanations of Buddhist meditation by Western scholars are *E. Conze, *Buddhist Meditation* (New York: Harper, 1956); and W. L. King, *Theravada Meditation: The Buddhist Transformation of Yoga* (University Park: Pennsylvania State University Press, 1980).

Three books which introduce Zen training and awareness by masters who founded Zen communities in the United States are *S. Suzuki, *Zen Mind, Beginner's Mind* (New York: Weatherhill, 1970); *J. Sasaki, *Buddha Is the Center of Gravity* (San Cristobal, NM: The Lama Foundation, 1974); and R. Aitken, *Taking the Path of Zen* (San Francisco: North Point Press, 1982).

*S. Shibayama, *Zen Comments on the Mumonkan* (New York: New American Library, 1974) provides comments by the late master of the Nanzenji Monastery in Kyoto on a famous Zen text of koans. R. Masunaga, trans.,

A Primer of Soto Zen (Honolulu: East-West Center Press, 1971) gives a translation of the thirteenth-century Zen master Dogen's *Shobogenzo Zuimonki*, a series of brief talks on Zen practice and awareness.

Two comprehensive introductions to the practice of yoga by teachers who explain the interaction of physical and mental control are S. M. Majumdar, *Introduction to Yoga: Principles and Practices* (New Hyde Park, NY: University Books, 1964); and Sri Swami Sivananda, *Practice of Yoga* (Sivanandanagar, India: The Divine Life Society, 1970).

Two translations of the classical text *Yoga Sutras* by Patanjali with commentary by contemporary practioners are *I. K. Taimni, *The Science of Yoga* (Wheaton, IL: Theosophical Publishing House, 1961); and *Swami Hariharananda Aranya, *Yoga Philosophy of Patanjali* (Albany: State University of New York Press, 1983; first published in 1963).

A Practical Guide to Integral Yoga (Pondicherry, India: Sri Aurobindo Ashram, 1965) is a collection of excerpts from the writings of Sri Aurobindo and the Mother, which introduces the reader to a broad scope of the thought and practice of Sri Aurobindo.

D. Goleman, *The Varieties of the Meditative Experience* (New York: Irvington, 1977) is a brief introduction to meditative paths from different religious traditions.

F. J. Streng, C. L. Lloyd, Jr., and J. T. Allen, *Ways of Being Religious* (Englewood Cliffs, NJ: Prentice-Hall, 1973), Chapter 4, "Spiritual Freedom through Discipline (Mysticism)," gives excerpts from advocates, sympathetic interpreters, and critics of this way of being religious.

Mysticism in Western thought is an umbrella term under which several experiences and practices tend to cluster. Included in them are the means to ultimate transformation discussed especially in Chapters 2 and 4. Several general introductions to mysticism that provide data for and discuss several of the elements described in this chapter are:

*E. Underhill, *Mysticism* (New York: Dutton, 1961; first published in 1911). This is still regarded by many as the classic exposition of mysticism. It emphasizes the goal of union with absolute reality through personal, introspective awareness.

*M. L. Furse, *Mysticism: Window on a World View* (Nashville: Abingdon, 1977). The approach in this book is to view mysticism as a pattern of seeing the depth of life and recovering an immediate awareness of oneself in the present.

R. M. Jones, *New Studies in Mystical Religion* (New York: Macmillan, 1928). A series of lectures that analyze the relation of mystical awareness to psychology, personal discipline, and institutional religious forms, showing what this awareness might mean in the context of twentieth-century Western society.

General introductions to mysticism most often emphasize the disciplined effort of the individual mystic to be reunited with the one eternal reality. Representative of this interpretation are J. Politella, *Mysticism and the Mysti-*

cal Consciousness Illustrated from the Great Religions (Kent, OH: Kent State University Bulletin, 1964); and *S. Spencer, *Mysticism in World Religion* (Baltimore, MD: Penguin, 1963).

103
*Attaining
Freedom
Through
Spiritual
Discipline*

Two philosophical analyses of mysticism are W. T. Stace, *The Teachings of the Mystics* (New York: New American Library, 1960), in which this noted philosopher views mystical experience as nonintellectual and transsensory identification of oneself with all things; and *F. Staal, *Exploring Mysticism* (Berkeley: University of California Press, 1975), a methodological reflection and critique, which affirms that mysticism is compatible with reason and vigorous social interaction.

A still popular introduction to the transforming states of consciousness is W. James, *The Varieties of Religious Experience* (New York: Random House, 1929; originally published in 1902). Chapters 11–14, 16, and 17 focus on the mystical path and experience, which are understood in the context of a psychological interpretation of a unified or divided self.

Students who want to interpret Eastern awareness in terms of the psychological framework of the Eastern theories of human nature can profitably read Swami Akhilananda, *Hindu Psychology* (London: Routledge & Kegan Paul, 1948); *Lama Anagarika Gorinda, *The Psychological Attitude of Early Buddhist Philosophy* (London: Rider, 1961); and *R. E. A. Johansson, *The Dynamic Psychology of Early Buddhism* (Atlantic Highlands, NJ: Humanities Press, 1979).

Comparisons between Eastern spiritual therapies and Western psychological therapies are found in G. Coster, *Yoga and Western Psychology: A Comparison* (London: Oxford University Press, 1934); H. Jacobs, *Western Psychotherapy and Hindu Sadhana* (London: George Allen & Unwin, 1961); and *D. T. Suzuki, E. Fromm, and R. DeMartino, *Zen Buddhism and Psychoanalysis* (New York: Grove Press, 1960); Tarthang Tulku, ed., *Reflections of Mind: Western Psychology Meets Tibetan Buddhism* (Emeryville, CA: Dharma, 1975); and J. Welwood, ed., *The Meeting of the Ways: Explorations in East/West Psychology* (New York: Schocken Books, 1979).

Two important studies of comparisons in mystical awareness by noted scholars are *R. Otto, *Mysticism: East and West* (New York: Meridian, 1957; first published 1932); and *D. T. Suzuki, *Mysticism: Christian and Buddhist* (New York: Collier, 1962; first published 1957).

PART TWO

Modes of Human Awareness Used to Express Religious Meaning

In Part One we discussed four traditional models, or ideal types, of religious life. These models portray processes of ultimate transformation as experienced by advocates in different religious traditions. All of them share the assumption that ultimate reality must be found in some sort of transcendent force—the Holy Presence, the Sacred Realm, Pure Consciousness, or the Cosmic Law. In Part Two we look at some nontraditional ultimate transformations, often called humanistic religion. The emphasis in this part is on the transforming possibilities of experience, which are felt to be the deepest possible and the most comprehensive but which are derived only from the capacities of life and consciousness found in this world.

The chapters in this section reveal a point of view suggesting that the greatest human need is to find meaning and fulfillment in the here and now. Life need not be directed by the hope of eternal life nor caught up in the rhythm of an unchanging moral law. The ultimate is not what a few extraordinary teachers, guides, prophets and authorities regard as the transcendent, transtemporal, and often hidden ultimate reality. The ultimate reality for the advocates of nontraditional religious transformations is the meaning that the human being finds in life itself.

The strongest advocates of humanistic religion believe that humanity today is not fully mature but has considerable potential. They believe that people must put away such childish fantasies as life after death or nirvana. For example, the moral philosopher Kai Nielsen puts the case this way:

> To be free of impossible expectation, people must clearly recognize that there is no "one big thing" or, for that matter, "small thing" which would make them permanently happy; almost anything permanently and exclusively pursued will lead to that nausea that Sartre has so forcefully brought to our attention. But we can, if we are not too sick and if our situation is not too precarious, find lasting sources of human happiness in a purely secular world.[1]

The significance of this secular claim for ultimate transformation is the recognition that true joy, meaning, love, and insight are available without an eternal, transcendent ultimate reality. Whatever can be called "ultimate," "comprehensive," or "lasting sources of human happiness" is to be found only within the changing, temporal, conditioned everyday world.

Although those who follow traditional religions are willing to allow that traditional religious feelings can be usefully *expressed* in conventional, secular ways, they maintain that the ultimate reality or deepest value is eternal or "given." In the modern world, however, some people like Nielsen claim that the skills and procedures developed in strictly human dimensions can lead to the most profound processes of self-discovery and can create the deepest values. At this point you might say to yourself: Perhaps some people may *think* they have access to lasting sources of human happiness by using only secular, conditioned human capacities; but in reality these capacities are only minor reflections of the transcendent, unconditioned reality (God, Cosmic Law). A secular humanist would experience transcendent reality if he or she would use one or more of the traditional means to ultimate transformation, like personal awareness of the Holy Presence or sacred revelation! Such a response highlights the shift in orientation we are making in Part Two— from a transcendent ultimate that requires special resources or means for making it actual in life to an ultimate value that is effected by profoundly using a common mode of human activity, such as reasoning, working for social justice, realizing selfhood, or engaging in a significant livelihood.

Before we make a personal judgment about the true nature of ultimacy, we need to try to understand the assumptions of the humanistic claims just as we have done for unfamiliar or alternate traditional religious claims. A study of the dynamics of ultimate transformation in both traditional and nontraditional religious forms reveals two things: (1) Traditional ways of being religious (Part One) are not experienced by their advocates to be just extensions of human capacities, and (2) humanistic ways (Part Two) are not experienced by their advocates as just limited perspectives and skills drawn from traditional religious assumptions and activities. Both the traditional and the humanistic ways are distinct and proper subjects of an objective and comparative way of human religious life. We include both ways here because the advocates of both claim they are concerned with superlative (ultimate) values and the nature of being in existence.

The chapters of Part Two focus on five secular (or humanist) processes through which some people claim to achieve ultimate transformation. These processes are (1) fulfilling human relations, (2) social responsibility, (3) rationality, (4) artistic creativity, and (5) responding to physical existence. The modes of human awareness can function religiously inside of, as well as outside of, traditional religions, and we will look at both kinds of expressions. Chapters 6 through 10 are not organized identically to Chapters 2 through 5. Whereas each chapter in Part One was divided into a five-point process of ultimate transformation, the subject of each chapter in Part Two is placed in the framework of the five-point process only at the end of the chapter.

In the first part of each chapter, we look at how these modes operate *within* a religious tradition. Generally, they are expressions of an ultimate reality that transcends them. In this way, music, visual arts, thought, and social institutions are *forms* through which the ultimate, transcendent reality enters a person's life or is revealed in everyday existence. The singing of a hymn, the study of a theological claim, or the effort to implement dharma in daily life can express the aesthetic, rational, and social dimensions of life *within* a religious tradition. In the last part of each chapter, we look at social reform, rational reflection, personal relationships, art, and response to physical existence as they function religiously *outside* traditional religious institutions as means to ultimate transformation. These are processes through which human beings order their lives, find enjoyment, and understand themselves. Here again, we will follow the organization of the five-point process that we used in Part One to illustrate how these modes serve as means for the highest fulfillment in life.

107
*Modes of
Human
Awareness
Used to
Express
Religious
Meaning*

To understand that art, reason, or human relationships can lead to religious fulfillment, one must recognize the claim that some dimensions of reality can be understood only through these or other modes of human awareness. When some people become aware of their artistic sensitivity, their ability to use reason, and so forth, they become conscious of their truest capacity for "becoming" as human beings. "Being human," they claim, is something different from just "being." To exist as a human being means to deal with and to interpret existence as it appears in ideas, art, architecture, cities, and the cosmos. To be human means to make judgments, to select the important qualities of life, and then to construct meaning based on one's personal experience, on the experience of other people, and on considerations of the past and future.

From the humanist point of view, people should use their capacities as fully as possible in the present, instead of seeking final or absolute answers to life's problems in a realm beyond this life. Human beings must learn to eliminate pain, injustice, anxiety, boredom—even death—by making conscious decisions, learning from their mistakes, and rising above human failures. Human life is not something static, whose quality has been set for all time by some unseen and eternal standard. True spirituality involves using available techniques of human development, or secular development as traditional religious advocates call it. Julian Huxley, a renowned advocate of humanist religion, urges all people to participate in what he calls "transhumanism." He writes:

> The new understanding of the universe has come about through the new knowledge amassed in the last hundred years—by psychologists, biologists, and other scientists, by archaeologists, and historians. It has defined man's responsibility and destiny—to be an agent for the rest of the world in the job of realizing its inherent potentialities as fully as possible. . . . Whether he wants to or not, whether he is conscious of what he is doing or not, he *is* in point of fact determining the future direction of evolution on this earth. This is his inescapable destiny, and the sooner he realizes it and starts believing in it, the better for all concerned.[2]

From the humanist point of view, freedom from absolute ideals or eternal values does not necessarily result in the elimination of long-term responsibility, hope for a better future, or the need to decide what is and is not meaningful. It simply shifts the focus of these concerns from transcendent to conditioned life.

In the following chapters, the political, rational, interpersonal, aesthetic, and physical ways of ordering existence are discussed separately because each can become a different means of enhancing life. Although these modes of awareness have been integrated into the religious and cultural outlook of traditional societies, in modern societies they often are specialized disciplines, with skills and techniques based on different values, emphases, and evidence. Art and science, for example, are often viewed as opposite ways of approaching truth. Those who accept historical or scientific inquiry as the basic means of structuring human awareness and revealing ultimate reality believe that such inquiry allows people to transform life from a meaningless, crude, frustrated, and unhappy experience to one of significance, creativity, excitement, and growth. On the other hand, those who seek ultimate reality through aesthetic experience might argue that scientific or historical values are not the only ones that can ultimately transform human life. Thus, the final section of each chapter in Part Two focuses on a mode of human awareness that some advocates consider to be a spiritual technique to transform life at the deepest level.

CHAPTER 6

The Religious Significance of Fulfilling Human Relationships

Why consider the religious function of human relationships? First of all, ultimate transformations always take place with some human reference points. Therefore, interpersonal relationships form a dimension of life to which religious processes, traditional or otherwise, must relate. In addition, for those who regard spontaneity, intimacy, and self-fulfillment through interpersonal relationships as central to their being, human relations are at the core of their spiritual life.

If we maintain that human relationships define everyone's capacity for good and evil, then the ways in which human beings interact with each other become important religious concerns. Psychological studies confirm that the human personality requires stimulation from others to develop. Children who have been denied human contact from infancy seem unable to learn language or expected social behavior. So we first learn how to be human from other people. Our awareness of the world and our way of functioning within it comes in large part from models set by "significant others"—immediate family members, aunts and uncles, peers, close friends, coaches, or teachers. However, because interpersonal relationships belong to the daily routine of being human, it is possible to take them for granted. At that point, we lose sight of the power and the significance of our encounters with others.

Although people learn about themselves and grow from their experiences with other people, not all experiences have the power to transform. Human interaction can only become a religious encounter when a dynamic and living exchange with another leads to a life-changing self-discovery. In the experience of a sensitive touch, the warmth of companionship, or the feeling of being understood, many people become aware that their loneliness or fear is healed. Growing, sensitive, caring relationships that are deep and meaningful give people something to live for and the courage to excel. Such experiences may even provide the will to live under otherwise intolerable circumstances.

Because human relationships are complex, each important human encounter holds the possibility of creating problems or opening up unexpected dimensions of life. For example, the tensions between expectations (ideals) and reality may lead to unhappiness. A lonely man tries to buy friends and ends up with none; a little girl prays for her sick father who eventually dies; a husband and wife try but fail to change each other. Common reactions to such disappointments include suspicion, distrust, withdrawal from the possibility of future encounter, and even the development of neurosis and psychosis.

On the other hand, an awareness of the difference between human ideals and the reality of human relationships can have a positive effect. An ideal can spur individuals to grow beyond their present capabilities. For example, among certain American Indian nations, adolescent boys are sent to fast and meditate in a wilderness cave. When one of them is inspired by a vision, the elders of the tribe might prophesy that he will become a great chief. As a result of the prophecy and because of the trust the boy has in the wisdom of the elders, he rises to the occasion and cultivates the virtues of courage, patience, and concern for his people.

Another example of the power of human encouragement appears in the life of Helen Keller, who was born deaf and blind. Through the care and love of her teacher, Annie Sullivan, Miss Keller went beyond her family's greatest expectations (that their daughter lead a reasonably normal life) to become an internationally known author and lecturer. Through the inspired work of Annie Sullivan, Helen Keller became an inspiration herself.

In both these examples, the tension between ideal and real expectations was resolved through a transformation into a new reality. The strength and courage of a future chief replaced the weakness and fear of a hungry boy. The intelligence and love offered by a teacher helped to stimulate the development of a new self-identity filled with enthusiasm and hope. Transformation of these kinds may occur as a result of appeals to divine sources or may result from efforts on a purely human level. Either way, the transformation of ideal behavior (the behavior of a chief) into concrete behavior (the bravery of a boy) often removes the pain of separation from the familiar (from childhood to manhood), soothes fears of rejection, loneliness, and insecurity, and paves the way for more meaningful relationships.

In this chapter, we first examine the role of human relationships within traditional religious structures as one form of ultimate transformation in everyday life. Here the discussion focuses on the ministry to the lay community, the training of novitiates (new members of a religious community), and ethical teachings. Then we describe some ways in which personal, creative interaction can assume ultimate significance outside of traditional religious structures: participation in psychotherapeutic encounter groups, sensitivity to everyday relationships, and a sincere search for self-knowledge, leading to an integrated life marked by caring, honesty, and love.

A concern for human relationships characterizes all traditional religious structures. It is found abundantly in the teachings of the major religious traditions that advocate love of neighbor, compassion for all beings, or kindliness toward the needy. It is seen in the counsel and pastoral care given to people by priests, ministers, and spiritual teachers. It is expressed through both personal relationships and symbolic gestures of devotion and sacrament at especially important moments in a person's life. A Jewish bar mitzvah, a Christian confirmation, a Hindu sacred thread ceremony (*upanāyana*), a marriage, or a cremation all respond to the human needs for recognition, belonging, and reassurance. In the traditional theistic religious context, the source of this human concern comes from the personal discovery that one is a child or servant of God and must do his will, which requires compassion for all other members of creation. Human relations in this context are vehicles for reaching a higher understanding beyond the strictly human.

Devotional Services and Pastoral Care

Traditionally, two important functions of a priesthood organized to minister to the lay community have been (1) the performance of regular devotional and sacramental services for the community and (2) some form of pastoral care for individuals. In a worship service, the priest or spiritual guide, such as a Christian pastor or Muslim imam, leads the congregation or membership into a closer relationship with divinity. In turn, the believers feel closer to each other because they have shared the experience. Worship services include both the sober piety of a Catholic High Mass and Navaho group communion in a hogan during a peyote ceremony. In both cases, there is more than one relationship established. The priest or "road chief" acts as a translator for the divine. Through this translation, the believer may enter into a more intimate relationship with the transcendent power. In turn, the power (still transmitted through the priest or chief) frees the believer from past sins and self-destructive tendencies. It is important to remember that, for the participant, the religious service is more than a social function designed to make people feel good about themselves. The priest is more than a leader of a society, because the relationship among the people and between them and the leader takes on a sacred character. The symbolic acts of the priest and the experience of the believer are the means through which transformation is achieved (see Chapter 3), but the social experience of common worship provides the basis for a shared interpersonal relationship.

Although pastoral care deals mainly with individual concerns, it may be seen as an extension of the priest's mediation between God and human beings. Among the pastoral duties of the Roman Catholic priest are hearing the confessions of penitents and comforting the dying with the last rites (Extreme Unction). Pastoral care also characterizes the efforts of a Chippewa Indian shaman as he performs a healing ceremony for a sick member of the tribe by building a "shake lodge" to call healing spirits into the body of the sick person. Spiritual leaders take care of young people when they train them in the way of the Lord, in the Tao, or in the Buddha's path to spiritual freedom. Special ministries to jails, reformatories, and mental hospitals are also parts of pastoral care.

History of Christian Pastoral Care. We can see a specific example of the role of a spiritual leader in the Christian tradition. In Christianity, pastoral care is known in traditional terms as the "cure of souls." The efforts of the early church (before 100 C.E.) were directed at sustaining people through the troubles of the world, which many Christians believed was swiftly coming to an end. Once Christianity became a legal religion under Constantine the Great (in 325 C.E.), the church grew more concerned with guiding people to behave according to the norms of the newly formed Christian culture. By the beginning of the medieval period, about 500 C.E., pastoral care had evolved to become part of a well-defined sacramental system designed to treat all the spiritual ills of common life.

As changes occurred in the social structure of Western Europe, the character of pastoral care changed as well. During the Renaissance and Reformation (1500–1700), the notion of individual worth, first emphasized in art and philosophy, continued to grow and find support in scientific, economic, and political activity. These forces had their effects on "Christian nurture" in the eighteenth and nineteenth centuries, leading to a greater acceptance of individual convictions and value systems. Today pastoral care is administered in conjunction with the nonchurch-related helping professions of medicine, psychology, and psychiatry.

Functions of Christian Pastoral Care. Out of this historical context have grown the four general Christian pastoral functions of healing, sustaining, guiding, and reconciling. These functions may be described as follows:

Mental and physical *healing* may include such acts as anointing sacred places or body afflictions with holy water or oil, healing through contacts with religious relics (for example, the bones of a saint), the laying on of hands by charismatic persons, exorcism, or group therapy techniques administered by the clergy.

Sustaining is mostly employed during times of personal crisis to prevent a person's disintegration and give consolation and emotional support. Furthermore, it helps the sufferer discover personal resources (family, friends, occupation) that will help with recovery. Finally, sustaining confirms redemption in the eyes of God and the church in spite of whatever has happened.

Guiding is more of a counseling than a crisis-oriented activity. It may include listening, giving advice, and encouraging a person to make decisions.

Reconciliation restores strayed or lost souls to the community of the church. Its chief means are forgiveness for wrongdoing and the assignment of a penance.

Collectively, these four functions stress the importance of human relationships to the spiritual well-being of individuals and for the continued existence of organized religion.

Training of Novitiates

Another expression of the importance of human relationships within traditional structures of the world's religion is the training of novitiates and the maintenance of monastic communities. Of great significance in many Asian traditions is the relationship between the spiritual teacher (guru, *acharya, murshid, roshi*) and disciple. Of all obligations recognized by religious Hindus, for example, the *guru padashraya,* or servile veneration of the spiritual teacher, is considered one of the most important and is compulsory. In exchange for the household maintenance, systematic begging, and personal devotion of the disciple, the guru bestows esoteric teaching and spiritual power upon the disciple.

In the West, monastic training for novitiates is less codified than in the East. However, it is important for every Christian novitiate to have a guide skilled in the life in Christ. One cannot learn what there is to know from books and study alone. Human contact is essential.

Ethical Teachings

Perhaps the most important expression of the concern for human relationships within traditional religious structures lies in the values of kindness, patience, and compassion, taught by the founders or chief spokespersons of a tradition. The Jewish prophet Micah (around 700 B.C.E.), for example, summarized the importance of moral action after denouncing conformity to external religious rituals by saying:

> God has told you what is good;
>   and what is it that the Lord asks of you?
>   Only to act justly, to love loyalty,
>   to walk wisely before your God.[1]

A famous saying in the Confucian *Analects* shows the importance of reciprocal care between people:

> Tsekung asked, "Is there one single word that can serve as a principle of conduct for life?" Confucius replied, "Perhaps the word 'reciprocity' (*shu*) will do. Do not do unto others what you do not want others to do unto you."[2]

Jesus preached, "Do unto others as you would have them do unto you" and, as he was being crucified, said, "Father, forgive them for they know not what they do."

Likewise, the Buddha preached the *dhamma* (truth, law, practice) for forty years after his enlightenment so that all beings might be set free from suffering. Many Buddhist teachers instruct their followers to be friendly and compassionate and to experience sympathetic joy when another person attains clear-mindedness. In the Mahayana Buddhist scriptures, the goal and path of the bodhisattva (enlightenment-being) is portrayed. The bodhisattva combines the highest wisdom with compassion and seeks enlightenment, not for one's own sake, but for the sake of others. The great vow (determination) made by the bodhisattva demonstrates this concern for others. This unselfish being promises to remain in the world of suffering until all beings down to the most tortured creature in hell have been liberated. By integrating wisdom with compassion, an enlightened person participates in the changing nature of existence without attachment to it (see Chapter 5). The attitude of care for others by the bodhisattva is shown in the following lyric poetry from the manual, "Setting Forth in the Practice of Enlightenment":

> I am medicine for the sick and weary
> May I be their physician and their nurse
>   until disease appears no more
> May I strike down the anguish of thirst and hunger
>   with rains of food and drink
> May I be food and drink to them
>   in famine and disaster
> May I be an inexhaustible treasure
>   for those in need.[3]

These examples of care for other persons within the traditional religions show that significant human relationships result from a more basic reality, like God, Tao, or the Buddha-nature. The relationship between oneself and others has profound significance because it is an expression of transcendent reality or God's will. Within a traditional religion, human relationships are expressions of, or adjuncts to, other means to ultimate transformation because they are seen as a vehicle for a more basic source of change outside or beyond the strictly human situation.

FULFILLING HUMAN RELATIONSHIPS AS A MEANS TO ULTIMATE TRANSFORMATION

Although honesty, care for others, and love between people are advocated by the great world religions, some people who may not be followers of any traditional religion hold that these and other expressions of interpersonal relations should be not only part but also the core of quality living. Advocates of the centrality of human relationships assert that the development of concern for others and honesty in personal relations, which sometimes derive from traditional religious belief and ritual—for example, making a public marriage commitment in a church with the help of a priest or minister—can be had without recourse to the traditional religious belief system or any affiliation with a religious institution. Some advocates also assert that psychologically based techniques like psychotherapy, sensitivity training, or encounter sessions are a more powerful and direct means for transforming human beings into loving and caring people than traditional religious ways.

115
*The Religious
Significance
of Fulfilling
Human
Relationships*

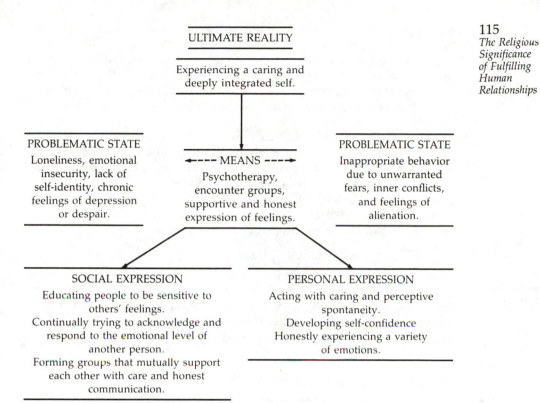

FIGURE 1.   *Fulfilling Human Relationships as a Means to Ultimate Transformation*

Because this humanistic approach does not appeal to a transcendent source, its advocates argue, the individuals involved in such a therapeutic relationship recognize their responsibility in promoting mental health, growth, and change. The inborn resources of the people engaged in inter-personal encounter—not God, an eternal transcendent moral order, or mystical awareness—are regarded as sufficient to transform human life at the deepest level. In the remainder of this chapter, we discuss the process of ultimate transformation through cultivating fulfilling human relationships by looking at the following elements: the human condition of emotional insecurity, loneliness, and self-deceit; the self-in-relation as the ultimate reality; therapeutic techniques as the means to transformation, and the social and personal expressions of this nontraditional way of being religious. Note the relationship between these elements in Figure 1.

The Problematic in the Human Condition: The Divided Self

From this point of view, the deepest problems in life arise from feelings of loneliness, fear, despair, and emotional insecurity. For example, a modern, technological world asks people to make fundamental changes in their lives and to make them quickly. Women, especially, are pulled between professional challenges and the traditional expectation to maintain a household for herself, a husband, and children. In India, the parents of three daughters must choose between the long-range economic advantages of a small family and the cultural need to have more children until at least one male child is born. Clearly, in times when major needs appear to contradict each other, the individual may have difficulty maintaining a clear self-identity.

Unless the "divided self" finds some means of reconciliation, the life of the individual may become actively or passively destructive. Unacknowledged feelings lead to inappropriate behavior, unexplained feelings of depression, and self-destructive tendencies in human relations. At an extreme point, repressed feelings of alienation may lead to an inability to perceive reality and a loss of self-control. It is not surprising that in the West, the nervous breakdown or psychotic break has become a part of many family histories.

In traditional religious processes, the divided individual would seek refuge and relief in ritual, in the experience of God's grace, in yogic meditation, or in a discovery of cosmic balance. Only in extreme cases might the traditional cure be supplemented by psychotherapy. There is, however, a nontranscendent ultimate reality that—according to some advocates—can respond to and cure the sickness of despair.

Ultimate Reality as an Integrated Self

The ultimate reality that counters all feelings of loneliness and fear is the integrated, fully functioning self. The assumption here is that every self has the potential to integrate all of its experiences in a mentally healthy way. This self enjoys life, experiences sorrow, learns from experiences, and accepts deficiencies. Through accepting all emotions and experiences, the individual develops skills for balancing his or her personal needs and responsibilities with the needs and responsibilities of others. Reality involves living here and now in relation to other people with integrity, honesty, and care.

It is no easy task for the individual to take responsibility for his or her actions and for the feelings that arise from them. For this reason, traditional religion and associated cultural habits have been important sources of comfort. At the same time religious attitudes and cultural habits, claim advocates of the humanist orientation, may block the way for an individual's full self-discovery by assigning ultimate answers to a transcendent reality. Although from a theistic perspective one must know God before one may know oneself deeply, in this humanist approach, the individual person has to probe deep and sometimes painful conflicts within his own consciousness. Beginning in the 1960s in the United States, the means for learning how to be a self-sufficient and caring person became available to the general population by way of encounter groups, self-discovery centers, and popular books on how to lead a richer, fuller life. The kinds of therapy that had been limited to the wealthy (and often regarded as slightly embarrassing) achieved a new acceptance and a new, larger audience.

Means to Fulfillment: Therapeutic Relationships

117
*The Religious
Significance
of Fulfilling
Human
Relationships*

Some basic forms of contemporary therapeutic techniques are being used within traditional religious structures in the West. Some therapists, however, suggest that personality therapies will eventually replace traditional religious institutions because transformation can be accomplished by human encounter alone. The clinical psychologist O. H. Mowrer, for example, believes that therapy groups will eventually replace the Christian church:

> I think there is a good possibility that these groups represent the emerging form of the church of the twenty-first century. They will very likely differ from conventional Catholic and Protestant churches in that they will not be specifically christocentric, nor will they be explicitly theistic (compare Confucianism and Buddhism). But they will, I think, be *profoundly religious*. . . . The term "religion," in its literal derivation, has no necessary relation to "theology." The former term comes from the Latin root *ligare*, which means connection, and *re-ligare*, from which our term "religion" comes, means reconnection. And this, more than perhaps anything else, is what the small-groups movement is concerned with: the reconnection, reintegration, reconciliation of lost, lonely, isolated, alienated, estranged persons back into a loving, concerned, and orderly fellowship or group of some sort.[4]

The ultimate character of personality development through psychotherapy is also noted by psychologist A. Maslow. Discussing the nature of a healthy society in a radio interview, he maintained that it is possible to find ultimate values by directing attention to the healthiest aspects of human life:

> In general, the consequences of psychotherapy are moves toward better values. The person in successful therapy generally comes out a better citizen, a better husband, a better wife—certainly a better person. He is more perceptive and more spontaneous—this practically always happens. These results are achieved through self-knowledge—the main path to discovering within ourselves the best values for all mankind. The more clearly we know these values, the more easily, spontaneously, effortlessly we can grope toward them.[5]

To suggest that creative human relationships within a therapeutic setting can be a source of personality transformation is not to claim that *all* human relationships are therapeutic. Some human relationships are too casual or superficial to promote any lasting change. Others are so destructive that they damage the individual, possibly preventing healthy relationships in the future. Furthermore, not all therapeutic relationships are intended to be means to ultimate transformation. Many psychologists do not place ultimate value on their work. Still, according to some exponents of the humanistic movement, therapeutic relationships and human relationships in general are connections that may be able to bring about the deepest possible personality transformation.

The Growth-Motivated Therapeutic Relationship. One of the most influential therapists of our time, who focused almost totally on the character of the therapeutic relationship, was Carl Rogers. Emphasizing that the therapist-client relationship must evolve in a permissive, accepting atmosphere,

Rogers proposed six basic points as necessary and sufficient conditions for therapeutic personality change.[6] As you read this list, notice that the conditions are distributed between the patient and the therapist.

1.   There must be a relationship, that is, psychological contact between two people.
2.   The patient must recognize an incongruence between his or her self-perceptions and the behavior that is causing anxiety.
3.   Within the therapeutic relationship, the therapist must be genuinely and freely him- or herself—in other words, integrated to the extent that the therapist's self-image and behavior are congruent (even if this congruency reveals that the therapist is not a perfect human being).
4.   The therapist must place no conditions on the relationship, such as "I like you only if thus and so," but must make an attempt to accept unconditionally and positively all aspects of the client's behavior whether it is deficient or growth oriented.
5.   The therapist should try to develop an empathetic understanding of the client's inner world of meaning, come to know that inner world as if the therapist were the client—without ever losing the "as if" condition—and communicate this understanding to the client.
6.   To a minimal degree, the patient needs to acknowledge this empathetic understanding.

Under these conditions, says Rogers, constructive personality change is certain. In addition, he emphasizes that any warm, accepting, and open person can fulfill the therapeutic role. Rogers's view that professional diagnosis and training are unnecessary suggests that the power for transformation potentially lies in the interaction between any two caring and sensitive people. In fact, if the patient becomes dependent on the therapist as the expert, just as worshippers have become dependent on priests, he or she does not develop inner resources for solving problems.

The idea of human relations that emerged as a result of the work of psychologists like Rogers and Maslow stresses two important points: (1) that a positive humanistic approach reveals the possibilities life holds for each person and (2) that it is important to search for ways in which to realize these potentials in society. The goal is not only to produce fully functioning people by appealing to their best character through love and approval but also to create a psychologically healthy culture by releasing individual creative power into it. So, from this perspective, psychological forces are seen as the most influential contemporary power in the development of personal and social values.

Evolution of Group Therapy. With the flowering of the humanistic movement in American psychology during the early 1960s, therapists were challenged from within their own ranks and by their clients to discover new ways of effectively communicating. Many people saw a need to bring the one-on-one exchanges between therapist and patient out of the clinic and into group settings. What emerged was the development of group therapy techniques such as psychodrama (the acting out of emotional difficulties in front of a group), family-oriented therapy, and the multiple-therapist approach. At present, almost every individual therapy system has been adapted for use in a group.

119
*The Religious
Significance
of Fulfilling
Human
Relationships*

As a result of this group work, therapists developed new techniques that focused on nonverbal forms of communication: touch, attentive looking, silence, and intuition. This new movement toward a general improvement of communication skills through group interaction led many to the realization that a person did not need to be "sick" to benefit from group work. As a result, the word *therapy* (which implied mental problems) was dropped from the description of group work. On a larger scale, "growth centers," such as Esalen in Big Sur, California, sprang up all over the United States, emphasizing that the same techniques (plus some new ones) that had made sick people well could also make well people better.

Along with Carl Rogers, other therapists like Fritz Perls, Ida Rolf, and William Shultz have widely implemented these techniques to transform people's lives. Rogers, for instance, in his *Freedom to Learn*, proposes a practical plan for a communication revolution in the classroom. He advocates the use of the intensive group experience, otherwise known as sensitivity training, the "T" group, or the encounter workshop, as the most effective means yet discovered for facilitating constructive learning, growth, and change—in individuals or groups:

> The intensive group, or "workshop" group, usually consists of ten to fifteen persons and a facilitator or leader. It is relatively unstructured, providing a climate of maximum freedom for personal expression, exploration of feelings, and interpersonal communication. Emphasis is upon the interactions among the group members, in an atmosphere which encourages each to drop his defenses and facades and thus enables him to relate directly and openly to other members of the group—the "basic encounter." Individuals come to know themselves more fully than is possible in the usual working and social relationships; the climate of openness, risktaking, and honesty generates trust, which enables the person to recognize and change self-defeating attitudes, test out and adopt more innovative and constructive behaviors, and, subsequently, to relate more adequately and effectively to others in his everyday life situation.[7]

Whereas William Shultz is well known for his effectiveness in leading encounter groups at a popular level and Ida Rolf for developing techniques of intensive therapeutic body massage, the late Fritz Perls developed innovative group techniques within a psychotherapeutic approach called "Gestalt therapy." The following is a brief account by a neurophysiologist of a group session with Perls where "the hot seat" is used. This is a vacant chair next to Perls, which is used by a person who wants to work with him:

> I got into the hot seat again, this time about the death of my mother. I had some unfinished business . . . having to do with guilt about her death. . . . I had spent seven years working to keep her alive and then, at the end, when the cancer finally killed her through a respiratory death, I blamed myself for having kept her alive by artificial means, so long.

I got into the hot seat and Fritz said, "Okay, go back to your mother's death." I went back to that particular day and began to hear her dying, became frightened, and came back to the group. Fritz said, "Go back." I went back again and started going through the fear, the grief, and the guilt connected with the doctors, with my own part in it. I examined very carefully the whole [sequence] having to do with her death. I cried. I became extremely fearful, got into a panic, then I cried with grief again. Three times Fritz put me through it and finally he said, "Okay, you haven't quite finished with that, but you have dealt with most of it." He let me off the hot seat.

I spent a total of two weeks and one weekend in his workshops and learned very much about myself and about others and about his technique. I was impressed with the fact that he could tune in on where one was and then program one to move even further into the space that one was reluctant to go into.[8]

Perl's handwritten and Original epigraph to his *Gestalt Therapy Verbatim* encapsulates the entire process most aptly:

To suffer one's death
and to be reborn
is not easy.[9]

These examples of group work indicate a few of the institutional forms that a concern with human relationships has taken. They express, from the standpoint of the committed participant, a possible means to ultimate transformation in the psychotherapeutic setting.

Social and Personal Expressions: Education, Action, and Self-Understanding

So far we have said that the ultimate reality in this religious process is achieved in the integrated, fully functioning self. The means to achieving this reality include formal psychotherapy and encounter group work, as well as informal but attentive relations with other people. How, then, do all of these realizations express themselves socially and personally?

The social expression of this ultimate reality happens through two processes: education and action. Education in sensitivity is necessary because certain racial habits and cultural biases that we take for granted may cause great discomfort to others who do not understand them. When former President Jimmy Carter kissed Anwar Sadat's wife on the cheek, his action horrified a largely Muslim nation. One should not touch the wife of the Egyptian prime minister, particularly as Mr. Sadat was a devout Muslim. Similarly, but without international significance, most of us recognize that some conversational habits are more reassuring than others. For instance, a simple nod of the head or an occasional sound of acknowledgment creates a sense of security and trust in a personal conversation or in a classroom dialogue. A responsive face stimulates communication; an unresponsive face can stop communication altogether.

The second way in which to express a belief in the power of human interaction is by putting the techniques for true communication into action. Recall that Carl Rogers suggested how encounter groups could improve classroom learning. Similarly, industrial psychologists use encounter and communication techniques to improve relationships between labor and management. The reasoning here is that the more effectively labor and management can communicate their needs to each other, the more production will improve. The Japanese, for example, seem to have perfected the concept of industrial teamwork and interaction. In Japan, small teams combine their various talents to solve problems at all levels within an industry. In each case, sensitive communication leads to a better life.

Although people need the aid and support of others to function well in a healthy culture, knowledge of the self is crucial. Such personal traits as honesty, sincerity, and courage are necessary for self-understanding if individuals are to deal effectively with the inner forces of their lives. A person must take the time to alter habits that could interfere with spontaneous and happy relations with other people. A person must learn self-trust before he or she can extend trust to others. Thus, it is only through self-knowledge that effective reconciliation can take place between people in an alienated and fragmented society.

To be a fully functioning person in a relationship means to be able to experience oneself fully through another, to discover that other, and to share a sense of direction and mutual enjoyment. At the same time, becoming a fully functioning person involves exploring and developing one's ability to relate on a deep emotional level. It means to give love, to be loved in return, and to have grown more fully human because of the experience. From this perspective, to love and be loved offers the deepest awareness of true joy in existence and thus becomes the highest goal of life.

SUMMARY

Human interaction is a religious encounter when a dynamic and living exchange with another leads to a life-changing self-discovery. This human interaction may occur either within or outside traditional religious expressions.

Within traditional religious structures, human relationships may take the forms of ministry to the lay community, the training of new members of a religious community (novitiates), and ethical teachings by the founders or chief spokespersons of a given tradition. In each case, there is an assumption that human contact is essential for knowing important things. In the religious context, a person makes a better guide than any set of instructions.

The relationships between medicine men and priests with their "congregations" are examples of ministry to the lay community. In Christian ministry, the character of pastoral care has changed with historical and cultural conditions. The functions of pastoral care include healing, sustaining, guiding, and reconciliation. Ethical teachings in the major religious traditions have emphasized the values of kindness, patience, and compassion in a person's relations with others.

Fulfilling human relationships may also be a nontranscendent religious expression. One of the primary means to such fulfillment is the therapeutic relationship, which began in private psychotherapy but has emerged in several group forms. The five elements of fulfilling human relationships are as follows:

1. The problematic in the human condition is the recognition that life is filled with loneliness, fear, despair, and emotional insecurity. These unacknowledged feelings lead to unexplained feelings of depression and loss of self-control.
2. The ultimate reality that cures the alienation of the human condition is the fully functioning self, which can take personal responsibility for its actions. This self enjoys life, experiences sorrow, and trusts others to participate in both kinds of feelings.
3. The means to achieving fulfillment in intimacy comes from encountering and relating with other people. Learning to relate with others may happen in structured encounter groups or in informal encounters with other people. In either case, the key to making contact is through expressing emotions honestly and sensitively.
4. The social expression of this reality occurs through education and action. A person or groups of people must become sensitive to the personal and cultural needs of others. The principles of honest communication can be put to work in education, business, and diplomacy.
5. For the individual, being fully integrated and capable of establishing caring relations with others results in feelings of spontaneity, creativity, self-confidence, and happiness. The divided self becomes whole again.

As you think back over the chapter, consider what O. H. Mowrer said: "I think that there is a good possibility that these [encounter] groups represent the emerging form of the church in the twenty-first century." What do you think?

SELECTED READINGS

Classical statements by psychologists and psychoanalysts that interpret the most profound awareness and attitudes about life in terms of personality development and interpersonal relationships include the following:

*G . W. Allport, *The Individual and His Religion* (New York: Macmillan, 1950). Here religion is described as a person's ultimate attempt to complete one's personality in a comprehensive social context.

*E. Fromm, *Psychoanalysis and Religion* (New Haven, CN: Yale University Press, 1950). A series of five lectures, including "The Psychoanalyst as 'Physician of the Soul'." He distinguishes the humanistic psychoanalytic therapy from both behavioral adjustment therapy and institutional religious practice.

*A. Maslow, *Religions, Values, and Peak-Experiences* (New York: Viking, 1964). Author advocates finding the sacred in ordinary experience and regards this as the lesson to be learned from all true mystics.

A. Maslow, *The Farther Reaches of Human Nature* (New York: Viking Press, 1971). Essays published posthumously that focus on the development of the deepest human values leading to self-actualization and creativity.

*R. May, *Man's Search for Himself* (New York: New American Library, 1953). An advocate of humanistic psychology discusses techniques for integrating oneself by getting in touch with one's feelings, perceiving goals, and recovering a relationship with one's subconscious.

*F. Perls, R. Hefferline, and P. Goodman, *Gestalt Therapy* (New York: Delta, 1951). Theory and application of Gestalt therapy before it became nationally known. *F. Perls, *Gestalt Therapy Verbatim*, compiled and edited by J. O. Stevens (Lafayette, CA: Real People Press, 1969). Verbatim accounts of intensive workshops and dreamwork seminars conducted by Perls at Esalen from 1966 to 1968.

C. R. Rogers, *Freedom to Learn* (Columbus, OH: Charles E. Merrill, 1969). Advocates a humanistically oriented approach to the educational process, particularly the training of scientists, by focusing on the person and his values. Contains interesting revolutionary tactics for renovating the educational process using the intensive encounter group experience.

Two anthologies that include sections on the use of psychotherapy as humanistic means for personal and religious development are F. J. Streng, C. L. Lloyd, Jr., and J. T. Allen, *Ways of Being Religious* (Englewood Cliffs, NJ: Prentice-Hall, 1973), Chapter 5, "Attaining an Integrated Self through Creative Interaction"; and E. Cell, ed., *Religion and Contemporary Western Culture* (Nashville: Abingdon Press, 1967), Chapter 6, "Religion and Psychotherapy."

Three accounts of personality training through encounter groups, which intend to transform one's life and which emphasize living in the here and now, experiencing one's feelings, and acknowledging the paradox of control and being controlled are G. B. Leonard, *Education and Ecstasy* (New York: Delacorte Press, 1968); R. B. Levy, *I Can Only Touch You Now* (Englewood Cliffs, NJ: Prentice-Hall, 1973); and A. Bry, *EST: Sixty Hours that Transform Your Life* (New York: Harper & Row, 1975).

R. A. Harper, *Psychoanalysis and Psychotherapy: Thirty-six Systems* (Englewood Cliffs, NJ: Prentice-Hall, 1959). A brief but informative collection of sketches covering most of the major psychotherapeutic systems in America prior to the rise of the humanistic movement. See especially Chapter 9, "Group Psychotherapies."

W. A. Clebsch and C. R. Jaekle, *Pastoral Care in Historical Perspective* (New York: Harper, 1964). Useful information on the history and functions of the Christian pastoral care movement with extensive examples of eminent theologians discussing various aspects of the topic.

*Ram Dass, *The Only Dance There Is* (Garden City, NY: Anchor Press/Doubleday, 1974). A former Harvard professor-turned-yogin calls on health science professionals to place their therapy in the context of the Eternal Present, as he humorously tells stories of his own experiences.

123
*The Religious
Significance
of Fulfilling
Human
Relationships*

CHAPTER 7

The Religious Significance of Social Responsibility

People grow up with the recognition of social limitations and possibilities. Part of the maturing process is acquiring the sense that individuals are partially regulated by their interactions with other people. As a member of a community, a person can do some things, but not others, and learns that there is a difference between good and bad.

Social relationships provide channels for expressing human values, especially those sets of values that we call "morality" or "ethics." Moral actions reveal the parts of human existence that deal with rights and obligations in relation to others. In discussing morality or ethics, the term *justice* has particular significance. For the advocates of social responsibility as ultimate reality, there is an unbreakable link between what is moral, just, and right.

As we have discovered in Part One, the role of correct behavior (morals, ethics) has been an essential ingredient in traditional religious expressions. In fact, correct behavior is so much a part of the traditional religious life that it may seem unnecessary to give social responsibility a place of its own as a means to ultimate transformation. Furthermore, including strictly secular movements, such as the feminist movement, in a study of religious life may seem to stretch the definition of religion. But this is our aim.

Modern history suggests that the urge to seek social justice or to establish an ethical society inspires and transforms people whether or not they believe in God. Without appealing to divine or to natural law, dedicated reformers may find ultimate meaning in their work to make human life better for everyone. To understand them, we must ask: Is the work of Che Guevara, the revolutionary, less religious than that of evangelist Billy Graham? Or consider Mother Teresa as she moves through the night streets of Calcutta, picking up discarded humans so they may die in clean beds. No one would question the compassion and power of such a mission. But suppose that Mother Teresa wore no habit and was just Teresa. Would her work transform her less or allow less dignity to the dying?

This chapter, then, focuses on the proposition that for some social reformers, a moral relationship to other human beings (expressed through social action) can be a means to ultimate transformation either through a variety of traditional religious expressions or outside recognized religious communities. Those who express their religiousness outside of traditional forms do not appeal for guidance to a transcendent natural law or to God's law. For them, being religious is recognizing and acting on behalf of the value of human life; social action leads to ultimate expressions of social justice and equality. In this context, the full development of social-ethical relationships gives a life religious significance.

ETHICS AS A MODE OF BECOMING HUMAN

Figure 1 outlines the discussion of this chapter. Imagine that the inverted triangle in the upper portion of the figure is an electrical circuit and that the points of the triangle represent those forces that supply a charge to human existence. There is the self, there are other people with whom the self must interact, and there is an ideal (in this case an ethical ideal) that completes the circuit.

While the ethical ideal represents only one point on the circuit, it may draw its power from one of several sources. In this depiction, two of those sources are associated with traditional religious forms (columns 1 and 2) and one of them with secular institutions (column 3). In traditional religions, the ultimate source of goodness in a society is not found in governmental legislation nor even in a particular type of government. In theistic traditions (Christianity, Judaism, Islam), the ultimate source of goodness is God. In traditions based on natural moral law, such as in the traditional Brahmanical understanding of dharma in Hinduism, the purpose of social life and political government is to administer the eternal law, not to legislate social life according to the people's will. Similarly in China, the Confucian cultivation of true humanity nurtures such virtues as propriety, wisdom, and honesty. The Confucians considered these virtues to be reflections of the universal moral order. The emperor was supposed to be the chief moral example for all society as the connection between heaven and earth. His failure to administer justice and provide peace and minimal prosperity was grounds for rejecting his rule. Even if a ruler's administration of the law might be called into question, the law itself was beyond debate.

A third orientation makes no appeal to God or to natural law. Instead, it bases morality on the human capacity to have rights and responsibilities in relation to others. In this context, moral relationships are determined by the strictly human capacity to set goals, assess their values, and construct social mechanisms, such as legislatures and courts of justice, to implement the goals. A basic notion in this orientation is that all people, regardless of birth or religious views, have legal *rights*. If people recognize they have rights simply because they are human, they must recognize that this human quality extends to other people as well. So, rights automatically become *obligations*. A person's claim to rights implies that others are obliged to recognize those rights and that they, in turn, have rights that place obligations on others.

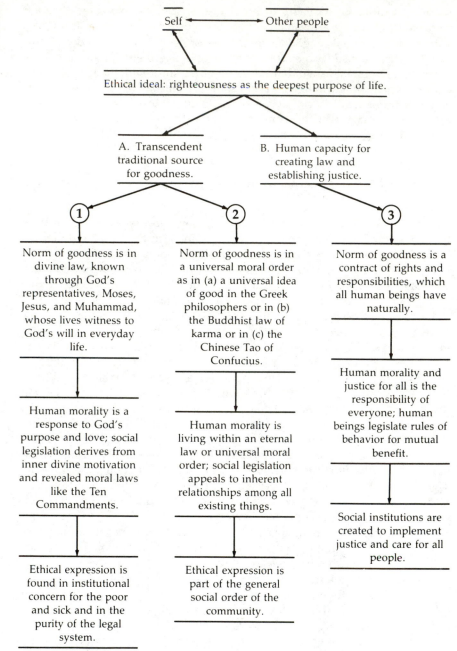

Self ←————————→ Other people

Ethical ideal: righteousness as the deepest purpose of life.

A. Transcendent traditional source for goodness.

B. Human capacity for creating law and establishing justice.

1

2

3

Norm of goodness is in divine law, known through God's representatives, Moses, Jesus, and Muhammad, whose lives witness to God's will in everyday life.

Norm of goodness is in a universal moral order as in (a) a universal idea of good in the Greek philosophers or in (b) the Buddhist law of karma or in (c) the Chinese Tao of Confucius.

Norm of goodness is a contract of rights and responsibilities, which all human beings have naturally.

Human morality is a response to God's purpose and love; social legislation derives from inner divine motivation and revealed moral laws like the Ten Commandments.

Human morality is living within an eternal law or universal moral order; social legislation appeals to inherent relationships among all existing things.

Human morality and justice for all is the responsibility of everyone; human beings legislate rules of behavior for mutual benefit.

Ethical expression is found in institutional concern for the poor and sick and in the purity of the legal system.

Ethical expression is part of the general social order of the community.

Social institutions are created to implement justice and care for all people.

FIGURE 1. *Righteousness as the Deepest Purpose of Life*

The concept that every human being has certain natural rights that society is expected to guarantee establishes a new context in which to consider ethical relationships. This concept can exist without reference to an organized religion and may even constitute a religious expression in its own right.

In this chapter, we look at the claim that justice, freedom, and human rights can be built into a society without an appeal to a transcendent power. As we might expect, this claim has been the source of lively debate among theologians. As you read, participate in the debate by asking yourself the following questions: (1) Is it possible to achieve social justice through secular institutions (such as government or public service organizations)? (2) Is it possible to achieve the highest, the ultimate, expression of social rights and obligations without an appeal to God or eternal natural law?

ETHICS AS AN IMPLEMENTATION OF DIVINE WILL

In a theistic society (one that recognizes God's will as preserved in divine laws), the morality of an individual's activity is often measured against the ideal ethical behavior expressed by the patriarch, seer, or founder of the community (see Figure 1, column 1). Thus, the revelations and the lives of Moses, Jesus, and Muhammad are the true expressions of God's will and purpose for "His people." Community members imitate the goodness of God (to the best of their ability) and live according to divine prescriptions for a good life. When a Christian loves his or her neighbor, that Christian is living according to the laws set down by God in Christ. When a Muslim accepts the direction of a religious leader (imam) in political matters, he is living according to Allah's will.

The logic behind supposing that divine law asserts a clear set of ethical values runs something like this. God is a caring God of justice and has created a world in which that justice is an active force. Because justice is a part of God's will, the divine law is an expression of God's loving care. God has revealed the patterns of righteousness through certain representatives—Moses, Christ, Mohammad. If one follows the models inspired by God, one will live the moral life; and if a society is structured according to revealed law, that society will be a just one. Therefore, human morality in all of its expressions is ideally a response to God.

When people respond to divine revelation, ethics takes the form of putting God's will into practice in their personal, social, and political lives. The revelation becomes the focus for creating a community of God's people. People in such a community are related to each other through their being called by God. From this perspective emerge two ways to express an awareness of God's will in ethical-moral behavior: (1) through accepting and supporting social obligations revealed by God to a community of his people or (2) through a demonstration of personal faith modeled after the lives of God's representatives. The former pattern stresses conforming to divine laws and emphasizes the consequences of social behavior for the total communal life. The latter emphasizes purity of heart, clarity of conscience, and right motives.

Traditional Religious Ethics Expressed Through Social Order

The ethical alternative that focuses on communal life is typified by the medieval Roman Catholic church and by the Sunni Muslims (who constitute more than 80 percent of the Arab world). The Roman Catholic church found God's will both in natural law, which governs human relations, and in revealed truth, whereby humanity is related to God through grace. The medieval theologian, Thomas Aquinas, for example, claimed that European society—and finally all people—ideally should embody the eternal order and so demonstrate God's law. Both secular life and the church were realms of the Christian life, each having its proper role in establishing God's law. The Christian man or woman in the Middle Ages could not have imagined a separation of church and state: both were expressions of God's care and justice.

In traditional Sunni Islam, as found in North Africa and Saudi Arabia, all social and political life derives, ideally, from divine revelation. Until the twentieth century, there was no separation of secular and religious law in the Muslim community. The law (*fiqh*) that prescribed social actions was based on the Qur'an and on the words and deeds ascribed by tradition to the Prophet (*sunnah*). Among the Sunni, four schools or systems of the *fiqh* were accepted for interpreting moral action. From the handbooks of these schools and from the explanations of the religious scholars (mufti), orthodox Muslims learned what they must do in all matters, from religious celebrations to personal hygiene. It was the responsibility of the Muslim ruler (*khalifah* or *imam*) to administer this ethic.

Traditional Religious Ethics Expressed Through Personal Faith

The second, more personal, means of expressing divine will through ethical behavior may be found in the Jewish prophetic tradition and in the Reformation of Western Christianity. Key terms in this expression are *pure heart* and *personal obligation*.

The Jewish prophetic tradition and the Old Testament psalms exemplify the ethical perspective that stresses moral actions originating in purity of heart. In the prophetic tradition, the holiness of God stands behind human moral action. God's communion with the patriarchs should lead each generation to teach the next one how to act. In relationships with others, a person should reflect God's care for the world; then blessings will abound.

The psalmist's ideal of the pure heart is expressed in Psalms 24:2–3.

> Who may go up the mountain of the Lord?
> And who may stand in his holy place?
>   He who has clean hands and a pure heart,
> Who has not set his mind on falsehood,
>   and has not committed perjury.
> He shall receive a blessing from the Lord,
>   and justice from God his saviour.[1]

Here is the point at which knowledge of God and a decision to do his will meet in human life. A person's moral duty is to witness to the Lord's holiness and blessing. We see this concern, for example, in the daily life of the Jewish community in the United States, which abounds in welfare and social agencies to care for community problems. On a more personal level as well, the fellowship of the tradition means that Jews coming into a strange city for the first time need only make themselves known to members of the local Jewish community to find an immediate "family" relationship and a concern for their personal needs. This deep social identification also produces religious scholars, historians, and writers who dedicate their lives to the preservation of the Jewish tradition.

With such an emphasis on outward action as the result of inner divine motivation, it is not surprising that the Jewish tradition stresses the importance of an ethical life. A person ideally expresses personal religious motives in practical moral activity. It was proclaimed by the prophet Isaiah (56:1–2):

> These are the words of the Lord:
> Maintain justice, do the right;
> for my deliverance is close at hand,
>   and my righteousness will show itself victorious.
> Happy is the man who follows these precepts,
> happy is the mortal who holds them fast,
>   who keeps the sabbath undefiled,
> who refrains from all wrong-doing![2]

People cannot be deceitful, unjust, or unkind without polluting the divine power at work in their hearts. Where the Holy One impinges on humanity, there one has a moral obligation that must be fulfilled, lest one break the covenant with God and become guilty.

The emphasis on personal obligation was also a part of the Reformation of Western Christianity. Well-known Protestant leaders expounded on the moral significance of the individual life: *Martin Luther* (1483–1546, Lutheranism) regarded every moral secular calling as a possible field for a full Christian life. Taking religious orders added no special virtue. *John Calvin* (1509–1564, Presbyterianism) attempted to establish a Christian society through local political action. His efforts became a model for positive involvement in social institutions. *John Wesley* (1703–1791, Methodism) reacted against the formality in the Anglican church and worked for a revitalization of the Christian's inner life to bring about a self-conscious life of social responsibility.

Perhaps the most dramatic expression of the Protestant Christian ethical imperative is the social gospel movement in England and America, especially as it existed between 1900 and 1930. The social gospel was a program of secular social reform that sought to give practical expression in political and economic areas of life to the Christian experience of redemption. Not only did it lead to the development of social services within Christian churches, but it also led to cooperation among church bodies on moral issues and aided the growth of such religious social agencies as the Salvation Army, the Young Men's Christian Association (YMCA), and the Young Women's Christian Association (YWCA).

So far, we have looked at one source of power for the ethical ideal as a way of being religious. In general, theistic religious traditions include ethical living as an expression of God's will. Ethical behavior may be expressed through the social order or through personal faith and a pure heart.

In the next section, we consider the ethical ideal as it receives power from an eternal order or law. In this orientation, there is no suggestion that humans are basically evil or cannot be morally perfect. As expressions of an eternal orderly process, people have the full potential to live in social harmony (see Chapter 4). The morality of an action is judged in relation to an individual's role in cosmic harmony. The task of an ethical person is not to legislate or create goodness but to administer or expose it.

ETHICS AS A REFLECTION OF THE NATURAL GOOD

As the previous section illustrates, one way of identifying oneself as an ethical being is to recognize that God's will is preserved in sacred scriptures. A person may bear witness to those laws by accepting particular social patterns (as the Sunni Muslims or Orthodox Jews do) or by accepting the moral obligations that God's will implies (as the modern, reformed Jew or some Christians might do).

Another way of identifying oneself as an ethical being is by paying attention to the natural and eternal "good" which is a part of the natural law (see Figure 1, column 2). Those who accept this point of view make two important assumptions: (1) There are (in some sense) eternal human values, and (2) human beings have a natural capacity to know what the highest truth is. Working within these two general assumptions, we find several conceptions of how one learns of, and then demonstrates, ethical knowledge. We analyze two of them here. One conception comes from the Greek philosophers, Socrates, Plato, and Aristotle. The second comes from the Buddha.

Ethics in Ancient Greek Moral Philosophy

During the fifth century B.C.E. in Greece, there was a general philosophical revolt against the mindless acceptance of social conventions and rules. A century later, a group of philosophers known as the Cynics claimed that popular convention offered no basis on which to judge right and wrong. They did not regard even commonly accepted moral positions as an eternal good. Although the extreme view of the Cynics was unacceptable to Socrates, Plato, and Aristotle, they did share the notion that the mere existence of a habit or accepted social attitude did not justify its acceptance as an ultimate value. For them, there was a direct link between philosophical reflection and knowing what moral action or virtue meant. The meaning was available in the natural order; it just had to be searched out.

Knowledge for Socrates (470–399 B.C.E.) meant practical wisdom, as distinct from a mystic intuition. He believed it was possible to know virtue and to teach it. The object of moral concern is the good, but to know the good requires analyzing the conditions in which it can be expressed. Laws that help to bring about the good do so because they are reasonable. These laws

should be followed because they bring about useful effects rather than because they are divine commands.

Similarly, Plato (428–348 B.C.E.) held that virtue cannot be identified with
custom or political authority; rather, virtue is dependent on knowledge.
Knowledge is available through contact with the supreme ideas that transcend every particular expression of them. There was, therefore, a gap between the appearances of actual existence and transcendent reality. In the
sphere of ethics, Plato distinguished between the everyday rules of civil and
political life and the virtue of the philosopher. Rules could be expressed in
the conduct of a statesman by moral effort, whereas virtue could be attained
only by inquiring into the nature of absolute virtue. In the last analysis, the
survival of society depended on its ability to discover ultimate ends.

The concern to define virtue and law in terms of ultimate ends was
continued by Aristotle (384–322 B.C.E.). His *Politics*, however, reflects
a deep concern for civil administration, which is supposed to provide opportunities, especially for property-owning males (the aristocrats), to live
noble lives. He believed that moral relationships promised a noble and full
life for those who could perceive values above wealth and power. The state
existed to prevent some members of this upper class from exploiting other
members.

Ethics in Early Buddhism

Like the Greek philosophers, the Buddha (560–480 B.C.E.) and his followers emphasized that moral action is not valuable unless it is related to
a radical mental critique (similar to what the Greeks called "inquiry")
and spiritual reassessment of life. In contrast to the Greeks, however, the
Buddha claimed that no idea in itself is eternal. Ideas are only useful as temporary guideposts along the road to liberation from worldly illusion and
sorrow. According to the Buddha, the goal of life is not to express a universal moral ideal but to achieve freedom from all mental and emotional
bondage—including ideals. Nevertheless, although social ethics are relative
to the goal of freedom from sorrow, they are a vital part of what it means to
follow the path of the Buddha.

Verse 183 of the Dhammapada (one of the most widely read Theravada
Buddhist scriptures) reads: "Not to commit any sin, to do good, and to
purify one's own mind: that is the teaching of [all] the Buddhas." This
suggests that morality is not a trifling matter. Other teachings elaborate the
view that evil action arises from human greed ("craving"), which is produced by mental and moral actions (karma) as long as people delude themselves by accepting the conventions of life as eternal truths. The origin of sin
does not lie in something external to human life, such as a devil, but is a
product of human greed and ignorance. Similarly, virtue is not simply
obeying certain social prescriptions; it is living in such a way as to free
oneself from all the attachments to mind and emotion.

In this light, the highest virtue is to teach the *dhamma* (truth, law) of the
Buddha. This was the social responsibility that the Buddha accepted after he
attained enlightenment in Northeast India. This teaching includes following
certain rules of morality, such as refraining from taking life, stealing, and

lying, as well as perfecting such virtues as charity, wisdom, and forbearance. These ethical prescriptions emphasize personal and interpersonal ethics and stress that the individual should change within if outward actions are to have any spiritual meaning. Although it is true that personal perfection does not require the development of a system of political ethics—as Aristotle advocated—the welfare of society requires that the Buddha's *dhamma* be taught and that the state protect and support perfected beings and those seeking perfection.

In summary, ethical standards are important forces in determining how people should behave, both personally and within society. In some systems, such as in traditional Christianity and in the city (*polis*) of fourth-century B.C.E. Greece, the very nature of society was determined by the standards of justice and morality established either by God or by nature.

As we move to the third part of this discussion (see Figure 1, column 3), there is another important point to remember about the traditional forms. Both of them assume that reality has already been established by God or by natural law. The last section makes no such assumption. Whatever else this mode of religious expression inherits from tradition, such as the significance of moral social action, it begins with the assumption that reality has not been determined once and for all.

SOCIAL-POLITICAL REVOLUTION AS A MEANS TO ULTIMATE TRANSFORMATION

In the course of this discussion of social ethical action as a means to ultimate transformation, we cover the same five elements of religious process that we did in Part One. Like the traditional forms, nontraditional forms involve (1) the problematic in the human condition, (2) the ultimate reality or ideal, (3) the means to ultimate transformation, (4) personal expressions of transformation, and (5) social expressions of transformation. First, however, we look at the influences that caused a secular religious expression to split off from the transcendent religious expression. This consideration is important because it sets up a dialogue between advocates of traditional forms and advocates of the new expression. This dialogue might begin with the question: What caused people to seek and (they say) find ultimate fulfillment without appealing to some transcendent force?

Preindustrial Society and the Secular-Ethical Mode

A look at Western history from the eighteenth century on points out where human rights began to emerge as an issue of high concern. The fact that religious institutions were not able to settle matters of injustice for the masses may have contributed to the religious-secular split.

The most dramatic expressions of the Western urge to freedom occurred in the late eighteenth century, first with the American Revolution and then with the French. In both cases the populations in revolt had been systematically denied economic freedom and justice. Furthermore, neither population was willing to depend solely on the power of prayer for deliverance. So, the old order was overthrown and a new one devised by the will of the people put in its place. The Preamble to the Declaration of Independence declares:

> We hold these truths to be self-evident, that all men are created equal, that they are endowed by their creator with certain unalienable Rights, that among these are Life, Liberty and the pursuit of Happiness. That to secure these rights, Governments are instituted among Men, deriving their just powers from the consent of the governed. That whenever any Form of Government becomes destructive of these ends, it is the Right of the People to alter or abolish it, and to institute new government . . .

People are not subjects governed by a lord; they are citizens with certain guaranteed rights. They accept responsibility for legislating, as well as administering, rules. Such rules permit all citizens to have freedom to pursue happiness if all citizens accept the responsibility to allow their neighbors the same freedom.

The matter of human responsibility in constructing a government responsive to social needs is even more apparent in the French Declaration of the Rights of Man and of the citizen. Announced as a part of the judicial revolution, August 27, 1789, this document makes no reference to a creator at all. Here humans possess certain rights because of a natural law.

> The representatives of the French people, organized in National Assembly, considering that ignorance, forgetfulness, or contempt of the rights of man are the sole causes of public misfortunes and of the corruption of governments, have resolved to set forth in a solemn declaration the natural, inalienable, and sacred rights of man, in order that such declaration, continually before all members of the social body, may be a perpetual reminder of their rights and duties; in order that the acts of the legislative power and those of the executive power may constantly be compared with the aim of every political institution and may accordingly be more respected; in order that the demands of the citizens, founded henceforth upon simple and incontestable principles, may always be directed towards the maintenance of the Constitution and the welfare of all.[3]

Postindustrial Social Action

The Industrial Revolution in the nineteenth-century Western world extended the reforms of the social structure based on natural human rights. Industrialization and its attendant ills prepared the ground for Karl Marx (the philosopher of communist economics) to formulate his ideas about radically restructuring industrial production.

From the point of view of nineteenth-century social critics, from Karl Marx to Charles Dickens, industrial England increased its productivity by exploiting British factory workers for labor and British colonies for raw materials. Colonies were dependent because they had no factories to produce their own clothes, bicycles, or machine parts. Factory workers were dependent because they were kept so poor. Such a disparity between rich and poor might have been acceptable when kings were thought to have divine right of rule. However, revolutions had since been won in the name of *human rights;* human rights and industrialization made an explosive blend. It is no surprise, then, that both Karl Marx (1818–1883), who wrote the *Communist Manifesto,* and Mahatma Gandhi (1869–1948), who led India's liberation movement, woke up to their missions in England. England was the most industrialized nation of the nineteenth-century world and the most obvious example of how great wealth for some could cause great misery for others.

Although the spiritual quality of Gandhi's work for freedom is more apparent than Marx's, Gandhi (a devout Hindu) himself states that there is no religion higher than truth and righteousness. Likewise, Marx and Gandhi would have agreed on the ideals that should shape a society after the revolution. Gandhi was horrified by the violence of the 1917 Russian Revolution but considered socialism as the best means for achieving social and economic equality.

The modern world is now five revolutions away from the time when human value was derived from divine revelation. The American Revolution, the French Revolution, the Industrial Revolution, the Russian Revolution, and the Chinese Revolution have all made claims in the name of social justice and equality. They have all aimed at creating a moral society. To what extent they have achieved their aims may be questioned. However, there is no question that proponents of social change believe that ultimate reality is achieved when people live freely in just, productive, and mutually enhancing relationships.

Figure 2 illustrates political and social life as a means to ultimate transformation.

Abuse of Power Corrected by Political Freedom and Social Justice

Figure 2 shows us that within the human condition, or problematic state, the priests and teachers who are the traditional guides for religious life have become a part of the problem. They belong to a group of people who are interested in maintaining a status quo that keeps the oppressed in line. For example, some claim that during the days of slavery in the United States, the Protestant churches played an active part in keeping slaves quiescent by promising a better life in the next world rather than here and now. Traditional institutional religion is regarded as an opiate when it makes the masses of people believe they are helpless and powerless. In turn, these masses become apathetic toward tyranny, oppression, and injustice.

As in other religious expressions, this one challenges the human condition with the cure of ultimate reality. In this case, ultimate reality means freedom, justice, social harmony, and equality. This reality assumes that the true life of the human being is a social-political-economic life. In the last analysis, social dynamics control everything from education to art to technology. Therefore, the highest goal of humanity is to achieve social, political, and economic freedom, which will allow people to live in just, productive, mutually enhancing relationships.

ULTIMATE REALITY

Political freedom, justice,
equal opportunity, appropriate
distribution of wealth.

PROBLEMATIC STATE	←--- MEANS ---→	PROBLEMATIC STATE
Individual accumulation of political and economic power at the expense of other people. Discriminating legal and social structures that prevent the exercise of human rights.	Legislating and structuring social institutions for the general welfare and justice. Exercising personal effort and sacrifice.	Injustice, tyranny. Apathy, fear, and the feeling of powerlessness. Control by a small group by propaganda, misinformation, or physical force.

SOCIAL EXPRESSION	PERSONAL EXPRESSION
Creating political, economic, educational, and legal institutions that ensure human rights and general welfare. Developing government on the basis of a social contract between equals; participatory government. Public discussion and "grass-roots" legislation by an informed population.	Developing a sensitivity to injustice and manipulative control of social institutions. Cultivating a sense of urgency, courage, persistence, and often confrontation for continuing social-economic improvements.

FIGURE 2. *Social Responsibility as a Means to Ultimate Transformation*

Ethical Means: Legislation and Personal Effort

This means to ultimate transformation makes two requirements of its adherents: *effort* and *trust*. The effort is a social-political effort to inform and organize society in order to legislate and structure society for the general welfare. The trust is in the basic ability of all human beings to create (or revise) social-political institutions for the benefit of all people. Because the trust factor does not depend on God as a source of human goodness, this means to ultimate transformation is one of the most difficult and optimistic of all religious expressions. Albert Camus points out the difficulties of social action in *Resistance, Rebellion, and Death*:

> There is no ideal freedom that will someday be given us all at once, as a pension comes at the end of one's life. There are liberties to be won painfully, one by one, and those we still have are stages—most certainly inadequate, but stages nevertheless—on the way to total liberation.[4]

As Camus suggests, this mode emphasizes the value of modification and change for developing new possibilities. Thus, the essential character of a socially sensitive system of government, scientific theory, or technology is the capacity for continual change. What is not socially useful is crushed and buried. The very notions of rights and responsibilities change with the times, but the acceptance of human responsibility sets in motion the social, scientific, and political energies that make the pursuit of happiness possible for all citizens.

Social and Personal Expressions: Liberation Movements

Because one of the key terms in the ethical orientation is *action*, it is sometimes difficult to separate its social and personal expressions. The creation of a just society for all people as expressed in law courts, common economic opportunities, and equal political power requires a personal, inner sense of urgency, courage, and persistence. Many revolutionaries are willing to die for their cause: the enhancement of life for all people. The call for social change requires people to have a heightened awareness of implicit as well as explicit injustices, as in institutional racism or sexism. A new vision of possible social and economic structures must be kept in mind. For example, the South American revolutionary Che Guevara stated in a speech "On Our Common Aspiration—The Death of Imperialism and the Birth of a Moral World":

> Socialism cannot exist if a change does not take place in man's consciousness, that evokes a new fraternal attitude toward humanity. Such a change must be of an individual nature, in the society in which socialism is being built or has already been built, as well as of a worldwide nature in relation to all the peoples who suffer from imperialist oppression.[5]

We could distinguish social from personal ethical expression by pointing as examples of the former to the effort to change institutional forms through U. S. federal laws to withhold federal funds until businesses and state agencies comply with court orders to implement equal opportunity or through legislation to ensure due process before the law in criminal cases. Such open social structures express the ideal of enhancing the general social welfare of a society by assuring every individual his or her inalienable rights. This means to ultimate transformation emphasizes implementing social change through legislation or political revolution. Just having a vision or awareness that justice is an ideal is not enough. Nevertheless, some social changes are effected gradually, and there is a constant battle between those who want to legislate social and political equality and those who hold other values more highly.

To indicate how social and personal expressions of a human rights ethic interact, we look briefly at two American liberation movements. The first of these, the civil rights movement, appears to be equally moved by traditional religious forces and by the human urge to freedom. The second, the feminist movement, is more clearly secular in its origins and aims.

The most dramatic movement for social and economic self-determination in recent U. S. history has been the civil rights movement, and the most visible and effective force in that movement rose from the black Christian church. However, the connection between the church and political action had more to it than a need for God's helping hand. For years, the church was the center of black social activity. Until churches became targets for bombing and cross burnings by the Ku Klux Klan, they were safe places to assemble to discuss problems, as well as to worship. Throughout the more violent times in the movement, Martin Luther King, Jr. (like Gandhi), depended on traditional religious principles to lead his followers in the path of nonviolence and to give coherence to the movement. The church was the glue that held civil rights together in a familiar setting. As the movement has progressed, however, its most public expressions have tended to call attention to secular matters: education and economic justice. The Reverend Jesse Jackson does not simply teach black students how to pray; he teaches them to say, "I *am* somebody!"

The more clearly secular modern American freedom movement is the feminist movement. Partly because the male-dominated hierarchy of most Christian churches contributed to the systematic denial of economic and social rights to women, women could not easily appeal to religious tradition for aid. The staunchest opponents of the feminist movement argue that it is contrary to standard interpretations of divine law. These opponents also feel that changes in the status and role of women threaten the institution of the family and a general social morality derived from the Bible. An important indicator of social change is the use of language that includes rather than excludes women. Because language points to the assumptions and values of a culture, the language for expressing general humanity and the Supreme Being, feminists argue, must not simply convey a masculine image.

While some recent feminist action has focused on theological language and the role of a priest, minister, or rabbi within a religious institution, the earliest and dominant issues gathered around economic, legal, educational, and social rights. Since colonial times, self-help women's groups have worked for the right to attend medical school, the right to vote, and the right to equal pay for equal work. Feminists claim that without equality for all, there can be no general well-being for any.

Is Human Effort Sufficient?

The ideals expressed by ardent social reformers have the capacity to stir and to move the listener to action. Historically, however, there does not seem to be much evidence that people are good enough and willing enough to endure the risk and insecurity of constantly ensuring that government remains a servant of the people. In fact, some philosophers claim that the task is an impossible and irresponsible one without reference to God. J. E. Smith, a professor of philosophy at Yale University, states this point of view clearly when he writes: "No morality not based on religion possesses a principle of self-criticism, precisely because it possesses no transcendent reference to which it is itself subject and which judges it . . . Morality is both unsure and incomplete without a living connection with religious faith."[6]

Still, although it acknowledges no transcendent force, there is an urge in this mode of ultimate reality that moves volunteers to help develop the resources of the third world by joining the Peace Corps, to work for legal services for the poor, and to work for the elimination of political imprison-ment and torture through Amnesty International. Is there morality in these actions independent of religion? For the individual, dedication to these var-ious causes requires courage and persistence—often confrontation—for con-tinuing social improvement. The results of this dedication may lead to accomplishments as small as the occupation of an abandoned and otherwise useless house by a homeless family or as epic as the Long March that marked the beginning of the Communist China revolution.

SUMMARY

The combination of ethics, morality, and justice has always been an impor-tant part of traditional religious expressions. In theistic traditions—Islam, Judaism, Christianity—morality is seen as an extension of God's will that shows itself in individual behavior and in the way rulers govern society.

In traditions that assume there is a natural law at work in the universe—fourth-century B.C.E. Greek philosophy and Buddhism—human expres-sions of goodness and virtue (morality and ethics) actively reflect the corre-sponding transcendent values of virtue.

In a third way, advocates assume that there is no transcendent reality at all. Here the ethical life expressed through social action becomes a religious expression of its own with its own five essential characteristics:

1. The human condition is marked by fear, injustice, apathy, and tyranny. The masses are held in check by powerful self-serving leaders.
2. The ultimate reality that cures a condition of fear and apathy is a state of freedom and equality for all. This condition is marked by social responsibility and harmony and leads to social, political, and economic well-being.
3. The means to this ultimate reality are social, political, and educa-tional action. Taken together, these restructure the way things are (the status quo) and establish a pattern of flexible goal setting. In this context, goals are not set forever but change as the meanings of justice, freedom, and general welfare develop.
4. When the only religious life is the ethical life, social expression in-volves working for change through social institutions. One goal is to make sure that the government remains a servant of the people rather than the other way around.
5. For the individual, this religious conviction means to be aware that the struggle for justice is never-ending, and to have the courage and persistence to struggle for continued social improvement.

In thinking back over the three different ways of being an ethical being, recall how you have defined your own moral standards. Do they derive from traditional religious convictions or from nontranscendent consid-erations? Also, do you agree or disagree with J. E. Smith when he says "morality is both unsure and incomplete without a living connection with religious faith"?

Remember that secular expressions of the religious life offer the advocates of traditional religious expressions an opportunity to examine their beliefs and to consider how some people seem able to function as ethical beings without referring to a transcendent power of any sort.

SELECTED READINGS

Explorations into the importance of social responsibility and the power of social structures for effecting a comprehensive enhancement of human life are found in the following:

C. A. Moore, ed., *Philosophy and Culture: East and West* (Honolulu: University of Hawaii Press, 1962), Part IV, "Ethics and Social Practice," and Part V, "Legal, Political, and Economic Philosophy." A collection of papers by well-known scholars from various continents.

*J. Wach, *The Comparative Study of Religions* (New York: Columbia University Press, 1958), Chapter 4, "The Expression of Religious Experience in Fellowship." Wach's emphasis is on the expression of a person's confrontation with ultimate reality in a cult-community and institutional structure.

Introductions to the variety of responses to social responsibility made within European (Christian) culture can be found in:

E. Cell, ed., *Religion and Contemporary Western Culture* (Nashville: Abingdon, 1967), Section 8. A selection of eight readings from the writings of well-known contemporary Christian theologians on the relationship between religious life and social order.

H. R. Niebuhr, *Christ and Culture* (New York: Harper, 1951). A classic analysis of Christian social ethics. The author distinguishes among five types of patterns in which Christian faith has been related to cultural patterns in Western history.

The variety of ethical forms taken by religious commitments in different Asian contemporary societies can be seen in C. K. Yang, *Religion in Chinese Society* (Berkeley: University of California Press, 1961), Chapter 14, "Communism as a New Faith"; M. K. Gandhi, *The Gandhi Sutras*, edited by D. S. Sarma (New York: Devin-Adair Co., 1949), Chapter 2, on the spiritual importance of *satyagraha;* *W. L. King, *In the Hope of Nibbana* (La Salle, IL: Open Court, 1964), Part II, "Content and Application— Buddhist Ethics in Practice"; *G. E. von Grunebaum, *Modern Islam: The Search for Cultural Identity* (Berkeley and Los Angeles: University of California Press, 1962), especially Chapter 2, "The Problem of Cultural Influence," and Chapter 9, "Problems of Muslim Nationalism."

Reflections on the need for all humanity to create the social structures for political freedom, justice, and fair economic opportunities as a basic condition of human existence are presented in the following sources:

F. S. C. Northrop, ed. *Ideological Differences and World Order* (New Haven, CT: Yale University Press, 1949), Chapters 1, 8, 11, 15, and 21. Various professors of law, economics, and philosophy express their views on the conditions, attitudes, and social organization needed to provide peace and justice in an international context.

J. Ortega y Gasset, *The Revolt of the Masses* (New York: W. W. Norton, 1957; originally published in 1930). This classic statement by a Spanish philosopher is an impassioned call to implement moral ideals in the apparently chaotic and unprincipled social-political changes of the twentieth century.

C. J. Friedrich, *Transcendent Justice: The Religious Dimension of Constitutionalism* (Durham, N.C.: Duke University Press, 1964). After analyzing different forms and developments of constitutionalism in Western culture, the author in the last chapter discusses the implications of a humanist constitutionalism in the present age, when the traditional religious foundations of constitutionalism have almost vanished.

F. J. Streng, C. L. Lloyd, Jr., and J. T. Allen, eds., *Ways of Being Religious* (Englewood Cliffs, NJ: Prentice-Hall, 1973), Chapter 6, "Achievement of Human Rights through Political and Economic Action." A collection of readings expressing advocacy, sympathetic interpretation, and critiques of religious life discussed in the final section of this chapter.

Advocates for, and analyses of, specific liberation movements are found in *A. D. Austin, ed., *The Revolutionary Imperative: Essays Towards a New Humanity* (Nashville: National Methodist Student Movement, 1966); *D. Dellinger, *Revolutionary Nonviolence* (Indianapolis: Bobbs-Merrill, 1970); C. Oglesby and R. Shaull, *Containment and Change* (New York: Macmillan, 1967); and *R. Morgan, ed., *Sisterhood Is Powerful: An Anthology of Writings from the Women's Liberation Movement* (New York: Random House, 1970).

Introductions to the ethical ideals necessary for nonviolent political-economic change according to M. K. Gandhi can be found in M. K. Gandhi, *India of My Dreams* (Ahmedabad: Navajivan Publishing House, 1947); *J. V. Bondurant, *Conquest of Violence: The Gandhian Philosophy of Conflict* (Berkeley: University of California Press, 1969); and *T. Merton, ed., *Gandhi on Non-Violence* (New York: New Directions, 1964).

Resources for examining the ideals and effects of Marxian Communism as a means to ultimate transformation include E. Fisher, ed., *The Essential Marx* (New York: Herder and Herder, 1970); K. Marx and F. Engels, *The Communist Manifesto* (New York: Appleton-Century-Crofts, 1955); and T. Ling, *Karl Marx and Religion* (Totowa, NJ: Barnes and Noble, 1980).

CHAPTER 8

The Power of Rationality

Reasoning power—like social responsibility—is one of the modes of human awareness people use to construct their daily existence. Reasoning involves the ability to see a similarity or cause-effect relationship in two different experiences and to give that similarity or relationship a name. For example, people sense heat in both sun and fire, but they also know from experience that sun and fire are different things. They may abstract an attribute such as heat from these two different phenomena for one kind of comparison, but they may also abstract other elements of sense experience and relate sun to moon, planets, and stars, forming a classification of "heavenly bodies." In this way, most often without being conscious of it, people experience and mentally order the world by selecting and relating identifiable elements in life.

In this chapter, we discuss the human ability to reason as it relates to a person's self-awareness. Reason enables people to learn who they are, to think about similarities and differences, and to express those thoughts in words and other symbols. These reasoning abilities have long been important in the rational discussion of traditional religious matters, particularly in interpretation, justification of norms, and criticism of alternate religious positions. But can words (known in logic as "verbal abstractions") and their logical relationships lead a person to ultimate understanding? The goal of rationality as we discuss it in the last part of this chapter is to provide such a means.

It is not possible in these few pages to discuss all the procedures and problems of logic, the formation of language, and the discipline of syllogistic logic (formal deductive reasoning). For our purposes, it is enough to say that reasoning is a process that determines *how* reality is known—not only *that* reality is known. Reason in the history of humanity has been seen as a useful aid to traditional human religiousness. Different world religions use reason as one means for grasping the truth of religious texts. However, if one assumes that nothing—not a god, nor superconsciousness, nor an eternal cosmic law—exists beyond what can be understood through the intellect, then logic and philosophy themselves can become means to ultimate transformation. We consider these issues in the following three sections: (1) the power of defining experience with words, (2) uses of reason and reflection in traditional religious thought, and (3) applied and reflective rationality as the means to ultimate transformation.

THE POWER OF DEFINING EXPERIENCE WITH WORDS

Most people assume that the distinctions among objects like trees, buildings, and airplanes or between values such as good and bad are self-evident. They accept their understandings as reality. However, serious investigation often breaks down commonsense concepts and judgments. On critical analysis, some supposed facts, such as "The sun rises" or "A person's body lasts as long as his life," are recognized as *interpretations*. Whereas most people see the sun "rise," some, using mathematical analysis, conclude that the earth turns as it goes around the sun. Some think of the human body as basically the same body from maturity until death; for others it changes constantly as old cells die and new cells replace them. Although commonsense definitions are useful in interpreting many ordinary human experiences, they are less helpful for a philosophical or theoretical physical analysis of human experience that focuses on hidden causes or structures of life. Such an analysis requires definitions that can make fine distinctions among the specific features of human experience. Therefore, the formulation of definitions becomes an important element in the reasoning process as it is used in both traditional (theological) and nontraditional religious discourse.

The Constructive Power of Words

Definitions establish the distinctive character of something in comparison with something else; for example, the differences between cardinal bishops and priests in the Catholic hierarchy. Some terms are taken to be self-defining. For instance, in theistic traditions, *God* always means a personal god. Similarly, the word *savior* carries within itself the notion of someone who needs saving. Such self-defining concepts give the one who understands the definitions a mental set for experience; for example: "If I believe in a savior, I must require saving." If definitions somehow direct the ways in which a person thinks, then they become powerful forces in the process of self-awareness.

As a definition becomes more general or more abstract, it extends the range of its power. When we define things within our personal experience, the power of the definition is limited to ourselves. However, many kinds of definitions go beyond the personal. For example, when Joseph Smith, the founder of the Mormon church, was given an expanded definition of the Christian savior by the angel Moroni, Smith's new definition was only a perception within his personal experience. However, as soon as he convinced others to accept the definition, his experience was no longer merely personal.

The more abstract, or general, a word becomes, the farther removed it is from any particular person's experience. Words like *love, truth, reality,* and *meaning* are inexact and general, for they abstract meaning from multiple sense impressions and meanings and apply to many individual experiences. The abstract value of a word grows along with the growing human mind. Take the word *love.* An infant may be able to feel love from his or her parents, but does not think about love. As the child grows, the word *love* begins to make sense and applies to mom and dad. Then comes puberty and romance. Suddenly there is more than one kind of love. The influence of that word is spreading. The youngster who pursues religious studies as well as romance may believe that there is a divine love at work in the world. This love exists inside of, but transcends, human experience. Nevertheless, because a human being has the ability to abstract, he or she is able to understand the sentence "God so loved the world that He gave His only begotten Son"—regardless of the analysis or judgment the person makes about the sentence. To understand a word in its most abstract character requires a full capacity to reason in order to reach out and incorporate a concept (such as love) into one's understanding.

In fact, the unique capacity of a concept to mean something quite arbitrary or unfixed in relation to a specific event is what makes it so useful and, at the same time, so problematical. Suppose representatives from two nations sit down to discuss their "God-given rights" to a certain territory. The first thing these representatives will have to establish is what they mean by the word *God.* If they can agree on a definition (they would probably never agree on a name), they must decide what they mean by *rights* in the context of God's action. In clarifying the meaning of terms, the representatives are constructing a realm of discourse in which they can participate. The difficulty that people from different backgrounds often have in creating a realm of discourse indicates how tightly our definitions are tied to our experience. Somehow the concepts that are formed by cultural experience have the power to construct a person's self-awareness whether the person is aware of that construction or not.

How a Definition Functions

Philosophers have different explanations of the way a definition functions. Each way interprets the relationship between a mental concept and reality differently. Here we discuss two prominent explanations given in Western philosophy.

The first explanation of how a definition functions comes from the Greek philosopher Aristotle. In Aristotle's imagery, a definition is "a phrase signifying a thing's essence." The essence is that unchanging character of something, the bottom line. Any superficial variation must still lead back to the essence. For example, if a Christmas tree is defined as "an evergreen tree decorated with ornaments at Christmas," something would be classified as "a Christmas tree" when it presented these essential characteristics. Notice there is no indication whether the tree is natural or artificial or whether the ornaments are organic or manufactured. Those details are superficial variations, not a part of the essence.

The attempt to know something by learning its essential character, its definition, has played a large role in Western logic—as well as in Indian thought and in Chinese philosophical reflection. To suggest that there are such essences and then to define and ever more perfectly redefine experienced phenomena to conform to an ideal image of a pure nature (reality) is one way to relate knowledge to reality. In summary, this way of relating knowledge to reality depends on three assumptions: (1) There are essences; (2) these essences can be defined; and (3) these definitions will produce an ideal image of a pure nature.

The second prominent explanation of how a definition functions is that it may be considered valid if it is appropriate to a particular context of thought. For example, the validity of a definition of *tree, star,* or *person* does not depend on its perfectly expressing all possible trees, stars, or persons. Instead, its validity depends on the purpose for which it is used. However, if definitions are only valid and helpful in a particular context (rather than as true reflections of essences), then two consequences follow.

The first consequence is that, as the philosopher Ludwig Wittgenstein (1889–1951) noted in his later writings, the definitions of everyday speech are "pliable." The same word does not refer to exactly the same thing each time it is used. For example, the term *Christmas tree* can refer to various objects that have some things in common but no single element common to all. One tree may be an evergreen with a pointed top covered with candles; another may be an evergreen with a round form and electric Christmas lights on it; a third may be a metal tree with a pointed top and Christmas lights on it. But the term *Christmas tree* may apply to all of them.

The second consequence of definitions depending on context is that as the context surrounding the word changes, so does its definition. Thus, the purpose of a biologist classifying human beings as one of the vertebrates is different from that of the Hebrew psalm writer who claimed that "man" was "little lower than God." Similarly, the elaborate classification of animals among the American Indians has a quite different purpose from that of contemporary zoologists. Look at the following definitions of *coyote.* The first one is by Humishuma (Mourning Dove), an Okanogan Indian. The second comes from the *Fieldbook of Natural History.*

Definition 1.

> The animal people were here first—before there were any real people.
> Coyote was the most important because, after he was put to work by the Spirit Chief, he did more than any of the others to make the world a good place in which to live. There were times, however, when Coyote was not busy for the Spirit Chief. Then, he amused himself by getting into mischief and stirring up trouble. Frequently, he got into trouble himself, and then everybody had a good laugh—everybody but Mole. She was Coyote's wife.
> My people call Coyote Sin-ke-lip, which means Imitator. He delighted in mocking and imitating others, or in trying to, and, as he was a great one to play tricks, sometimes he is spoken of as Trick Person.[1]

COYOTE:
Canis latrins
Length, snout to tail tip about 4 ft., 1/3 being tail. Average weight, male to 50 lb.; female to 30 lb. Ears conspicuously large and erect, providing excellent field character. Color, pale brown sprinkled with gray, black, or sometimes white, with underparts nearly white, with ears darker. Looks like a rather large grayish collie dog or pale yellowish, small German shepherd dog with drooping tail. Breeds in January. Three to 10 young born 63 days later, blind, but furred; nurse two weeks; may be taken from den at 3 weeks; at 6 weeks, may venture out on own; run with parents by July. Family together until at least early fall. Breeds first winter. Life span, if lucky, about 13 years.[2]

Obviously, the writers of these two definitions had different purposes in mind when they wrote them. From the latter explanation of how a definition functions, we may consider both definitions to be correct.

REASON IN TRADITIONAL RELIGIOUS THOUGHT

All the religions that emphasize a direct revelation of God (like Judaism, Christianity, and Islam) as recorded by prophets, tribal leaders, or disciples, as well as religions that revere an honored tradition (like orthodox Hinduism and classical Confucianism), use human rationality to define and interpret "the given truth." In the effort to interpret correctly the original revelation or insight, theologians use reason in at least three ways: (1) to interpret a statement of eternal truth or revered tradition by a close analysis of the meaning of words and their use in sentences; (2) to set religious standards that help decide when to apply the ultimate assertions about life to a particular situation, whether the situation occurs a generation after the original expression of truth or thousands of years later; and (3) as a supplementary resource for knowledge for living the religious ideal.

The Power of Reason to Interpret Revelation or Spiritual Insight

The concern to preserve meaning has led to the growth of libraries of commentaries, each of which strives to offer a correct yet dynamic interpretation of various religious topics. These libraries are important as centers of learning for various schools and denominations. The Jewish Talmud, the Hindu Smriti, the Confucian commentaries, and the writings of Martin Luther, John Calvin, or John Wesley in Protestant Christianity are all examples of human efforts to interpret correctly both the letter and spirit of the original "word." Similarly, in the Japanese Buddhist Pure Land schools, dating from the thirteenth century C.E., the writings of the founders of these schools are studied and elaborated upon by their followers as much as, and often more than, the Buddhist writings in the ancient Sanskrit and Pali languages of India. Indeed, the history of the development of the major world religions can be understood only by seriously examining the changing interpretations within a tradition. These changes have often resulted from the reinterpretation of a particular portion of the sacred documents or the reevaluation of an earlier tradition.

The effort to get back to the true intention of the original sacred law, divine story, or metaphysics is complicated by the fact that religious symbols (images or concepts) are not facts; they are indications of, and vehicles for, deep and comprehensive realities that adherents claim are inaccessible through simple designations. The symbols for ultimate reality have different dimensions, which lead to many interpretations. Symbolic notions such as "the divine nature of Jesus Christ," "Brahman," "God's will," and "emptiness" give rise to a variety of interpretations, which are often paradoxical or logically contradictory. How, for instance, can Jesus Christ be both God and man? That claim is logically self-contradictory. In fact, the attempt to explain the meaning of the most profound religious symbols may lead to tensions within a religious community. Such tensions, for example, contributed to the Protestant Reformation (1500–1650). One of the debates between Martin Luther and the priests speaking for the pope's position in the Roman Catholic church had to do with the nature of faith. Luther argued that faith, defined as personal commitment, is the power by which a human being is saved. If that was true, it meant that priests, who were extremely powerful at that time, were not necessary to an individual seeking salvation. Taking away the authority and power of the priests who were affiliated with the pope in Rome upset the structure of the Christian church. In the end, the interpretation of a single word split the European Christian world in two. The split has continued to reverberate throughout the subsequent four centuries as Europeans expanded their influence in North and South America and many other places in the world.

The Power of Reason to Set Religious Standards

Why are religious interpretations so important that people are willing to fight wars over them? Interpretations are important because they set standards. The correct, or otherwise most acceptable, interpretation holds the power to set important social, theological, and ethical norms. For instance, rational interpretations of the true meaning of nonrational religious visions may determine social relationships, the use of certain rites instead of others, ethical decisions, and beliefs themselves. The power of theological formulation to clarify and perpetuate certain religious concepts from generation to generation has clearly been as important in religious life as the original expression.

Why else would the United Methodist church hold long debates over whether to accept homosexual individuals into the ministry? Is the deepest meaning of the New Testament to love one's neighbor no matter what? Or are there limits beyond which one cannot go and still be a part of the community? Does the authority of I Corinthians 6, which says: "Make no mistake: no fornicator or idolater, none who are guilty of adultery or of homosexual perversion, not thieves or grabbers or drunkards or slanderers or swindlers, will possess the kingdom of God,"[3] have more authority than

I Corinthians 13:4, which states: "Love is patient; love is kind and envies no one . . . . Love keeps no score of wrongs; does not gloat over other men's sins, but delights in the truth. There is nothing love cannot save; there is no limit to its faith, its hope, and its endurance."[4] The debate continues. This and every other attempt to clarify the original intention of the revered writings (the Bible, the Qur'an, the Vedas) require the interpreters to use reason expressed through concepts and language.

Two specific examples show how reason has been used in parts of major religious traditions to communicate a vision of truth that transcends logic. In Islam, the standard for belief and practice is the Qur'an, God's "recitation." Within several generations after Muhammad, who recited Allah's own word in the Qur'an, several schools of interpretation had been established in the Islamic world. These interpretations ranged from the literal ones of a fundamentalist sort to more liberal interpretations in which some questions were left open. Most Muslims regard the Qur'an as having the answers to all basic questions about doing God's will. In the third century of the Islamic tradition (parts of the eighth and ninth centuries C.E.), a dialectical theology (one based on logic and critical examination) called *kalam* emerged, which tried to articulate the truth of the Qur'an and to refute with logic those schools that tended to innovate rather than to preserve the original claims. For example, Al-Ash'ari (who died A.H. 324, in the tenth century C.E.) was an orthodox theologian who, in his later life, tried to affirm the traditional Islamic position with the help of logical demonstration and philosophical argument. Although for him reason had no independent validity and his central concern was to reveal the meaning of the prophet's words, his method was different from that of Islamic scholars who appealed only to the literal meaning of the words of the text.

In ancient India, as the Aryan culture (which moved from Persia into northern India, perhaps 1500–1000 B.C.E.) spread from North India toward the south and east (roughly 1000–300 B.C.E.), the Vedic religious leaders had to crystallize and systematize their understanding of eternal truth (the Veda) that had been handed to them from the remote past. These leaders knew that vague understandings of truth would not travel well or remain coherent in a changing cultural environment. Their efforts took the form of aphorisms (sutras) into which they put their religious insights. In turn, these sutras became the subjects for interpretation. By about two thousand years ago, there were several orthodox religious perspectives (*darshanas*) claiming to provide the insight and proper techniques for knowing the highest truth. Because no one school could win adherents simply by asserting its superiority, the teachers of the different perspectives finally had to justify their views by reason and clear articulation.

Like the Muslim Al-Ash'ari, the orthodox Hindu scholars used philosophical concepts to point people in the right direction, to set standards for them. The final realization of truth required some form of spiritual practice. Nevertheless, the power to cleanse the mind of error and ignorance depended, in part, on knowing the nature of things—which was partially stated in logical propositions. Throughout, the commentaries demonstrate an intellectual capacity for clarifying, classifying, and explaining by means of logical inference.

Reason as a Supplementary Resource for Knowledge

So far, we have looked at those situations in religious history that have called on reason and logic as they were needed to clarify one point or another. In no sense was rationality considered to have a life of its own. However, there is another perspective, which suggests that reason is a more equal partner with revelation or eternal law in understanding the truth centuries after it was first made known.

The human capacity for reason is a particularly potent force for those theologians who assume that divine or eternal power reveals itself in every moment of existence. Also, when a historical religious tradition spreads into new cultures and new times (as Islam has spread into Africa, Indonesia, and the United States), tensions may arise between those using the symbols that had persuasive power for the originators of the tradition and those using new symbols to redefine the meaning in their own terms. For instance, should an American woman who is a black Muslim expect to wear a veil, have no job, and walk at a "suitable" distance behind her husband? Should she be stoned to death if she commits adultery? Lose her right hand if she steals? Exactly how should the prescriptions of Islam be translated into contemporary life?

Christianity. The degree to which reason is accepted as a positive force in learning the truth pivots on the question of how reason is related to revelation. The Roman Catholic theologian Thomas Aquinas (1224–1274) argued that reason could and should be used in proving God's existence independently of any revealed knowledge. This was so, he asserted, even though philosophical reflection was not the only or highest form of religious knowledge—the highest truth could be known only through special revelation and had to be taken on faith.

Similarly, Anglican Bishop Joseph Butler (1692–1752) claimed that God revealed himself through the natural and moral order as well as through the special revelation of Jesus Christ. He argued in *The Analogy of Religion* that we know the moral perfection of God by an examination of our own nature. He felt that, just as there are natural physical laws, so there are general moral principles to be discovered through firsthand investigation and comparison. Butler maintained that these moral principles are identical to those revealed in Scriptures.

A more recent Christian theologian who has taken the use of reason seriously is Paul Tillich (1886–1965). The use of reason, he claimed, is important to spiritual reflection as a tool for asking questions about the nature of humanity. Christians are told to love God with heart, soul, and mind. So what does it mean to love God with one's mind? Tillich held that philosophical truth is concerned with ultimate reality, as is religious faith. Such philosophical truth deals with the structure of being that transcends any concrete form of existence (or any particular concept). Although there are basic differences between the theologies of St. Thomas, Bishop Butler, and Professor Tillich, each of them used a theological method that grants reason a positive role on the grounds that rational order, moral principles, and special divine revelation ultimately derive from the same source.

Islam. The Muslim tradition, similarly, has grappled with theological questions about the relationship between reason and revelation. One of the most dramatic uses of reason for formulating truth in Islam is found in the Mu'tazila tradition. The Mu'tazilites criticized fellow Muslim theologians who claimed to present a theology exclusively on the authority of the Qur'an and the tradition (the *Hadith*). They insisted on using logical principles to assert the unqualified character of God's unity. Where this character was challenged by apparently conflicting statements in the Qur'an or the *Hadith*, the Mu'tazilites used logic to justify their theological claims. The heavy use of reason often put them at the opposite pole from orthodox theologians, especially on such complicated questions as the relationship of human freedom to God's absolute determinism and whether the Qur'an was the creation of God or an attribute of God.

Buddhism. So far, the examples in this section may suggest that the use of reason by religious scholars always leads them to argue for a universal essence (Allah, God) that exists beyond, and is the source of, every particular religious expression. However, another example will show how logic has been used in another way. This way does not assume that there is a universal essence at all. Logic here is used to prepare one to perceive the highest truth. This perspective is found in the assertion of the second-century Indian Buddhist philosopher Nagarjuna that "all things are empty." In his *Fundamentals of the Middle Way*, Nagarjuna denied that there can be a self-existent essence such as god, matter, time, or universe, as the object of human knowledge or intuition. He expressed his point through a logical (dialectical) criticism of all positions that maintain the reality of all essences. When Nagarjuna was criticized by his opponents for assuming more reality for his own argument than for theirs, he maintained that his use of logic was relative, not absolute, as in the case with any means of knowing. On the one hand, reason is not just a first step in a knowledge to be dropped when either revelation or intuition takes over. On the other hand, reason does not achieve certainty from a perfect deduction based on an essential premise. He maintained that concepts and inferences are as useful as any other means for realizing the truth when they are recognized as being empty of essential reality as any forms in existence.

REASON AS A MEANS TO ULTIMATE TRANSFORMATION

> Reason is to the philosopher what grace is to the Christian. Grace causes the Christian to act, reason the philosopher. . . . [The philosopher] takes for true what is true, for false what is false, for doubtful what is doubtful, and for probably

what is only probable. He does more, and here you have a great perfection of the philosopher: when he has no reason by which to judge, he knows how to live in suspension of judgment.[5]

So far in this chapter, we have considered reason and rationality as means for probing and conveying the word as it comes from the traditional religious processes. We have seen that rationality has been used as one of many helpful human tools in the study of religious truth. Logic has also served as an important associate to revelation; together, logic and revelation maintain contact with the truth as it reaches over the centuries and into a variety of cultures. In the following sections, we move to a third position, which holds that rationality is a suitable means to ultimate transformation without an appeal to transcendence. Whereas the process of rational thinking is the same both inside and outside traditional contexts (they both use definitions, formal logic, and abstraction), the ends of rationality are quite different for the two. Figure 1 illustrates transformation through rational reflection alone.

Unclear Thinking Corrected by Reflection on Truth

Those people who accept rationality as sufficient means to the ultimate see the difficulties in human existence rising from an inability to think clearly. First of all, people tend to use language in a careless way, which causes them to sound like Humpty Dumpty in the following excerpt from *Through the Looking Glass.* Humpty has just determined that there are 364 days in a year when one might get an *un*birthday present.

> "Certainly," said Alice.
> "And only *one* for birthday presents, you know. There's glory for you!"
> "I don't know what you mean by 'glory,'" Alice said.
> Humpty Dumpty smiled contemptuously. "Of course you don't—till I tell you. I meant 'there's a nice knockdown argument for you.'"
> "But 'glory' doesn't mean 'a nice knockdown argument,' " Alice objected.
> "When *I* use a word," Humpty Dumpty said in a rather scornful tone, "it means just what I choose it to mean—neither more nor less."
> "The question is," said Alice, "whether you *can* make a word mean so many different things."
> "The question is," said Humpty Dumpty, "which is to be master—that's all."[6]

When the power of definition gets out of control, then the flexibility of abstract concepts such as "truth" and "freedom" may be used to mislead rather than to establish a dialogue as a search for the truth.

In a world where words lose their logical connections, emotion substitutes itself for reason and people lose the ability to understand reality. Such a disconnection from reality, say the adherents of this view, permits an absolute authority in social affairs, such as the Ayatollah Khomeini of Iran or the Christian church of the Middle Ages, to destroy the most significant possibilities of human life or life itself. The destructiveness caused by irrational behavior suggests that, without appealing to reason, no one can achieve an understanding of oneself or the world.

ULTIMATE REALITY

Accurate knowledge and judgment:
truth known through analytic reflection,
conceptual clarity.

PROBLEMATIC STATE	◀----- MEANS -----▶	**PROBLEMATIC STATE**
Confused and unclear ideas.	Logical analysis,	Unanalyzed ideologies and vague claims.
Behavior based on irrational decisions and emotional compulsions.	systematic reflection. Clarity of ideas and accurate linguistic usage. Formulation of ideas to be tested by public analysis and common experience.	Faulty use of language or logic.

SOCIAL EXPRESSION
Educating people in logic, reflective philosophy, mathematics, and clear communication. Rationally determining law and political economic policy. Communicating persuasively and clearly.

PERSONAL EXPRESSION
Feeling the pleasure of knowing with some certainty. Experiencing the security in detecting good and bad arguments. Developing a sense of order and meaning through understanding.

FIGURE 1. *Rationality as a Means to Ultimate Transformation*

There is, however, an ideal that, if achieved, will counter the chaos caused by emotional compulsion, conceptual confusion, and inappropriate language. This point of view assumes that there *is* truth in the world and that the human mind can perceive it. The mind seeks the truth through the language of logic, natural science, and mathematics. In turn, logic and mathematical formulas are used to express the truth once it has been found. The clarity of such expression reflects an order and a balance of relationships in nature that give people a sense of security and a means to control irrational social decisions.

Rational Means: Logical Analysis

The process of rational thought can become an independent means to ultimate transformation when adherents view it as the primary or only valid source of knowledge. In the Western intellectual tradition, some philosophers, especially logicians, regard human reasoning as the most distinctive feature of human existence. They would agree with Diderot, who said that for the philosopher, reason functions as grace. These people hold that the development of rational skills and clarity in thinking are absolutely necessary for having worthwhile personal relationships (for establishing a realm of discourse) and for making social-political decisions. The following elements are central to this nontraditional process.

Clear and distinct ideas are the power for ordering human life.

Knowing not only what is true but also why it is true is primary. The question "why" is answered through a logical inquiry into the necessary relations among things.

Concepts and logical procedures correspond to the most profound nature of reality, since philosophy deals with universals and timeless realities.

With the aid of education, human beings can use the natural rationality they were born with.

These are optimistic statements. The late philosopher A. N. Whitehead expresses the high hope of human rational capacity in the following definition of speculative philosophy:

> Speculative philosophy is the endeavour to frame a coherent, logical, necessary system of general ideas in terms of which every element of our experience can be interpreted. By this notion of "interpretation" I mean that everything of which we are conscious, as enjoyed, perceived, willed, or thought, shall have the character of a particular instance of the general scheme. Thus the philosophical scheme should be coherent, logical, and in respect to its interpretation, applicable and adequate.[7]

History of Rational Means. The means to ultimate reality through a rational approach took shape in Western Europe during the Enlightenment of the eighteenth century. Philosophers of this time (among them Diderot and Voltaire) spoke of a new awakening of the human spirit through critical and analytical thought. Although the leaders of the Enlightenment still used the word *God* in their discussions of reason, they did not mean exactly the same thing that theists did. At that time, *God* was often used to express the depth of the force of reason, as it is in the following discussion.

To claim that rationality is a legitimate means to ultimate transformation, Enlightenment philosophers had to justify the claim that reason was basic to human beings. They held that human beings are born with a rational capacity—we are *Homo sapiens*—and that rationality influenced the human ability to know things even before humans were aware of the influence. The French philosopher Descartes (1596–1650) argued that the ways or modes by which people understand things are innate, not learned. These fundamental modes, or ideas by which people in all cultures know the world, are God, mind, and physical existence (the general condition of things occupying space). His conception is important because it considers how human beings can know the true nature of things. The reasoning goes like this:

> *If* fundamental ideas exist in the consciousness before humans are aware that those ideas exist, and

If these fundamental ideas are equally available to all people through the exercise of thought,

Then human beings have access to ultimate transformation through the perfection of natural means—rationality.

It is not surprising, then, that Descartes's philosophy is based on the now famous phrase, *cogito ergo sum:* "I think, therefore I am!"

The Dutch philosopher Spinoza (1632–1677) offered an even more specific statement of how reason could be used to arrive at a system outside of theology that could account for all phenomena. In the following excerpt, Spinoza expresses an important part of the method for understanding the source of everything:

> Now it is clear that the mind apprehends itself better in proportion as it understands a greater number of natural objects; it follows, therefore, that this portion of the method will be more perfect in proportion as the mind attains to the comprehension of a greater number of objects, and that it will be absolutely perfect when the mind gains a knowledge of the absolutely perfect being or becomes conscious thereof.[8]

It is worth noting here also that in his writings Spinoza used the word *God* to mean "the source of everything," what he called "a substance consisting of infinite attributes." Perhaps the easiest way in which to distinguish between Spinoza's God and the God of the theists is to remember that the goal of Spinoza's reason was to comprehend God perfectly, a goal not even the saints would dare set. The form of comprehension was a mathematical system so complete that it would account for all possible thought and experience.

Moving from the seventeenth century to the twentieth brings us to the school of logical positivism. Represented by such philosophers as R. Carnap and A. J. Ayer, this school makes two fundamental assumptions about the nature of reality and its relationship to human comprehension: (1) Discursive thought (moving from premises to conclusions) is the primary or even sole means for expressing thought, and (2) feeling is whatever human beings express that cannot be projected into discursive language and then verified through observation (that is, any formulation of thought that attempts to give information must be scientific).

These two assumptions may sound complicated. Actually, they are a familiar part of an ongoing battle between scientists, who assume that the earth is millions of years old and fundamentalist Christians, who take the words of the Bible literally. Part of what makes science interesting is that every scientific proposition is only good until there is conflicting evidence. In addition, the rules in the game of science state that every proposition must be open to being proven wrong; that is, a proposition that truly conveys knowledge must include evidence that can be tested—otherwise, it is not a real proposition. When the Christian makes the proposition that the earth was created in six days, the scientist can test that proposition against the geological record. However, when the Christian claims that in the beginning God made the heavens and the earth, the scientist cannot respond because there is no evidence to test. The logical positivist asserts that the latter claim of the Christian is like an exclamation or an emotional gesture, but it gives no information about life.

Summary of Rational Means. Those who hold that the power of rationality is the power of transformation make a two-part assumption about how the truth may be known. First, they assume there is an order to reality and that order is a natural, inborn part of human thinking. Then they assume that, if reason is cultivated, the knowledge gained from that cultivation not only improves human existence in the present but may also be passed on to future generations for further improvement. However, as tedious as some of the analysis may sound to a person not trained in logic, the passions of the intellect are neither dry nor cold. The following passage reflects some of the energy and excitement of thinking:

> This is man, the heaven-stormer. This is man the adventurer. He is man spiritual, standing in awe before the wonders of the universe in which he finds himself. He is man religious, filled with wonder, thinking, yearning to know, aspiring to understand. He is the heretic, the seeker, the everlasting questioner. He is man the inquirer, whose restless mind constantly re-examines all knowledge he possesses, testing it, seeking to discover whether it really is knowledge, or whether perchance it is the kind of superstition that so often passed as knowledge in earlier times.[9]

Here we can feel the sense of adventure that comes with an inquiring mind. It is this spirit combined with careful, logical reasoning that marks rationality as a means to ultimate transformation.

PERSONAL EXPRESSION: INTELLECTUAL EXERCISE

For the individual, the power of rationality has both practical and pleasurable possibilities. On the practical side, a person who is able to spot a good or bad argument is going to be able to make sound business decisions, whereas a person with poor ability to reason will not. Suppose a medium-sized company is trying to decide which computer system to install or whether to install one at all. Those who make executive decisions for the company must be able to sift through the arguments coming from IBM, Wang, or Texas Instruments to tell which system is the most reasonable choice. First-time computer buyers are advised not to rely on their intuition.

Other practical applications for rationality are being able to evaluate a political argument, a presidential speech on foreign policy, or a directive from a superior (a parent or a boss). When people can locate a good and bad argument and when their own thinking is clear, they will not be misled and they can be persuasive in talking with other clear-thinking people. They can make decisions in light of a comprehensive view of the world.

In addition to having practical value, rationality carries with it a special kind of pleasure. From time to time, every person confronts a problem or an idea that must be thought through. Many people have experienced the combination of relief and joy that comes as a result of attacking a knotty problem, thinking through it, and as a result, arriving at a solution and understanding. Rational thinking is not necessarily grim, serious business; done well, it may lighten the weight of the world.

SOCIAL EXPRESSION: EDUCATION

The dominant social form of this type of transformation is education, especially in philosophy, logic, mathematics, and natural science. When parents and boards of education declare that we need to return to the basics, they generally mean "reading, 'riting, and 'rithmetic"—the three R's. Looking closely at those three basics, we find most of the necessary ingredients for rational thinking. Through reading, people become acquainted with both an abstract vocabulary and concepts that may reach beyond their own experience. When people write, they are learning how to express their ideas in a coherent, logical fashion. An outline prepared before writing an essay is a picture of a logical progression. Mathematics at all levels is a system in which the results of formulation may be tested for accuracy. The mind trained in the basics and then expanded through the natural sciences, philosophy, and physics holds the promise for describing the order of the universe.

Because education is the first step in the perfection of rationality, twentieth-century cultural philosophers such as Julian Huxley or F. S. C. Northrop have asserted that the university will become to the modern world what the medieval church was to twelfth-century Europe. At one time, the church could offer a person everything he or she needed to know about reality. These days, at its best, the university provides similar information. People understand themselves through the social sciences, develop skills in creative imagination and reflection in art, literature, and religious studies, and learn to modify natural processes through the physical sciences. Philosophy serves an even greater need because it analyzes how people *know* reality—as distinct from how to describe and classify information, imagine a scene, or love someone. Reason is the key to comprehension and the clearest basis for making satisfactory decisions.

SUMMARY

The power to reason involves the power to recognize similarities and differences among things and to give those qualities names. When we use this definition of reason in a discussion of religious processes, we consider the power that words have in structuring religious concepts. At some level, language is necessary to pass on the important religious ideas within a community and to explain those ideas to others outside the community.

Once we understand how basic reason is to religion, we may understand the part it has played in religious processes. Reason may supplement traditional religious expressions, and it may be a religious process of its own.

Christians, Muslims, Hindus, and Buddhists have all used reason to interpret key ideas within their traditions. Those advocates of a certain point of view who could express its validity most logically and persuasively could, in turn, establish certain norms based on that point of view. However, although reason was an important tool for theologians, it was only of secondary importance to being religious.

Reason also was used to keep traditional religious expressions fresh in spite of changes in habits and culture. Here the use of reason becomes quite important, particularly in interpreting religious meaning when it crosses cultural boundaries and centuries of economic and technological change.

Finally, rationality is used as an independent means of ultimate transformation. As in the case of revolutionary social action, rationality may function as a separate, nontranscendent religious process. The five elements of rationality as a religious process include the following:

1. The human condition is often marked by uncontrolled emotion, confusion about the meaning of concepts, and a loss of understanding. Absolute or fanatical authorities pervert language to gain power for themselves.
2. The ideal that cures the confusion of humanity is clear thinking and clear expression of ideas. Through precise thinking and expression, we can see through the smog of faulty reason and find the truth.
3. The means to achieving rational clarity is to practice being logically precise in mental and linguistic expression. The path to ultimate reality is characterized by a careful analysis, leading to clear thinking and an improvement in the human condition.
4. The personal expression of this process is in the excitement of figuring out a tough problem or in spotting unreasonable arguments of others. Clear thinkers cannot be misled by a poor argument.
5. The social expression of this means to ultimate transformation is education: particularly in philosophy, logic, and science.

When you have your next informal discussion on religion with a friend or acquaintance, consider how you use logic and reason and how their use affects the quality of the conversation.

SELECTED READINGS

Introductions to the power of language, reason, and philosophical inquiry for structuring what is true in human experience are found in the following sources:

*S. K. Langer, *Philosophy in a New Key* (Cambridge, MA: Harvard University Press, 1942), Chapters 3, 4, and 5. In these chapters, especially in Chapter 4, "Discursive Forms and Presentational Forms," the kind of meaning available through conceptual abstractions and the logical relationships of concepts is analyzed.

*F. S. C. Northrop, *The Meeting of East and West* (New York: Macmillan, 1960). See especially Chapters 7 and 8. The theoretic character of Western knowledge is described as central to the forms and values of Western civilization.

*K. Burke, *The Rhetoric of Religion* (Berkeley: University of California Press, 1970; originally published in 1961). Using evidence from Christian sources Burke argues that the use of words (verbal action) is the basis for knowledge of that which transcends empirical verification.

C. G. Vaught, *The Quest for Wholeness* (Albany: State University of New York Press, 1982). Philosophical inquiry is portrayed as the quest for wholeness whereby human beings explore both their origin and the indefinitely expanding outer world.

*B. Russell, *Mysticism and Logic and Other Essays* (New York: Longmans, Green, 1925). Essay I, "Mysticism and Logic," Essay 3, "A Free Man's Worship," and Essay 4, "The Study of Mathematics," are popular articles that declare the importance of perceiving necessary relationships between classes of things and using laws of thought to determine human choices.

For an introduction to contemporary analyses of the relationship between religious language (mainly Western) and the use of language and logic for learning truth see E. Cell, ed., *Religion and Contemporary Western Culture*, Section 5, "Religion and Philosophy," which includes readings from E. Brunner, P. Tillich, and J. Wisdom; *I. T. Ramsey, *Religious Language* (New York: Harper, 1961); W. A. Christian, *Meaning and Truth in Religion* (Princeton, NJ; Princeton University Press, 1964); *R. Trigg, *Reason and Commitment* (New York: Cambridge University Press, 1973); and M. L. Diamond and T. V. Litzenburg, *The Logic of God: Theology and Verification* (Indianapolis: Bobbs-Merrill, 1975).

Analyses of the use of reason in the classical cultural traditions of South Asia can be found in:

K. N. Jayatilleke, *Early Buddhist Theory of Knowledge* (London: George Allan & Unwin, 1963), especially Chapter 6, "Analysis and Meaning." An authoritative discussion of the importance of ideational classification and logical analysis in early Buddhism.

S. Bagchi, *Inductive Reasoning: A Study of Tarka and Its Role in Indian Logic* (Calcutta: Calcutta Oriental Press, 1953). An in-depth survey of the use of reason in Indian philosophy.

K. H. Potter, *Indian Metaphysics and Epistemology* (Princeton, NJ: Princeton University Press, 1977), Part I: Introduction to the Philosophy of Nyaya-Vaisesika. Basic terms, philosophical issues, and modes of analysis are examined.

*B. K. Matilal, *Epistemology, Logic and Grammar in Indian Philosophical Analysis* (The Hague: Mouton, 1971). This series of essays provides a depth analysis of basic philosophical issues.

For an introduction to the role of reason in Chinese philosophy, see *Fung Yu-lan, *A Short History of Chinese Philosophy*, translated by D. Bodde (New York: Macmillan, 1948), especially Chapters 23, 24, and 28; *Fung Yu-lan, *The Spirit of Chinese Philosophy*, translated by E. R. Hughes (Boston: Beacon, 1947), Chapters 9 and 10; and Wing-tsit Chan, ed., *A Source Book in Chinese Philosophy* (Princeton, NJ: Princeton University Press, 1963), Chapters 32–34 and Chapter 42.

The use of reason for knowing truth by Western philosophers such as Spinoza, Locke, or Leibnitz is seen in readily available translations of their works, or in books of readings in the philosophy of religion. For example, see N. Smart, ed., *Historical Selections in the Philosophy of Religion* (New York: Harper, 1962).

*M. White, ed., *The Age of Analysis* (New York: New American Library, 1955). This brief anthology of twentieth-century philosophers clearly indicates the role of reason in the analysis of human experience.

Two books present some basic analyses and arguments of the logical positivists: R. Carnap, *Logical Syntax of Language* (New York: Humanities Press, 1937); and *A. J. Ayer, *Language, Truth, and Logic* (New York: Dover, 1936).

F. Ferré, *Language, Logic and God* (New York: Harper & Row, 1961) is a critical philosophical analysis of logical positivism applied to Christian theological speech.

Two significant philosophical attempts to redefine and reformulate the classical Western approaches to the ontological arguments for God are found in *C. Hartshorne, *The Logic of Perfection* (Lasalle, IL: Open Court, 1962); and S. M. Ogden, *The Reality of God* (New York: Harper & Row, 1966).

CHAPTER 9

The Power of Artistic Creativity

Beauty has religious significance because whatever is truly beautiful is a perfect expression of what is. Beauty, in this sense, is different from prettiness or attractiveness, which may be deceptive and superficial. Something that is pretty or appealing does not necessarily have religious meaning. Beauty, on the other hand, is that quality that brings harmony, mystery, and vividness to art and lends truth to lines, colors, rhythms, sounds, and space. Taken together, the elements of art are all potential means of revealing the deepest meaning of existence. The meaning of a work of art is not primarily a representation of something else, such as a natural form. Through imagination and skill, an artist creates something to which people can directly respond with deep emotion through aesthetic contemplation. Beauty, through art, however delicately or roughly expressed, has the power to transform life.

THE RELIGIOUS IMPORTANCE OF ART

Art is a basic part of being human. The art that grabs and engages the senses is not the luxury of a few sophisticated connoisseurs nor the activity of a few disciplined artists. In a religious context, the artistic effort expresses what it means to be human at the most profound level. Recall how folk and rock music rallied a spirit that cracked the rigidity and conformity that seemed to characterize the United States in the 1950s. Young people, poor people, and people of racial minorities turned to artistic expression to create order and transcendence in a world that seemed to them brutal and chaotic.

Because of its transformational qualities, art of religious significance involves more than simple depiction. Whereas a snapshot might capture an image of the world as we observe it, art interprets the world in the context of human sensitivity to many levels of awareness. Through artistic creativity, some people structure their universe, not simply by assembling lines, form, and space to suit a commercial end, but by putting those elements together in a way that reflects their internal life at its most intense. Langdon Gilkey, professor of theology, describes the connection between art and religion in the following way:

> When an event that we label art . . . stops the heedless flow of time into an enhanced moment, a moment of new awareness or understanding, a moment of intense seeing and of participation in what is seen, then (as the Zen tradition has taught us) the transcendent appears through art, and art and religion approach one another.[1]

What do we mean when we say that spiritual truth is expressed in beauty? Are there differences in the way that beautiful things express truth? This chapter focuses on two contexts in which religious meaning is expressed through art. These are (1) liturgical art and drama as visual theology and (2) art as a means to ultimate transformation as it releases creativity and beauty into the world.

LITURGICAL ART AS VISUAL THEOLOGY

By *liturgical art* we mean art that makes visual the content of a religious tradition. Such art is commonly found in churches and church architecture, but may also be found in drama and dance. Liturgical art depicts the specific images of myths, such as gods, saviors, and saints, and plays an important role in the architecture of holy places. In most cases, the individual artists, choreographers, or architects responsible for these creations have conformed their styles to the conventions of traditional religious art. For this reason, St. Sebastian is always depicted tied to a tree and pierced with arrows, no matter who paints him (Figure 1). Likewise, it hardly matters whose mind designed or sculpted the figures of the apostles who look down from the entrance of the Cathedral of Santiago in northwest Spain. The important point is that people entering the church be able to recognize the figures above them. Liturgical art, then, is the art of the familiar in religion.

The Religious Image

Liturgical art, like theology, is an expression of the infinite through the use of finite form. Unlike theology, this art depends on visual symbolism, rather than on verbal or written description. A single image must be worth 1,000 words. We see this symbolic quality in animal-headed gods or multiple-armed deities in ancient Egyptian and living Indian religions (Figures 2 and 3). Within cultural boundaries, the religious artist strives to express the content of a religious tradition in the most perfect way. Therefore, it is correct—in the context of Hinduism—to depict that part of divinity that overcomes obstacles (Ganesh) as a god with the head of an elephant. With the strength of an elephant, Ganesh can knock down any barrier. Those

FIGURE 1. *St. Sebastian*

who pray to Ganesh, pray for his strength. Likewise, the believer finds nothing outrageous or unreal about an artist's depiction of Christ, whose open cloak reveals the Sacred Heart, or of the monkey-king, Hanuman, the devotee of the Lord Rama in Hinduism, who pulls open his chest to reveal that he has Rama in his heart.

In the context of conventional religious art, the artist seeks to lose his individuality and to become a medium for God's self-expression. In India, for example, the art manuals suggest that the artist eliminate distracting influences through yoga and thereby visualize perfectly the divine power, even in its terrible, supernatural characteristics (recall Arjuna's vision of Krishna in Chapter 2). What is revealed by the true artist in every religious tradition is not a repetition of what people usually see but a recognizable depiction of the way things are—good or bad.

To guide the one who seeks to understand the divine through art, the artist may draw on certain cultural conventions whose meanings the ob- server may immediately identify. Christian theology, for example, focuses

FIGURE 2.   *Egyptian God and Goddesses*

on Jesus Christ. The specific images of Jesus teaching, healing, dying on the cross, or the infant Jesus lying in the manger are central to the Christian's perception of God's revelation. The aesthetic skill of the artist combines with the familiar image to release religious meaning.

In contrast to the Christian emphasis on Jesus Christ, Hinduism makes use of many images and forms to express the infinity and otherness of the divine. Hundreds of myths and stories compiled over the past 4,000 years are the background for the varied images of divinity found in Hindu temples and shrines. In Hindu mythology, there is no story of resurrection (a story that makes the otherness of Christ very clear). Therefore, the otherness of God is portrayed through various suggestions of the nonnatural, such as the unusual use of color. When Lord Krishna appears with a midnight-blue face, the artist reminds the viewer that Krishna is not only different from the rest of us but also that he is infinite and eternal—blue is the color of eternity and infinity. A boyish, blue-faced god with long hair and bright red lips may seem peculiar to the Western eye. To the believer who

FIGURE 3.   *Ganesh*

understands the symbolic value of such a strange appearance, Krishna is a friend and inspiration.

Just as the artistic conventions for conveying religious meaning vary from culture to culture, the conventions within a culture may change because of new ways of looking at old truths. In the context of liturgical art, a change in style may suggest a change in interpretation. The early seventeenth-century Spanish painter, El Greco, portrayed Christ's resurrection as a mystical, nonnatural event. In contrast, the sixteenth-century Italian, Il Tintoretto, painted the same event as a fact more real than the trees, grass, and animals that serve as the background. Is one of these visions a truer reflection of the resurrection than the other? As far as either creates a visual reflection of the divine, and to the extent that the viewer is moved by the rendering, each articulates the truth.

Similarly, in the history of Buddhism, the Buddha may be depicted in various ways. He is sometimes portrayed in the stillness and solemnity of meditation, his eyes half-closed and his bearing expressing total serenity, or he may be seated, teaching the *dhamma* (truth, practice). A favorite way for artists to indicate different activities or events in the Buddha's life is to use standardized hand gestures (*mudras*), one for teaching, another for meditation, another for expressing compassion. There is also a difference in the style of expressing the nature of enlightenment. In the Gandharan art of second century C.E. India, for example, we see a shift from a material human form showing muscles and bone structure to a spiritualized and formalized Buddha with soft, curved lines, who is beyond physical limitations.

The Religious in Motion

The impulse to reach ultimate transformation by reenacting religious truth and cosmic order through dance, drama, and music is as ancient as the use of visual arts for this purpose. In some cases, music serves as the background accompaniment; often, however, it possesses its own power to transform.

If we follow the history of Western drama beginning in fifth century B.C.E. Greece, drama declined. By the twelfth century C.E., however, drama had Dionysus, the patron of the arts and wine. After its high period in classical Greece, drama declined. By the twelfth century C.E. however, drama had regrouped in the medieval churchyard to emerge for public viewing in plays about Christian morality. These dramatizations served in part to bring revealed truth to an illiterate populace in a fashion that would awaken them to God's word. Because Greek and medieval Christian drama belonged to cultures that kept written records, the history and content of many performances are well documented and tend to dominate textbook treatments of religious enactments. However, religious dance and drama is still one of the central religious expressions in traditional cultures in Africa and North America today.

An African dancer wearing the antelope headdress becomes the spirit force (god) and moves in the control of the spirit's power. To know the dancer's human identity would be unthinkable because, during the dance, that identity ceases to exist. Likewise, among the Hopi of Arizona, the ceremonial dancers become powers of life depicting the Kachinas Hummingbird, Cloud Maiden, or the harvest corn (Figure 4). Beautifully masked, the Kachinas serve as conductors for the powers of the universe. Not only are the dancers transformed through the ritual of the dance but observers, absorbed by the movement, also join in transcendence. The beauty of the costumes and the solemnity of the occasion create a religiously artistic movement comparable to that created by the celebration of high mass at Christmas in Rome.

MUSIC AS BENEDICTION

Some of the world's most magnificent music expresses itself through religious motifs. It is unfortunate that the great cathedrals of Europe do not come equipped with a memory for sound. The stone figures and religious

FIGURE 4.   *Kachina*

art that adorn the walls appear to be as lasting as the messages they bear. But the liturgical music that was meant to fill church interiors is not permanent and may be taken for granted by worshippers. Certain occasions do, however, make the religious power of music obvious. During the Mozart festival that takes place each year in Salzburg, Austria, organ concerts are given in the city's great cathedral. During rehearsals, the grandeur of the music fills the cathedral with a unique religious force. Even after the organist stops, the music hangs in the cathedral like a blessing.

Clearly, humans have a special connection with music of all sorts. Song steadies the spirit and binds the singer to a cause. Soldiers sing as they march, the oppressed sing their tribulations, the cantor sings a Jewish synagogue into life. The muezzin chants a call for devout Muslims to prayer; the holy men sing as Hindus bathe away past sins in the Ganges. King George III of England was so moved by the Hallelujah chorus of Handel's *Messiah* (written in 1741) that he jumped to his feet. Easter worshippers have been standing ever since when the Hallelujah chorus is sung.

ART AS A MEANS TO ULTIMATE TRANSFORMATION

Unlike the other nontraditional religious expressions, which conform rather easily to the five-part structure of religious processes, art as a religious process is difficult to outline. For the sake of continuity, this discussion is arranged according to our familiar structure (Figure 5). However, keep in mind that the means to ultimate reality are a part of the ultimate reality itself.

It is possible that the elements of artistic expression are hard to separate from each other because art is so built into what it means to be human. What the art historian Victor Zuckerland has to say about music could apply to the other arts, as well:

> If we cannot separate man, time, and music in our thinking, then it is impossible to think of a beginning of music. . . . As legend has it, music was the gift of a god to mankind. What this means is quite clear. It could not have been that a god intoned a song for people to sing after him. Gods do not give in this way, from the outside. A god's gift comes from the inside; he opens men's hearts and unseals their lips. . . . At the beginning, music comes from men, not to them—or, rather, also to them but on the rebound. The singer or player cannot help hearing what he sings or plays: the circle must be closed. Here the notion of a confrontation between listener and work makes no sense. Music is both the gift and the giving, the musician both giver and recipient.[2]

Sterility of Imagination Corrected by the Power of Artistic Creation

From the point of view of those who take art to be the highest expression of what it means to be human, the problematic character of the human condition is marked by a lack of sensitivity to the beauty that exists in all life forms. People have become so rational, practical, and cautious that they have lost the ability to respond to the mystery of human life. As a result, life has become sterile and imagination dead.

What will counter this death of the imagination is art. The practicing artist is most often the one who embodies the surge of creative possibilities. The artist reveals—say those who view aesthetic production as part of ultimate transformation—the deepest reality of what it means to be human. Etienne Gilson, the late lecturer in fine arts and professor at the University of Toronto, describes the apprehension of beauty as fundamental to "being" as a human being; this he calls an "ontological experience." He writes in *Painting and Reality*:

> If . . . the beautiful is being itself as an object of a pleasing apprehension, then it must share in the intrinsic character of being, which, because it is the first principle in reality as well as in knowledge, escapes description and definition. If we say of a being that it is *this* rather than *that*, we simply define it by itself. In short, we can absolutely not think otherwise than in terms of being, which is the very reason we cannot place it in front of us as an object to be seen. The same is true of the beautiful. If and when it is there, it confronts us with the wonder of a man-made being whose apperception alone is enough to fill us with pleasure. . . . This is a primary ontological experience; as such, it is ultimate in its own order.[3]

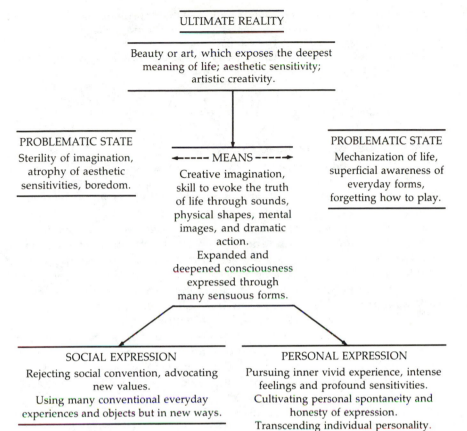

ULTIMATE REALITY

Beauty or art, which exposes the deepest
meaning of life; aesthetic sensitivity;
artistic creativity.

PROBLEMATIC STATE

Sterility of imagination,
atrophy of aesthetic
sensitivities, boredom.

◄----- MEANS -----►

Creative imagination,
skill to evoke the truth
of life through sounds,
physical shapes, mental
images, and dramatic
action.
Expanded and
deepened consciousness
expressed through
many sensuous forms.

PROBLEMATIC STATE

Mechanization of life,
superficial awareness of
everyday forms,
forgetting how to play.

SOCIAL EXPRESSION

Rejecting social convention, advocating
new values.
Using many conventional everyday
experiences and objects but in new ways.

PERSONAL EXPRESSION

Pursuing inner vivid experience, intense
feelings and profound sensitivities.
Cultivating personal spontaneity and
honesty of expression.
Transcending individual personality.

FIGURE 5. *Artistic Creativity as a Means to Ultimate Transformation*

The apprehension of beauty, then, is a power to create what truly "is" in
the artist and the perceiver. The observer or audience joins the artist in the
creative expression as both enter the harmony, mystery, and vividness of
the sensuous experience. The artist's presentation has the power to introduce the perceiver to a new world that lies beyond habitual and conventional awareness. When Keith Jarrett plays the piano or Ravi Shankar plays
the sitar, the men and their music become one to create a force that magnet-
izes the audience. Marian Anderson the singer and Pat Benatar the rocker
both have the capacity to wrap an auditorium in music that carries singer
and listeners beyond their surface selves.

Although the immediate interaction between artist and audience is not as
common in the visual arts as it is in the musical arts, some pictorial traditions suggest that there is a three-way mystical union among the object, the
art, and the artist that may be joined by the observer as well. This shift to
another dimension of reality is dramatically described in the following story:

One day, while the emperor was admiring Wu Tao-tzu's glorious painting of a
landscape with mountains, forests, and clouds, Wu Tao-tzu pointed to a doorway

on the side of one of his mountains, and invited the Emperor to enter and behold the marvels within. Wu Tao-tzu himself then climbed up the painting and entered, beckoning to the Emperor to follow. But the Emperor paused, afraid. The door then closed and Wu Tao-tzu was never seen again. It seems only Wu Tao-tzu was willing to discover whether his work was art.[4]

So, according to T. R. Martland, does art "provide new parameters by which [humans] expand into unknown territory."

Artistic Means: Creative Imagination

The means to ultimate reality in this nontraditional religious expression bears some interesting similarities to the traditional form of reaching the ultimate through myth and ritual (Chapter 3). Recall that those who find ultimate transcendence through myth and ritual use the ritual act as the bridge from the profane world to the sacred world. Artistic religious expression also requires a concrete act (the production of music, art, or dance) to carry the participant-observer into a new understanding of beauty. In this case, however, the goal of the event is not to infuse the Sacred Realm into profane existence but to create beauty here through any conventional forms, made more real through imagination and skill in presentation. Sacred and profane become meaningless concepts that only limit an artist.

Art as a means to ultimate reality appears in all developed cultures and in all historical periods. For the past thousand years in Japan, and longer in traditional Chinese culture, a profound concern for aesthetic expression has marked the common, everyday lives of people.[5] Cultured Chinese believed that natural beauty and human perfectibility expressed life's deepest meanings. These people had little concern about a future life or transcendent reality. Their intention was to live happily, which meant wisely, and to enjoy the flow of life in everyday activities. Indeed, much Chinese poetry has dealt with the subjects of daily living. The poet Li Po (701–762 C.E.) expresses his appreciation for such beauty in his poem "In the Mountains on a Summer Day":

> Gently I stir a white feather fan,
> With open shirt sitting in a green wood.
> I take off my hat and hang it on a jutting stone;
> A wind from the pine-trees trickles on my bare head.[6]

In creating moods of peace, harmony, or loneliness, the Chinese landscape artist, as well as the poet, sought to stimulate the mind and enoble the spirit for enriched living. In cultivating an aesthetic sensitivity, the Chinese produced a sense of the rhythmical relationships of things and enhanced their own capability to enjoy life spontaneously.

The concern for rhythmical vitality was equally important in Japan. The appreciation of nature is evident, not only in the formal religious expression of Shinto, but also in the cultivation of gardens, the imagery found in poetry, and the subject matter of ink line drawings. Since the days of the Heian court (ninth to twelfth centuries C.E.), when refinement was of great importance, the cultivation of taste in the perfect expression of beauty has filtered down through the military classes to the peasantry. At present, one of Japan's new religions focuses on the aesthetic as the truest expression of religion. The first precept of this religion, PL Kyodan (perfect liberty order), is that "life is art."[7] To fulfill one's potential constitutes artistic creativity, which is held to be the most profound religious statement.

Social Expression: Advocacy of the New

Perhaps the most obvious comment on how the artistic life presents itself to society is that it is nonconformist, avant-garde, bohemian. Traditionally, artists have a distaste for social conventions and programmed ways of life. They tend to cluster together in certain parts of a city, often where the rents are lower and where other artists live. Paris and New York have been the most well-known settings for the gathering of artists. Imagine Picasso, Hemmingway, Gertrude Stein, Fitzgerald, Monet, and Renoir all living in Paris at the same time. Furthermore, they were friends. It seems that artists are best stimulated by other artists, even if the final expression of beauty results from solitary effort.

The artist is, of course, only half of the formula of art as religious expression. The other half belongs to the audience. At least from the time that concert halls were built, participant observers have confirmed the transforming power of art by attending the ballet, the opera, the symphony, the theater, and more recently gallery openings. In the 1960s in the United States, the role of the audience was extended by the now-famous Woodstock music festival, where the interaction among the artists, the music, and the masses gave new meaning to the artistic experience.

Personal Expression: Pursuit of Experience

In this mode of awareness, personal expression emphasizes pursuit of inner vivid experience, feeling, and sensitivity. The highest values are individual spontaneity and honesty of expression. As we mentioned earlier, these feelings and sensitivities may be expressed through dance, music, and design or in daily activities. In this sense, the farmer who plows straight furrows and judges correctly just when to plant so that crops can be harvested at a particular time is an artist. So is the merchant who builds up trade through attractive advertising, fair prices, and good taste. Here art is the functioning of any individual in a way that conveys the proper rhythm or form of the particular activity. This kind of personal expression counteracts mechanical living, which is a part of the problematic of the human condition.

For individuals who produce art, rather than live aesthetically, personal expression may be different. Artists, in their performances or works, embody the human urge to give meaning to experience. Thus, their lives are caught up in the question of what it means to be human. Of course, most artists are not systematic theorists. On the contrary, they express meaning in ways different from philosophical discourse. The artist's power of creativity, however, often transcends his or her individual personality. Vincent van Gogh, to take one well-known example, felt driven by a creative power that was unknown to his conscious self. What this power is, or the goal toward which the artist strives, is difficult to name. The composer, Igor Stravinsky, once commented:

> I care less about my "work" than about composing. This is partly because one never composes exactly the piece one sets out to compose, just as I am not now saying exactly what I had in mind to say but what the extenuating words that come to mind as I go along lead me to say.[8]

Albert Hofstadter, professor of philosophy at Columbia University, explains that in the creative process, artists do not know exactly what the goal is, nor what they want to say. The reality they wish to express takes form *during* the process of creation; it is not preconceived. Artists reveal truth to the extent that the creative forms they adopt truly derive from the relationship between their natural capacities and the realities they perceive. Then the symbols they create become true to the experience of life; in turn, the beauty in the art is invested with the power to transform.

To understand art as a dynamic process rather than simply as an object of perception is to see that art is a capacity shared to some extent by everyone. To experience meaning in concrete forms is to experience concrete life as a *human being*. The artist is not a different species of animal but has a unique role in every culture to show the spiritual significance of the totality of human life, rather than to perform one task well, such as farming or teaching. The artist can embody the elemental forces of humanity that seek spiritual expression. Similarly, patterns of the American square dance or the rhythm of the blues derived from songs sung by blacks in the cotton fields or of the movements of a policeman directing traffic in Rome show that people can expose a deep meaning in all activities of life.

SUMMARY

Beauty expressed through art is a perfect expression of what is. Art in this context is creation of a significant level of human reality; through art, some people structure their universe. Artistic expression may function in traditional religious contexts or outside those contexts as its own means to ultimate transformation.

When art functions as a part of a religious tradition, it is called liturgical art. Its purpose is to reveal religious truth through "visual theology," dance, and music. The personal expression of the individual artist or composer is always subordinate to the conventional symbolic requirements of the tradition. Also, this art intends to express divine reality rather than earthly reality, so depictions of the divine are not required to be realistic.

When art functions as its own ultimate reality, it can be expressed in many ways. Some of these ways are quite ancient. Both cultured Chinese and Japanese considered life itself a kind of art, whereas some Western artists tried to create a mode of reality called beauty.

The characteristics of the way of being religious through artistic creativity are as follows:

1.   The problematic of the human condition is a loss of creativity and death of the imagination. Human life has become mechanical, and people have forgotten to look for the beauty in all forms of life.
2.   The ultimate reality that counteracts the lifelessness of common human living is the creative act. This act may use sound, sight, touch, or any other sense form to present the way things are. The artist who through imagination offers the perceiver a vision of beauty also offers the perceiver a vision of truth. In this reality, there is an unbreakable connection between the artist, the art, and the audience.
3.   The means to the ultimate reality, a life of beauty, come from combining form (a picture, a composition) with creativity and integrity. The artist shows the audience reality by using a particular style and medium to break through to a new experience. Unlimited by convention, the artist is free to choose any form to convey the truth of life.
4.   Commonly, the social expression of the artist is anticonventional. Sometimes artists gather in small communities for mutual support. The role of the audience may be more conventional, but it can make an enthusiastic public contribution to the art-artist-audience triangle.
5.   The highest values for the individual in this expression are spontaneity and honest expression. Artists in their works or performances give meaning to human experience, and transform themselves and their work into clear channels for expressing the deepest possible sense of reality.

As you reflect on this chapter, try to remember how you feel when you hear good music that is well performed or when you see a work of art that affects you in a particular way. Also, consider what part liturgical art and music have played in your religious or cultural upbringing.

SELECTED READINGS

G. van der Leeuw, *Sacred and Profane Beauty: The Holy in Art,* translated by D. E. Green (New York: Holt, 1963; first published 1932). An eloquent discussion of the religious significance of dance, drama, rhetoric, the pictorial arts, architecture, and music, concluding with a general Christian theological aesthetic. Still one of the best statements on art as a sacred act. The book deals predominantly with the art of archaic society, the ancient Near East, and Europe.

Two useful introductions to the role of art in traditional religions, which include pictures and references to film and slides as well as further readings, are D. L. Eck, *Darśan: Seeing the Divine Image in India* (Chambersburg, PA: Anima Publications, 1981); and R. B. Pilgrim, *Buddhism and the Arts of Japan* (Chambersburg, PA: Anima Publications, 1981).

S. G. F. Brandon, *Man and God in Art and Ritual* (New York: Charles Scribner's, 1975). A study of religious images, architecture, and vestments from around the world, documented with many pictures, which shows the relation of art forms to traditional religious ritual and narratives.

Two collections of essays on the expression of truth and reality through Western art are J. B. Vickery, ed., *Myth and Literature* (Lincoln: University of Nebraska Press, 1966); and E. Cell, ed., *Religion and Contemporary Western Culture* (Nashville, TN: Abingdon Press, 1967). In the former collection see especially Section 2, "Myth and Literature"; in the latter, Section 3, "Religion and Modern Art," and Section 4, "Religion and Modern Literature."

For an introduction to a variety of philosophical analyses of the truth expressed in aesthetic experience, the following are suggested: P. Wheelwright, *Metaphor and Reality* (Bloomington: Indiana University Press, 1962); A. Hofstadter, *Truth and Art* (New York: Columbia University Press, 1965); J. Hospers, *Meaning and Truth in the Arts* (Chapel Hill: University of North Carolina Press, 1946); E. Gilson, *Painting and Reality*, Bollingen Series XXXV.4 (Princeton, NJ: Princeton University Press, 1957); E. B. Feldman, *Varieties of Visual Experience: Art as Image and Idea*, 2nd ed. (Englewood Cliffs, NJ: Prentice-Hall, 1972); and F. D. Martin, *Art and the Religious Experience: The 'Language' of the Sacred* (Cranbury, NJ: Associated University Presses, 1972).

The importance of expressing Christian faith through pictorial and literary art has been recognized in recent decades. The following books will introduce the reader to some of the theological and aesthetic problems involved: J. W. Dixon, *Nature and Grace in Art* (Chapel Hill: University of North Carolina Press, 1964); R. Hazelton, *A Theological Approach to Art* (Nashville, TN: Abingdon, 1967); N. A. Scott, *The Broken Center: Studies in the Theological Horizon of Modern Literature* (New Haven, CT: Yale University Press, 1966); A. N. Wilder, *Theology and Modern Literature* (Cambridge, MA: Harvard University Press, 1958).

For an introduction to the presentation of truth through art in non-Western cultures, the following books are readily available: *A. K. Coomaraswamy, *The Dance of Shiva: On Indian Art and Culture* (New York: Noonday, 1957); *A. K. Coomaraswamy, *The Transformation of Nature in Art* (New York: Dover, 1934); Lin Yutang, *The Chinese Theory of Art: Translations from the Masters of Chinese Art* (New York: Putnam, 1967); *L. Warner, *The Enduring Art of Japan* (New York: Grove, 1952); *F. Boaz, *Primitive Art* (New York: Dover, 1955); F. S. C. Northrop, *The Meeting of East and West* (New York: Macmillan, 1960), Chapter 9, "The Traditional Culture of the Orient," and Chapter 10, "The Meaning of Eastern Civilization."

*T. R. Martland, *Religion as Art: An Interpretation* (Albany: State University of New York Press, 1981). A provocative analysis that identifies religious forms with artistic objects and actions as free, forceful, and creative frames of meaning by which people order their lives.

*E. Deutsch, *Studies in Comparative Aesthetics* (Honolulu: University of Hawaii Press, 1975). A philosophical reflection on the nature of aesthetics from Japanese rock gardens to American oil paintings, showing that humanely created objects express beauty, latent inner states in the perceiver, the mysterious, and a kind of knowledge.

G. Bazin, *The Loom of Art* (New York: Simon & Schuster, 1962). An analysis of art as a "play of images" in which style is a "transcendent vocable" that makes explicit an ideal in a civilization.

*F. Frank, *Art as a Way: A Return to the Spiritual Roots* (New York: Crossroad, 1981). A personal statement advocating art as a discipline of seeing the reality of existence in such a way that it contributes to the regeneration of the world.

Alternative understandings of the way in which art exposes the reality of life can be seen by comparing Shin'ichi Hisamatsu, *Zen and the Fine Arts,* translated by G. Tokiwa (Tokyo: Kodansha International, 1971); and R. Meryman, *Andrew Wyeth* (Boston: Houghton Mifflin, 1968). These volumes are oversized and contain pictures and reproductions. Hisamatsu describes how Zen art is vigorous when it expresses the awakened "formless self," whereas the painting of Andrew Wyeth expresses an intensity felt through the realistic depictions of people or things. Both, however, focus on everyday objects and scenes and show a deep identification with nature.

*E. L. Wade, C. Haralson, R. Strickland, *As in a Vision: Masterworks of American Indian Art* (Norman, OK: University of Oklahoma Press, 1983). Photographs of Native American art—clothing, baskets, masks, and musical instruments—are interwoven with descriptions, songs, and prayers to portray the continuity of an aesthetic within a view of life.

CHAPTER 10

The Religious Response to Physical Existence

Do the following exercise. Close your eyes and try to recall everything that you know exists in the physical universe. Recall pictures sent back to earth from deep space, the tiny organisms that you have seen through a microscope, mountains, deserts, oceans, lightning, and the Big Dipper. Then ask yourself the following questions: How did all of those things get there? What is it that keeps everything in place? Having asked those questions, you have put yourself in the company of cosmologists whose business it is to construct theories of the universe as an ordered whole and to determine the general laws that govern it. A cosmology provides human beings with a picture of the way things are; it serves as a map of the physical world.

COSMOLOGIES AT WORK IN THE WORLD

Various models have been used to form a cosmological picture. In the West, the best known model of the world pictures it as a product created by God. From that initial divine act of creation follows every detail of a person's physical and spiritual life. Lines from the familiar Christian hymn "How Great Thou Art" illustrate how this cosmology has been fully integrated into a religious expression:

> Oh, Lord, my God, when I in awesome wonder
> Consider all the worlds thy hands have made.
> I see the stars, I hear the rolling thunder,
> Thy power throughout the universe displayed.

However, the familiar image of God standing at the beginning of creation is not the only cosmology at work in the world. The ancient religion of India used a biological model, picturing the world as a cosmic egg from which emerged all possible forms of existence. Modern astronomers use yet another model. For many of them, the world is a product of the "Big Bang," a whirling speck in one of the smaller galaxies in an expanding stream of energy. Each of these models not only describes where everything comes from but also suggests ways in which a person may think about him- or herself in the universe. On a fundamental level, it matters that we were created by a personal God, hatched from the impersonal cosmic egg, or evolved organically from some yet unknown primordial event.

A cosmology, then, is not simply a set of notions about the order of the physical universe. It is also a force that selects, labels, and patterns our perceptions of the potential of the universe. So, it should not be surprising that as new views of the universe are discovered and the old cosmologies are revised or abandoned altogether, one's deepest sense of self is affected. What, for instance, happens to the person singing the hymn when that person is confronted with the possibility that there were no hands that made the universe—that the force behind existence is either impersonal or that there is really no ultimate force at all except gravity or electromagnetism?

In forming a world view, people consider at least two religious issues: (1) existence before birth and after death and (2) the relationship between personal decision making and the nature of the universe.

The first issue, existence before life and after death, is sometimes phrased as two questions: Where do we come from? and Where are we going? From a religious perspective, these questions are closely related. They reflect the assumption that human existence is not an isolated phenomenon but part of a larger whole. In recognizing the facts of birth and death, many people within and outside organized religions seek to relate their (apparently) limited physical existence to some (apparently) more lasting reality, which is the source of existence. Because a person's self-image is partly based on a recognition of the source of existence, it makes a difference whether that source is the hand of God or a primordial pool of amino acids shocked into life by a bolt of lightning. Further, bolts of lightning are unlikely to make any promises about life everlasting; experiences of God do.

The second religious issue asks another two-part question: Is there order in the universe, and, if so, what relationship is there between that order and my actions? The recognition of a relationship between individual action and the universal order of things poses problems of morality. For example, Do I have real freedom of choice? Are my actions predominantly determined by conditions over which I have no control? Moreover, morality—which has to do with right and wrong—needs some norm or standard by which to judge whether an action is right or wrong. Among other things, cosmologies set standards and so become measures for right and wrong behavior. Therefore, if I do not obey God's will as defined in the Qur'an, will Allah destroy me? If I live in contradiction to the natural order, will I destroy myself?

This chapter deals with the impact of various cosmologies on individuals as they attempt to understand the reality of their physical presence in the world. The cosmologies discussed in the first three sections are secondary aspects of the processes of ultimate transformation found within traditional religion. The last two sections, however, examine contemporary humanistic scientific views of the world. There the concern with historical and physical existence expresses a religious significance independent of a transcendent power.

THE WORLD AS GOD'S CREATION AND TIME AS REVELATION OF GOD'S PURPOSE

In this world view, people are aware of existence as the creation of an eternal God. Here the world is not the natural product of an impersonal force but the stage on which people express their obedience or disobedience to God's will. Such a view is represented by the prophetic tradition of Judaism, by Western Christian orthodoxy following the fourth-century theologian St. Augustine, and by the orthodox (Sunni) tradition in Islam. In this view, humanity's true life is lived in response to unique revelations of God's will and love in human history. Present existence is dependent on sacred reality (God, Allah), with which the passing moment is never to be confused.

Time and the physical world began with God's creative act, and they remain meaningful only in relation to his ultimate purpose. As God's creations, time and the physical world were once full of possibilities for human happiness. But human beings have misused their opportunity to enjoy God's creation, and so humanity experiences turmoil and suffering. Nevertheless, God uses a few people, certain historical events, and some societies as the means for revealing his will and love through which all people can live in at least limited happiness. The special moments of revelation, for example, God's gift of the Torah to the Jewish people and the prophetic tongue to interpret it properly, the incarnation of the divine word in Jesus Christ, or the recitation (Qur'an) of God's will to Muhammad, signify a qualitatively different moment than can be found in the natural world. Special revelation illuminates the true order of existence and its ultimate goal of fulfillment.

In the three Western religions of revelation, the moment of revelation is closely connected to the hope of an eventual fulfillment of God's purpose. This hoped-for goal can be expected either in this world or after death, although the ultimate realization comes at "the end of the age" (the end of time). Human beings, together with the rest of creation, find ultimate reality in following the laws of God. In Christianity and Islam, people depend on God's mercy and love; those who respond to him are brought into a blessed situation (heaven) that transcends the anxieties, pains, and sins of this existence. It would be presumptuous for people to find their deepest meaning in their own efforts; only God's love, justice, and mercy are powerful enough to overcome evil. God, as the uncreated source of everything, is the wholly other (see the section on ultimate reality in Chapters 2 and 3). His mysteries surround temporal existence, both in the beginning and at the end of the age.

THE WORLD AS THE ETERNAL RHYTHM OF PRIMAL ENERGY

A world view commonly found in the East sees human beings as part of a dynamic nature. Concrete experiences of life, natural phenomena, a person's self-awareness in relation to others in everyday events—all these hold ultimate reality, the potential of bliss, the power of God. Here the whole cosmos has the potential for expressing the transcendent order of things, the terrible-blissful power that brings all things into existence. The divine reality may be found in such common elements as water and fire or in human intellectual and political achievements. In Japan, the Shinto apprehension of the divine (*kami*) in natural phenomena is such a cosmology. In India, this cosmic power shows itself in the ancient Vedic awareness that the world is the appearance in many forms of the divine energy, Brahman, as controlled by the cosmic order (*rita*). Similarly, the Chinese Confucian writer Tung Chung-shu (about 179–104 B.C.E.) sees human life as part of a totally interrelated cosmic order:

> The vital forces of Heaven and earth join to form a unity, divide to become the yin and yang, separate into the four seasons, and range themselves into the five agents. "Agent" in this case means activity. Each of the activities is different, therefore we speak of them as the five activities. The five activities are the five agents. In the order of their succession they give birth to one another, while in a different order, they overcome each other. Therefore, in ruling, if one violates this order, there will be chaos, but if one follows it, all will be well governed.[1]

This view is part of living harmoniously with Cosmic Law (see Chapter 4).

The view of human life as part of a cosmic order appears in both polytheism (many personal extraordinary powers) and monism (an impersonal universal power). The devout Shinto, Hindu, and Confucian live with all other existing beings in a vast community of forces and fulfill their natures and values by conforming to the inner necessity of the cosmos. Those who live in the flow of the eternal rhythm realize the most profound level of awareness; they are "blessed."

Human beings can learn of the eternal rhythm by looking at the sequential patterns of change in the natural and social worlds: summer becomes fall, a son becomes a husband, a citizen an official. Although the rhythm is too profound and mysterious for any simple mental formulation, sensitive people can know it directly because they participate in it. This external rhythmic power, as it appears in the concrete events of life, offers answers to the most perplexing questions about the human situation. Sometimes special divination (foretelling) techniques have been used to reveal the mysterious universal rhythm. For example, the ancient Chinese classic *I Ching* (Book of Changes) gave its users a special lens through which they could perceive their proper relationship to the ever-changing social and physical rhythm of the universe. Once individuals know where they are in relation to the whole, they can make appropriate personal decisions for attaining success in a particular situation.

Figure 1 shows how a cosmology may affect the individual's sense of self. Those who perceive existence as a never-ending succession of beginnings and endings, moving in time to eternal rhythms, have quite a different view of their place in the cosmos from those who see human time as linear, beginning at the moment of God's creation.

One of the key religious implications of the notion that humanity is an integral part of the cosmos (see Figure 1(b)) is that the terms *divine* and *natural* can be used interchangeably. Nature is not a dead mechanism. The sun, rivers, mountains, and trees are divine in that their life force, the dynamics of their growth, movement, or stability, derives from the inherent order of cosmic energy. Human participation in the cosmic rhythm of nature makes physical existence the normal place for spiritual fulfillment. From this point of view, a person's central religious concern is not to learn the unique revelation of God's will, as a Christian, Jew, or Muslim would, but to express spontaneously the natural order and rhythm of life. Human beings can be comfortable in this world without seeking a transworldly existence.

THE EVERYDAY WORLD AND THE REALITY BEYOND

While some view the physical world as God's creation and others view it as a part of an all-inclusive natural order, a third group regards the world as less than real. Unless the world reflects the reality that exists beyond it, it is meaningless or evil. From this point of view, the world achieves significance when it exposes reality through ritual action (Chapter 3), mental inquiry (Chapter 8), or an experience of divine self-enjoyment.

The first orientation distinguishes between divine and human realms. Human activity is only valid insofar as it duplicates and reforms human existence in the divine pattern. The symbolic construction of a person's cosmos through ritual action is seen in a wide variety of expressions. Among them are the religious dances found in some African societies, the rites of Osiris (the god of both life and the underworld) in ancient Egypt, the building of the Vedic fire altar in ancient India (see the Vedic hymn on page 32), the setting up of Roman altars to the *soter* (savior) who guaranteed peace and prosperity, and the practice of the Eucharist within medieval Christianity (see the discussion of communion on page 50). Through the ritual, structure and order are given to chaos. Value is infused into the fleeting, unstable moments of time.

Besides ritual activities and sacred symbols, certain mental activity has given stability and consistency to human experience. The second orientation to locating eternal order in fleeting time is to find pure and eternal ideas. This activity uses logical principles and concepts by which people analyze and organize their awareness into a meaningful system (see Chapter 8). The Greek philosopher Plato asserted that there is a realm of eternal

(a)

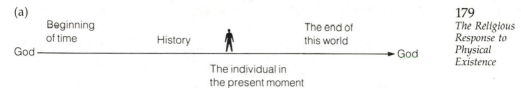

(b)

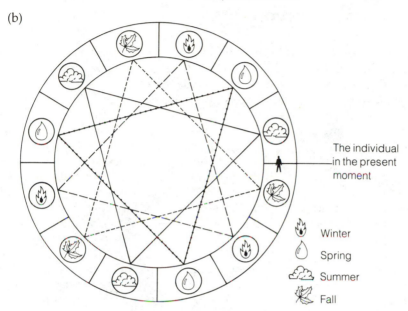

FIGURE 1. *The Individual in the Cosmos. (a) A linear representation; (b) A cyclical representation: Each moment, lifetime, year, world, universe is part of an eternal rhythm of change.*

ideas more real than the experienced forms of human life. However, a gulf exists between the realm of universal, eternal abstraction and the concrete things of life. Through inquiry that gulf can be bridged. The idea that abstractions, universal laws, or principles are tools by which people know the truth has been a basic position in Western philosophy.

Whereas the ancient Greeks employed analysis to discover order, the Hindus saw phenomenal existence as God's "play" (*lila*). In this perspective, all existence—the sun, moon, or a religious thought—is God's activity manifest in concrete events and things. These events can reflect the divine reality of Vishnu, Shiva, or the great goddess Shakti. The continuing creation of the world, for example, is the cosmic dance of Shiva, just as the continual process of maturing, decay, and death is the relentless activity of the goddess Kali, one of the many forms of Shakti. Although all life's activities are divine expressions, they are regarded as brief moments of divine exposure. As the Lord Krishna says in the Bhagavad-Gita, the everyday realm of action (karma) is to be transcended by being absorbed in Krishna: "From the realm of Brahma downwards, all worlds are subject to return to rebirth, but on reaching Me . . . there is no return to birth again" (VIII, 16). The world, which is divine expression, is ultimately an illusive delight from which people must separate themselves if they are to return to the divine essence.

THE POWER OF COSMOLOGIES

From the variety of world views, we can see that no single world view has so far satisfied the needs of people in all cultures. In the contemporary world where there is continual exchange of ideas between cultures, the variations among cosmologies and claims for the exclusive value of one can produce serious conflict, demonstrated by continuing strife between Hinduism, with its many images of God, and Islam, with its imageless monotheism.

In case there is any doubt about the hold a particular cosmology may have on its adherents, we should review the Copernican revolution in Western thought. Before the astronomer Nicolaus Copernicus (1473–1543) "rearranged" the cosmos, devout Christians (as well as others) accepted the view proposed by the geographer and astronomer Ptolemy (about 130 C.E.), which put the earth in the center of the universe. This geocentric, or earth-centered, arrangement seemed to be self-evident, natural, and a correct expression of the importance of human beings in God's creation. The planets, the sun, the moon, and the stars all revolved around us, bearing witness to God's care and love. Nevertheless, this perception of the heavenly bodies did not fit exactly with what could be observed in the heavens; some planets even appeared to go backward from time to time. Astronomers had difficulty mapping the heavens with any degree of certainty until Copernicus advanced the theory that the sun, not the earth, was at the center of a *solar* system.

This new perspective in astronomy made sense out of the planetary motions; but in the process, it evicted humanity from its central location in the universe. Even more important, the new scientific method of observation based on mathematical calculation was seen to threaten the Christian church. Churchmen feared that in asserting there was a method for discovering how the world worked, the new scientists were questioning the omnipotence (all-powerfulness) and transcendence of God. The prospect of displacing revelation with scientific method was so frightening to some of the most powerful church officials that they forced the astronomer and founder of experimental physics, Galileo Galilei (1564–1642), to withdraw his views supporting Copernicus and kept him under house arrest for the final eight years of his life.

Although modern Christians have no difficulty accepting the world as a small planet in a greater solar system, and many are willing to integrate scientific discovery with faith, the initial wrench from the accepted world view was painful and disruptive to every social structure that depended on the old cosmology as a model.

With some ideal of the emotional and religious attachment that individuals and cultures may have for a particular view of how the universe operates, it is possible to understand how some of the recent discoveries in science and technology have confronted tradition, or in some cases, left the boundaries of tradition altogether.

The Scientific World View

So far, we have considered cosmologies as an adjunct to traditional religious expressions, that is, the dominant world view in a particular religious tradition helps to establish the metaphysical (or transcendent) aspects of religion in the physical world. A physical world that operates by cause and effect with apparent consistency everywhere makes possible a view in which God is the prime cause of all effects. Whether a cosmology maps divine or natural order, its depiction of the physical world reveals a certainty and predictability.

What happens to eternity when, as physicist Albert Einstein first suggested, the physical laws that appear to operate here on earth are proven to have no particular connection to physical laws that operate elsewhere. What does it mean for some contemporary physicists to assert that time and space no longer exist as separable entities but function as a single unit. Furthermore, until this century, no Western cosmologist suspected that mass and energy were different forms of each other; and no one would have guessed that light could be bent by the force of gravity.

In addition to grappling with physical laws that are relative rather than unchangeable, the modern seeker must also learn to cope with the concept of uncertainty. A half century ago, the theoretical physicist Werner Heisenberg pointed out that, at least in the subatomic world, it is impossible to determine at the same time both the position and the speed of a fast-moving particle. So, not only is the physical world relative, it is also uncertain. If there are immutable laws of physics, they exist beyond our current realm of understanding.

With the capacity of modern science to reach into the world of subatomic particles (which may not be particles at all) and out to the world of space, humanity seems obliged to at least acknowledge this reformulation of the nature of existence. Nevertheless, what may be scientifically true may not be theologically acceptable. Hence, reactions to the new physics have been mixed. Three typical responses to this most recent encounter with uncertainty have been outright rejection, separation of two distinct worlds of experience, and reformulation.

Those who reject the experimental findings of the new science recall that false prophets have always been at work to obscure the true vision of the eternal divine revelation. They would not have approved of Galileo's findings, and now decline to accept the evidence that the earth is quite ancient. Geologist Claude C. Albritton has called them "chronophobiacs": they fear time itself.

The second group, the separatists, includes both scientists and theologians who would deny that scientific analysis and traditional religious activities have anything in common. Religion and science are, they say, two separate activities that need not be in conflict precisely because of their distance from one another. The procedures in a chemistry or physics laboratory share nothing with the activities that go on in a church, mosque, or Zen monastery. Those who hold the separatist point of view may maintain a tolerant ignorance of the other realm or dismiss it as idle speculation or superstition. In either case, the separatist is left using one world view most days a week and a different one on holy days.

The first two reactions to the modern scientific world regard the new cosmology with suspicion and doubt, a point of view that inhibits rather than expands understanding. Today, however, some interpreters of both science and traditional religion hold a different stance. Some contemporary religious leaders recognize the contribution of the scientific world view in expressing the relationship between traditional religious claims and other expressions of life. This integrated view of science and theology reaffirms the idea expressed in the last paragraph of Charles Darwin's *Origin of the Species* (published in 1859):

> It is interesting to contemplate a tangled bank, clothed with many plants of many kinds, with birds singing in the bushes, and various insects flitting about, and with worms crawling through the damp earth, and to reflect that these elaborately constructed forms, so different from each other, and dependent upon each other in so complex a manner, have all been produced by laws acting around us . . . There is grandeur in this view of life, with its several powers, having been originally breathed by the Creator into a few forms or into one; and that, whilst this planet has gone cycling on according to the fixed law of gravity, from so simple a beginning, endless forms most beautiful and most wonderful have been, and are being evolved.[2]

Although Darwin's theory of evolution has been modified, the wonderment that attended his discovery is felt by other scientists to be no less potent than it was for him in 1859. It is that joy of discovery and reverence for the visible world that permits a scientific world view to assume the status of religious expression.

SCIENCE AND TECHNOLOGY AS A MEANS TO ULTIMATE TRANSFORMATION

As a religious expression, science often deals with the same concerns that traditional religions do. Among those concerns is the ability to imagine an order that accommodates both the seen and the unseen. Consider Albert Einstein's explanation of energy, expressed as the equation $E = mc^2$ (where c equals the speed of light). He asks us to imagine what the world would look like if we were riding on a beam of light. If we do that, he suggests, the physical world would appear (among other things) to become shorter laterally and time would slow down. Now, although Einstein's assertions have been substantiated in the laboratory, those particular features of the universe are beyond apprehension by human senses. Today people are asked to accept certain laws of physics (that appear to contradict logic) as the most useful hypotheses for a general explanation of how energy works at a subatomic level. People are also asked to believe that what they can measure with their senses is no longer a measure of very much at all.

Not only is time-space relative, but also Heisenberg's principle of uncertainty suggests that at the subatomic level, we can only make educated guesses about how the smallest unit of energy (a photon) operates. Measuring the speed of a particle dislocates its position; establishing the location of a particle interferes with its speed. Hence, all that a scientist may reasonably do is make suppositions about movement in the microcosm. Relativity and uncertainty are two new considerations in drawing the map of existence in the physical world.

As do other religious expressions, the religious response to physical existence through science and technology can be seen to have five properties (see Figure 2): (1) the problematic in the human condition, (2) the ultimate reality, (3) the means to ultimate transformation, and (4) the social and (5) personal expression of that reality.

Lack of Control Corrected by Engineering Physical Welfare

In this view of ultimate transformation, the human condition is marked by uncontrollable physical conditions that limit human potential. If people are hungry or diseased, they disrupt the economic and political well-being of the society. Furthermore, psychological disorders cause distress for the individual, the family, and, by extension, the community. At the root of the human condition—say the advocates of scientific and technological solutions—are biological and psychological deficiencies that cause hungry people to riot and emotionally disturbed people to murder.

When people concentrate on the physical world as the most fundamental source of human well-being, the physical world functions as the ultimate reality. For these people, the cure for the human condition is with us and at hand. The highest good involves the fulfillment of primal needs: food, warmth, physical security, health, and reproduction. This reality breaks down the barriers between natural and artificial because genetic and social engineering ultimately express themselves through *human* enjoyment. In this reality there is no reason for an untimely death caused by, say, liver failure. Science and technology will produce a substitute liver, install it, and send the patient home to family and work. Perhaps even natural death can be indefinitely postponed.

Physical Means: Technological Manipulation

Whereas the science of the unseen (which includes studies in genetics and consciousness, as well as physics) provides the philosophic background for a religious apprehension of the physical world, it is the technological culture of that science that supplies the means for expression. Recall that the human condition includes lack of control over our own physical states, whether those involve aging, spastic muscle behavior, or genetic malfunctions. Through human inventiveness, science-based technology has made it

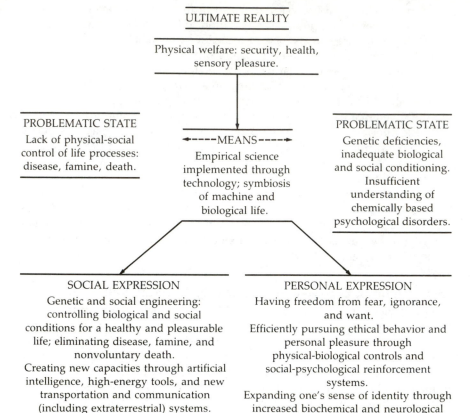

FIGURE 2. *Science and Technology as a Means to Ultimate Transformation*

possible to begin to unlock the mechanisms to control human misery, or at least to counter it.

In the first place, a growing understanding of genetics has brought medical technology to the verge of being able to repair "bad" genes in utero (in the womb), such as the one that causes Down's Syndrome. Such repair would relieve the expectant mother and father of the difficult decisions of whether to terminate a pregnancy.

Technology may also counter physical disability. Perhaps one of the most dramatic innovations is the creation of a computer-generated speech mechanism for people with acute spastic conditions. For example, multiple sclerosis sufferers may be locked into their own consciousness, speechless except for unintelligible grunts. These people are able to use their limited muscle control to activate computers that can "speak," thereby achieving communication. Military technology is giving fighter pilots the capacity to fire rockets with eye movement; the same technology will in time give frustrated intelligence the means to communicate.

It is possible to accommodate much of what the new science and technology have to offer within traditional religious understanding, but not all modern people think that accommodation is necessary. They find joy in discovery and transcendence in the means within a real (as opposed to strictly illusory) physical world to correct problems that have always been considered inherent in the human condition.

At some point in the development of "ultimate" technology, the line between the human and the machine will become even less distinct. Already, bionics (the electronic enhancement of biological functions) have been developed to an incredibly sophisticated level. Much of the work in bionic limbs has been carried on by Walt Disney, Inc., whose initial goal was to create bionic limbs that would permit the electronic model of Abraham Lincoln to sit down in the Hall of Presidents at Walt Disney World without breaking the chair. Artificial movement that can imitate the subtlety of natural human movement holds stunning possibilities for the fields of robotics (suppose robots could be sent to do dangerous jobs like coal mining) and in the replacement of lost limbs.

Social Expression: Biosocial Engineering

The social expression of this type of ultimate transformation is genetic engineering and biosocial conditioning to extend human control of the universe. Human beings must have selective mastery of their social and physical environments by controlling population and by wiping out the conditions of famine, disease, and nonvoluntary death. In these ways, the technology of the modern age can dramatically enhance the quality of life.

The visionary scientist R. Buckminster Fuller has proposed a huge computer-fed game, How Do We Make the World Work? which dramatically illustrates the effort to create a better world. In this learning game, teams of players win by making humanity a continuing success at the earliest moment possible:

> The general-systems-theory controls of the game will be predicated upon employing within a closed system the world's continually updated total resource information in closely specified network complexes designed to facilitate attainment, at the earliest possible date by every human being, of complete enjoyment of the total planet earth, through the individual's optional traveling, tarrying, or dwelling here and there. This world-around freedom of living, work, study, and enjoyment must be accomplished without any one individual interfering with another and without any individual being physically or economically advantaged at the cost of another.[3]

Although many adherents of traditional religions would be skeptical about the possibility of providing "complete enjoyment" for everyone, those who claim ultimate power for the technological revolution urge people to have courage and patience and to make a great effort. Human beings, they insist, will be able to change their biological and cultural capacities. In *Technological Man: The Myth and Reality*, V. C. Ferkiss writes:

Humanity today is on the threshold of self-transfiguration, of attaining new powers over itself and its environment that can alter its nature as fundamental as walking upright or the use of tools. No aspect of man's existence can escape being revolutionized by this fundamental fact—all his self-consciousness that we call culture, his patterns of interaction that we call society, his very biological structure itself. . . . [A] complex of events has altered the nature of man, the complex of discoveries and powers that we glibly speak of as modern technology.[4]

Scientists and others holding these views raise many basic religious and philosophical questions about human freedom and identity. The questions are ancient, but they are now formulated with a sensitivity to physical control of self-images, values, and consciousness.

Personal Expression: Forming a New Self-Identity

In an order that includes the potential for radical genetic change and the intimate interaction between human beings and electronic beings, how does the individual identify him- or herself? Imaginative literature suggests that genetic control (as portrayed in Aldous Huxley's *Brave New World*) will destroy human vitality and creativity. The movie *2001* draws its drama from the battle between humans and the computer HAL who (which?) has decided to take control of the spaceship. It is possible that to the individual who has accepted a cosmology answering to the divine or natural order, this new cosmology, which answers to neither, is terribly threatening. Even the answers to the fundamental religious questions may seem to lack reassurance. "Who am I?" "Why am I in this world?" "What is this world *really*?" "What is life all about?" "Where do I fit in?" If we take a view of the physical world as it runs through contemporary science and technology, the answers might run something like this: "You are physical-chemical-biological energy." "You are in the world because you arose from a genetic mix similar to the rest of the organisms that happen to be here." "This world—organic and inorganic—is the expression of physical energy in its many combinations." "Life is all about achieving the highest good through the fulfillment of primal needs; and this is becoming possible by genetic and social management." Finally, "You fit in where you find the optimal conditions for your physical-biological energy. There you will find what is called care, love, trust, and insight."

SUMMARY

A cosmology is a theory of the universe and the general laws that govern it, that is, a cosmology tells us how the physical world is arranged and what keeps that arrangement in place.

Different cultures use different cosmologies or universal models. In traditional Christianity, all physical life was created by God. In ancient India, the physical world originated from a cosmic egg. For some modern scientists, everything in our universe came from the Big Bang; our world is a tiny fragment of the original explosion. Each of these cosmologies holds power for those who accept it, because *where* we believe we came from and *how* we believe we keep going affects the way we understand ourselves in the physical world.

In traditional religious expressions, cosmologies may help answer two kinds of questions: (1) those concerning existence before and after death and (2) those concerning relationships between personal decision making and the nature of the universe. These kinds of questions have been answered by three different traditional ways of understanding the physical world: (1) the world as God's creation and time as a revelation of his purpose, (2) the world as the eternal rhythm of the original or cosmic energy, and (3) the world as fleeting impressions of a different (eternal) reality. In each case, the cosmology expressed a connection between religious life and physical existence. As Galileo discovered, the power of a cosmology within a culture can be considerable.

The religious response to physical existence alone can be categorized according to the five elements of a religious process:

1. When physical reality is the center of religious concern, the problematic of the human condition is experienced as physical suffering. This suffering is caused by an inability to control the problems arising from genetic and biochemical causes. Disease, famine, and death limit all human possibilities.
2. The ultimate reality that cures the condition of biophysical deficiency is the fulfillment of all physical needs: food, warmth, physical security, health, and reproduction. In this context, experiences of enjoyment, pleasure, and beauty are produced and controlled by mental and physical programming.
3. The means to this transformation come through science and technology. Technology, in particular, can help overcome physical and mental limitations. Genetic engineering can produce better varieties of living organisms such as wheat, chickens, or cattle. Genetic surgery can correct genetic errors in unborn children. Through machinery of all kinds (including computers), humanity can improve the quality of life. Eventually, the distinction between what is natural and what is artificial will lose its importance.
4. Social expression of this ultimate transformation involves applications of science and technology. If people begin to live better because they are healthier and relieved of physical suffering, then the distinction between social and physical realities fades away. Behavior modification and genetic improvements will lead to the good life for all.
5. For the individual, accepting this ultimate reality means to be free from fear, ignorance, and want. Through chemical and social reinforcement, each individual can realize his or her highest potential for care, love, trust, and insight.

As you reflect on this chapter, keep in mind that many writers and philosophers are suspicious of genetic and behavioral programming. In his book *Brave New World*, Aldous Huxley suggests that genetic and social conditioning will make the world a boring place in which to live. Also, consider whether a world cured of human suffering through technology is different from a world cured of human suffering through Buddhist meditation, Christian faith, or the moral cultivation of a truly humane person (Confucian). Do you think that continual technological change is inevitable? If so, will it necessarily change our perception of who we are?

SELECTED READINGS

The religious significance of the way people view the world is explained in W. B. Kristensen, *The Meaning of Religion* (The Hague: Nihoff, 1960), Part I, "Cosmology," and in *G. van der Leeuw, *Religion in Essence and Manifestation* (New York: Harper, 1963; first published in 1933), Part IV, "The World." These important phenomenological studies deal predominantly with religions of the Near East.

A more general discussion of the importance of cosmic imagery, with emphasis on linear and cyclic world processes to contrast the Judaeo-Christian-Muslim orientation with archaic and Eastern religions, is found in W. L. King, *Introduction to Religion*, rev. ed., Chapter 8, "Cosmogonies and Cataclysms: The Mythos of World Beginnings and Endings."

A more comprehensive discussion of the variety of cosmologies in human history is found in two studies by S. G. F. Brandon: *Time and Mankind* (New York: Hutchinson, 1951), and *History, Time and Deity* (New York: Barnes & Noble, 1965).

M. K. Munitz, *Theories of the Universe* (New York: Free Press, 1957). A volume of selected readings from Western sources on cosmology from Babylonian culture to modern science, for the general reader.

H. Corbin et al., *Man and Time*, papers from the *Eranos* Yearbooks, Vol. 3 (New York: Pantheon, 1957). A collection of papers on the imagery of time by specialists in different religious and cultural traditions.

An introduction to the importance of historical study for understanding human life can be found in the selections in P. Gardiner, ed., *Theories of History* (New York: Free Press, 1959), which includes representative philosophies of history and recent views on the nature of historical knowledge and explanation; and *K. Löwith, *Meaning in History* (Chicago: University of Chicago Press, 1949), in which the theological implications of some basic Western interpretations of time are analyzed.

The nature of modern science and its contribution to human understanding of existence is discussed in I. G. Barbour, *Issues in Science and Religion* (Englewood Cliffs, NJ: Prentice-Hall, 1966); and H. K. Schilling, *The New Consciousness in Science and Religion* (Philadelphia: United Church Press, 1973). For both authors, "religion" means predominantly Protestant Christianity, and the central focus is on understanding the differences, together with the interrelatedness, of these two sources of human meaning. Barbour's book includes an analysis of four specific problems (e.g., determinism vs. human freedom, evolution vs. creation), and the discussion presents Christian theology and modern science as alternative languages applied to human life. Schilling affirms the possibility of sensing an ultimate quality of existence through the integration of scientific data and biblical faith.

Statements by scientists that describe the impact of scientific understanding of human life and contemporary technology on human self-awareness are found in R. H. Haynes, ed., *Man and the Biological Revolution* (Toronto: York University, 1976); and *Committee on Science, Engineering, and Public Policy of the National Academy of Sciences, *Frontiers in Science and Technology* (New York: W. H. Freeman, 1983).

Introductions to the contemporary view of humanity as basically a result of biological evolution and an entry into a biocultural revolution are found in D. M. Rorvik, *Brave New Baby: Promise and Peril of the Biological Revolution* (Garden City, NY: Doubleday, 1971); J. Salk, *Man Unfolding* (New York: Harper & Row, 1972); L. Thomas, *The Lives of a Cell* (New York: Viking Press, 1974); and C. Sagan, *Dragons of Eden* (New York: Random House, 1977).

P. McCorduck, *Machines Who Think: A Personal Inquiry into the History and Prospects of Artificial Intelligence* (San Francisco: W. H. Freeman, 1979). A sensitive and strongly argued case for understanding the information processing of computers in terms of human intelligence, culminating in a provocative final chapter, "Forging the Gods."

*K. Baier and N. Rescher, eds., *Values and the Future: The Impact of Technological Change on American Values* (New York: Free Press, 1969). Seventeen essays by sociologists and economists, which consider the impact of technological innovation on individual and group values. Various methodological questions regarding the conceptualization of issues, gathering data on value changes, and the difficulty of forecasting are explored.

F. J. Streng, C. L. Lloyd, Jr., and J. T. Allen, eds., *Ways of Being Religious* (Englewood Cliffs, NJ: Prentice-Hall, 1973), Chapter 7, "The New Life through Technocracy," provides excerpts from advocates, sympathetic interpreters, and critics of a scientific transformation of life.

Books that explore the integration of images of, and orientations to, time and space from traditional Eastern philosophies and contemporary Western theoretical physics are *F. Capra, *The Tao of Physics* (Berkeley, CA: Shambala, 1975); *L. Dossey, *Space, Time and Medicine* (Boulder, CO: Shambala, 1982); *A. de Riencourt, *The Eye of Shiva: Eastern Mysticism and Science* (New York: William Morrow, 1981); and *G. Zukav, *The Dancing Wu Li Masters: An Overview of the New Physics* (New York: William Morrow, 1979).

*W. Heisenberg, *Physics and Philosophy: The Revolution in Modern Science* (New York: Harper, 1958). A classic statement by a physicist whose theory of indeterminancy of quantum mechanics is named after him, with a very useful introduction by the renowned philosopher F. S. C. Northrop.

PART THREE

*Approaches to an
Objective Study of Religion*

Since the late 1800s, scientific investigation has been one of the most important influences on the study of religion. The scientific approach, with its emphasis on reason and analysis, was developed first in Western Europe and then adopted by academic centers throughout the world. Its adherents assume that all matters of human concern make proper objects of study. No matter may be excluded as too sacred. So, in the second half of the 1800s, the study of religion, together with anthropology, sociology, and psychology, became an academic discipline, taking its place alongside mathematics and physics.

The purpose of the scientific approach to religious life was assumed to be radically different from the theological concern to interpret life to bring a person to salvation. The advocates of objective study also rejected the claim that revelation and mystic experiences were absolute modes of knowledge. The sacred in human life was brought under the scrutiny of objective investigation. Investigators did not view religious conviction as the result of divine grace or supernatural power, but interpreted religious beliefs and symbols in the context of human forces and institutions. In scientific study, the investigator's personal value systems were supposed to be excluded.

Nevertheless, the personal element in religious studies always seems to appear. In presenting some of the basic tasks, procedures, and assumptions of the scientific study of religion, we should keep in mind that these understandings of religious phenomena are often based on cultural assumptions and presuppositions of Western religious scholarship. Nevertheless, one of the most prominent characteristics of this effort has been the accumulation of a large body of descriptive information about what people throughout the world think and do. From this perspective, the best scholarship is based on firsthand information—direct communication with the sources through field research and language study. A major assumption is that there are commonalities in differing human experiences. The accumulation of information can thus stimulate comparisons that may reveal broad human patterns. Ideally, a wide range of information about human behavior elsewhere—from the eating habits of a people thousands of miles away to the art of an ancient civilization or an unfamiliar vision of life after death—will enrich people's understanding of their own humanity.

As important as it is to point out the cultural roots of scientific thinking, it is just as important to recognize that different attempts to understand religion objectively have emphasized different aspects of life and developed various principles of interpretation and explanation. Within religious studies, scholars have taken several approaches, four of which we explore in this part. In the order in which they have engaged scholarly opinion and efforts, these four general approaches to understanding religion are as follows: (1) to find the earliest religious expression; (2) to discover how religion functions culturally, socially, and psychologically; (3) to understand human religiousness by comparing concrete historical religious expressions; and (4) to find the deepest meaning of religion through dialogue.

One of the continuing problems of religious studies is to decide which of these approaches (or combination of approaches) will lead to the greatest understanding. The solution depends, of course, on what kind of result is considered most useful. For instance, those desiring to predict future behavior on the basis of a social science model will not ask the same questions as those seeking to interpret the meaning of a particular cultural symbol or institutional form. Nevertheless, studies in one discipline, say, anthropology, may illumine the understanding of a rite or symbol in another, say, a comparative study of religious art.

We have chosen to review here a few key researchers and problems of interpretation and to indicate some of the difficulties basic to their approaches for two reasons. First, it is important to be aware of the academic context out of which the subject matter of this book emerges. Second, it is helpful to know what questions have been asked about religion and the range of answers given. Some questions have been based on faulty assumptions; some answers are limited in their interpretive power. Further explorations may reveal new perspectives that go beyond those covered in this book. We hope that by understanding how different scholars in the past hundred years have wrestled with understanding the religious life, you, as reader, will be able to formulate some new questions and answers of your own. In the last chapter, you will have the opportunity to apply your new knowledge to some current interpretations of religion.

CHAPTER 11

The Origins of Religious Life

Traditionally, one of the major efforts in the scientific study of religion has been the attempt to find the beginning of religion, the source from which more recent expressions derive. Especially from 1850 on, some scholars sought to understand the nature of religion by investigating the earliest religions then known. They felt that if they could find the origin of religion, they could understand its nature and properly interpret the sequence of changes in religious history.

When looking for the beginning of religion, scientific investigators considered only those sources that were objectively measurable. They rejected as unmeasureable the traditional religious descriptions of the origin of the world and humanity as found, for instance, in the biblical account of Adam and Eve or the creation stories in other sacred writings, such as the Muslin Qur'an, the Hindu Veda, or the Japanese Kojiki. From the scientific perspective, researchers could not regard God, as revealed in any of the sacred scriptures, as the actual source of human religious reflection or worship. Scientific scholars studied religious mythologies, but they did not believe that the myths described actual happenings. For these scholars, the myths and rituals did not accurately explain the nature of personhood, the development of life, or the source and conditions of the deepest meaning, joy, and wholeness in human experience. Rather, mythic material presented the investigator with information that could be interpreted objectively to explain the linguistic, psychological, and social causes of religion.

Although nineteenth-century investigators attempted to stay free from theological assumptions, they began their studies with another set of assumptions that sound very much like those used in theories of biological evolution. Some key assumptions of nineteenth-century religious investigation are as follows: (1) All religions began at a single source; (2) historically, religions have progressed from simple forms to more complex ones; (3) the contemporary religious practices of "primitive" groups (those without a written tradition) reveal how religion began; and (4) more technologically advanced cultures (those having a literary tradition) have more advanced religious practices.

It is not surprising that this list echoes the assumptions of biological (and geological) evolution. The nineteenth century was bursting with discovery in the natural sciences. Some of the best minds in all disciplines were looking for sources. In religious studies, scholars searched for the sources that *produced* religious expressions. What makes these studies different from theological studies is that the scholars of religious studies regarded the sources of religion as necessarily different from God, Tao, or pure consciousness. In this chapter, then, we follow the scholars who tried to define which religious forms were the earliest. Some concluded that religion is a product of faulty thinking; others thought that religion rose from intense personal feelings. Still other scholars proposed that the first religious expressions evolved from a need for social control. Table 1 outlines some of the answers to the question of the evidence for religion.

TABLE 1. What Is the Earliest Evidence for Religion?

Source	Scholar	Theoretical Justification
Names of gods	F. Max Mueller (*Essays in Comparative Mythology*, 1856)	Natural phenomena were taken to be expressions of spirits or divine personal agents
Early reflection on dreams and death	Edward Burnett Tylor (*Religion in Primitive Culture*, 1871)	Preliterate cultures divided reality into the physical world and a spiritual world populated by invisible forces; an inferior stage of mental development could not express the idea of a single deity
The emotion of awe	Robert H. Codrington (*The Melanesians, 1891*)	*Mana* was a force of life that preceded mythology and belief in spirits; it was effective extraordinary power
	Robert R. Marett ("Preanimistic Religion," 1900)	Awe of impersonal supernatural power (*mana*) predated naming gods or believing in spirits
Totemism	Emile Durkheim (*The Elementary Forms of the Religious Life*, 1912)	A society cannot exist without a group identity; the totem unites the members of the society through its sacredness

TABLE 1. (continued)

Prelogical social mentality	Lucian Levy-Brühl (*Primitives and the Supernatural*, 1931)	Primitive people were sensitive to invisible powers, not to concepts like God
Magic	James G. Frazer (*The Golden Bough: A Study in Comparative Religion*, 1911–1919)	Magic predated the worship of nature or the dead; it is less complex than the operation of supernatural agents
	Bronislaw Malinowski (Magic, Science, and Religion," 1925)	Magic and religion are used for different social purposes and function simultaneously
The high being	Wilhelm Schmidt (*The Origin of the Idea of God*, 1912)	Modern primitive societies at the extremities of cultural diffusion use "late" religious forms; but *traces* of worship of a high being suggest that such worship was the original expression
Symbolic pattern formation	Raffaele Pettazzoni (*The All-Knowing God*, 1955)	A high being predates monotheism because monotheism assumes polytheism; all earliest expressions reflect a need to create a symbolic world
	Mircea Eliade (*Patterns in Comparative Religion*, 1949)	People need to live in an orderly world and so use sacred symbols to overcome change and disorder

RELIGION AS A PRODUCT OF FAULTY THINKING

F. Max Mueller. A fairly common approach to understanding myths during the last half of the nineteenth century was to view gods as personifications of natural phenomena. For example, the volcanic building force in Hawaii is personified as Madame Pele; the force of the ocean that smashes away at the volcanic islands is understood as the retaliation of Pele's jealous sister. During the 1800s, the accepted scholarly opinion was that the worship of many gods (polytheism) was earlier, or "more primitive," than the exclusive worship of one god (monotheism). This conclusion was based on the assumption that before people developed clarity of thought—which found its highest expression in modern times—their expression was dominated by intense feelings and a confused use of words. This view had important implications for an investigation of the language of religious myths (recall the power of language, in Chapter 3).

F. Max Mueller, who is sometimes called the father of the "science of religion," explained the origin of religion as a mental slip in thinking that the natural *objects* of our senses were "acting *subjects*." (We observe a volcano erupting and conclude that Madame Pele is at work.) In his early work, *Essays in Comparative Mythology* (1856), Mueller held that natural objects or events (lightning, tornadoes, sun, and mountains) incited terror, wonder, trust, and security. From this point of view, religion was first experienced as the mental response to rapture or fear before natural phenomena; for example, in the experience of daybreak. The earliest human expression of the experience of joy at dawn might have been to exclaim, "The dawn is coming!" However, as soon as the structure of language indicates the possibility that dawn is capable of doing anything—in this case, arriving someplace—the process of personification has already begun. According to Mueller, the first expression of religion was a "disease of language" by which people mistook a way of speaking for an indication of reality. Once the dawn can *do* anything, it is just a short step to giving dawn a name and a sex and calling her Aurora.

Mueller's reconstruction of the origin and growth of religion is essentially that when a person perceives the infinite, he or she gives this experience a name; the object of religious awe becomes a personified creature and its name is passed on. Human beings became aware of the infinite, named the infinite, passed on the name, separated the name from the original meaning, and ultimately rejected the name. The process works this way: (1) The people of Greece observe that the sun *follows* the dawn; (2) they personify the sun and call it Apollo and name the dawn Aurora; (3) stories are told in which Apollo follows Aurora; (4) Apollo becomes a recognizable god in human form complete with his own oracle and worshippers; (5) Apollo becomes a name for an inexplicable power and loses his particular connection with the sun. Mueller called this process, which takes place over centuries of human experience, "the dialectical growth and decay" of religion.

Mueller's theory suggested that the names of the gods were like footprints that could be traced through time. Therefore, by making a comparative study of the language about God (the naming of the infinite), the scholar could trace the history of religions.

Edward Burnett Tylor. Another attempt to find the origin of religion in faulty thinking was made by Edward Burnett Tylor in his *Religion in Primitive Culture* (1871). Here he claimed that the earliest form of religion was animism—the belief that all of life was full of spirits or powers (anima). For Tylor, the rational nature of humanity is the clue to understanding how religion was produced. People in preliterate cultures, he felt, had the same kind of mental faculties as modern people—though in an inferior stage of development. Although they recognized spirits as invisible forces of life, they did not clearly express the idea of a single deity (a more advanced development).

Tylor felt that religious ideas arose because thinking people in a low level of culture were deeply impressed by two groups of biological problems: first, the difference between death and life, and second, the appearance of human shapes in dreams and visions. He maintained that, as early humans considered these two phenomena, they concluded that everything is composed of two aspects—the physical and a spirit or soul. By accepting a usually unseen spirit, they could explain the visual similarity of a live body, a dead body, and an unconscious body. At the same time, they could explain how human forms appear in dreams and visions—they are spirits. Once the reality of human experience had been divided into physical life and spirit life, it was only a short logical step to three important religious doctrines: (1) Souls may move from one life to the next (transmigration); (2) the personal soul may have a future spiritual life (as in heaven); and (3) very powerful spirits live in other realms (higher or lower). For the rest of the nineteenth century, this theory of animism dominated scholarly thinking on the earliest expression of religion.

RELIGION AS A PRODUCT OF AWE

Robert H. Codrington and Robert R. Marett. Although the theory that animism represented the source of all religion was widely accepted, it did not go unchallenged. There were several scholarly attempts to show that the cause of religious phenomena came well before the rather complicated logic that connects language and reflection on dreams and death to the notion of spirits. The most persuasive arguments came from men who had done fieldwork among the primitives themselves. Robert H. Codrington, a Christian missionary who carefully observed the people among whom he worked, in his book *The Melanesians* (1891) described the religion in Melanesia as based upon ancestor worship, magical practices, and *mana*. *Mana* was an overwhelming force that existed everywhere and could act for good or evil. Codrington saw possession and control of *mana* as a type of religious experience that preceded mythology and belief in spirits. Other terms expressing this impersonal supernatural power, such as *wakan, orenda,* and a type of Polynesian *mana,* were soon discovered in various peoples throughout the preliterate world.

In 1900, the Oxford anthropologist Robert R. Marett published an article entitled "Preanimistic Religion," confirming Codrington's observations. This article became one of the most famous expositions of the theory that the first stage of religion was not naming the gods or asserting the existence of nonphysical spirits, but rather was an emotion of awe evoked by a feeling of personal relationship with the impersonal supernatural power of *mana*. This theory has played a very important role in understanding preliterate religious expressions, and it is still assumed by many in the general reading public to be the best explanation of religious origins.

RELIGION AS A PRODUCT OF SOCIAL IDENTITY

Emile Durkheim. In his famous book *The Elementary Forms of the Religious Life* (1912), sociologist Emile Durkheim tried to locate the causes of the basic forms of religious acts and notions. For him, the purpose of religion was to regulate human relations with spiritual beings. In contrast to the scholars who saw the beginning of religion as an incorrect understanding of life or as products of a personal overwhelming experience, Durkheim held that religion was created by pressures of social obligation related to what primitive people perceived as a supernatural realm. Thus, religion began when a group of people began to understand itself as a society and recognized a sacred realm identical to the ideal self-understanding that the society had of itself. Gods or spiritual forces were ideal and imaginative representations of the community.

Seeing the origin of self-awareness in group interaction, Durkheim looked for the earliest expression of religion in the symbolism of natural phenomena through which a group of people identified themselves. He found this expression in the practice of totemism, which expresses the idea that there is some magical connection between a society and a plant or lower animal form. The totem is the object of awe and reverence (a species of tree, a crab, or a particular stone) and has a special relationship to the group that identifies itself in terms of this object. The totem is not merely an idea; it is a symbol for the sacred whereby the individual becomes one with the sacred. As evidence, Durkheim pointed to the totems found among the Australian aborigines, where the totem symbolized sacredness and the clan at the same time. He argued that the clan could not exist without the totem because there was no other way for the members to be united; therefore, totemism must be the earliest expression of religion.

RELIGION AS A PRODUCT OF PRIMITIVE MENTALITY

Lucien Levy-Brühl. In the attempt to locate the characteristics of primitive reflection, experience, and social habits during the first quarter of the twentieth century, a continuing concern was the comparison of primitive and modern systems of thought. The French anthropologist-philosopher Lucien Levy-Brühl championed a theory—the focus of discussion for several decades—emphasizing the differences between the mentalities of primitive societies and modern rational reflection. In *Primitives and the Supernatural* (1931), Levy-Brühl explicated the view that religion resulted from the primitive person's "irrational mental life" as an experienced world of ancestral spirits, witchcraft, omens, pollution, and purification. Such notions as "supreme God" or even "a religion," he maintained, correspond to nothing in the minds of primitive people. Instead, such people are sensitive to the presence of invisible powers that have greater or lesser influence throughout their existence. These invisible powers are always present, and the primitive man, woman, and child learn to cope with them by following various rules and regulations.

Levy-Brühl, like Durkheim, saw religion as deriving from social thought. The primitive mentality was a pattern of social expectation and learning. Personal interests and experiences were conditioned by social symbols and appropriate behavior. Primitive people experienced everyday events in a nonlogical manner, and accounted for their experiences and actions in terms of mystical or supersensible forces. This did not mean for Levy-Brühl that primitive people have no logical principles or means of explaining phenomena; rather, their categories of thought are different from modern European thought. The primitive person gives conscious attention to everyday things and events in a manner different from that of contemporary Westerners. This primitive mentality accounts for the belief in spirits, magic, omens, and healing rituals.

Subsequent discussion of this theory indicates that it is an oversimplification and does not take into account the variety of thought and experience in preliterate societies. Nevertheless, Levy-Brühl's concern to see religious meaning as part of a community's pattern of perception and behavior accords with the present recognition that different kinds of reasoning provide explanations for those who begin with the assumptions and categories found in them.

THE RELATION OF RELIGION TO MAGIC

James G. Frazer. Another theory that has influenced the study of religion is James G. Frazer's notion that religion was an appeal to supernatural beings for solutions to problems not satisfactorily solved by magic. He held that religion functioned as a primitive science. This perspective is found in Frazer's *The Magic Art*, which is part of the twelve-volume work entitled *The Golden Bough: A Study in Comparative Religion* (1911–1919). The principles on which magic is based are (1) like produces like, or an effect resembles cause, and (2) things once in contact with each other continue to act on each other even at a distance. Both principles are based on the assumption that things act on each other through an invisible or secret "sympathy." Nevertheless, although partially successful, magic was deficient as an explanation of hidden causes. The idea of the operation of supernatural agents is a more complex idea, claimed Frazer, appearing later than sympathetic magic.

For Frazer, knowledge of the supernatural began when people experienced certain extraordinary emotions and came up with extraordinary ideas for which they could not account in ordinary ways. The solution was to assign these emotions and ideas to the work of a powerful spirit or deity. Once religion is achieved, says Frazer, it assumes one of two forms, which may be found simultaneously. These forms are (1) the worship of nature (animism) and (2) the worship of the dead. It is hard to say which form came first, but the belief in spirits soon evolved into totemism, the worship of some special natural object. According to Frazer, a god experienced in a human form completes the evolutionary process to the present time: magic to belief in spirits as causal agents to totemism to a god in human form. To document this theory of religious progression, Frazer argued that most primitive evidence of religious life comes from the aborigines of Australia, where magic is universally practiced and where an appeal to a higher power is nearly unknown.

During the past fifty years, Frazer's theory has influenced students of archaic religions. However, he has been severely criticized for not interpreting his data in relation to levels of cultural development. For example, the event of a group of people drinking wine together, butchering a lamb or goat, or worshipping a corn goddess can have certain cultural meanings in an agriculture-dominated village and others in an urban, commerce-dominated setting.

Bronislaw Malinowski. Not all anthropologists have separated magic and religion in the way Frazer did. For instance, Bronislaw Malinowski ("Magic, Science and Religion," 1925) rejected Frazer's assertion that magic is an inferior science. Malinowski claimed that primitive people clearly were aware of the difference between magic and naturalistic laws. Magic was the spontaneous activity in human situations of stress when recourse to all naturalistic laws had failed. Magical force was generated and transferred in the atmosphere of the supernatural—not the natural—world. The distinction Malinowski saw between magic and religion, then, was that religion creates values and poses ultimate ends directly, whereas magic simply has practical, utilitarian purposes and is only a means to an end.

The dominant notion of magic today, expressed by such prominent anthropologists as Ruth Benedict and Claude Levi-Strauss, is that magic and religion are not two alternatives or stages in evolution; rather, they are two parts of human self-awareness reflecting two ways of interpreting the universe.

RELIGION AS AN EXPRESSION OF HIGH BEING

Wilhelm Schmidt. During the first quarter of the twentieth century, while Marett, Frazer, and Durkheim were developing their notions of *mana*, magic, and totemism, respectively, students of ethnology (the study of racial groups) were criticizing them for not distinguishing among the evidence found at various levels of social and cultural development. One of the leading ethnologists of the time, Wilhelm Schmidt, claimed that the origin of the idea of God cannot be found without using a scientifically based historical method to distinguish and clarify various levels of development within preliterate societies.

Schmidt thought that by identifying levels of development in the living remnants of the oldest civilization and arranging these in a developmental sequence, a scholar could establish a historical line of "before and after." Although he recognized that no living culture represents the earliest human life, he held that one could reconstruct the original religion by projecting backward from the available evidence. Schmidt's approach to locating

201
The Origins of Religious Life

general levels of cultural development, which then allows investigators to specify earlier or more recent cultural forms, is based on two principles. The first is that there is cultural diffusion from an area having a moderate climate (for example, the Mediterranean Sea area) to the polar extremities of the Asian and American continents. The second principle is that the latest or youngest element in a culture complex is the one that appears to be strongest; older elements appear weaker. Thus, the most prominent elements (*mana*, totem, magic) among preliterate societies living today in either isolated places (jungles, deserts, islands) or at the extremities of the Asian and American continents are only later modifications of an original religious phenomenon.

In the first volume of his large work, *The Origin of the Idea of God* (1912), Schmidt argues that the least technologically developed tribes indicate through their beliefs and cultic practices a distorted but positive reflection of the earliest religious experience—the worship of a "high being." Whereas some scholars today reject Schmidt's thesis outright, others accept his evidence that a high being is recorded in the myths of the least technologically developed cultures today. For these scholars, the problem of an original monotheism or of the nature of a high being is a crucial issue.

THE COEXISTENCE OF MULTIPLE RELIGIOUS FORMS: EXPRESSIONS OF A SYMBOLIC WORLD

Raffaele Pettazzoni. Raffaele Pettazzoni, who has made detailed studies of preliterate peoples and has helped to define the contemporary discussion of early religious forms, discusses the problem of original monotheism in *The All-Knowing God* (1955). Pettazzoni denies the presence of monotheism among preliterate societies, as monotheism is historically defined, since this term suggests a denial of all other gods and, as such, presupposes polytheism. He affirms the existence of a high being in the most primitive tribes as *one* kind of religious expression. Nevertheless, he does not wish to approach the study of religious phenomena with preconceived notions of the attributes of a supreme being—notions that he claims have been formed in a comparatively late stage of philosophical development. A religious myth, Pettazzoni maintains, is not just a pleasant contemplation or a result of logic; rather, it is the mental and spiritual orientation by which a person achieves self-identity. A myth of creation, for instance, is not primarily the reflection of a primal cause; rather, it is a guarantee for the existence of humanity and the universe through symbolic meaning.

Mircea Eliade. Mircea Eliade, a contemporary scholar of archaic religious symbols, accepts that we cannot find a pure form of the earliest religion among living peoples and that in preliterate societies today there are various religious expressions. However, he holds that human beings must have had an early vital need to bring some symbolic order to life. The most archaic living societies affirm some belief in a supreme being, but they do not give the supreme being a central role in religious life; other religious forms are also found in these societies. Eliade acknowledges the ethnological distinctions among various levels of religious life according to the cultural development of humanity, and as a result, he finds that the symbolism, imagery, and rites of different peoples reflect their particular needs and orientation to existence. But in spite of the cultural differences, says Eliade, religious symbols come from a universal human need to live according to a symbolic world that gives ultimate meaning to life.

THE ARCHAEOLOGICAL RECORD

Recently, the effort to locate the earliest expressions of religion has shifted from a study of living preliterate cultures to prehistoric archaeological discoveries. Some scholars, for example, E. O. James in his *Prehistoric Religion*, use both archaeological data and studies of contemporary preliterate people to interpret archaic religion. However, in the last fifty years archaeological evidence of prehistoric religion has generally been used to supplement theories about the earliest form of religion.

Archaeological evidence suggests that we can classify the presumably religious artifacts into three periods: The Old World, or the Upper Paleolithic period, 100,000 to 300,000 B.C.E.; the Late Stone Age, or the Mesolithic period, 30,000 to 10,000 B.C.E.; and the Neolithic period, 10,000 to 3,000 B.C.E. In the first period, we find no art, but we do find careful burial of various cultural implements with the corpse. In the next period, we find Homo sapiens (or Cro-Magnon man) and evidence of deliberate and careful burial in which the dead bodies were decorated with red ochre and shells and various cultural implements were placed alongside them. The art during this period includes painting, engravings, carvings in relief, and models of animals in clay, suggesting the practice of magical rites to ensure productivity and success in hunting. The Neolithic period is said to begin with the discovery of agriculture and the domestication of animals, and there is much evidence of agricultural rites and worship of a fertility goddess, as well as the goddess's male partner, a cult of the spirits of the dead or ancestors, and a cult of the powers in the earth.

Even such a brief summary of the framework into which archaeological findings are placed indicates the difficulty of using those findings to draw clear conclusions about the origins of religion. Not only is there lack of sufficient evidence, but also there are serious problems in knowing how to interpret the information that *is* available.

CAN THE FIRST RELIGIOUS EXPRESSION BE FOUND?

The attempt to define the original religious experience through a study of preliterate societies assumes continuity between them and prehistorical religious life and between them and modern, science-oriented cultures. If we judge that present ideas and life activities are dependent on those of the past and that the past is significantly related to present personal and cultural awareness, then it is important to look into the earliest expressions of religion to understand ourselves and the contemporary scene. As we have seen, however, the study of preliterate cultures has produced evidence of *different* expressions of supernatural power. We even find that a contemporary notion of supernatural being may not apply exactly to the earliest awareness. So, an investigator must be open to several possible meanings and images of religion.

It is most likely that the earliest religious experiences were diverse and that the history of development cannot be formulated as a simple, evolutionary scheme in which the variety of religious expressions derive from a single source. Social anthropologist E. E. Evans-Prichard has summarized the attitude of many investigators toward the origin of religious life when he writes:

> I think that most anthropologists would today agree that it is useless to seek for a *primordium* in religion. . . . It has been clearly established that in many primitive religions peoples' minds function in different ways at different levels and in different contexts. So a man may turn to a fetish for certain purposes and appeal to God in other situations; and a religion can be both polytheistic and monotheistic, according to whether Spirit is thought of as more than one or as one. . . . I suppose it would be agreed that the kind of cause-and-effect explanation which was implicit in so much earlier theorizing is hardly in accord with modern scientific thought in general, which seeks rather to reveal and understand constant relations.[1]

The study of origins has seldom resulted in positive conclusions—other than that the problem is complex. Today the general trend of inquiry into religion by social scientists is the investigation of the sociocultural role of religion, discussed in Chapter 12. Here the subject of the origin of religion is usually omitted entirely. The purpose of contemporary studies of low-technology societies is to record data as accurately as possible and to define the type or structure of religious beliefs, rites, and religious institutions. This concern seems to confirm the feeling of many social scientists and historians that the effort to find the first expression of religion is not only a frustrating problem but also a false one.

SUMMARY

In the nineteenth century, scholars asked themselves: How can we know the most about the deepest meaning of religion? Their answer was to look for origins. If they could understand where religion came from in the first place, they could more clearly understand why it was so important to human life.

Scholars who searched for origins shared the following assumptions: (1) All religions began at a single source; (2) religions progress from simple to complex forms; (3) the contemporary religious practices of preliterate groups reveal how religion began; and (4) technologically advanced societies have more morally and philosophically advanced religious practices.

Although researchers shared these assumptions, they tended to locate the original source of all religions in different places. Max Mueller and Edward B. Tylor attributed the earliest religion to faulty thinking about the natural world. In contrast, Robert H. Codrington and Robert R. Marett maintained that the first religious response came from overwhelming feelings of awe for the action of invisible powers. Lucien Levy-Brühl argued that religion originated in a primitive mentality.

Three other scholars, Emile Durkheim, James G. Frazer, and Bronislaw Malinowski assigned the origins of religion to three different places altogether. Durkheim said that groups of people found religious union by identifying with a plant or lower animal called a totem. Frazer claimed that religion emerged when magic could not solve important problems. Malinowski countered Frazer by suggesting that magic and religion coexisted and served different community needs.

Three other important points of view were proposed by Wilhelm Schmidt, Raffaele Pettazzoni, and Mircea Eliade. Schmidt placed the earliest religious experience in the worship of a high being, whereas Pettazzoni denied the possibility of monotheism among preliterate societies. Eliade, as well as Pettazzoni, suggested that religion emerged from multiple forms, all of which provide symbolic significance for the society.

In reviewing the efforts of scholars to find the origins of religions, we find two recurring problems: (1) The same evidence can yield different interpretations; and (2) there does not seem to be enough evidence available to resolve the disagreements. As a result, the search for origins as *the* means for understanding the deepest meaning of religion has lost its scholarly appeal. The archaeological record of ancient civilizations, which was once seen as a source for answers, is now used as a source for developing new questions and raw data.

SELECTED READINGS

A selection of ten readings by leading social scientists on the origin and development of religion is found in W. A. Lessa and E. Z. Vogt, eds., *Reader in Comparative Religion: An Anthropological Approach*, 3rd ed. (New York: Harper, 1972), Section I, "The Origin and Development of Religion." These readings provide a basic introduction to the problem of locating the earliest form of religion.

Paperback reprints of some early studies of the origin of religion are available. Among these are *E. B. Tylor, *Religion in Primitive Culture* (New York: Harper, 1958); S. Freud, *Totem and Taboo* (New York: Random House, 1946); *J. G. Frazer, *New Golden Bough*, abridged, edited by T. H. Gaster (New York: Macmillan, 1959); *E. Durkheim, *The Elementary Forms*

of the Religious Life (New York: Collier, 1961); *P. Radin, *Primitive Religion*
(New York: Dover, 1957); *L. Levy-Brühl, *Primitives and the Supernatural* (New York: Dutton, 1935; first published in 1931); *R. H. Lowie, *Primitive Religion* (New York: Grosset & Dunlap, 1952; first published in 1924); and *B. Malinowski, *Magic, Science and Religion and Other Essays* (Garden City, NY: Doubleday, 1955; first published in 1948).

*E. E. Evans-Prichard, *Theories of Primitive Religion* (London: Oxford University Press, 1965). A critical assessment of the major theories that attempt to account for the religions of primitive peoples. The author, a renowned social anthropologist, shows the cultural biases in the together archaeological information and anthropological studies of living and resulted more often in confusion than understanding.

*E. O. James, *Prehistoric Religion: A Study in Prehistoric Archeology* (New York: Barnes & Noble, 1957). Here a renowned historian of religion brings together archaeological information and anthropological studies of living preliterate cultures to present an overall picture of prehistoric religion.

E. Norbeck, *Religion in Primitive Society* (New York: Harper, 1961). An anthropologist's statement on the role of religion in primitive society. Chapters 2 and 3, "Origins" and "Conceptions of the Supernatural," are clear summaries of the problems in trying to find the original expressions of religion.

Two classic expositions that, while somewhat dated, still contain some interpretive insights are:

A. E. Jensen, *Myth and Cult Among Primitive People* (Chicago: University of Chicago Press, 1963; first published 1951). An interpretation by a leading ethnologist of the religious configurations found in primitive culture.

J. Maringer, *The Gods of Prehistoric Man* (New York: Knopf, 1960; first published 1952). A description of the evidence in an interpretation meant for the general reader. Pictures and diagrams are included.

Recent introductions to the interpretation of artifacts and archeological evidence for understanding prehistorical peoples, including religious life, are Grahame Clark, *World Prehistory in New Perspective*, 3rd ed. (London: Cambridge University Press, 1977); Grahame Clark, *Mesolithic Prelude: The Palaeolithic-Neolithic Transition in Old World Prehistory* (Edinburgh: University Press, 1980); and *Brian M. Fagan, *People of the Earth: An Introduction to World Prehistory*, 3rd ed. (Boston: Little, Brown, 1980).

Two books that explore the religious meaning of cave art found from Spain to the Black Sea and dating from about 30,000 to 10,000 B.C.E. are:

André Leroi-Gourhan, *Treasures of Prehistoric Art* (New York: Harry N. Abrams, 1967). This oversized volume contains many colored illustrations, discusses the methodological difficulties in dating the art forms, and suggests interpretations of their significance.

Paul Shepard, *The Tender Carnivore and the Sacred Game* (New York: Charles Scribner's, 1973). A synthetic interpretation of the world view, rituals, and social attitudes of a hunting culture based on the art and design of the "cave temples" found in Western Europe.

Two interpretive analyses of prehistoric evidence for the worship of the Mother-Goddess are E. O. James, *The Cult of the Mother-Goddess* (London: Thames and Hudson, 1959); and S. von Cles-Reden, *The Realm of the Great Goddess: The Story of the Megalith Builders* (London: Thames and Hudson, 1961).

CHAPTER 12

Psychological and Social Functions of Religion

When the scholars discussed in the previous chapter were unable to find the basic character of religion in its origin, those scholars who followed them shifted their focus to studies of the role, or function, of religion in social interaction. This approach to the study of religion attracted mainly researchers from the social sciences, which were taking shape at the beginning of the present century. These scholars, whom we will call "functionalists," shared the following assumption: Both the *fact* of religiousness and the *variety* of religious forms are the products of cultural, psychological, and social conditions.

Viewed in this way, religion becomes one of several forces in the life of a culture, a society, or an individual. Social scientists who study religion as it functions in society may, for example, examine religious rites in terms of their psychological ability to relieve the fear of death, or they may analyze how religion has served as a means for self-affirmation among the powerless and poor. In both cases, they are treating religion as a *part* of human living, rather than as the center of life.

In this chapter, we describe the functional approach to the scientific study of religion. Although this approach is not the only one found in the social sciences, it has been important to the study of religion during the past century and still provides an important general method of interpretation today. This approach assumes that societies are systems of interdependent parts and forces. Functionalists regard religion as both a product of society and a contributing factor to it. In addition, religious institutions may be an important influence on the personal development of an individual. In combination with the family, the educational system, and government, religion helps make up a total cultural system. Functionalists define culture broadly as a complex set of symbolic, institutional, and physical systems that interact with each other to structure human life.

Whereas some social scientists limit their studies to the description or clarification of specific data (such as what economic class of people attends the Episcopal church), others define the strength of their discipline as its ability to test theories of social interaction through experimental methods. Through observation, social scientists (including psychologists, sociologists, and cultural anthropologists) construct theories that will tell them about the basic character of religion as it functions in developing personality, molding social institutions, and creating cultural patterns. To highlight the way that the social sciences study religion, we briefly examine in turn the basic issues, key figures, and interpretive views found in psychology, sociology, and cultural anthropology.

RELIGION AS THE SUBJECT OF PSYCHOLOGY

The term *religion* is used in at least two basic senses in psychological studies. In the first sense, religion is defined as a set of accepted forms (prayer, worship, mystical experiences; see Part I) that are set off from, but related to, other forms of *personality* expression. In this context, religion has only limited significance for the human personality, since it is only one of several organizing factors—and not even the most important of these. From some psychologists' standpoint, religion provides a certain kind of social conditioning that can have either beneficial or detrimental effects on the person who is trying to adjust to society. For instance, the psychologist might ask: "Do the Baptist restrictions on dancing, smoking, and drinking add to or subtract from an individual's mental health?"

In the second psychological sense, the term *religion* is sometimes used to mean self-fulfillment. This definition recognizes religion and its functions as basic to personality integration, spiritual wholeness, and self-fulfillment. The study of religion in this sense does not require that the investigator accept a particular theological proposition—for instance, ahout the reality of God as the object of worship. It only assumes that the human personality requires moral and spiritual values to achieve self-fulfillment.

These two definitions have caused a split within psychology. The first, religion as accepted forms, is used by many researchers who follow experimental behaviorism. This approach stresses the use of repeated experiments and interprets human behavior as the sole result of a stimulus-response mechanism. The first definition is also used in the clinical psychology of Sigmund Freud. The second definition, religion as central to human wholeness, is found in the work of Gordon Allport, Carl Jung, and some of the more contemporary approaches in the humanistic movements in American psychology (see Chapter 6).

The Experimental and Analytical Approaches

William James. Elements of both approaches to the psychological study of religion appear in the work of the founder of American psychology, William James. As early as 1874, James set up the first laboratory for psychological testing. In 1890, he published his seminal *Principles of Psychology*, in which he introduced, among other concepts, the notion of a stream of consciousness in mental life and of a self making decisions within that consciousness. For James, a spiritual self was an identifiable aspect of personality develop ment. Then, in *The Varieties of Religious Experience* (1902), James excited the general public with his interpretations of religion and his analysis of differ- ent forms of personal religious experience. In applying scholarly investiga- tion and scientific method to the study of religion, James demonstrated (1) the effects that personality factors had on observable religious phenomena and (2) the role of personal religious experience in personality growth.

Wilhelm Wundt. The position that human religious behavior could be studied experimentally (developed by William James) influenced a late nineteenth- century movement that attempted to pattern psychology on the natural sciences. A major spokesman for this approach was the German psycholo- gist Wilhelm Wundt, who founded his experimental laboratory for psycho- logical testing in 1879. The influence that this laboratory method had on American psychological studies was enormous; much of psychology came to be limited to that which could be observed and measured. As a result, psychology developed into the scientific study of behavior. In this ex- perimental context, *religion* was defined as both (1) conventional institu- tional activity and (2) one of many influences that condition peoples' observ- able and measurable social behavior. Notions of a religious consciousness that could not be measured as a part of this natural world were regarded as unscientific and therefore not a subject of psychological analysis.

This attitude, which reduced religion to the status of observable emo- tional behavior, is responsible for a number of recent studies that regard religion simply as the internalization of ritual forms in the culture. This data-based view of religion is often found in questionnaires for mental and personality testing. Some scholars have pointed out that the measures of religiosity in religious-preference questionnaires are designed (either con- sciously or unconsciously) to indicate how close a person is to certain tradi- tional religious practices, rather than to uncover the nature of his or her religiosity. Responses to questions like "Is there a life after death?" "Is the Bible inspired?" "Does the devil exist?" indicate only whether an individual subscribes to certain accepted forms. A person who has dropped out of a fundamentalist sect to work for peace, civil liberties, and open housing in non-church-related organizations might get a low score on such a religiosity test, although he would score high on a preference test given by members of a social action association. There are many other difficulties in drawing up a questionnaire that will reveal the deepest values of a person or of a signifi- cant sample of the population. Unless questionnaires, which the general public may depend on for information, can be designed to explore both traditional and nontraditional religious experience, they lead to invalid con- clusions about religious life in a modern world.

Sigmund Freud. Sigmund Freud also influenced studies of the psychology of religion. Freud held that religion is a self-imposed psychological mechan- ism, which people use to control their feelings of helplessness, fear of aggression, and sexual energies. A person's conscience, in Freud's view, is an internalized control mechanism—the civilizing force learned from one's family and culture. The violated conscience produces psychic pain and guilt. For instance, if a culture says that adultery is against God's law, the adulterer will make that rule an internal one. It is that internal rule, or conscience, that will cause the adulterer to feel guilty and distressed. Indeed, a well-conditioned conscience may produce guilty feelings even before the bad act.

In general, Freud regarded organized religion as a kind of fantasy people use to recover a lost sense of childlike intimacy with parents. Now largely discredited, Freud's theory about the origin of religion was that it arose from an organized community guilt over the sons' original murder of their tribal father (remember the Oedipus complex?). Nevertheless, Freud's effort to locate psychic powers and forces below the level of consciousness (the subconscious) has made a major contribution to the psychological study of religion.

For Freud, religion (by which he meant the Judeo-Christian morality of his time) was the social control over an individual's inner, psychic, energy, which is instinctive. When psychic energy is repressed, he claimed, its natural expression is redirected into socially acceptable religious and artistic forms. Such expressions relieve the anxieties caused by the repression. Sometimes, however, the psychic energy is so strong that it breaks through the conventional modes of regulation. This breaking out is called neurosis. Religion as a defense against instinctual drives and irrational forces was satisfactory in an earlier, nonscientific culture in which myth was alive and ritual actually controlled human self-awareness (see Chapter 3). However, Freud warned that in an intellectual and rational age, traditional religion is only an infantile attempt to use the psychic force creatively.

Clyde Kluckhohn and Edwin O. James. An interpretation closely related to Freud's places a higher value on the function of religious activity. This view assumes that the function of religion is to give people something to hold on to in times of personal crisis. Scholars such as anthropologist Clyde Kluckhohn and historian E. O. James emphasize the fact that human beings live in an environment full of dangers and hazards. Religion helps people maintain their integrity in the face of biological, physical, social, and psychological threats—the most profound of which is death. Religious rituals are social forces that offer stability and reinforcement to the person and to society in the face of disaster. These rituals promise rewards more significant than those ordinary life can offer. Consider the Christian crusader or the Muslim who goes to war for a holy cause. War is terrible, but the committed believer may be fearless for if he dies, he will attain a higher reward in paradise. Through religious beliefs and rituals, humans may anticipate potential threats and, as a result, be better able to handle them when they come. Notice that, even on a happy occasion like a marriage, the vows in the Christian church anticipate the triple sadnesses of sickness, poverty, and death.

The Humanist Approach

Not all psychologists and psychiatrists define religion as organized ritual and moral practice or interpret its basic significance as control of fear and irrational drives. To some, as suggested earlier, religion represents the most complete human awareness and means to achieving self-fulfillment. Religion is the most profound expression of personhood whether through "normal," socially acceptable religious practices or through "abnormal" attempts to preserve self-integrity. Here *abnormal* can mean either neurotic responses to fear and anxiety or simply a healthy, religious expression that rises above the do's and don'ts of one's culture (recall St. Theresa and Miki in Chapter 2). Religious institutions may add to or subtract from self-fulfillment, but religiousness always leads to freedom and completeness. Among those who stress the life-enhancing powers of religion are Gordon Allport, Carl Jung, and those who represent more recent trends within existential-humanistic and transpersonal psychology (described later).

Gordon Allport. Allport's classic statement is *The Individual and His Religion* (1950). He argues from the standpoint of a scientist interested in the uniqueness of each individual's expression of religious awareness, in particular, the function of this awareness in the mature personality. For Allport, the individual's religiousness begins with an introduction to outward religious forms, which she or he personally interprets. However, no matter how similar those outward forms might be (such as everything in a Roman Catholic church on Sunday morning, including the celebration of a mass), the enormous variety of ways in which people can combine them makes the spiritual response of each individual unique. Indeed, there are as many varieties of religious experience as there are religious people.

Once the religious forms have been introduced by the family or the culture, an individual's religious development is affected by such factors as bodily needs, intelligence, interests, curiosity, and cultural symbols. The combination of these factors, Allport feels, creates a religious "sentiment." For his purposes, Allport defines *sentiment* as an organized system of thoughts and feelings directed toward some identifiable object of value. In the case of religious sentiment, the object of value has such ultimate importance that a person's conditioned religious behavior takes on a life of its own. At that point, one can no longer say that religion is just another stimulus. An individual has formed a mature religious sentiment when he or she has succeeded in integrating such influences as parental hopes ("Grow up and raise a family!"), legal restraints ("It is illegal to take merchandise without paying for it"), personal relations with others ("You are my friend"), and body sensations ("Oh, that feels good!") into a feeling of individual responsibility and a sense of meaning in life. From Allport's point of view, a religious sentiment is mature when it develops along avenues of widening interest and self-unification and when it creates a discriminating, dynamic attitude that leads to moral living and a comprehensive picture of existence.

Carl Jung. Carl Jung, who also offered psychological insights into the meaning of religion, saw religion as the strongest value within the organizing process of the human psyche. "That psychological fact," he said, "which is the greatest power in your system is the god, since it is always the overwhelming psychic factor which is called god. As soon as the god ceases to be an overwhelming factor, he becomes a mere name."[1]

Jung understood humanity not simply as a combination of biological and chemical forces but as a totality that includes both conscious and unconscious existence. The integration of these two parts of mental life is the highest point in the evolution of the unique spiritual possibilities of the human personality. This integration, according to Jung, does not just happen. It can be achieved only through discovering and struggling with the depths of consciousness. According to Jung, the unconscious forces are always religious, for they are the most profound influences on people as they create their own humanity. Jung's insight has been reinforced by other psychologists who point out that, when parents, society, or the church itself blocks the religious urge, it may destroy a person's basic religious potential. This destruction may result in neurosis or psychosis.

Contemporary Psychological Trends

Many contemporary psychologists assume there is a universal human need to express one's full potential, no matter how that fullness is defined. From this point of view, the neurotic person and the dramatic convert (say, from Methodism to Krishna Consciousness) share a common personality conflict. As a result of this conflict, both the neurotic and the convert adopt behavior that may appear to be inappropriate to preserve their center, their own existence. The psychotherapist Rollo May and other scholars of existential psychology address this issue when they speak of the basic need for self-affirmation. Existential psychology is an understanding of the personality that focuses on a description of the "immediate experiencing" people have as they perceive existence and make decisions about their lives. This position suggests that neurosis or radical conversion cannot be identified with a failure to adjust to social standards. Human social and religious conduct cannot be defined simply as adaptive behavior in reaction to appropriate stimuli, as the behaviorists would say. In fact, defining religion as socialized adjustment ignores the larger part of human life that requires a comprehensive goal or purpose. From May's point of view, people achieve that goal through expressing the uniqueness of their individual personalities—a uniqueness that does not fit within the behaviorist mold.

Some other contemporary (and nontraditional) trends in the areas of humanistic (secular) and transpersonal (requiring a transcendent goal) psychology also focus on the life-enhancing values of religion that go beyond simple socialized adjustment. The humanistic movement emphasizes meaning and values in science and the development of healthy relationships between people. In this movement, investigators are concerned with religious values as they function in mental health. By contrast, representatives of the transpersonal movement emphasize the psychology of spiritual growth within the evolving personality. This group emphasizes techniques and states of consciousness associated with acting out religious values inside or outside organized religious institutions. Both humanistic and transpersonal psychologists maintain that a person's religious self-fulfillment may or may not be expressed within the forms of an historical religious tradition.

RELIGION AS THE SUBJECT OF SOCIOLOGY

Whereas psychologists have looked at religion as it affects the personality development of an individual, sociologists focus on religion as it interacts with other social forces. In general, sociologists interpret religious phenomena either in terms of religious functions within the society (recall Chapter 3 on myth and sacrament and Chapter 4 on cosmic order) or in terms of the interaction among religious structures and other social structures.

Religion is an appropriate study for sociologists because it provides both integrating and conserving forces for a society. First of all, religious affiliation gives people a sense of identity and belonging. The basic meaning of religious symbols and rituals in this context is found in socially integrating images; such symbolic forms define what is true and good for all members of a society. These images contain an implicit obligation, namely, that one should live according to the values expressed in the religious symbols. To do otherwise is to move toward self-destruction and the destruction of all humanity.

The second significant role of religion in society is that religion helps establish a system of social relationships that preserve the social order. These social relationships extend beyond the bounds of the religious institution into other social institutions. Consider the connection between the American legal system and Judeo-Christian morality. Although the Ten Commandments have no secular authority, they stand firmly behind legal and social definitions of good and bad conduct in the society. For all actions, a person can expect rewards for conforming to the highest norms and punishments for deviating from them.

A third role of religion in society, which is connected with the two preceding, is the power to relate the society to a value beyond the society. Religious institutions furnish or support the norms of other social institutions by placing not only ritual activities but also all life activities under the judgment of an ultimate purpose (such as God's will or Buddha Amida's vow to bring all beings to the Pure Land). Ideally, the moral taught in a Sunday school lesson should carry over into a Christian's work and family life. How religion fits in with a variety of society's integrating and controlling systems, then, is the focus of the sociology of religion. The following pages describe the major contributions of some of the historically important figures in the sociology of religion.

Emile Durkheim and Max Weber. Two famous scholars who interpreted religious life in relation to social forces were Emile Durkheim and Max Weber. For Durkheim—who made his major contributions early in the twentieth century—religion was real when it expressed the vital energy of social interaction. Religious life had its roots in a cause more basic than individual thought or feeling, namely social forces (page 198). What human being designated as God was basically a symbolic expression of society's group (or corporate) definition of itself. Durkheim stressed that religious self-fulfillment was determined by a person's participation in the group norms, ideals, and expectations through which he or she gained a self-image. Personhood, for him, depended heavily on how well an individual took the values of the social order and turned them into internal expressions. So, the more able the orthodox Muslim Saudi Arabian is to conform to the social structure prescribed by the Qur'an, the more he or she is fulfilled individually.

A few years after Durkheim had formulated his approach to religion in the social structure, Max Weber approached the same topic from a different direction. Durkheim took religious expression as a universal condition of all human societies; Weber suggested that different religious forms functioned according to specific self-awareness as expressed in particular historical situations. Weber did not reduce religious feeling to social forces; rather, inner religious meaning and social forces interacted. Not only did social norms influence individual behavior but individual answers to such universal human problems as suffering, evil, and death had profound consequences on social development. For example, Weber related charisma, the unexplainable spiritual power that some people have to lead others, to social processes. In his view, religious leaders who are charismatic individuals, such as Muhammad in the seventh century C.E., or the Reverend Sun Myung Moon, who leads the Unification church today, have power due to deep psychic links with their followers. Such individuals embody the reorganization of social patterns for their followers and develop new religious movements. In this way, Weber focused on the interaction of social forces within the individual and the group to account for the changes found in a religious tradition or a cultural way of life.

Durkheim and Weber influenced many later scholars who applied social science concepts to the interpretation of religion. A number of them relegated religion to the role of a "social mobilizer and integrator of a social group." They regarded social forces as the basic reality and saw social organization as the fact that is necessary for the development of an individual self.

Joachim Wach. In his *Sociology of Religion,* Joachim Wach defined religion in relation to natural groups (family, kinship, racial cults), different forms of religious organization, different social strata, political systems, and types of religious authority. By this approach, Wach was responding to the contemporary assumption that religion can be expressed differently at different times in the same culture and can be defined in different ways. In fact, in a single society, religion may have both complementary and antagonistic functions. Wach's purpose was to examine the interaction of various religious functions as they were expressed in different social institutions.

Wach found a variety of roles within religious communities, as well as multiple relationships between the religious community and the rest of social life. Applying a scheme similar to Wach's, many recent sociological studies have analyzed particular religious institutions and their relationships to social patterns. The social structures or institutions are the lenses through which values in personal belief are examined. A single religious practice, such as the singing of hymns, may appear in variations depending on the social factor (national groupings, sex, age, and class) through which it is viewed. Religion in this view is not culturally constant but culturally relative to other social institutions.

Robert Bellah, W. Lloyd Warner, and Thomas Luckmann. Another recent trend in the sociology of religion challenges the notion that "church" and "religion" are naturally linked. Some sociologists have criticized the identification of church with religion on the grounds that it provides too narrow a definition of religion and religious institutions. Besides omitting much relevant data, they say, such an approach fails to recognize that, in a twentieth-century industrial society, the established institutions of religion constitute neither the source nor the expression of the most important values.

Robert Bellah and W. Lloyd Warner have pointed out the impact of "civil religion" in America.[2] They regard as religious activities such cultural expressions as annual Memorial Day ceremonies, the funeral rites for President John F. Kennedy, or honor paid to the ideals of heroes of American history—especially those who were killed, such as Kennedy or Abraham Lincoln. Similarly, American editorials and speeches about democracy, patriotism, the virtues of the early (European) settlers, or values like strength, endurance, and energetic effort are imbued with a sacredness that places the American people and the "American way of life" in the dimension of ultimate values.

In an analysis not restricted to the American scene, Thomas Luckmann, in *The Invisible Religion,* says that every society has "a configuration of meaning," which is internalized by the individuals of that society.[3] This configuration has various levels of significance, and the highest level in the hierarchy of meanings expressed in special symbols is the religious expression of a society. Luckmann suggests that sociologists look for religious forces in modern industrial society under such themes as "self-realization," "mobility," "sexuality," and "familism."

The contemporary phenomenon of secularization is an example of this thinking. Some scholars point out that the notion of secularization as the loss of power by the traditional institutions of religious activity is inadequate as sociological theory as it fails to recognize all the ways in which the transcendent fits within the social fabric. According to the critics, the sociological understanding of religion cannot be limited to the analysis of certain institutions that have been labeled "religious," but must encompass all structures of society whereby people seek and express their most profound self-awareness. Technology, politics, psychiatry, or art may be regarded as secular by traditional theological norms, but for a scientific study, they may represent the most powerful social expressions of value change.

RELIGION AS THE SUBJECT OF CULTURAL ANTHROPOLOGY

Students of cultural anthropology—the intellectual heirs of Durkheim, Weber, and Freud—have taken religion seriously as one aspect of cultural patterning. Like these predecessors, anthropologists usually assume that religion is derived from cultural and social needs. From the anthropological point of view, religion serves those needs in at least two ways: (1) It establishes patterns of cultural self-awareness, and (2) it reestablishes a balance within society after a crisis such as war or the death of a leader.

In the first case, anthropologists regard religion as a system of ideas and emotional responses to life through which a culture creates and defines certain habits of action like rituals and ceremonies. Through these cultural habits, the society develops a cultural self-awareness. The basis for interpreting religious forms as "cultural habits" is that a framework of human activity underlies any particular formal expression of culture, such as initiation ceremonies. As a matter of fact, cross-cultural comparison starts with the assumption that behind the different religious expressions, all people have the same common needs. All people face the problems of obtaining food and shelter and the events of birth, illness, war, and death. Although different value systems, rites, and beliefs provide various answers to human problems, the problems are defined by human biology and social interaction.

Other anthropologists have concentrated on religion's second function of establishing a balance in a society after some crisis. In early studies of tribal societies, anthropologists determined that the function of religion was to preserve the social order through rites and rituals. For these scholars, religion was the human effort to control the unexplainable aspects of life; the social phenomena of magic, religion, and science were attempts by people to reach progressively higher levels of social awareness in order to fill gaps in knowledge and to deal with uncontrolled natural forces in an orderly manner. Although this interpretation has been criticized by scholars who have made detailed studies of magic, religion, and science as social expressions, it is still influential in generalized anthropological interpretations of religion.

In studying this second function, some anthropologists interpret myths and rituals within the more general context of social tensions and crises common to all cultures. Religion becomes the symbolic dramatization of a common system of sentiments, which is repeated not only periodically to condition the culture but especially at points of danger or threat to the personal or cultural life. Such crucial personal experiences as birth, puberty, marriage, and death, as well as experiences that hold a society of individuals together as a culture (for example, recounting the origin of the culture or community, reaffirming the necessity to keep a specific community in hostile or friendly relations, or celebrating the relation of humankind to the cosmos) all require symbols and symbolic activities whereby the community identifies itself and preserves the value patterns that are at the root of self-identification.

The following paragraphs explain the views of two important scholars of the anthropological study of religion.

Alfred L. Kroeber. As we noted, from an anthropological view, religion is seen as a system of ideas and emotional responses used by a culture to create, define, and establish habitual ways of action through which the society interprets and validates itself. This view of religion is found in the works of Alfred L. Kroeber, who emphasizes that the essential elements of a culture are its patterns.[4] For example, a comparison of Japanese, Indian, Saudi Arabian, and American social life show significant differences in child-rearing, incorporation of young adults into adult society, and attitudes toward aging and death. These patterns integrate people into an organization and provide the channels whereby segments of society can function as a culture. The particular relationships among individuals, between individuals and small groups, among small groups, and between the individual and the whole culture are established and conditioned by overriding organizations (sometimes by traditional religions) that play a powerful, conservative role in society.

At this point in Kroeber's argument, one might think he is saying that impersonal powers alone form society. On the contrary, individual human agents both create and embody cultural events. When viewed from a long-range perspective, individuals predominantly express established cultural traits rather than individual forms, which are different from those of that culture. At the same time, individuals act as *if* their individual personalities do change cultural events, and occasionally a few individuals may stretch and sometimes tear the fabric of society, which must then be rewoven. History gives such examples as Napoleon Bonaparte, Joseph Stalin, and Mao Tse-tung.

Claude Levi-Strauss. The work of the French cultural anthropologist Claude Levi-Strauss exemplifies the approach called "structuralism," a concept used by a diverse group of scholars who attempt to discover the meaning of myth. The problem for structuralists is to determine how myth operates below the level of consciousness in people's minds. This effort searches for the significant meanings and the structural laws beneath surface patterns of meaning and intention. Such meaning is to be found in sets of symbols in cultural communication systems, including mathematics, music, literature, ritual, language, art, and myth.

Structuralists do not dismiss myths, stories, and sayings from ancient and contemporary peoples as meaningless superstition. On the contrary, they believe these expressions operate with strict logic to communicate meaning. For example, Levi-Strauss, in his four-volume *Introduction to a Science of Mythology*, analyzes the myths of the Indians of North and South

America in terms of the abstract ideas within concrete images. He points out that these people recognize that certain objects, animals, plants, people, places, and events (whether real or imagined) have sacred status in a community, not because they are sublimations of repressed emotions (as Freud believed), not because they have social force for preserving group identity (as Durkheim claimed), and not because they have practical uses to control social groups (as Karl Marx asserted), but because they communicate meaning. The stories embody general ideas; they make comprehension of the world possible in terms of dramatic images.

From his studies of preliterate peoples and myths, Levi-Strauss formulated general hypotheses about symbol making that he claims are valid, historically and cross-culturally. In *The Savage Mind* (1966), he argues that human beings have equal capacity for thought; the differences among groups lie in the concrete experiences they have to think about. The mind (thought) of the modern scientist is in no sense superior to the mind of the primitive hunter. Levi-Strauss rejects the often-assumed contrast between primitive and advanced societies, the notions of historical progress and the evolutionary superiority of any race or people or of any human symbol system. From Levi-Strauss's point of view, all religions and myths are valuable and meaningful for the people participating in them. Finally, no one can prove that any particular symbol system within a society (such as mathematics or science) is basically more meaningful than any other symbol system (such as music or myth). All operate with the same organ of the body—the brain—for the same purpose: to communicate meaning to other human beings.

SUMMARY

The key notions of the approaches to the function of religion in social scientific study are the following:

Religion first became the subject of social scientific exploration as the social sciences began to apply the scientific methods of observation and experimentation to the ways in which religion operates in a culture. Each discipline brought its own particular perspective to the search for the answer to the question: How do we understand what religion really means?

Psychologists found their answers in the individual's integration of religious experience and behavior into his or her personality. For them, religion was either one of several organizing factors or it was central to the whole effort of self-development; it was a controlling or liberating mechanism in the formation of one's personality.

Sociologists look at religion a little differently. To them, it seems limiting to try to understand the deepest meaning of religion through individual personality development. Sociology has taken the view that the deepest meaning of religion expresses itself in one of two ways: either as a force that gives coherence to societies or as the ultimate structure for justifying rewards and punishments within the culture. In any case, religion is the cultural glue that keeps societies from falling apart.

Although cultural anthropologists hold a view that sounds similar to the sociologists', their approach is less concerned with contemporary trends in social patterning than with the question of when and how religion is most potent, which they have tried to answer through cross-cultural observations. There are two dominant responses to this question. One group maintains that religion works to establish the most important general patterns in the culture. Others assert that religious forces are most powerful and purposeful when they rise to meet a crisis: birth, death, war.

SELECTED READINGS

An excellent statement briefly explaining the scientific study of religion is "Religion," *International Encyclopedia of the Social Sciences*, edited by D. L. Sills (New York: Macmillan, 1968). Three prominent scholars, an anthropologist, sociologist, and psychologist, discuss past and present studies of religion in their respective fields. Each essayist places the study of religion in the context of Western intellectual history.

Introductions to social scientific study of religion can be found in the following anthologies, which give both historically important and recent interpretations: W. A. Lessa and E. Z. Vogt. *Reader in Comparative Religion: An Anthropological Approach*, 3rd ed. (New York: Harper & Row, 1972). W. M. Newman, ed. *The Social Meanings of Religion: An Integrated Anthology* (Chicago: Rand McNally, 1974); O. Strunk, ed., *Psychology of Religion* (Nashville: Abingdon, 1971).

Psychological studies of religion include:

*G. W. Allport, *The Individual and His Religion* (New York: Macmillan, 1950). This classic in the psychology of religion examines the nature, development, and influence of subjective religious life in the mature personality. See especially Chapter 2 for an example of methods used to collect data on religious beliefs, using a traditional approach to psychological inquiry.

*W. James, *The Varieties of Religious Experience* (New York: Modern Library, 1929; first published in 1902). A classic exposition of a scientific study of religion, available in an inexpensive edition.

*R. May, ed., *Existential Psychology* (New York: Random House, 1960). A collection of essays by R. May, A. Maslow, H. Feifel, C. Rogers, and G. Allport reflecting the need to deepen concepts that define the human condition.

*J. White, ed., *Frontiers of Consciousness: The Meeting Ground Between Inner and Outer Reality* (New York: Julien Press, 1974). A book of readings on contemporary topics in transpersonal psychology, which focuses on the relevancy of consciousness as an object of study and as experience of transcendent awareness.

C. T. Tart, ed., *Transpersonal Psychologies* (New York: Harper & Row, 1975). Various scholars analyze religious expressions from around the world to expose the psychological significance of spiritual experiences.

Sociological studies of religious life include:

*M. Weber, *The Sociology of Religion* (Boston: Beacon, 1963; first published 1922). One of the most famous social scientists of this century exposes his approach to religious phenomena in an analysis of the relationships between religious convictions and human conduct, especially in terms of economic patterns and social grouping. The book also contains a very helpful analysis by T. Parsons of Weber's contribution to the study of religious life.

*J. M. Yinger, *The Scientific Study of Religion* (New York: Macmillan, 1970). A substantial, but introductory, account of methods and problems in the study of religion by social scientists. Besides introducing the reader to the field of sociology of religion, Yinger discusses several prominent areas of current investigation in light of a field theory of religion.

*P. Berger and T. Luckmann, *The Social Construction of Reality* (Garden City, NY: Doubleday, 1966). This study in the sociology of knowledge is an introductory analysis of the objectivation, institutionalization and legitimation of "reality," which is seen as the product of social construction.

*J. W. Sutherland, *A General Systems Philosophy for the Social and Behavioral Sciences* (New York: Braziller, 1973). A discussion of some of the implications of general systems theory for study in the social and behavioral sciences; it is meant for advanced students of social sciences.

B. Wilson, *Religion in Sociological Perspective* (New York: Oxford University Press, 1982). A reflective analysis of the history, development, and areas of present research in the sociology of religion. The author is sensitive to the need to reformulate the basic theoretical concepts of this discipline to reflect a truly worldwide and comparative study of diverse social contexts in which religion is found.

R. Wuthnow, ed., *The Religious Dimension: New Directions in Quantitative Research* (New York: Academic Press, 1979). Summary essays by noted scholars on the state of research in religious institutions and beliefs that emphasize quantifiable data as found during the 1970s.

Anthropological studies of religion are found in :

*E. Norbeck, *Religion in Human Life: Anthropological Views* (New York: Holt, Rinehart & Winston, 1974). A brief but clear introduction to religion, defined as belief and behavior in relation to supernatural beings as part of socially created human culture.

*A. F. C. Wallace, *Religion: An Anthropological View* (New York: Random House, 1966). A contemporary representative analysis of religion from a naturalist perspective, which typically focuses on the social-cultural functions of the religious forms in preliterate and Western societies.

*C. Levi-Strauss, *Structural Anthropology*, trans. by C. Jacobson and B. G. Schoepf (Garden City, NY: Anchor Books, 1967; first published in 1963).

See especially Part III, "Magic and Religion," for an introduction to this contemporary anthropologist's structural approach to mythology. See also his *The Savage Mind*, translated by G. Weidenfeld (Chicago: University of Chicago Press, 1966).

T. van Baaren and H. Drijvers, ed., *Religion, Culture and Methodology* (The Hague: Mouton, 1973). A series of papers primarily by European sociologists and anthropologists emphasizing the limitations in the empirical methods and theoretical formulations in the "science of religion."

CHAPTER 13

The Comparative Study of Religion

Before embarking on the comparative approach to the study of religion, let us review where the discussion in Part Three has taken us so far. In Chapter 11 we looked at the study of religion's origins as a way to know about the meaning, function, and development of religion itself. This scholarly direction was dominant in religious studies during the latter half of the 1800s and into the early 1900s.

During the twentieth century, religious studies changed its emphasis from a search for origins to a search for the functions of religion in personality development and society. This direction was influenced by sociology, psychology, and anthropology, all of which were emerging disciplines in their own right. Those scholars who searched for functions believed that religions could be best understood if they could define how religious processes operated within the society and within the individual consciousness. Although their approaches are still being used in religious studies, some social scientists focused on a comparison of different forms and images of the major religious traditions themselves.

This chapter brings our discussion on the methodologies of religious studies well into the present century. Although the search for connections among religious expressions began with Max Mueller in *Comparative Mythology*, 1856, it really became important in the last quarter of the nineteenth century and into the twentieth. Basically, this approach asks two questions: (1) How are we to understand the religious expression of another person in a different culture and in a different time? and (2) How are we to perceive whatever is religious in others and in ourselves? These questions arise from the obvious fact that there exist dramatic differences in religious claims and forms of expression. Are these differences merely superficial? Does a common religiousness exist at a deep level in spite of apparent differences? If common ground could be found between conflicting religious expressions (Buddhist and Hindu, Muslim and Jew, Catholic and Protestant), would this common understanding contribute to the cause of world peace? So, the pursuits of these scholars are not idle exercises. Answers to their questions might affect humanity on the most fundamental level.

There is not one but three established ways of comparing religious expressions. The first is called the historical method and focuses on religious expressions as they fit within a historical context. The second approach, phenomenology, attempts to discover the intention of religious phenomena and to locate the structures of religious life in symbols, rites, and doctrines. The third approach examines the relation of religiousness to cultural systems. Although each approach has a different emphasis, all three attempt to be primarily *descriptive* rather than *normative* (value setting). For example, when the sixteenth-century Protestant reformer Martin Luther comments on the New Testament or the contemporary Zen master Shibayami Roshi speaks of the empty self, these are primarily normative statements even though they describe historical or psychological events. A normative statement is an exposition of a life commitment or conviction by an advocate. A descriptive statement, on the other hand, portrays the distinctive character or meaning of a religious phenomenon in relation to a general notion of religion, a historical context, or a universal set of social and cultural conditions. In general, students using the comparative method try to be descriptive as they seek to reveal the meaning of religious expression as it is felt and understood by those who follow it.

Predictably, any scholar who attempts to walk in the shoes of someone from another culture and to be objective at the same time is going to have some difficulties. Some of the problems that the student of comparative religion faces are as follows: (1) how to maintain objectivity in understanding a view or practice different from one's own; (2) how to avoid cultural bias by not implicitly defining religiousness in a way that frames the questions of the investigator; (3) how to cope with the lack of a neutral language of religious life so that one can make both unbiased *and* profound comparisons; and (4) how to take seriously the fact that all religious life is formed by historical-cultural forces without reducing religion to a function of some cultural force.

THE HISTORICAL METHOD

The historian of religions has had two major concerns: (1) to describe as objectively as possible the conditions and elements of a historical situation and (2) to recognize the changes in religious life that result from interactions with many cultural conditions surrounding a religious event. Historians have based their interpretations of religion on historical documents and other empirical evidence. Such documentation, they claim, permits them to gain an objective understanding of a religious event that divine revelation or transcendent insight cannot provide. For example, a historian might look at the historical Jesus as a person whose ideas derived from his culture and historical circumstances (he lived in a country occupied and governed by the Romans). This approach shifts the concern from Jesus as the son of God, which is a theological claim, to Jesus as a man existing in time, which can be verified by data compiled through the study of ancient texts and languages. By looking at the figure of Jesus from a historical perspective, historians attempt to discover the contextual meaning of the religious forms that grew out of teachings of Jesus.

Once an event or a practice has been placed in a historical framework, it may be properly compared with other similar events or practices in other cultures. Take the practice of sacrifice, for instance. From the historian's point of view, the general term *sacrifice* does not mean the same thing in all respects in different languages and social contexts. Human events are better understood by analyzing specific cultural contexts than they are by abstracting similar-looking forms from one historical framework and comparing them with forms taken from an entirely different historical framework. For example, historians maintain that a close study of the ancient priestly sacrifice in India, as expressed in the Brahmanas, reveals a meaning quite different from the "sacrifice of God's son" as described by Paul in the Christian New Testament. Sacrifice may be a common form of religious expression, but its meaning is more closely related to its cultural context than to a comparable form from another cultural context.

Historians of religion believe that the details of human life are more important than the universal patterns of human life. Although the historian assumes that men and women of the past and of different cultures are sufficiently similar to us so that we can understand them, he or she emphasizes that it makes a real difference whether a person was born in first-century Rome, in ninth-century China, or in the twentieth-century United States. The historian is concerned with the meaning of these differences; to know these distinctions is to get an understanding of oneself that can be had in no other way. Birth in a particular time and place conditions the forms and meaning available to a person. Time limits a person's possibilities, but any particular moment in time also has great potential meaning. Thus, the historian values the uniqueness and the significance of historical data.

As a result of this emphasis, the abstractions and generalizations used in common speech begin to lose their usefulness as definitions. For instance, such terms as *Islam, Hinduism,* or *Buddhism* are convenient but very rough abstractions for groups of beliefs and practices that may vary enormously in different cultural and historical settings. Historians, therefore, are not content to understand the meaning of religious life by describing only the dominant or orthodox position of a religion. Instead, they emphasize the changes brought about by particular people or events, the differences between subgroups or movements within a tradition, and the particularities of the organizations, practices, and symbols used by different people. When they study the religions of the world, historians most often focus on cultural factors as the greatest determinants of human meaning. From this perspective, to say that the practice of Islam varies considerably from border to border in the Middle East is to say more than "Iran and Saudi Arabia are both Muslim countries."

So far in this discussion of the historical approach to comparative religion, we have touched on two important historical assumptions: (1) The meaning of religious forms depends primarily on a particular historical-cultural context, and (2) the accurate description of a historical context is basic to understanding any human phenomenon—including religion. Both assumptions suggest that measurements are at the core of understanding. A third assumption that historians make is: (3) *Human* data presents the investigator with an "incalculable individuality," which makes any study less than 100 percent objective or predictable. This last point is important because it is this human element that separates historical studies from studies in the natural sciences.

According to German theologian and philosopher Ernst Troeltsch (1865–1923), historical causes and effects cannot be measured like natural causes and effects because of the human element. Causality in natural science, Troeltsch said, takes the form of an unchanging give and take. If the basic material of the world is energy, cause may be seen as the transformation of energy from one form to another, which follows an observable pattern of change. In contrast, historical causation is mostly a matter of psychological motivation and sensitivity.

Because historical reality is an expression of human consciousness, historians see cultural changes in relation to the conscious, as well as unconscious, efforts of human beings. What is unique about the causal force in human consciousness is that the initiative for change is found not only in a person's past but also very forcefully in an expected result, goal, or purpose. This complexity of motives gives a particular character to human events. The freedom in psychosocial conditions of the individual or group introduces an incalculable element. So, human life includes the possibility of generating something new, something more than what might happen because of impersonal forces.

It is, in fact, this incalculable individuality, this ability to form a new reality, that is at the center of historical studies. Historical study does not attempt to learn the universal laws by which all particular phenomena are understood, but rather tries to understand the uniqueness of the historical phenomena it investigates. It attempts to reconstruct as closely as possible the human events under investigation as they occurred within their own specific and unique historical setting. Historical reality, then, is quite different from natural or physical reality, which can be understood through universal laws.

We can summarize this discussion in the following way: In comparing religions, historians maintain that the comparisons must be made between culturally similar events and rituals rather than between nominally similar ones. Historians also hold that religions change and develop according to surrounding events. Finally, historians are quick to remind us that religious changes are not the result of impersonal forces in history in the same way that natural change seems to be absolutely moved by cause and effect. In historical studies, human unpredictability must be figured into the equation.

The historical method in religious studies has called attention to the importance of comparing like to like and to differences to arrive at accurate and objective results.

THE PHENOMENOLOGICAL METHOD

Descriptive phenomenology in the study of religion can be defined as the art of interpreting the *intention* of religion, that is, the phenomenologist studies the meaning of concrete religious data, not according to historical influences, but according to the intentions of the advocates. In general, phenomenologists share the four following assumptions: (1) The intentional structure in the consciousness of religious advocates exposes the deepest meaning in concrete religious forms (like ritual, sacrifice, and so on); (2) the meaning of religious forms (phenomena) is most clearly exposed by comparing typical patterns or processes of religious life; (3) religiousness has its own unique quality or character that cannot be reduced to, or simply caused or explained by, other human forces; and (4) it is necessary for the investigator to participate empathically in the intention of the religious advocate being studied while setting aside his or her personal value perspective.

What these assumptions come down to is that one cannot get to the real meaning of religion through any route other than the self-understanding of religious people or through any other mind but the believer's. Thus, phenomenologists set themselves the difficult task of laying aside their own cultural biases and religious conditioning, entering the consciousness of the devotee as much as possible, feeling what the devotee feels, then looking at the information that their empathic nets have collected. A social scientist might not be satisfied with the intuitive knowledge that the phenomenologist brings out of an empathic study, but for the phenomenologist there is no other way to really understand the meaning of religious phenomena.

In the phenomenological study of religion, there are two main areas of concern: (1) the attempt to find the specifically religious power or intention of religious phenomena and (2) the attempt to locate structures or patterns of religious life in symbols, rites, and doctrines that human beings have used at different times. We look here at the work of three different scholars who have been influenced by the concerns. Only one, Gerardus van der Leeuw, has seen himself as a phenomenologist of religion per se; however, the other two are recognized by other scholars in comparative religion as being very influential in the effort to understand the intention found in religious phenomena.

Rudolf Otto. Otto, a German professor of Christian theology, wrote one of the classic books highlighting the unique quality of religious phenomena. In *The Idea of the Holy* (1917), Otto assumed that the holy is a unique quality that is not identified with anything else in life and that religious awareness is a unique part of human consciousness. For him, the essential character of all religious awareness was a feeling of awe toward, yet fascination with, this wholly other reality (God). God was not simply a human idea of a feeling. God was a mysterious reality confronting the individual person with an incomparable, overwhelming power—a power that struck awe, even horror, into people's hearts but that also had a captivating charm for people (recall Krishna and Arjuna in Chapter 2).

Otto, like other phenomenologists of religion, tried to avoid a clearly defined philosophical orientation. As a group, scholars who are sensitive to a phenomenological approach have asserted that any method of interpreting religion must include the recognition that *religious experience cannot be reduced to other elements of human life.* The lack of such awareness, they say, limits the study of religion to nonreligious factors. It is like reducing the aesthetic value of a great painting to the value of the canvas and pigments and the number of brush strokes made by the painter. In contrast, if investigators seek to expose religious meaning, they should make a detailed study of the peculiarities that make religious life significant for the religious adherent.

Gerardus van der Leeuw. Phenomenologist G. van der Leeuw, who was a member of a Protestant theological faculty in Holland, explained in *Religion in Essence and Manifestation* (1933) why studying the nature of religious phenomena requires an approach different from that of either the physical or the social sciences. Religious life, he said, is neither simply a subjective feeling nor an objective expression that can be isolated and studied as an independent entity. Every religious phenomenon (symbol, rite, feeling, awareness) involves an interaction between the object of attention (say, a communion wafer in the Christian Mass) and the subject of attention (the communicant). A phenomenon is "what appears." Whereas many people think of what appears as brute fact, van der Leeuw (like many phenomenologists) held that all facts include a person's interpretations of sensory input. Whatever is recognized as given in human experience (say, the wafer) is, at the same time, reconstructed by (the communicant's) visual perspective, emotional patterns, and evaluative ordering processes. What appears, then, is a result of a significant organization of the awareness of reality according to a structure of apprehension.

It is important to locate the phenomenon in the interaction between subject and object to avoid making religion either so exclusively subjective that it is inaccessible to anyone other than the devotee or so exclusively objective that it has no relation to the person's experience. In practice, the religious meaning of religious data is so profound that it is inexhaustible. For van der Leeuw, the significance of the inexhaustible meaning of religion was that God, in the last analysis, revealed himself; and human beings—including phenomenologists—could not understand divine utterance in its fullness. Human beings stood always at the frontier of mystery. Only when God came to people could they break out of their limited perceptions. Not all descriptive phenomenologists follow van der Leeuw's theological understanding of the relation between the unfathomable reality and the conditioned expression known in a particular moment of life. Nevertheless, they do recognize that the use of limited historical or symbolic forms to express the unfathomable source of all meaning is an important problem in interpreting religious significance.

As mentioned before, a central feature in the descriptive phenomenology of religion is grasping the religious meaning of an action or belief through the study of its structure. On the basis of his studies, van der Leeuw held that there were three fundamental structures of religious life: dynamism, animism, and deism. *Dynamism* refers to an ultimate impersonal power, like the Sioux Indians' *wakan* or the Melanesian notion of *mana*. *Animism* is power of life experienced as an encounter between spirits, souls, or other beings who have will power. *Deism* is a general term for the worship of a supreme being. These are the three basic patterns, he suggested, for apprehending the source of all religious life.

From the standpoint of Hindu, Buddhist, or Confucian understanding of human experience, this conclusion is quite narrow and reflects a Western—perhaps more specifically a Protestant Christian—bias. Very few Western scholars at present organize their general understanding of religion under these three headings. Nevertheless, the phenomenological method, with its focus on clarifying religious meaning by locating the basic structures of meaning, has been influential in academic circles, paralleling and sometimes overlapping with the structuralism of the social science.

Mircea Eliade. Eliade, emeritus professor of the history of religions at the University of Chicago, has tried to describe patterns of religious meaning through comparisons of specific myths and symbols. In his book *Patterns in Comparative Religion* (1949), Eliade interprets religious data according to various kinds of symbolic awareness (modalities) in light of his definition of religion as "the appearance of the sacred." Humanity has perceived the sacred dimension of life through different modalities, he says. Some of these modalities are symbolized by the sky, water, the waxing and waning of the moon, seasons and cycles of vegetation, and the earth. Each modality, which is defined by a different symbolic structure, is an expression of the nature of life. For example, the transcendence of God is revealed in the infinity, inaccessibility, and creative power (rain) of the sky. There are, however, many forms of religion, each of which is an appearance—often an eruption—of the sacred in common, profane existence. Awareness of the sacred is the exact opposite of profane awareness in life; what is sacred is what is real. People apprehend the sacred through symbols and myths, and according to Eliade, the task of the interpreter of religion is to expose the religious value found within the different modalities in which sacredness appears. The patterns of religious forms show the organization of human experiences. When these experiences have *religious* value, they are imitations of the creative acts and models found in the sacred or divine realm.

For Eliade, symbols, myths, and rites—especially those found in preliterate societies—represent a reevaluation of human self-awareness in terms of a transcendent, ultimate reality, a kind of evaluation that is radically different from that expressed in historic, everyday situations. These mythical patterns of awareness (which Eliade also calls "modalities of the sacred") can be isolated and studied. They have a power that is not derived from a particular historical or social set of circumstances; rather, they represent a unique dimension of human awareness that takes different forms according to different historical periods and cultural uses. The structures continue beyond a particular cultural form and reveal the religious meaning of similar particular expressions. By comparing the historical expressions of a religious phenomenon, says Eliade, the interpreter of religions can write a history of a symbol and uncover the religious meaning of religious symbols.

In summary, although scholars who are ifluenced by a phenomenological approach may differ in their specific interpretations of religious phe-

nomena, they share important assumptions about how to arrive at interpretation. The phenomenological approach focuses on an investigator's
empathetic or intuitive experience of the ultimate meaning expressed by a
religious devotee. The success of this approach depends on two things: (1)
how well the investigator is able to expose the meaning of a religious phenomenon by setting aside his or her own religious assumptions and (2) how
well the investigator can express a general religious intention in a vocabulary that transcends the cultural bias of his or her own language. From the
point of view of phenomenologists, unless the intention of religion can be
exposed through empathy, scholars will never be able to grasp the truest
meaning of religious expression.

THE RELATION OF RELIGIOUSNESS
TO CULTURAL SITUATIONS

Eliade's effort to understand religious meaning according to different modalities of sacredness in particular cultural-historical situations shows a
deep sensitivity to the fact that religious experience is always formed within
a particular cultural context. This fact has become a central concern for
several scholars who recognize the inexplicable quality of religion while
emphasizing that religious meaning is heavily dependent on cultural forces
and human capacities. One difficulty many interpreters of religion have is
that people (whether scholars or devotees) use the same modes of
apprehension (for example, language, emotion, social relations, visual experience, attitudes) in both religious and nonreligious experience. How can
a scholar distinguish between religious and nonreligious elements if every
religious form is conditioned by cultural conventions? How can a person
apprehend the religion experienced by someone from a different cultural
background or religious tradition?

The studies of three scholars of comparative religion have dealt specifically with cultural forces in the formation of religious expression without
reducing the religious content to social, historical, or semantic elements.
These three men share with other comparative religion scholars the concern
to describe the differences and similarities of religious data objectively. At
the same time, they understand religion as a set of relations between religiousness and historical-social-cultural contexts of meaning.

The first representative of this point of view is Joachim Wach who,
although recognizing the special religious quality of the data he studied,
was particularly conscious of social-cultural modes of expression. The
second, Wilfred C. Smith, emphasized the uniquely personal quality of
religious faith as it is manifested in historical traditions. The third, Ninian
Smart, is particularly interested in the relation between religious experience
and conceptual symbols, including philosophical formulations.

Joachim Wach. Wach was a professor of the history of religions at the University of Chicago. In his posthumous book, *The Comparative Study of Religion* (1958), Wach attempted to relate the dynamics of religious awareness to

social life, cultic acts, and conceptual formulations. Although he asserted that religious expression always reveals ultimate reality to the adherent (and thus religious life cannot be reduced to other cultural forms), he was very conscious that in religious life people use modes of expression that are also used in the secular world. Wach, who was also a noted sociologist of religion (see page 214), sought to expose the meaning of religious experience found in different human modes of apprehension: thought, ritual action, and fellowship.

For Wach, the core of religious life was a special kind of experience, for which he gave four criteria: (1) It must be a response to what is experienced as ultimate reality; (2) it must represent a total response of the whole being; (3) its intensity must be such that it is the most powerful, comprehensive, shattering, and profound experience of which people are capable; and (4) "it involves an imperative; it is the most powerful source of motivation and action."[1] A genuine religious experience must be expressed socially, ritually, and conceptually if it is to be identified and preserved in history as a religion. Every religious tradition has developed social, cultic, and conceptual forces to express this experience. Therefore, those who want to comprehend a religious life that is not their own must be sensitive to all three forms of expression. To understand another person, Wach claimed, means to comprehend the dominant traits in another person's self-expression by grasping intuitively the other's orientation and piecing together clues to his or her intellectual meaning. As the phenomenologists also maintain, such understanding requires that the investigator be sensitive to the significance of others' concepts and presuppositions.

Wilfred C. Smith. In his book *The Meaning and End of Religion* (1963), W. C. Smith, formerly director of the Center for the Study of World Religions at Harvard University, criticizes some scholarly attempts to describe a person's religious experience in terms of an impersonal entity called "religion." He maintains that because religious phenomena are human expressions, one must be sensitive to the character of the individual's involvement as that person expresses him- or herself in prayer, ritual, or social responsibility. The investigator, maintains Smith, must distinguish between a religious person's personal faith and the cumulative tradition that is the object of study of the historian and of the scholar who studies forms.

Is there a method that can expose the "unfathomability of that personal faith"? A first step, replies Smith, is to understand the role that personal faith has played in the religious history of humanity. This understanding involves not only observing cultural phenomena but also recognizing that the interaction between a human being and the transcendent takes place through cultural forms.[2] The transcendent, of course, cannot be directly observed. However, the believer's apprehension of the transcendent can be inferred by an imaginative sympathy disciplined by intellectual rigor, and cross-checked by vigorous criticism. Human faith can be studied, then, by being sensitive to the living quality of religious people who have expressed this faith in cultural forms. Smith advocates an approach that emphasizes the individual's inner and inexplicable character as a corrective to the objective studies that have emphasized methods based on observation and analysis of religious forms.

Ninian Smart. Ninian Smart, a British philosopher of religion, has given a somewhat different focus to the problem of the relation of religiousness to cultural expression. He recognizes that what Western scholars term "philosophy of religion" is really a series of reflections on Christian theology in the light of Western philosophical problems. Unhappy with this limited perspective, he has studied the religious thought of India and has wrestled with the problem of adequate religious terminology for comparing the claims of the major religious traditions. In his book *The Phenomenon of Religion* (1973), Smart criticizes a common assumption of such scholars as Otto and Wach that some kind of universal core experience is common to every religious phenomenon. Such an assumption, he suggests, is contradicted by the deep differences among various religious activities and among truth claims described in empirical studies. The major religious traditions have different "foci," and these differences must be taken into account in a descriptive phenomenological analysis.[3]

The focus of a religion is both the object of cultic activity and the public norm for group behavior. In a theistic tradition, the focus is the god worshiped; in Theravada Buddhism, however, it is nirvana. Faith in the focus of any religious group is expressed in practices, as well as reverence before images and heroes, but the most sophisticated expression, according to Smart, is in systematic thinking. Thus, in Christianity, the focus is most clearly articulated in theology. The focus transcends the practice, doctrines, and experiences of the faithful, but any apprehension of it includes an account (and in any tradition there are several interpretations) of the way the focus manifests itself.

Different kinds of understanding of the same religious data are quite possible, Smart claims. A scholar's interpretation of the focus will differ from that of a devotee. Likewise, a sophisticated group of monks or scholars within a tradition will not interpret the focus in the same way as outside social scientists and historians. Similarities in the data (such as similar forms of ritual) do not mean there are no important differences among subgroups within a tradition. In practice, cross-cultural comparisons of the religious foci need not be based on a belief in a single transcendent reality (such as God) or a single cultural process (such as rational interpretation). Likewise, although the "principles of numinous power"—the essential qualities of divine influence—in theistic worship and sacraments provide a special content for believers, they cannot be understood independently of the linguistic, psychological, economic, and political structures of society in which myth making occurs. The myth-making forces depend on specific cultural conditions, and so, myths function in different ways for different social groups.

In summary, the concern to explore the interaction of social, historical, and conceptual forces and what is distinctively religious in a cross-cultural context has become an important part of the comparative study of religion. Each of the scholars mentioned in this subsection focus on a different cultural force; however, they are all sensitive to the distinctiveness of par-ticular religious communities' claims of ultimacy in determining a cross-cultural definition of religion, or faith, as a universal human factor. For each, the religious factor in human life cannot be reduced to other human factors found in culture; yet religious expressions are seen to be strongly conditioned by cultural forces. This concern highlights the question about how we can understand religion, since religion is recognized to be an "un-fathomable" field of experience that also has conditioned processes of expression.

SUMMARY

The various approaches to the comparative study of religions reflect differ-ent answers to the questions "How are we to understand the religious expression of another person in a different culture and a different time?" and "How are we to perceive whatever is religious in others and in our-selves?" Such questions assume that we can talk meaningfully about reli-gion or religious life, but in human experience religion is related to other forms of human awareness.

The last three chapters have surveyed various attempts to locate and interpret the meaning of what is religious in human existence. Although these approaches to the objective study of religion differ, they have several common concerns:

1. Each interpretation stresses historical religious expressions and empirical documentation. A student of religion must have specific knowledge of the cultural background, historical situation, and con-cepts and acts of the people he or she is studying.
2. Each interpretation emphasizes the fact that no single religious ex-pression provides the only valid norm for understanding all other religious forms. The social scientist, historian, or phenomenologist of religion cannot be bound to only one cultural tradition and its expression of religiousness if he or she intends to say anything about general religious behavior, institutions, and symbols.
3. Finally, each interpretation is concerned with the meaning of reli-gious life. The purpose of the study of religion is not only to collect unrelated facts about religion, but also to explore the forms and processes of religious life to understand the conditions for creat-ing particular expressions and the significance of the forms for hu-man life.

Every interpretation, however, involves the investigator's sensitivities, concerns, and presuppositions. If the investigator is not self-conscious about his or her pattern of thinking as a religious or nonreligious person, he or she will predominantly seek and find those elements in an unfamiliar religious expression that are familiar. The investigator's conclusions will simply represent the religious data that fit into the investigator's bias. Stu-

dents of religious life need not accept as valid the ultimate norm of the
devotee. They should, however, be aware of their own presuppositions, be
able to expose the assumptions and structures of another's religiousness,
and even see relationships the adherent may overlook.

SELECTED READINGS

E.J. Sharpe, *Comparative Religion: A History* (London: Duckworth, 1975). A
useful description of the basic approaches, issues, and positions of scholars in the objective study of religion, from the beginnings of comparative
and social scientific investigation at the end of the nineteenth century to
the debate over the use of interfaith dialogue during the 1960s.

*J. de Vries, *Perspectives in the History of Religions,* translated by K. W. Bolle
(Berkeley: University of California Press, 1977; first published 1961). An
informative summary of the variety of methods used by European scholars in the nineteenth and first half of the twentieth century to study
religion. Emphasis is on various approaches for understanding religious
ritual and myth.

J. Waadenburg, ed., *Classical Approaches to the Study of Religion* (The Hague:
Mouton, 1973), Vol. I, introduction and anthology. An 80-page historical
survey of the last hundred years of the European scholarly study of
religion, followed by 600 pages of brief excerpts from deceased major
European contributors to research in religion. Volume II contains a bib-
liography and evaluations of the scholars mentioned in Volume I.

Volumes of essays by scholars in the history of religions who discuss methodology and exhibit interpretive techniques as applied to religious data
include M. Eliade and J. Kitagawa, eds., *History of Religions: Essays in
Methodology* (Chicago: University of Chicago Press, 1959); J. M. Kitagawa,
ed. *(The History of Religions: Essays on the Problem of Understanding* (Chicago: University of Chicago Press, 1967); and U. Bianchi, C. J. Bleeker,
and A. Bausani, eds., *Problems and Methods of the History of Religions*
(Leiden: E. J. Brill, 1972).

The historical approach to understanding man's spiritual life is discussed by
*W. Dilthey, *Pattern and Meaning in History* (New York: Harper, 1961);
and E. Troeltsch, "Historiography," *Encyclopaedia of Religion and Ethics,*
edited by J. Hastings (New York: Scribner's, 1951); 6:716–23; and is exem-
plified by C. P. Tiele, *Outlines of the History of Religions* (Kegan Paul,
Trench, Truebner, 1896); and G. F. Moore, *History of Religions,* 2 vols.
(New York: Scribner's, 1949, first published 1913, 1920).

A thoughtful analysis of historical studies of religion and a critique of some
recent scholarship labeled "history of religions" is found in R. D. Baird,
Category Formation and the History of Religions (The Hague: Mouton, 1971).

Two volumes of essays by renowned historians of religion who discuss
methodological issues while interpreting ancient, traditional, and con-

temporary religious forms are J. Z. Smith, *Map Is Not Territory: Studies in the History of Religions* (Leiden: E. J. Brill, 1978); and R. J. Z. Werblowsky, *Beyond Tradition and Modernity: Changing Religions in a Changing World* (London: Athlone Press, 1976).

The phenomenological approach is found in *G. van der Leeuw, *Religion in Essence and Manifestation.* (New York: Harper & Row, 1963; first published in 1933). See also W. B. Kristensen, *The Meaning of Religion,* translated by J. B. Carman (The Hague: Nijhoff, 1960); *M. Eliade, *Patterns in Comparative Religion,* edited y R. Sheed (New York: Sheed & Ward, 1958; first published 1949); and G. Mensching, *Structures and Patterns of Religion,* translated by H. F. Klimkeit and V. S. Sarma (Delhi: Motilal Banarsidass, 1976; first published in 1959).

A volume of essays by M. Eliade, which provides a basic orientation for the general reader to his interpretive approach, is *The Quest: History and Meaning in Religion* (Chicago: University of Chicago Press, 1969).

J. Waardenburg, *Reflections of the Study of Religion* (The Hague: Mouton, 1978). A series of thoughtful essays by a renowned Dutch scholar defending the phenomenological study of religion as the exploration of the intention in religious expressions.

W. L. Brenneman, Jr., S. O. Yarian, and A. M. Olson, *The Seeing Eye* (University Park: Pennsylvania State University Press, 1982). An analysis of the relation between phenomenology of religion and the philosophical tradition of hermeneutical phenomenology, plus a defense of hermeneutical phenomenology as a method for the study of religion.

J. G. Arapura, *Religion as Anxiety and Tranquility: An Essay in Comparative Phenomenology of the Spirit* (The Hague: Mouton, 1972). An analysis of two types of consciousness expressed in the Christian West and "the Indian spiritual sphere" as different "ultimate religious sources of insight," ending with a chapter on the difficulties and alternate roles played by these two types in interfaith dialogue.

*J. Wach, *The Comparative Study of Religions.* See especially Chapter 1," Development, Meaning and Method in the Comparative Study of Religions." An introductory summary of the discipline of comparative religion and the mature conclusions of a notable scholar about the elements inherent in interpretation of religious phenomena. Wach deals specifically with the methodological problems of comparative religion in *Types of Religious Experience: Christian and Non-Christian* (Chicago: University of Chicago Press, 1951). Chapters 2 and 3.

W. C. Smith, *The Meaning and End of Religion* (New York: Macmillan, 1962). See Selected Readings in Chapter 1 for the basis of Smith's provocative reassessment of common assumptions in Western studies about the religious traditions of mankind.

N. Smart, *The Phenomenon of Religion* (New York: Herder and Herder, 1973). This short but substantial book presents a critical assessment of some recent attempts to study religious expressions cross-culturally and analyzes the nature of ritual with special attention to the Christian Eucharist.

CHAPTER 14

Understanding Through Interreligious Dialogue

How can human beings deeply understand the processes of ultimate transformation? Is it by using a social scientific method that explains the function of religious life (Chapter 12) or by using a comparative method to classify and interpret diverse forms (Chapter 13)? Some scholars suggest that neither of these approaches is satisfactory. Only through a person-to-person dialogue—talking with, not about, a religious person—can one gain the deepest understanding of religious life.

In interreligious dialogue the focus is on sharing one's sense of authentic living with another person. Such sharing, say the advocates, makes it possible to learn about another person's religious commitment while exposing one's own deepest sense of what is true, good, and deeply enriching in life. In wrestling with such questions personally, an investigator will become aware of the sensed but unexpressed depth and richness of an alternate attempt to probe the mystery of living. If dialogue takes place in trust and regard for the other person as a significant resource for one's own religious awareness, it reveals the most profound similarities and differences between ways of being religious.

An approach for understanding that centers on interreligious dialogue includes some of the same assumptions as those in a comparative study of religions:

1. The deepest aspects of the human spirit are unique and cannot be reduced to psychological, sociological, economic, chemical, or physical forces.
2. Whatever is an authentic religious activity proceeds from an ultimate context, whether that is defined in transcendent, cosmic terms (Part One) or human deep-structure terms (Part Two) that go beyond personal or group determinations. Beyond any individual's religious beliefs or a group's set of moral and aesthetic expectations, there is a general or universal religious capacity.

3. For any person to know the nature of religious life or of authentic living at the deepest level, he or she must seek out alternate religious forms and compare them. Ideally, to know one's religious tradition deeply one must know all religions.
4. Not only are there different religious symbols, rituals, moral standards, and social institutions in various world religions, there are different kinds and levels of understanding *within* a religious community. Thus, some expressions are more central or vital than others within the same religious tradition. It is important to know which these are for understanding particular data.
5. The drive toward spirituality is as basic to human life as love, emotional security, and a sense of order. This basic quality of human life is experienced as the pursuit of the highest value or as the realization of the deepest possible resource. Ideally, it should flow through a person's moment-by-moment life consciously and unconsciously.

PROCESS OF DIALOGUE

The advocates of interreligious dialogue claim that their procedure for understanding is different from the general comparative and phenomenological approach to understanding religion and is also an improvement on it. The key difference is that instead of the investigator affirming a kind of objectivity that requires setting aside his or her own religious or value orientation, both (or all) participants in the dialogue express their own deepest value judgments. Some advocates of dialogue point out that no investigator can totally eliminate all value orientations or biases, so the best procedure is to recognize the biases about which a person is conscious and let the dialogue expose the rest.

Other dialogue advocates stress the opening of oneself as a person to another human being without trying to place oneself in an artificially neutral position. They recognize that to be most honestly humane in approaching a person who acts, speaks, and behaves in a very different way, one must enter such an engagement on equal terms and not regard the person as an object of study. Because the content of religious life involves a transformation of attitudes and perceptions, a significant encounter with another person requires sharing one's own understanding of the truth, as well as trying to understand the differences and similarities of the other position.

The advocates of dialogue stress that the object of the investigation is not a piece of historical information nor a cultural form that an investigator can then compare with an idea in his or her mind. The object, rather, is the unspeakable mystery, the unspoken dynamic, which gives value to the best in life, even as this mystery is expressed in particular words, gestures, and actions that in some ways may be very unlike one's own. The engagement, then, is as much in the *process of dialogue* as with a symbol, pattern of behavior, or institution.

At this point we should note that the concern to engage the personal attitudes of the investigator is highly criticized by some scholars. To focus on the personal significance of a religious commitment, they say, is to move from an objective study of religion to a theological evaluation or a critical philosophy. For them, objective understanding can only be gained through historical and phenomenological descriptions and social scientific explanations. As you read the views expressed by the proponents of dialogue in this chapter, ask yourself how they interpret the notions of "understanding" and "objectivity." Do you think that the human expressions of the "unspeakable mystery" found in different religious claims can be investigated intersubjectively (that is, through different personal subjective perceptions), if not quite objectively? Is the goal of objectivity best achieved by the application of a general principle or concept, such as universal law, to particular, continually changing moments of experience? Does every description and explanation of religious experience involve an implicit, if not an explicit, evaluation of the basic value or truth claimed by the advocate? If so, is greater objectivity gained by bringing the investigator's religious or antireligious attitudes out into the open?

In this chapter, we consider several aspects of interreligious dialogue as a way to understanding religious life. We first describe three ways in which scholars understand the relation between ultimate truth, goodness, or insight (divine revelation, transcendent awareness) and the particular cultural and historical forms (claims) of truth or righteous behavior. Because this approach emphasizes exposing one's own value position, it must deal with the issue of the nature of authentic religious life, which neither the social scientific explanation of religious forms nor the general comparative phenomenological description of religious life sought to pursue. Then we examine the common emphasis on the personal character of this approach, in which people rather than ideas or actions are the object of understanding. Last, we point out some issues that arise when dialogue is used to engage others in situations of turmoil and conflict.

DIALOGUE AS RECONCILIATION OF RELIGIOUS PLURALITY AND ULTIMATE REALITY

When committed believers from different religious traditions or advocates of a traditional religion and of a "secular means to ultimate transformation" talk with each other, they intend to reveal the deepest spiritual resources at their disposal. In doing so, they participate in a paradoxical activity: They try to communicate the eternal universal truth or righteousness although necessarily using shifting language and cultural understandings. In this situation, the concern for integrity of one's own view or the view of one's community's view needs to be matched with a rare generosity and skill in listening to another's view. It is the genius of true religious leadership, say the proponents of interfaith discussions, that it is willing to stand in the tension between the deepest awareness of ultimate reality and the relative, culturally determined, and shifting needs of the moment. When the values represented in dialogue become an internal dialogue within each participant, the participants begin to understand the religious reality that each attempts to express.

Part of the dynamic of dialogue is the unrestricted search for ultimate truth. In this effort, say the advocates of dialogue, it is impossible to bracket out, or eliminate, one's own deepest motivations and processes of valuation. Similarly, the participants need to keep in mind that it is the truth, insight, compassion, or righteousness transcending the dialogue that is the purpose of the dialogue. That kind of truth or righteousness cannot be possessed exclusively by any participant; rather, it emerges where the dialogue is successful, where there is spiritual growth by all the participants. To this degree, mutual understanding is a spiritual process that opens the depth of reality as it emerges in honesty, mutual respect (regardless of disagreements), and courage for creating genuinely new possibilities. For example, in a Muslim-Hindu dialogue, both (ideally) try to expose the transcendent power that makes possible the love people should have for each other; or both Christians and Buddhists who are in dialogue (ideally) claim from the depth of their experience that patience and compassion are necessary to develop a community of true righteousness.

This suggests that entering into a serious dialogue to discover the deepest meaning of religion requires a special kind of awareness. Participants must be willing to reveal the depth of their own convictions and to accept as equally real the depth of another's convictions. Such awareness allows the participants to approach the question at the center of dialogue: What is the relation between the highest human insight into religiousness and the specific religious formulations in history? Although this question has been answered in many ways, we discuss three of the major alternatives here:

The first way is to perceive a mystical, undifferentiated unity above or beneath all temporal and physical differences. This view is sometimes called "perennial philosophy" and suggests that, at some point, all differences among specific religious formulations disappear.

The second way is to recognize that different traditions and cultures have alternative and complementary strengths, which, like aesthetic tastes or emotions, cannot finally be reconciled. Dialogue, in this understanding, focuses on specific critical world problems, such as oppression and injustice, or they are concerned with specific philosophical issues, such as how to interpret the claim for truth. In this way, truth or justice need not be considered a transcendent reality but a general regulating notion or an ethical issue common to all reflective people.

The third approach to relating diverse religious and ideological commitments and a general ideal or ultimate reality is to focus on the experience of interpersonal encounter. The commonality of the participants is found neither in a transcendent spiritual reality nor in an abstract idea or social ideal. Rather, it is found in the humanness of dialogue with all its complexity and ambiguity. The deep reality that makes dialogue possible and necessary is simply humanity affirming an ultimate context for all people, who paradoxically yearn for and fear "otherness."

Perennial Philosophy

The first alternative is found in the writings of the mystic Frithjof Schuon *(The Transcendent Unity of Religions)*; of the emeritus professor of religion at Syracuse University Huston Smith *(Forgotten Truth)*, and of the late Indian philosopher Sarvapali Radhakrishnan *(An Idealist View of Life)*. In this approach, the world we experience is seen to contain different levels of reality. Smith points out that in the "primordial tradition," an ancient view that pervades every major culture, existence occurs at four levels: the terrestrial (earthly) plane, the intermediate (psychic) plane, the celestial plane, and the infinite. Although not all those who subscribe to perennial philosophy accept the same classification of things, they all affirm that there is a gradation of existence from the physical reality in time and space (the terrestrial plane) to a wholly different order of reality at the highest level—an undifferentiated infinite beyond all form. The differences in religious belief, ritual, and institutional forms that seem to be so important in our everyday, ego-centered experience fade away when we see and affirm the timeless and infinite reality that is no longer broken or differentiated into various forms. In perennial philosophy, infinite reality is like light. When light passes through a prism, we can see the various shades of blue, yellow, green, and red. No one of these colors, which are like the different cultural forms of religion, is light itself. But taken together, the individual colors of the spectrum become a single light—invisible and illuminating.

As there are different levels of experienced reality, so there are four parallel levels of selfhood: body, mind, soul, and spirit. The deepest level of reality, the infinite, is known by the parallel level of selfhood, the spirit. At this level, the individuality of particular religious traditions—specific beliefs and rituals—is unimportant, and the source of all particulars is directly intuited. The spirit in human consciousness *is* the infinite, which is without any distinctions. The center of changing, developing religious traditions is the common core—both the beginning and the end—of all human spiritual effort. The differences of ethical claims and the different evaluations of life expressed in the physical world, psychic experiences, and theological-mythical expression disappear and become one in a limitless, wholly transcendent pure consciousness, or infinite self. (In this option, all religions come to a common point, which is the essence of human spirituality; an undifferentiated, infinite awareness.) The dialogue functions to bring forth a deeper apprehension of the spirit, the inner identity of all religions.

Rational Inquiry and Ethical Decision

The second form of dialogue does not concern itself with the question of the spiritual nature of religious claims; rather, it focuses on issues of ethical decision, the general quality of human life, and the meaning of philosophies and ideologies that can be analyzed by social scientific and rational means. This form of dialogue emphasizes general understanding, critical analysis, and the development of social and legal structures to correct social problems on a worldwide scale. For example, Roscoe Pound, formerly dean of the Harvard Law School, in discussing the possibility and necessity for a world-wide system of justice, says:

> In order to understand our fellow men—and we must understand them if we are to live with them—we must understand both our own picture of things as they should be and their picture. We shall not understand them, and we shall only live with them at the cost of much friction, if we assume as a fixed starting point, with no critique of our own picture, that theirs is bound to conform in all its details to ours. . . .
>
> It is not easy for the machinery of social control to operate [if people uncritically assume their own view is superior to others]. If it is to operate effectively, men must be led to criticize the details of their pictures of things as they ought to be. They must be led to ask whence they derive their details, . . . In particular, they need to inquire whether their pictures of the nature of things are anything more than an idealization of the conditions of their childhood, projected into another time and used as a measure for a different society.[1]

Pound goes on to advocate an education policy that exposes people to the ideals of others, even when they are very different, and that trains them to assess views critically and sympathetically for their usefulness in developing a global community.

The self-critical effort necessary to develop a just social order is also a fundamental principle in considering the various cosmologies, philosophies, and traditional religious explanations of the world. The philosopher and mathematician Alfred N. Whitehead claims in his book *Religion in the Making* that the three organized systems of thought that have contributed most to human self-understanding in the modern world are Christianity, Buddhism, and science. They are basic to contemporary life because they attempt to define the nature of the world and organize thinking about the goal of human life. In dialogue the participants must be sensitive to the fact that their own theories (doctrines) and perceptions of the sensory world grow into, and take root in, their ultimate values. Such ultimate values, or ideals, direct the way in which a person views all life and its possibilities. Therefore, one must be aware of well-rooted and hidden assumptions in every position.

In contrast to the perennial philosophy perspective of a transcendent, undifferentiated spirituality at the core of all value orientations, White-head's understanding emphasizes that the forms of concrete experience are always at the heart of the value determination. This means that whatever continuity there is between religions and between traditional religion and secular cosmologies will be determined by decisions in a here-and-now consideration of truth claims, selection of ethical priorities, and practical decisions in implementing ideals, not in an undifferentiated mystical plane.

In a similar way, Professor of Theology John Hick has pointed out that in the dialogue between representatives of the world religions, there must be a concern for truth that is not defined simply by the sincerity of the advocates nor by the emotional and aesthetic significance of a religious truth claim for the believer. The issue of religious truth in interreligious dialogue must be dealt with by recognizing that the normative, standard-setting, character of one tradition's religious claim—for example, that "You are Brahman" in Hinduism or that Muhammad is the seal (the final one) of the prophets in Islam—is not the final normative value for all the participants in the dialogue. One cannot simply say that an absolute claim is true for one religion's devotee and that a conflicting claim is true for a different religion's devotee. The religious knowledge claimed by one of the adherents needs to be recognized as true by the others in the dialogue, or at least that the claim is not based on false information or faulty judgment. Hick recognizes that when the object of knowledge is the infinite, various conflicting truth claims may be complementary, as all propositions are conditioned, and thus limited, by assumptions about the nature of knowledge and perception and by linguistic (thought) structures. At the same time, in the context of interreligious dialogue, all the participants are called on to become critical of their own traditional religious claims in light of alternative claims and become sensitive to the problem of the functions that religious truth claims have in giving meaning to life and in directing social decisions.

In summary, although each of the three advocates of dialogue described here derives his concern from different contexts, all of them emphasize the following matters: (1) the need for each participant to be *self*-critical of traditional and culturally biased views, (2) the significance of specific historical situations and concrete conditions in which the ultimate spiritual ideals take form, and (3) the power of general human skills, such as reason, or a sense of justice that goes beyond communal assumptions or cultural biases to provide solutions to the deepest problems of life.

Personal Faith Affirmations

The third approach to the problem of relating multiple religious expressions and truth claims to ultimate reality or to a universal ideal is what we might call exchanging personal faith affirmations. This approach is characterized by the confidence that participants in the dialogue have in their own personal faith stances, while remaining open to developing new formulations of their belief systems. Likewise, through gaining familiarity with the living conditions of others, they are open to reconsidering their own social habits in the light of the worldwide interdependence of all communities. This approach incorporates two concerns of the perennial philosophy and the rational-ethical humanist dialogue: (1) It affirms the need for interaction of people of different religious and ideological communities, and (2) it maintains that each participant should express his or her own value orientation to evoke the depth of human spirituality in the encounter. Nevertheless, this approach is distinct as it recognizes important differences in value orientations that go to the root of spiritual reality (in distinction to the perennial philosophy approach), and it affirms the importance of a transcendent reality that is a mystery and unthinkable presence (in distinction to the rational-ethical approach). The three spokesmen for the dialogue of exchange whom we consider are Christians by personal faith. Since they acknowledge the value of dialogue for a person who intends to stay within a traditional religious community, they also are called exponents for a "theology of world religions."

Wilfred C. Smith emphasizes the dialogue of exchange as a way to understand personal faith. Dialogue focuses on the meaning that a religious tradition has for a believer's total grasp of life. To understand another person deeply, says Smith, is to engage him or her at such a depth that the investigator can see the world through the person's eyes. Only then can a person understand someone else at a level where one's own world view is placed in judgment. To engage another religious person requires strong personal faith. However, here faith does not mean that a person holds an "exclusivistic view." In the exclusivistic view, one *avoids* questioning or doubting one's own viewpoint. In this dialogic position, one's faith is strongest when a person can confidently consider alternate expressions of faith as a way to deepen and expand one's own.

In this adventure a Muslim, for example, begins and ends life as a Muslim, but with a growing sense of religious self-consciousness about what he or she shares and does not share with others. Similarly, a Jew with a sense of openness can learn from other religious traditions while interpreting the variety of religious experiences for her- or himself in expanded Jewish terms. Or a Buddhist will remain a Buddhist by continuing to take refuge in the Three Jewels (Buddha, Buddhist teaching and practice, and the Buddhist community), while extending the implications of the Buddha's way into new social and cultural forms.

Developing a strong and open faith, for Smith, is to answer the most critical challenge for religion today: to collaborate in building a common world in which there is mutual understanding. This challenge is a moral imperative. Without presuming that there will be one religion throughout the world, Smith holds that believers in each religious tradition need to become aware that they are part of a developing religious history of humanity. By talking to people of other traditions, a person will get a different sense of the power of the symbols and ideals of that tradition than if one just learns about them in the abstract. In dialogue, an honest and open person not only gets information but also is already collaborating in developing a community for mutual understanding. In such a community, the participants will wrestle with conflicting views and judgments, as well as share points of general agreements. Such collaboration is not easy, but it is necessary for human survival; and it is an expression of both confidence and humility, produced by a deep personal faith.

A second advocate of the dialogue of exchange is the Roman Catholic scholar and priest Raimundo Panikkar, professor of religious studies at the University of California, Santa Barbara. He, too, claims that the most authentic approach to understanding the fact of religious plurality is to engage the faith of the investigator. Dialogue itself takes a deep faith. How is the committed religious person to express the universal ideal in the concrete present situation? Panikkar answers:

In the contemporary scene, where everything is in the fires of revision and re- form, in which every value is contested and the *metanoia* ["turn about," conver- sion] almost total, the authentically religious Man cannot shut himself off, close his ears and eyes, and simply gaze toward heaven or brood over the past; he cannot ignore his fellow-Men and act as if religion has assured him he has no more to learn, nothing to change. He must throw himself into the sea and begin to walk, even if his feet falter and his heart fails. Who are we to stifle the growing seed, to choke humble and personal buds, to quench the smoking wick.[2]

The purpose of dialogue is mutual personal spiritual growth. This makes dialogue an important spiritual act that transforms conflict into understand- ing, disregard for others into care for them, and fear into confidence.

For Panikkar, the ultimate resource for this transformation is the Divine Presence, which addresses each person through another human being. As Smith distinguishes tradition from faith, Panikkar calls attention to the fact that beliefs and creedal systems are culturally determined and that they are different from faith—a universal human experience that probes and remains open to the transcendent reality.

If each participant in religious dialogue remembers that every authentic encounter with another person is also an opportunity for genuine tran- scendence to enter their lives, the dialogue can be a means to expand a narrow, culturally centered point of view. At the same time, the function of a dialogue is not to reduce all the various beliefs and religious concepts to one position; different theological and philosophical formulations will flour- ish. Nevertheless, by opening oneself to a person with another ultimate commitment in an authentic exchange, the transcendent reality that is effec- tive in one's own life (and everywhere) will, in an indirect and hidden way, become evident.

A third example of the personal faith approach in dialogue comes from the late Roman Catholic scholar (formerly professor of eastern religions, at Oxford University), Robert C. Zaehner. He affirms that scholars should understand another religion from within and that mutual enrichment of the participants is a valid goal in interreligious dialogue. However, he is less willing than either Smith or Panikkar to speak of a transcendent mystery in the general human religious consciousness that is expressed in significantly different ways by different traditions. Also, he is not ready to go as far as they do in affirming that religious dialogue might provide truly new insights and formulations that improve the traditional spirituality of all participants, including the Christian. Dialogue can, at best, deepen the Christian's reli- gious life and illumine aspects only dimly perceived before.

For Zaehner, there is no fundamental unity of all world religions—as the advocates of perennial philosophy assert. To claim that all religions are different paths to a single, undifferentiated truth, he insists, does not take the central claim of God's revelation in the prophetic religions (Judaism, Christianity, and Islam) seriously. Likewise, he is critical of the general claim made that mystical experiences in all major religions express a com- mon insight. He points out that there are differences in mystical experi- ences, especially between a monistic type that seeks identity between the mediator and the undifferentiated infinity and a theistic mysticism that evokes love between the devotee and a personal God. The relationship between the best in world religions and the ultimate reality is, for Zaehner, an assimilation of all humanity's highest aspirations into God, who is incarnate in Christ. Likewise, the concrete social form of the divine word is the Christian church. To say this does not mean that other religions should, or will, die; each has a genuine quality. However, to express the deepest truth about revelation in the prophetic traditions, Zaehner claims, requires a clear statement that there is an exceptional quality about divine revelation and that the differences among religions cannot be considered only as differences of outward forms.

DIALOGUE AS A DISCOVERY OF PERSONAL VALUES

Within the dialogic approach, the key concern is to put the process of religious understanding in a human context. To understand another person requires not abstract analysis but human encounter—engaging the depth of another person's life. Dialogue engages two or more people in a dynamic process only when the inner core of each participant's life is touched and his or her ultimate orientation to life is exposed.

In a religious encounter, this response of one person to another can evoke a deepened and expanded sense of one's ultimate values. Such an engagement is to perceive someone's heart with one's own. To "perceive with one's heart" is a metaphor used in several world religions to mean seeing below the surface, or seeing what most people often do not want to see or cannot usually see. Philosopher of religion Maurice Friedman reminds us of the difficulty in deepening a superficial encounter into true communication:

> True communication is not a technique, but a unique event that may or may not recur, depending upon the commitment of the relationship, the personal resources, the difficulty of the situation, the tension of understanding and misunderstanding.[3]

When dialogue exposes the deepest values and character of human life, it can become *ultimately* significant for the participants. To share one's deepest religious commitment with another person in a mutual exploration of the fullest and freest living, say the proponents, is to evoke an expression of the ultimate context of life. Dialogue requires the assumption that there is a real boundary between individuals; each individual must have a distinctive character if he or she wants to share something distinctive with another individual. At the same time, both individuals in a dialogue participate in a context of awareness beyond either. The famous Jewish philosopher Martin Buber has pointed out that in dialogue, a person "turns with attention" to another person. Such turning with attention requires the attitude "that out of the incomprehensibility of what lies [immediately at] hand, this one person steps forth and becomes a presence."[4]

The reality of personhood, then, is neither simply subjective experience nor objective behavior. The reality of personhood is both inner and outer.

Meeting others is a necessary aspect of becoming an individual. We cannot become aware of ourselves at any depth without others to evoke and engage that which is our own personal reality. If this is true, suggest the advocates of interreligious dialogue, a person understands the character of religiousness in a manner evoking personhood; also one becomes a religious person by engaging the depth of another person in an awareness that both people stand within an ultimate context. To engage another person in a full way requires exposing the depth of one's own personal being—that is, exposing honestly one's true religious commitment—at the moment of being addressed by the other person.

The advocates of dialogue are the first to admit that to engage a person from another religion or value orientation includes risk and trust. The risk is of several sorts, ranging from arousing anger and hostility to receiving unexplored insights about oneself to discovering new horizons of meaning and truth. In real engagement with another person, we cannot fully foresee what will happen. Likewise, to expose ourselves or our deepest feelings and attitudes to the challenge of another person requires trust. One must trust that the other person is also caring, is secure enough in her or his view to allow for differences, and is open to learning new dimensions of his or her orientation or tradition that may be evoked in dialogue.

DIALOGUE AS A WAY OF MAKING CHOICES AND RESOLVING CONFLICT

Some advocates of dialogue have called attention to two negative aspects of life in the twentieth century that make dialogue imperative. One is that traditional cultural and religious value systems are no longer taken for granted as providing the spiritual and moral guidance for humanity. Modernization has undercut the philosophical assumptions and the social-economic power bases in many cultures. Present-day communications expose millions of people in each continent to a variety of religious and moral options. Scientific knowledge requires whole cultures to make constant adjustments in traditional theological and moral answers.

The confusion caused by competing value orientations and rapidly changing ideas has led many people to indifference and despair. A number of cultural philosophers have called attention to the fact that people are losing confidence in the traditional answers in virtually every culture today. New ideas break down the social norms and symbolic models formerly held sacred. The turmoil resulting from the rapid changes and multiple options prevents people from rational choice. People sometimes say, "Nobody knows, so what difference does it make?" or, "Technology is taking over, we don't make any real decisions anyway." To deal with this problem, the advocates of dialogue call for clear, interpersonal engagement in which people make decisions about themselves, their local communities, and the world community.

A second problem that dialogue would help to alleviate is intolerance. One way that some people have responded to modernization, scientific discovery, and intercultural communication is to retreat to some form of tradition that claims exclusive absolute truth, transcendent insight, or divine revelation. One group, identifying its ideological or social-economic position exclusively with the cosmic purpose or divine will, will clash with another community using the same kind of justification (God is always on "our" side), leading to religious hatred, class hostility, and racial antagonism. Exclusiveness was possible in a day when city walls, mountains, or oceans protected people from conflict, but today, the advocates of dialogue point out, there is no such defense. We are all living together on one spaceship called "earth," where groups with different languages, world views, and social organizations must live together or not live at all.

The solution to this problem of conflict arising from intolerance is not easy, say the dialogue advocates, but positive action in today's threatening situation requires people to understand the deepest sense of value of others. If people can just see each other as human beings who have common problems, they can help each other while acknowledging important and valuable differences. To engage in dialogue on practical problems also means that the people needing help have the right to determine how they are going to be helped. Dialogue allows for the possibility that there may be several solutions that may be effective in different places at different times.

In summary, the advocates of interreligious dialogue claim that reducing world tensions requires a sensitivity to the quality of personhood, which opens one person to another. In dialogue, one will not only learn about another person but about the particularity that is oneself. The advocate of dialogue says: "When I see the importance of another person to the revelation of my deepest humanity, then I can be neither indifferent to, nor intolerant of, the diversity of ultimate commitments that determine the quality of life in which we both live."

It is important to note both poles of the bipolar process of dialogue. At one pole is the continuity—some would want to say the commonality—of all true or authentic spirituality. At the other pole are the important differences—differences that, according to some analyses, are at the deepest level of religious life.

When engaged in interreligious dialogue, a person begins by acknowledging that the reality that is the object of religion extends beyond one's individual range of understanding to include the partner who is in dialogue. Such an attitude rejects the exclusivistic view that one's own view is of a totally different order—divine or absolute—from that of a person not identified with one's own religious position. This is to say that the ultimate reality in which one lives is not contained by one person's, one scripture's, or one community's statements, attitudes, or activities. That reality might be called "the mystery of being," in Western philosophy, the "suchness of form and nonform" in Buddhism, "the lord of life and death" in the theistic traditions, or the "peak experience" in humanistic psychology. It is the fundamental religious reality that causes scholars of religion and religious people of all cultures to stammer, speak in paradoxes, and remain silent when they try to spell out its power and depth.

Assuming that all parties speak out of an unspeakable ultimate context, the participants of interreligious dialogue attempt to evoke the best, the deepest, the most enlightening aspects of the alternate tradition. They are not looking for ways to discredit the dialogue partner. Each participant must continually ask if he or she has apprehended the deepest religious dynamic of the other person's view or whether there is a misunderstanding over the use of a term, a spiritual practice, or a practical alternative to communicate the core of one's religious life. At the same time, honesty in the dialogue prevents a superficial agreement where deep differences become evident.

SUMMARY

The advocates of interreligious dialogue maintain that the deepest understanding of religious life can be achieved through the interaction of religious people. This means that both partners in the dialogue expose their personal religious commitments or deepest value judgments. The dialogic process is basic, they say, for understanding religion, because religious life is a comprehensive orientation to life that includes the manner in which people evaluate life. Religious expression is personal in the sense that one's personhood is evoked in the process of expressing it and in getting a response from another.

People participating in religious dialogue can have various attitudes about the relationship between religious expressions and universal truth or ultimate awareness. Three of these attitudes are expressed in the approaches of perennial philosophy, rational inquiry and ethical discussion, and an exchange of personal faith affirmations. Though there are different understandings of the nature of the ultimate context in which the dialogue takes place, all participants emphasize that a dialogic understanding leads to a discovery of one's deepest personal values.

Religious dialogue is seen as a communication not only *about* values and ideals but also as a catalyst for evoking new dimensions in the religious awareness of the participants. At the same time, those who have engaged in dialogue are aware that the differences among religious advocates cannot be taken lightly. A continuing concern for those engaged in dialogue is simultaneously developing a sensitivity for understanding the particularity of the partner's position, communicating the depth of one's own value system, or faith, and remaining open to learn from another person for mutual benefit in living in a global community.

SELECTED READINGS

M. Friedman, *The Human Way: A Dialogic Approach to Religion and Human Experience* (Chambersburg, PA: Anima Books, 1982). A philosopher of religion calls for an experientially based understanding of the deepest awareness of other people, which enriches and draws forth the particularity of one's own deepest sensitivities.

D. K. Swearer, *Dialogue: The Key to Understanding Other Religions* (Philadelphia: Westminster Press, 1977). A Christian professor of religious studies whose speciality is Theravada Buddhism perceptively analyzes key religious issues, such as community, experience, morality, and a view of the world, in light of some Christian and Buddhist perspectives. The final chapter is a statement by a Thai monk, Buddhadasa, on several aspects of Christianity.

Representative statements by scholars who are also active participants in different religious communities and who seek to understand the faith of others for their own religious benefit are found in D. G. Dawe and J. B. Carman, eds., *Christian Faith in a Religiously Plural World* (Maryknoll, NY: Orbis Books, 1978); S. J. Samartha and J. B. Taylor, eds., *Christian-Muslim Dialogue* (Geneva: World Council of Churches, 1973); and P. Ingram and F. Streng, eds., *Buddhist-Christian Dialogue: Possibilities for Mutual Transformation* (Honolulu: University of Hawaii Press, 1984).

Two recent statements by philosophical theologians that portray incisively the "internal dialogue" within a reflective person who takes another religious position seriously are R. C. Neville, *The Tao and the Daimon: Segments of a Religious Inquiry* (Albany: State University of New York, 1982); and *J. B. Cobb, Jr., *Beyond Dialogue: Toward a Mutual Transformation of Christianity and Buddhism* (Philadelphia: Fortress Press, 1982).

Wilfred C. Smith's understanding of a dynamic and probing personal faith as found in diverse traditions, which makes possible and necessary a dialogue for developing a world perspective, is found in his books *Faith and Belief* (Princeton, NJ: Princeton University Press, 1979); and *Towards a World Theology* (Philadelphia: Westminster Press, 1981).

Raimundo Panikkar's call to remain open to transcendent reality by personally engaging and even participating with people who live in other religious traditions is found in his books *The Trinity and the Religious Experience of Man: Icon-Person-Mystery* (New York: Orbis Books, 1973); *Intra-religious Dialogue* (New York: Paulist Press, 1978) and *Myth, Faith and Hermeneutics* (New York: Paulist Press, 1979).

Robert C. Zaehner's position of the absolute character of religious truth, which remains in tension with particular forms of religious belief and action, is found in *Christianity and Other Religions* (New York: Hawthorn Books, 1964); and *Concordant Discord: Interdependence of Faiths* (Oxford: Clarendon Press, 1970).

Other recent statements by Christians who recognize the value of sensitive dialogue with people of other religious traditions for deepening their own spiritual awareness are J. S. Dunne, *The Way of All the Earth* (New York: Macmillan, 1972); P. Clasper, *Eastern Paths and the Christian Way* (Maryknoll, NY: Orbis Books, 1980); and W. G. Oxtoby, *The Meaning of Other Faiths* (Philadelphia: Westminster Press, 1983).

Clear statements by renowned spokespersons for perennial philosophy that emphasize the transcendent common inner meaning of diverse expressions of religious life are *F. Schuon, *The Transcendent Unity of Religions*

(New York: Harper & Row, 1975; first published in 1948); and H. Smith, *Forgotten Truth: The Primordial Tradition* (New York: Harper & Row, 1976).

The need to raise the question of the nature and criteria of ultimate truth as found in diverse religious traditions in order to understand religious beliefs is cogently argued in D. Wiebe, *Religion and Truth: Toward an Alternative Paradigm for the Study of Religion* (The Hague: Mouton, 1981). The need to raise the question of ultimate truth in conflicting truth claims is the basis for the essays by various renowned scholars in J. Hick, ed., *Truth and Dialogue in World Religions: Conflicting Truth-claims* (Philadelphia: Westminster Press, 1974). See also J. Hick, *God Has Many Names* (Philadelphia: Westminster Press, 1982).

Two volumes that focus on the issues of diverse religious traditions and their impact on the present need for realizing a world community are R. L. Slater, *World Religions and World Community* (New York: Columbia University Press, 1963); and S. J. Samartha, ed., *Faith in the Midst of Faiths: Reflections on Dialogue in Community* (Geneva: World Council of Churches, 1977).

CHAPTER 15

Consequences of Understanding Religious Life

"The future of religion is extinction." So say some social scientists and cultural philosophers. By this they mean that the beliefs, values, and spiritual practices of the past are no longer useful. The modern world, with its increasingly rapid changes, requires different insights than the historically important beliefs, values, and practices can provide. Although the claim that religion will come to an end may shock some readers—and appear obvious to others—it serves to stimulate reflection on the point of view of this book.

Our basic thesis is that religion is at the center of human life. The dynamics of religions (as opposed to any particular historical form this dynamic takes) will not become extinct as long as people exist. The religious dynamics that continue through various religious traditions and their different subgroups, as well as in nontraditional expressions of comprehensive value orientations, has been called "the means to ultimate transformation." As noted in Chapter 1, religious life always involves two separate but related aspects: (1) the outward, historical forms and (2) the internal dynamics. Therefore, the ways in which people seek ultimate transformation have both internal and external effects. These effects have an impact on, and are affected by, social and historical forces and lead people to alternative views of the nature of reality. The processes of ultimate transformation that people experience are said to bring about a more complete realization of the nature of things, rather than just changes in historical-cultural forms.

Looking at religion from this perspective, we can see that, although the dynamics of religion are unchanging, the forms those dynamics take may change in consequence of other changing processes of human life. A religious structure that provides the concrete awareness of ultimately transforming power is not isolated from modes of human awareness such as thought patterns, aesthetic sensitivities, or social relationships. Furthermore, religion functions in relation to historical, psychological, economic, and other conditions. Although one structure of ultimate transformation may be the most important one to an individual or a community, there may also be several subordinate structures with various historical forms.

The fact that a variety of religious processes may exist at the same time in one of the world's great religious traditions makes it possible for a person to shift from one process to another without shifting traditions. For example, a Roman Catholic who has participated in the elaborate symbolism of the Mass, institutional religious education, and the reverence for priestly authority (Chapter 3) may have an overwhelming charismatic experience of the Holy Spirit (Chapter 2) and then embrace the latter as the deepest expression of the Christian life. Sometimes a person may move from a traditional religious structure to a humanistic means to ultimate transformation. This kind of shift has been made by some modern Western thinkers whose early lives reflect a structure of a personal awareness of a Holy Presence or of sacred myth but whose later writings reflect a structure affirming human relationships or rational thought as the basic means to ultimate transformation. The flexibility of religious expression as it interacts with all the other elements of human life allows the dynamics of religious life to endure while personal experience, cultural processes, and historical forms of religion continue to change.

The history of religions is a record of changes. A study of history shows that both external and internal pressures have changed the content and expression of religious awareness. If one forgets that being religious means opening new vistas of meaning, stretching (and at times tearing) the traditional forms, and also recognizing oneself in the symbols, spiritual practices, and ethics of the past, religion becomes an empty husk or dissolves in the mirage of abstraction. The recognition of change raises the question of what religion can and should be today. If people realize that they are on a religious frontier, they must acknowledge at least three concerns: (1) religious pluralism and the significance of different processes of ultimate transformation, (2) the relevance of contemporary processes for ultimate fulfillment in life, and (3) the meaning of the personal or subjective element in religious experience as it relates to objective expression in understanding religion.

THE SIGNIFICANCE OF RELIGIOUS PLURALISM

Religious pluralism means that there are many different religious beliefs, practices, and institutions that are equally active in the world. In Part I of this book, we examined four different traditional religious processes: (1) personal apprehension of a Holy Presence, (2) creating community through sacred symbols, (3) living in harmony with Cosmic Law, and (4) attaining freedom through spiritual discipline. Although we discussed only four *proc-*

esses of religious life, we examined a much larger number of religious traditions: Judaism, Islam, Christianity, Hinduism, Buddhism, traditional Chinese family religion, and Native American religious life, among others. All of these traditions include ultimate claims, and all of them play key roles in the growth of contemporary self-consciousness.

Predictably, not all people respond to religious pluralism in the same way, although many respond in one of two ways: (1) Some reduce all religious reality to separate cultural entities that are the result of different historical and social factors; thus, they regard all religious views as secondary and relative to psychological and social needs. These we call "cultural reductionists." (2) Others reduce religious reality to some form of their own religious perspective; and whatever is significantly different from their personal viewpoint (or their religious tradition) is labeled nonreligious. These we can call "perspectival reductionists."

The Reductionist Views

For many people, the recognition that other religious people have different creeds, cultic forms, and symbols that have ultimate significance for them may be too overwhelming to consider. From a cultural standpoint, however, one may reduce all religious reality to one of several cultural forces. After all, no one expresses a religious dimension in life in isolation from historically and culturally determined religious forms. But the cultural reductionist holds that religion is to be understood simply as an ideology, a set of mores, or a cultural pattern, and these are regarded as having only relative validity. Another kind of cultural reductionism involves identifying the general meaning of a contemporary religion with particular historical forms. One may then regard different religions as self-contained, unrelated cultural entities. In this view, Hinduism is only for South Asians and Buddhism only for East Asians. Such a reductionist may regard other religions as just so many separate, unchanging systems of views, morals, and cultic acts—curious but dead objects of study.

The perspectival reductionist also reduces the complexity of religious life, but from a personal evaluative standpoint. This type of reductionist makes a value judgment that the only true religious expression is defined by the structure or form of religion most familiar to him or her. This point of view leads to two kinds of flaws in understanding the possible relations between the different forms and the ultimate context of religious meaning. To avoid the tension between many religious options and the claims to ultimacy of each, the perspectival reductionist tends to see either religious fusion or religious chaos in multiplicity. The first interpretation holds that all religions must eventually fuse into one powerful religious system, the form of which will be identical with that of a past or present religious system (preferably one's own). In this view, everyone would be forced to adhere to a single religion or ideology, accept one creed, and perform certain prescribed rituals. The other view suggests that considering various religious possibilities will necessarily end in chaos, confusion, and the denigration of all values.

Both types of reductionistic thinking tend to overlook the humanity of people whose values are different from one's own. Indeed, human history records countless instances of people who have tried to destroy all foreign influences—and their carriers. Both views also inhibit the efforts of individuals or religious communities to develop new insight about the meaning of religion for themselves or others.

The Empathic View

In a quite different kind of response to religious pluralism, a person recognizes that other human beings are (at least apparently) as moral, devout, intelligent, and religiously sensitive as her- or himself. Despite different religious views, other people are equally able to find happiness and peace and to perceive profound meaning in life. When the spiritual insight of others interacts with one's own means to ultimate transformation, then religious pluralism raises interesting personal questions. Why not participate in the joys and freedom witnessed to by a different religious option? Is it possible to understand deeply a religious tradition without joining a community of devotees? Does an appreciation of different religious options destroy the ultimacy claimed in each religious tradition?

A careful study of other religious people reveals that they, like oneself, are sometimes frustrated, sometimes successful. They wrestle with meaning and attempt to transcend the limitations of their tradition. Reformation and reinterpretation are part of the dynamics of every historical religious tradition. Certainly, each tradition contains norms setting the limits of orthodoxy (what is correct). However, even when the norms are generally accepted by those who practice within the tradition, there may be profound differences among practitioners, such as those that exist between Southern Baptists and Greek Orthodox in Christianity. To understand a religious tradition means, in part, to recognize the religious tensions and ambiguities between and within human beings who seek new horizons of meaning. Sometimes when people study their own traditions, they find surprises that require them to change both questions and answers.

The awareness that true religious commitment is not limited to one's own ethnic or linguistic background challenges a person to examine the theological and religious forms of other cultures. As a result, many people are exploring value systems today that their parents had never heard of in their youth. Those with this new awareness feel they can explore without assuming that conversion is necessary for understanding or that they must abandon their religious heritage to enter another's. However, although people should be willing to explore the values and forms of other religious traditions, they should not assume that all religions are really the same because they share some common elements. To overlook the differences between religious claims and religious structures is often to fail to see the intention of a particular, historical expression.

In summary, among the implications of religious pluralism for contemporary religious self-consciousness are the following: (1) A religion need not be regarded as an inherited system available only to those within that cultural tradition; (2) religious traditions allow significant internal differences and change in response to new historical situations; and (3) a person's religious commitment to one historical tradition can be enhanced by the incorporation of some values and practices found elsewhere.

One need not judge another person's faith as false just because one is committed to a given religious tradition. A more profound awareness of religious possibility can grow as one's own faith permits one to love another person—including the differences from oneself. By trying to understand new ideas while using ancient religious symbols, modern people can seek new definitions and concepts of what religion *might be*.

THE RELEVANCE OF CONTEMPORARY RELIGIOUS PROCESSES

The relevance of contemporary, nontraditional religious processes for understanding religion is that all spheres of life are seen as possibilities of ultimate transformation. By extending the definition of religion beyond traditional assumptions, any learning experience—in classrooms, at political meetings, or in the artist's studio—can be seen to have the capacity to develop insight, compassion, patience, and pursuit of truth. This does not mean that all human acts are intentionally religious. Rather, it suggests that religious elements pervade dimensions of human existence beyond those culturally and historically associated with religion. The investigator of religious life therefore should be aware of emerging possibilities for ultimate transformation, even though they appear to be quite different from traditional religious forms. In Part Two, we focused on five modes of human awareness that have become means to ultimate transformation for some people.

Gaining New Insights

Recognizing that new kinds of religious life may be emerging today implies that the study of religion is not limited to certain traditional human expressions labeled "religion." Such recognition raises questions about the inner dynamics of life. It also indicates that today, as in other times, there is an ultimate context of human awareness and commitment that is not limited by the specific cultural definitions of religion that have been used to expose that context.

In becoming sensitive to the dynamics of ultimate transformation in nontraditional processes, the investigator might become aware of one or more of these processes in which he or she participates. For example, the power of symbolic images and rational concepts (Chapter 8) and interpersonal relations (Chapter 6) often plays a role in the apprehension of religious data. As we saw before, the concepts people use signify what they consider real and important. Perhaps even the study of religion or the dialogue with others may itself become a means to ultimate transformation for some people.

Although religions show that people express an ultimate dimension within many different religious traditions and outside them, the study of new religious forms need not lead to the rejection of one's own tradition. It can enlarge one's range of religious options and may even make one more aware of the richness of one's own tradition. In describing some of the basic options, we make no overt judgments about their relative value, but simply indicate the claims made by people about the significance religion can have as a practical force in their lives. Each reader must decide on the advantages and disadvantages of particular forms and processes of religious life— recognizing that some forms and processes are already influencing that decision!

Extending the Definition of Religion

Religious forms die when they no longer furnish the direction and power for making decisions. Indeed, the great religious traditions have a history because they have met human problems differently in different times and places; their formulations and institutions have changed while preserving some continuity with past expression. One may feel regret and anxiety over the loss of a former structure of meaning and, in the same moment, experience a more profound order of reality that changes, yet deepens, a former understanding.

In a world of rapid change, we can benefit from keeping in mind three insights derived from a study of religious pluralism: (1) Changes in value orientations do not inevitably bring spiritual maturity or spiritual chaos. (2) The rejection of one religious alternative, such as that of one's childhood, does not ensure freedom from another kind of spiritual bondage. (3) All human living requires making ultimate value choices within specific, limited personal and cultural situations.

The accumulation of experience over the years does not always bring spiritual maturity to either a person or a community. To recognize this is only to admit there is no inevitable spiritual progress within the individual person or within the human race. It is to recognize that the creative power in discovery can be turned back on itself in a destructive way. For example, the concern to better oneself or to transcend one's limitations, although apparently springing from the highest motives, can turn into a struggle to control others for the benefit of oneself. Or, as many have warned, industrial power, technological discovery, and economic prosperity—although in themselves not to be equated with evil—may lead to dehumanization in the loss of self-respect and individual creativity in a mass society. Also, the legacy of the Western Enlightenment—freedom from absolute commitments—has furnished the conditions for a situation often recognized today: the monotony of uncommited lives.

The freedom attained by rejecting one value orientation does not necessarily mean freedom from the bondage of another value orientation that also turns out to be less than ultimate. The exchange of one idol for another is not spiritual freedom. How to avoid slipping into spiritual ignorance in the midst of the highest spiritual efforts is a continuing religious problems. The tools for a creative spiritual life may, without one's recognizing it, become weapons of spiritual death.

To have any kind of religious commitment is to make choices among the ideas we use, the relationships we have with other people, and the symbolic and aesthetic sensitivities we employ. The most profound limitation is not, however, in the finite (though vast) number of possibilities in a given situation; the greatest danger often is to crystallize the status quo with religious fervor and thereby reject the dynamic, the uncontrollable, the indefinable (and undefined) character of the spiritual.

SUBJECTIVITY AND OBJECTIVITY IN RELIGIOUS COMMITMENT

Faced with the possibility of accepting the notion of religious pluralism and nontranscendent religious expressions, a contemporary American often falls into an attitude of despair. In part, this despair comes from the Jewish and Christian attitudes, which are dominant in this culture, that emphasize the exclusive participation in one tradition. The admission of religious pluralism is interpreted as a defection from the teachings of the fathers. Some people have been overwhelmed with guilt at not being, say, good Christians simply because they have allowed the introduction of new scientific or cultural data to challenge the primary presuppositions upon which their parents' belief system rested.

Examining Conflict

People today cannot avoid engagement with neighbors of other faiths. Part of spiritual growth within any religious tradition requires considering alternate religious possibilities, not only as interesting intellectual options, but as influences on an individual's world view. This kind of consideration may challenge the way in which people regard their existence and even cause a personal identity crisis, but the outcome may be crucially important for further spiritual development. The choice in today's small world is not whether to engage people of other faiths or to respond to scientific discovery but whether to risk becoming aware of one's own religiousness in light of several cultural traditions. It is a question of whether to permit a deepening of religious experience from different sources, both past and present.

The situation becomes more complex when the individual is called upon to pay two possibly antagonistic roles: religious adherent and objective student of religion. What is one to do upon becoming sensitive to the value of life orientation that one did not know existed as a serious option? The scholar is confronted with an inner struggle of values between personal religious beliefs and objective methods of study. Three possible reactions to the conflict are defensive and negative: First, sometimes researchers cast aside religious beliefs instead of reexamining them. They regard belief as inferior to the more up-to-date methods of objective research. For example, behaviorist psychology might discard the traditional Christian notion of the soul as that which gives people the capacity and responsibility to make moral choices as this concept cannot be objectively verified. Second, investigators might reject the objective study of religion as impious and irreligious. They maintain that the original and unexamined belief system is better simply because they have dismissed all other arguments without giving them serious consideration. Third, the researcher who is also a believer may separate his or her experience and work. Eventually, such scholars may develop a double standard in which their belief system does not guide personal action and their actions do not support personally expressed beliefs.

Testing Understanding

We have suggested that people cannot understand religious phenomena as wholly external entities. Individuals' perceptions of the origins, functions, or meaning of religious life are conditioned by their concerns about it. It is important therefore to become aware of the questions and answers of scholars and devotees. Such an examination illumines some of the issues involved in the two roles and suggests how the differences and overlapping character of analysis and participation affect the outcome of claims made by each. Likewise, an investigator of religious life can become sensitive to the conflicts or benefits that may result when personal religious beliefs are related to objective methods of study.

Exploring various kinds of objective study and different traditional and nontraditional religious options can enhance a person's understanding of religious life and ability to make religious decisions. In the last analysis, some tension and, it is hoped, a healthy balance will remain between one's religious commitment and theoretical understanding of religious life. The latter aspect is important in the scholarly world, which needs to develop an intellectually disciplined method of understanding religious life that does not depend on the adherence of all researchers to a common belief system. Scholars need a theory about religious life, not an ideology—especially one based simply on the researcher's religious belief—and they need to be able to examine that theory from the joint perspectives of empirical study and philosophical reflection. At the same time, such study may open up the possibility of ultimate transformation in the researcher's life.

The engagement with alternate religious options, of course, always takes place in a particular cultural-historical context and may have unforeseen consequences. It is the matter of contexts and content that brings us to the conclusion of this book and to the application of some of its ideas.

THREE APPROACHES TO UNDERSTANDING RELIGION

In keeping with our two general assumptions that (1) the search for understanding the religious life is an ongoing process and (2) the fact of religious pluralism calls for the recognition of a variety of ultimate claims, we close this book with a description of three approaches to understanding the nature of religion. In these three points of view, both the need for understanding and the difficulty and the power of dialogue become clear. The difficulty is that the claims of the three spokesmen for these approaches seem to exclude the possibility for accepting other claims. The power exists in the possibility that one great tradition may inform another and together they will grow in understanding. Is one of these views better than the others? Are there aspects of each that can be integrated into a transcultural view giving equal value to the core claim of each perspective? Are they irreconcilable because each philosopher gives priority to different ways of evaluating the deepest aspects of life?

Each of these understandings of the nature of religion is given by a twentieth-century philosopher of religion. One is a Christian: Paul Tillich; another a Confucian: Chün-i T'ang; and the third a Buddhist: Keiji Nishitani. Each is aware of religions in the East and West and sensitive to the impact of scientific and analytical thought on modern life. Each of these philosophers tries to define religion, not in a particular tradition's history of religious ideas, but in the context of a worldwide human situation. In general, they try to answer the question of how people today can live authentically, given the limitations, selfishness, and weakness that seem to be part of the human condition. Each attempts to describe the nature of the deepest human need, how that need is fulfilled, and how life is enhanced at the most profound level.

Paul Tillich. For Tillich, human existence is the reality whose fulfillment is found through the creation of *meaning* as expressed in symbolic forms. Well-known symbols from the traditional religions include the cross and empty tomb in Christianity, Lord Shiva's third eye of insight and destruction in Hinduism, and the lotus, whose roots are in the mud but whose blossom opens above the water in Buddhism. Life without meaning is chaos; it has no value. To be human means that a person tries to unify all the elements of his or her consciousness, both the ideal and the practical aspects, in a meaningful gesture or symbol. Reality is not something outside the act of the human spirit. *Recognized at the deepest level, "reality" means to be aware of the unity of life in all its variety.* Tillich affirms a common theme in Western philosophy when he says:

> Meaning is the common characteristic and the ultimate unity of the theoretical and the practical sphere of spirit, of scientific and aesthetic, of legal and social structures. The spiritual reality in which the spirit-bearing form (*Gestalt*) lives and creates, is a meaning-reality.[1]

According to Tillich, there are three elements in every expression of meaning: (1) an awareness of the interconnection of the separate aspects of meaning, (2) the awareness that every particular meaning is related to an unconditioned and ultimate meaningfulness, and (3) an awareness that, although there is no complete unity of meaning in any existing (and thus conditioned) meaning, there is the *demand* experienced by people to fulfill the unconditioned meaning. Although any cultural form can express the spirit-bearing forces, not every cultural form expresses the unconditioned or ultimate meaning. In fact, there are demonic expressions at work when the true unconditional (divine) meaning is rejected. This rejection appears, for example, when a state claims to have ultimate authority and denies citizens freedom of conscience. However, there is the demand felt by many philosophers, prophets, seers, and artists as inherent in life to present the *unity of all meaning*. This all-pervading demand makes the unconditional meaning expressible at all times in some cultural forms, as in religious rituals, sacred writings, or righteous social action.

The consciousness of meaning, then, is the place where the spirit takes form. The formulation of a meaningful human expression is an act of ego consciousness in which finite human beings paradoxically express infinite self-transcendence. The highest value in human life appears in a personal act that depends on *infinite being-itself* (God) and that, at the same time, is a positive action within finite existence. The role of the personality in exposing both the partially unified cultural meaning and the unconditional ground for all meaning is made clear when Tillich states:

> The real meaning-fulfillment is one in which bestowal of meaning takes place in the sphere of individual reality bound to nature; an ideal fulfillment is one in which the giving of meaning involves no transformation in the material sphere, but, rather, a fulfillment of the existent thing in its immediate formation. . . . Personality is the place of meaning-fulfillment, both real and ideal.[2]

Nevertheless, Tillich makes clear that there is a distinction between the expression of (partially) unified meaning in culture and the self-conscious awareness of the unconditioned meaning of religious life. In this context, *religion is the attempt to grasp symbolically the unity of meaning that is directed toward that which exists unconditionally*. Tillich's definition of religion is "the sum total of all spiritual acts directed toward grasping the unconditional import of meaning through the fulfillment of the unity of meaning."[3]

The basic expression for the synthesis of form, content, and the unconditional is a *symbol*. This symbol of unity can never be regarded as absolute; otherwise, it is demonic. A true religious symbol is one that shows how any symbol cannot restrict the unconditioned source of everything (God) while yet evoking the sense of profound significance in the ordering of life through that symbol. In sum, the true spiritual consciousness, for Tillich, is the creation of a reality through meaning, which stands under the demand of unconditional reality; and the purest form of this is a symbol, which paradoxically unifies and judges all symbols.

Chün-i T'ang. For the Confucian scholar, Chün-i T'ang, "god" is not the central issue of spiritual life. Similarly, myths and symbol systems—while always found in religious institutions—are external to the core of the inborn religious spirit in all humanity. T'ang insists that Confucianism shares with all major religions the central demand of religious life; namely, "man lives to find a sure place to establish himself and his 'fate.'"[4] Human beings establish themselves within the order of the universe by realizing that their well-being is inseparable from that of all other beings. A person's fate (*ming*) is not an unchangeable predestination; it is the ultimate context in which particular personal obligations of an individual as a moral agent are set.

T'ang explains how a religious spirit and activity are needed beyond philosophic, scientific, or aesthetic interests to establish oneself in an ultimate context:

> [M]an can acquire the place for sure establishment only when his mind of infinity and transcendence, as much as this life and existence, are established or settled. This establishment depends on man's possession of the following things: religious belief or faith, the demand of the religious spirit through which the infinity and transcendence of the mind are manifested, religious morality, and moral deeds. This establishment can be found in most religions and the Confucianist religion.[5]

The basic human spiritual act, then, is any appropriate emotional, intellectual and physical expression of oneself in relation to the natural rhythm of change in the universe.

By doing an appropriate moral-spiritual action, a person expresses the essential value in the "human-heart." The highest expression of value in the universe is self-confidence arising from intuitive participation in the rhythm of change. T'ang says:

> [T]he final stage of the development of man's religious spirit ends in approaching the spirit of self-confidence. . . . Since Confucius and Mencius, the Confucianist has emphasized the spirit of self-reflection, self-awareness, and self-confidence. This spirit will become the convergence of all religions in the long run.[6]

This manifestation of the highest human value is not separate from the basic values within all nature. Ultimately, all existence is an expression of value, and the deepest sense of personal self-awareness is the avoidance of self-centeredness, which is also the expression of "human-heart" (*jen*). Even craving for survival and conflict between individuals are not morally neutral or without implications of value; they must be seen within the ultimate context of the harmony or internal order as a facet of the growth of things. Unless there is an implicit internal order, T'ang insists, the struggle or conflct between individual entities is impossible.

The realization of the "human-heart," when people continue and complete the inherent harmony of all things, is most clearly expressed for T'ang in the three objects of reverence: heaven-and-earth, a person's ancestors, and the great teacher (Confucius). For T'ang, the multiple objects of reverence express the deepest spiritual reality. Having multiple and, at the same time, particular personal experiences of a universal abstract spirit is important for the most profound kind of self-awareness. It is a conscious process in which one grasps the nature and movement of life. It is also a process whereby a person embodies values expressed in daily living.

Through a deep inner participation in the awareness of the origins and most fulfilling values of one's particular existence, a person can make appropriate decisions for applying this organic grasp of life to his or her individual situation. For example, a mother will care for her children; a government official will make plans to help a community prosper. Only after one has perceived the variety of interacting forces of one's present situation can one make the right moral choice in action. This kind of intuition does not result in an act of an isolated individual. Right moral choice in action expresses one's being as related to other people and one's environment at that moment in the rhythm of change. Acting in relation to the connected forces in life is a sign of spiritual integrity and establishes one's self and one's fate. T'ang summarizes the core of religious life as follows:

> The root of religious spirit lies in the transcendental completion and eternity of the demand for preservation and emergence of values. In the universe, growth of natural things, cultivation of human culture, the achievement of the realm of human integrity—all are activities of creating and actualizing values.[7]

Keiji Nishitani. Like Tillich and T'ang, the Buddhist philosopher Keiji Nishitani examines the self and the world to expose the nature of things. All three point out that without a deeper awareness than is commonly experienced, a person will be caught in the overwhelming sense of transience and meaninglessness. However, for Nishitani, the key to gaining a fulfilling perspective is not the personal creation of symbolic meaning that stands under the demand of unconditional reality; nor is it the establishment of a person in his or her proper position in the eternal rhythm of change; rather, it is *full* awareness of how we experience our existence.

Full awareness, in the Buddhist tradition, requires a breakthrough in the field of consciousness so that one no longer is aware of a separate ego, which is presumably to be fulfilled. To see the world in representations (symbols), or through a subject-object awareness, is only one—and a deficient—way to be conscious. It is a self-centered way of being in existence. To recognize that we participate in different modes of existence by experiencing different modes of consciousness is a basic step in attaining the deepest sense of life. This sense requires recognizing that at the core of one's being is the reality of death and nothingness of the self.

For Nishitani, religion is "the self-awareness of reality, or more correctly, the *real* self-awareness of reality."[8] Such inner awareness is more than a reflection on death or a skepticism about the ultimate significance of any human effort. Although he affirms that all of life is transient and human beings encounter the reality of nonbeing at each step, Nishitani claims that it is only in religion that human beings reach a deepening of the perception of their transience so that they see nothingness (or absolute emptiness) as the very condition of existence. In Zen, this awareness has been called "coming to oneself." Religion goes beyond philosophical doubt that there is intrinsic value in anything in this world. The special quality of the religious way of knowing reality is that "in religion one persistently pushes ahead in a direction where doubt becomes a reality for the self and makes itself really present in the self."[9]

For Nishitani, sin and morality are not simply questions of social expectations or even of decisions by an individual person. To think of sin as something that a person commits, such as disobedience against parents or God, is superficial; this is only a reflection of the fear generated by a false self understood as an entity over against another independent entity. Evil is, rather, a condition in the mental-emotional construction of oneself and other selves. Evil is a radical element of all conventional experience of existence as it is basic to a personal mode of being. To deal with the radical character of evil requires one to see how a dependence on the assumed personal self is hopeless.

The key activity that allows a person to perceive the nature of existence is shifting out of everyday consciousness to an intuitive identity with the absolute emptiness that is at the root of being. This awareness must be more than an intellectual comprehension of reality; it must be a total realization in spirit, soul, and body. As Tillich spoke of "meaning-reality"—the reality of our being known through meaning—and T'ang called for the actualization of one's "human-heart" to make oneself a "real" person, so Nishitani says that realizing absolute emptiness of oneself is the moment of "the reality realizing itself in our awareness."[10] In everyday consciousness, we rarely are in contact with things in the world, but with our ego-based response to them.

To shift out of everyday consciousness, a person must experience "Great Doubt." This kind of deep probing of the empty self is quite different from a common awareness of the transience and uncertainty of existence experienced by many people. It is a self-awareness more fundamental than ego consciousness:

> The Great Doubt represents not only the apex of the doubting self but also the point of its "passing away" and ceasing to be "self." It is like the bean whose seed and shell break apart as it ripens: the shell is the tiny ego, and the seed the infinity of the Great Doubt that encompasses the whole world. It is the moment at which self is at the same time the nothingness of self, the moment that is the "locus" of nothingness where conversion beyond the Great Doubt takes place.[11]

The Great Doubt that exposes the reality of the emptiness of self allows one to be released from the Great Doubt as perceived by the ego. If the Great Doubt is seen as a nihilistic void in which a self constructs an egoistic meaning—as it is in much contemporary French existentialist thought— it cannot free one from attachment to the self. Rather, the reality of absolute emptiness is the exposure of self and all things just as they are. Such an awareness of things is not a perception of emptiness (nothingness) as an object of ego consciousness, which would be just a representation or symbol.

To be aware of absolute emptiness is to affirm also the emptiness of a "nihilizing view" or of a negative attitude. It is a mode of awareness that discloses things as they are in both their particularity and relatedness. Nishitani suggests something of this awareness when he states:

> Only absolute emptiness is the true no-ground. Here all things—from a flower or a stone to stellar nebulae and galactic systems, and even life and death themselves—become present as bottomless realities. They disclose their bottomless suchness. True freedom lies in this no-ground.[12]

The goal of religion, then, is the awareness of "absolute emptiness" at the core of oneself, which eliminates selfishness at the deepest level. When this takes place, true charity, honesty, and justice can begin. By letting go of one's self-image, a person can be aware of existence at the deepest level and make practical decisions that do not lead to evil or pain.

CAN THE ALTERNATIVE APPROACHES BE RECONCILED?

By comparing the thought of Paul Tillich, Chün-i T'ang, and Keiji Nishitani, we can see that there are deep-set processes of evaluation that affect basic orientations to the nature of religious life. We can recognize three basically different approaches to authentic living: (1) through the creation of meaning by a person in community under the demand of "being-itself" (compare Chapter 3); (2) through the establishment of one's place in the cosmic rhythm of change by making moral choices (compare Chapter 4); and (3) through full awareness (insight) of the transience and related arising of existence that avoids attachment to a self-image (compare Chapter 5).

These three alternatives to the worldwide awareness of some fundamental problematic in the human situation and a proposal for a way to overcome it suggest a basis for understanding and the difficulty of doing so.[13] We need to recognize the differences in religious perspectives without either translating an alternate perspective into our own terms or considering our own perspective to be unchangeable. As the dialogue (or trilogue) proceeds, however, we recognize that each of us must understand an alternate view in relation to his or her own position. The question of how far people can go in reinterpreting their own position in light of the interreligious encounter remains open. As indicated in Chapter 14, in a dialogic approach to understanding religious life, an investigator is not only learning about another ideal for humanity but also is learning something about his or her own religious commitment.

The religious forms in which human beings have participated in the past and the tension within modern people's self-identity are part of the situation in the contemporary world. They are part of the limitations and possibilities we must consider to interpret who we are. In this light, understanding the religious life of all humanity and reflecting on the characteristics of religious life are not just abstract problems to be approached by a few specialists; they are directly related to the experience of what it means to be human at the deepest (and highest) level.

SELECTED READINGS

H. Ward, *Religion 2101 A.D.: Who or What Will Be God?* (Garden City, NY: Doubleday, 1975). An imaginative projection of a "new cosmic religion" based on current movements and discoveries in science, social history, and human consciousness.

G. Leonard, *The Transformation: A Guide to the Inevitable Changes in Humankind* (New York: Delacorte Press, 1972). A description of, and a call for, social experimentation in spontaneity and joy of living that requires intense effort, discipline, imagination, and a shift in awareness.

*J. Needleman, A. K. Bierman, and J. A. Gould, eds., *Religion for a New Generation*, 2nd ed. (New York: Macmillan, 1977). A book of readings exploring the nature of religion, methods for understanding the current situation of spiritual revolution, and religious dimensions of secular activities.

*R. Creel, *Religion and Doubt: Toward a Faith of Your Own* (Englewood Cliffs, NJ: Prentice-Hall, 1977). A brief introduction to different approaches and interpretations of religion focusing on issues arising from a personal development of a religious commitment.

*Dom A. Graham, *The End of Religion* (New York: Harcourt, 1971). A personal statement by a Roman Catholic who sees "ultimate religion" as a person "responding to the Existence in virtue of which he himself exists" and making use of insights from the whole history of human spiritual experience.

D. Howlett, *The Fourth American Faith* (New York: Harper, 1964). Here the fourth faith, the "faith of adventure," is described over against Protestantism, Catholicism, and Judaism.

Two books stating a religious perspective that includes the "best" in traditional religious expressions while emphasizing the capacities within human life are: *J. Dewey, *A Common Faith* (New Haven, CT: Yale University Press, 1934); and *R. Tagore, *The Religion of Man* (Boston: Beacon, 1931).

R. N. Bellah, ed., *Religion and Progress in Modern Asia* (New York: Free Press, 1965). A collection of papers by a variety of scholars on the influence of religious life and belief in different Asian countries. The epilogue provides an incisive analysis of the problems of defining and understanding the role of religion in contemporary Asian life.

A. Gehlen, *Man in the Age of Technology* (New York: Columbia University Press, 1980; first published in 1957). A perceptive examination of contemporary Western European life in which technological skill is seen as an expression of an unconscious law that progressively objectifies human labor and performance. Social institutions are seen as creations of human beings to give direction and purpose to individual consciousness.

*M. Katz, W. Marsh, and G. Thompson, eds., *Earth's Answer* (New York: Harper & Row, 1977). Papers given by well-known scientists, professors of law, and spiritual leaders at Lindisfarne Conferences on various topics in explorations of planetary culture.

*E. Laszlo, ed., *Goals for Mankind* (New York: E. P. Dutton, 1977). A report derived from the Club of Rome, containing a final section on the possible role of the great religous traditions in the development of world solidarity.

J. Needleman, *Consciousness and Tradition* (New York: Crossroad, 1982). A series of reflective essays by a prominent professor of comparative religion portraying the religious significance of specific cultural forms such as psychiatry, existentialism, and traditional religions. The author calls for an inner cultivation of spiritual arts as the deepest resource for people in contemporary society.

*A. Toffler, *Future Shock* (New York: Random House, 1970). A study of the impact of accelerating social, political, and technological change in the West; the author calls for a humanization of planning in social and political structures.

P. Slater, *The Wayward Gate: Science and the Supernatural* (Boston: Beacon Press, 1977). The author calls on contemporary readers to remain open to a consideration of a variety of "realities" when trying to understand themselves and their environment.

*C. Castaneda, *Journey to Ixlan: The Lessons of Don Juan* (New York: Touchstone Books, Simon & Schuster, 1972). Explores the consequences of opening a person to a new self-awareness.

Notes

CHAPTER 2: PERSONAL APPREHENSION OF A HOLY PRESENCE

1. *The Life of the Holy Mother Teresa of Jesus,* trans. by E. Peers (New York: Sheed & Ward, 1946), p. 121.
2. *The Pearl of Great Price: A Selection from the Revelations, Translations, and Narrations of Joseph Smith* (Salt Lake City: The Church of Jesus Christ of the Latter Day Saints, 1949), p. 50.
3. C. Isherwood, *Ramakrishna and His Disciples* (New York: Simon & Schuster, 1965), p. 66.
4. H. Van Straelen, *The Religion of Divine Wisdom: Japan's Most Powerful Religious Movement* (Kyoko: Veritas Shoin, 1957), p. 41.
5. Found in L. Renou, ed., *Hinduism* (New York: Washington Square Press, 1963), p. 187.
6. Found in H. H. Coates and R. Ishizuka, *Honen the Buddhist Saint* (Kyoto: Society for the Publication of Sacred Books of the World, 1949), p. 399.
7. Jacques Durandeaux, *Living Questions to Dead Gods,* trans. by W. Whitman (New York: Sheed & Ward, 1968), pp. 86–87.
8. Isaiah 1:4–7, found in *The New English Bible* (New York: Oxford University Press, 1970), p. 808.
9. Isaiah 1:18–19, Ibid., p. 809.
10. Sirdar Iqbal Ali Shah, *Lights of Asia* (London: Arthur Baker, 1934), p. 31. Many expressions of the Muslim awareness of the unique and incomprehensible nature of God are found in K. Cragg and M. Speight, *Islam from Within* (Belmont, CA: Wadsworth, 1980).
11. *Bhagavad-gita* 11: 10–12, 19, 25, 47, and 49, found in E. Deutsch, trans., *The Bhagavad Gita* (New York: Holt, Rinehart & Winston, 1968), pp. 95–97, 100–101.
12. R. Coles, "God and the Rural Poor," *Psychology Today,* January 1972, p. 36.
13. R. Fujiwara, trans., *The Tanni Sho: Notes Lamenting Differences* (Tokyo: Ryukoku University, 1962), p. 58.

14. *Vedic Hymns*, trans. by H. Oldenburg (Delhi: Motilal Banarasidass, 1964, first published 1897), Part II, p. 352.
15. J. Brough, *Selections from Classical Sanskrit Literature* (London: Luzac, 1952). p. 81. Reprinted by permission.
16. From K. Cragg and R. M. Speight, *Islam from Within*, p. 203.
17. Markandeya Purana 88:2–5, found in C. Dimmitt and J. A. B. van Buitenen, eds. and trans., *Classical Hindu Mythology* (Philadelphia: Temple University Press, 1978), p. 219.
18. R. Jones, *The World Within* (New York: Macmillan, 1918), pp. 18–19.
19. N. Ferré, *Making Religion Real* (New York: Harper, 1955), pp. 51, 54.
20. From *Daily Handbook for Days of Joy and Sorrow*, in P. C. Erb, ed., *Pietists: Selected Writings* (New York: Paulist Press, 1983), p. 185.
21. W. Pauck, trans., *Luther: Lectures on Romans* (Philadelphia: Westminster Press, 1961), p. 234.
22. Daien Fugen, trans., *The Shoshin Ge: The Gatha of True Faith in the Nembutsu* (Kyoto: Ryokoku University, 1961), p. 25.

CHAPTER 3: CREATION OF COMMUNITY THROUGH SACRED SYMBOLS

1. F. Waters, *Book of the Hopi* (New York: Viking Press, 1963), pp. 5–6.
2. *The New English Bible*, p. 72.
3. J. Neusner, *The Way of Torah*, 3rd ed. (North Scituate, MA: Duxbury Press, 1979), pp. 39–40.
4. Walter Abbott, S. J., ed., *The Documents of Vatican II*, trans. by Msgr. Joseph Gallagher (New York: Guild Press, 1966), p. 143.
5. See *Sunday Missal Prayerbook and Hymnal* (New York: Catholic Book, n.d.), p. 45.
6. An excellent Roman Catholic explanation of the unique character of sacred symbolic acts is found in V. Warnach, "Symbol and Reality in the Eucharist," in P. Benoit, R. E. Murphy, and B. van Jersel, eds., *The Breaking of Bread*, Vol. 40 of the series Concilium: Theology in the Age of Renewal (New York: Paulist Press, 1969), especially pp. 95–100.
7. R. B. Pandey, "Hindu Sacraments (Samskaras)," in *The Cultural Heritage of India*, rev. ed., 4 vols. (Calcutta: The Ramakrishna Mission, 1967), Vol. 2, p. 406.
8. See K. Cragg, *The House of Islam*, 2nd ed. (Encino, CA: Dickenson, 1975), Chapter 3.
9. See T. J. Hopkins, *The Hindu Religious Tradition* (Encino, CA: Dickenson, 1971), Chapter 2, "The Creative Power of the Sacrifice," and pp. 111–117 for a discussion of mantras in Vedic sacrifice and Hindu worship (*puja*).
10. Trans. by S. Beyer, ed., *The Buddhist Experience: Sources and Interpretations* (Encino, CA: Dickenson, 1974), p. 56. See pp. 46–64 and 116–153 for excerpts from various sources that assume the power of special words and actions in the Buddhist tradition.

11. J. S. Mbiti, *African Religions and Philosophies* (Garden City, NY: Doubleday, 1970), p. 165.

12. Ibid.

13. Ibid., pp. 165–166.

CHAPTER 4: LIVING IN HARMONY WITH COSMIC LAW

1. S. Radhakrishnan, *The Hindu View of Life* (London: George Allen & Unwin, 1961, first published 1927), p. 55.

2. Chün-i T'ang, "Religious Beliefs and Modern Chinese Culture, Part II: The Religious Spirit of Confucianism," *Chinese Studies in Philosophy*, Vol. 5, No. 1 (Fall 1973), pp. 52–53.

3. From the *Central Harmony (Chung Yung)*, trans. by Lin Yutang, in Lin Yutang, ed., *The Wisdom of Confucius* (New York: Modern Library, 1938), p. 105.

4. I:38–45; from E. Deutsch, trans., *The Bhagavad Gita* (New York: Holt, Rinehart & Winston, 1968), p. 34.

5. "Cosmologies in Ancient Chinese Philosophy," *Chinese Studies in Philosophy*, Vol. 5, No. 1 (Fall 1973), p. 15.

6. *Chung Yung*, XII:1 in L. G. Thompson, *Chinese Religion*, 3rd ed. (Belmont, CA: Wadsworth, 1979), p. 6.

7. Ibid., p. 4.

8. "The Philosophy at the Basis of Traditional Chinese Society," in F. S. C. Northrop, ed., *Ideological Differences and World Order* (New Haven, CT: Yale University Press, 1949), p. 28.

9. From *The Meditations of Emperor Marcus Antonius*, trans. by A. S. L. Farquharson (Oxford: Clarendon Press, 1944), p. 81.

10. D. S. Muzzey, *Ethics as a Religion* (New York: Simon & Schuster, 1951; reprinted New York: Frederick Unger, 1967), pp. 156, 158.

11. From the *Central Harmony (Chung Yung)*, in Lin Yutang, ed., *The Wisdom of Confucius*, p. 105.

12. From *The Mencius*, trans. by B. Watson, in *Sources of Chinese Tradition*, comp. by W. T. de Bary, Wing-tsit Chan, and B. Watson (New York: Columbia University Press, 1960), pp. 105–106.

13. *Li Chi: Records of Ritual and Protocol* XXI: 11, from *The Sacred Books of China: The Texts of Confucianism*, trans., by James Legge (Delhi: Motilal Banarasidass, 1966; first published in 1885), Sacred Books of the East Series, Vol. 28, p. 227.

14. Trans. by Lin Yutang, in Lin Yutang, ed., *The Wisdom of Confucius*, p. 229.

15. "The Philosophy at the Basis of Traditional Chinese Society," p. 20.

16. Trans. by Hung-ming Ku, in L. G. Thompson, *The Chinese Way in Religion* (Encino, CA: Dickenson, 1973), pp. 33–34.

17. M. Hiriyanna, "Philosophy of Values," in *The Cultural Heritage of India*, III (Calcutta: The Ramakrishna Mission, 1953), pp. 647–648.

18. Thompson, *Chinese Religion*, p. 136.

19. *Laws of Manu*, trans. by G. Buehler in Sacred Books of the East Series, Vol. 25 (Oxford University Press, 1886), pp. 30–31.

269
Notes

CHAPTER 5: ATTAINING FREEDOM THROUGH SPIRITUAL DISCIPLINE

1. *A Flower Does Not Talk: Zen Essays*, trans. by S. Kudo (Rutland, VT: Charles E. Tuttle, 1970), pp. 46–47.
2. Sri Aurobindo, *On Yoga I: The Synthesis of Yoga* (Pondicherry: Sri Aurobindo Ashram, 1965), pp. 768–769.
3. *Creativity and Taosim* (New York: Julian Press, 1963), pp. 130–131.
4. *Zen Mind, Beginner's Mind*, ed. by T. Dixon (New York: Weatherhill, 1970), pp. 21–22.
5. From W. T. de Bary, ed., *Sources of Chinese Tradition* (New York: Columbia University Press, 1960), p. 57.
6. Ibid., p. 53.
7. From the *Katha Upanishad* II. 1.1, 2, 4, 5, in *The Principal Upanishads*, trans. by S. Radhakrishnan (New York: Harper, 1953), pp. 630–632.
8. Sri Aurobindo, *A Practical Guide to Integral Yoga* (Pondicherry: Sri Aurobindo Ashram, 1965), p. 26.
9. From the *Digha-nikaya* (collection of long discourses), in S. Beyer, ed., *The Buddhist Experience*, p. 83. See also the other excerpts in Chapter 5, "The Stages on the Path."
10. From *Jaina Sutras*, trans. by H. Jacobi in Sacred Books of the East Series, Vol. 22 (Oxford: Oxford University Press, 1884), Part I, pp. 79, 80.
11. *The Perfection of Wisdom in Eight Thousand Lines*, trans. by E. Conze (Bolinas, CA: Four Seasons Foundation, 1973), p. 98. Italics added.
12. From Hui-k'ai, *The Gateless Barrier*, trans. by S. Beyer, in S. Beyer, ed., *The Buddhist Experience*, p. 268; see also other examples of koans on pp. 261–269.
13. Chapter 15, found in Chang Chung-yuan, *Creativity and Taoism*, pp. 126–127.
14. *The Heart of Buddhist Meditation* (New York: Samuel Weiser, 1962), pp. 19–20.

PART TWO: MODES OF HUMAN AWARENESS USED TO EXPRESS RELIGIOUS MEANING

1. K. Nielson, "Ethics Without Religion," in P. Kierty, ed., *Moral Problems in Contemporary Society: Essays in Humanistic Ethics* (Englewood Cliffs, NJ: Prentice-Hall, 1969), p. 21.
2. J. Huxley, "Transhumanism," in *New Bottles for New Wine: Essays by Julian Huxley* (London: Chatto and Windus, 1959), pp. 13–14. See also

his book, *Religion Without Revelation* (New York: New American Library, 1957), especially Chapter 9, "Evolutionary Humanism as a Developed Religion."

CHAPTER 6: THE RELIGIOUS SIGNIFICANCE OF FULFILLING HUMAN RELATIONSHIPS

1.   *The New English Bible: The Old Testament*, p. 1132.
2.   From Lin Yutang, ed., *The Wisdom of Confucius*, p. 186.
3.   From S. Beyer, ed., *The Buddhist Experience*, pp. 40–41.
4.   O. H. Mowrer, "The Problem of Good and Evil Empirically Considered, with Reference to Psychological and Social Adjustment," *Zygon: Journal of Religion and Science*, Vol. 4, No. 4 (December 1969), p. 12.
5.   A. Maslow, "Eupsychia—The Good Society," *Journal of Humanistic Psychology*, Vol. 1, No. 2 (Fall 1961), p. 8.
6.   See C. R. Rogers, "The Necessary and Sufficient Conditions of Therapeutic Personality Change," *Journal of Consulting Psychology*, Vol. 21 (1957), pp. 95–103.
7.   C. R. Rogers, *Freedom to Learn* (Columbus, OH: Merrill, 1969), pp. 304–305.
8.   From J. C. Lilly, *The Center of the Cyclone: An Autobiography of Inner Space* (New York: Bantam, 1973), pp. 103–104.
9.   F. Perls, *Gestalt Therapy Verbatim*, comp. and ed. by J. O. Stevens (Lafayette, CA: Real People Press, 1969), frontispiece.

CHAPTER 7: THE RELIGIOUS SIGNIFICANCE OF SOCIAL RESPONSIBILITY

1.   *The New English Bible: The Old Testament*, pp. 627–628.
2.   Ibid., p. 888.
3.   J. H. Stewart, ed., *A Documentary Survey of the French Revolution* (New York: Macmillan, 1951), p. 113.
4.   A. Camus, *Resistance, Rebellion, and Death*, trans. by J. O'Brien (New York: Alfred A. Knopf, 1970), p. 93.
5.   J. Gerassi, ed., *Venceremos! The Speeches and Writings of Che Guevara* (New York: Simon & Schuster, 1968), p. 379.
6.   "Religion and Morality," *Journal of Religion*, Vol. 29 (1949), p. 93.

CHAPTER 8: THE POWER OF RATIONALITY

1.   "Mourning Dove (Hu-mis-hu-ma)," *Coyote Stories* (Caldwell, ID: Caxton Printers, 1934); reprinted in J. F. Dobie, M. C. Boatright, and H. H. Ransom, eds., *Coyote Wisdom* (Dallas: Southern Methodist University Press, 1965), p. 66.

2. E. L. Palmer and H. S. Fowler, *Fieldbook of Natural History,* 2nd ed. (New York: McGraw-Hill, 1975), p. 693.

3. *The New English Bible: The New Testament*, p. 213.

4. Ibid., p. 221.

5. From the *Encyclopedie*, ed. by D. Diderot and J. d'Alembert, in F. le Van Baumer, ed., *Main Currents in Western Thought* (New York: Alfred A. Knopf, 1934), pp. 374–375.

6. L. Carroll, *Alice's Adventures in Wonderland and Through the Looking Glass* (New York: Harper, 1949), p. 127.

7. A. N. Whitehead, *Process and Reality: An Essay in Cosmology,* (New York: Humanities Press, 1929), p. 4.

8. B. de Spinoza, "The Treatise on the Improvement of the Understanding," in T. V. Smith and M. Greene, eds., *Philosophers Speak for Themselves: From Descartes to Locke* (Chicago: University of Chicago Press, 1940), p. 247.

9. D. Howlett, *The Fourth American Faith* (New York: Harper & Row, 1964), p. 180.

CHAPTER 9: THE POWER OF ARTISTIC CREATIVITY

1. L. Gilkey, "Can Art Fill the Vacuum?" *Criterion* (Autumn 1981), p. 8.

2. V. Zuckerkandl, *Man the Musician,* trans. by N. Guterman, Vol. 2 (Princeton, NJ: Princeton University Press, 1973), p. 13.

3. E. Gilson, *Painting and Reality* (Princeton, NJ: Princeton University Press, 1957), p. 210.

4. T. R. Martland, *Religion as Art: An Interpretation* (Albany: State University of New York Press, 1981), p. 158.

5. See Okakura Kakuzo, *The Book of Tea* (Rutland, VT: Tuttle, 1906), for an exposition and advocacy of "teaism" as an expression of the Japanese art of life.

6. Trans. by A. Waley, in *Translations from the Chinese* (New York: Alfred A. Knopf, 1941), p. 121.

7. See H. N. McFarland, *The Rush Hour of the Gods* (New York: Macmillan, 1967). Chapter 6, "PL Kyodan: An Epicurean Movement."

8. Quoted in T. R. Martland, *Religion as Art,* p. 149.

CHAPTER 10: THE RELIGIOUS RESPONSE TO PHYSICAL EXISTENCE

1. From *Ch'un-ch'iu fan-lu* [deep significance of the *Spring and Autumn Annals*], trans. by B. Watson, in *Sources of Chinese Tradition,* comp. by W. T. de Bary, Wing-tsit Chan, and B. Watson, p. 218. For further explanation of ancient Chinese cosmology, see L. G. Thompson, *Chinese Religion,* 3rd ed., Chapter 1; and L. G. Thompson, ed., *The Chinese Way in Religion,* Chapter 6.

2. Charles Darwin, *On the Origin of Species by Means of Natural Selection: Or the Preservation of Favoured Races in the Struggle for Life* (New York: Heritage Press, 1963; first published 1859), pp. 444–445.

3. R. B. Fuller, *Utopia or Oblivion* (New York: Bantam, 1969), p. 159.

4. V. C. Ferkiss, *Technological Man: The Myth and Reality* (New York: Braziller, 1969), pp. 17, 19.

CHAPTER 11: THE ORIGINS OF RELIGIOUS LIFE

1. E. E. Evans-Pritchard, *Theories of Primitive Religion* (London: Oxford University Press, 1965), pp. 104–105.

CHAPTER 12: PSYCHOLOGICAL AND SOCIAL FUNCTIONS OF RELIGION

1. C. G. Jung, *Psychology and Religion* (New Haven, CT: Yale University Press, 1938), p. 98.

2. See R. N. Bellah, "Civil Religion In America," in his *Beyond Belief* (New York: Harper, 1970), pp. 168–189; and W. L. Warner, *American Life: Dream and Reality* (Chicago: University of Chicago Press, 1953).

3. T. Luckmann, *The Invisible Religion: The Problem of Religion in Modern Society* (New York: Macmillan, 1967), pp. 53–56.

4. See A. L. Kroeber, *Anthropology,* rev. ed. (New York: Harcourt, 1948) and *Nature of Culture* (Chicago: University of Chicago Press, 1952).

CHAPTER 13: THE COMPARATIVE STUDY OF RELIGION

1. J. Wach, *The Comparative Study of Religions,* ed. by J. M. Kitagawa (New York: Columbia University Press, 1958), p. 30.

2. See W. C. Smith, *The Meaning and End of Religion* (New York: Macmillan, 1962), pp. 185–192.

3. See N. Smart, *The Science of Religion and the Sociology of Knowledge* (Princeton, NJ: Princeton University Press, 1973), pp. 67 ff. and *The Phenomenon of Religion* (New York: Herder and Herder, 1973), pp. 62 ff.

CHAPTER 14: UNDERSTANDING THROUGH INTERRELIGIOUS DIALOGUE

1. "Toward a New Jus Gentium," in F. S. C. Northrop, ed., *Ideological Differences and World Order* (New Haven, CT: Yale University Press, 1949), p. 10.

2. *Intra-religious Dialogue* (New York: Paulist Press, 1978), p. 73.

3. *The Human Way: A Dialogic Approach to Religion and Human Experience* (Chambersburg, PA: Anima Books, 1982), p. 100.

4. "Dialogue," in *Between Man and Man*, trans. by R. G. Smith (Boston: Beacon Press, 1947), p. 22.

CHAPTER 15: CONSEQUENCES OF UNDERSTANDING RELIGIOUS LIFE

1. *What Is Religion?* trans. by J. L. Adams (New York: Harper & Row, 1969), pp. 56–57.

2. Ibid., p. 64.

3. Ibid., p. 60.

4. "Religious Beliefs and Modern Chinese Culture, Part II: The Religious Spirit of Confucianism," *Chinese Studies in Philosophy*, Vol. 5, No. 1 (Fall 1973), p. 51.

5. Ibid., p. 52.

6. Ibid., p. 56.

7. Ibid., p. 79.

8. *Religion and Nothingness*, trans. by J. van Bragt (Berkeley: University of California Press, 1982), p. 5.

9. Ibid., p. 18.

10. Ibid., p. 5.

11. Ibid., p. 21.

12. Ibid., p. 34.

13. For a more complete analysis of these three positions, see F. J. Streng, "Three Approaches to Authentic Existence: Christian, Confucian, and Buddhist," *Philosophy East and West*, Vol. 32, No. 4 (October 1982), pp. 371–392.

Index

Advaita Vedanta, 95, 97
Al-Ash'ari, 147
Allport, Gordon, 208, 210
American Revolution, 132–133
Amida Buddha, 28
Animism, 199, 227–228
Anthropology of religion, 216–218
Aquinas, Thomas, 148
Archaeological record, 202
Aristotle, 130–131
Arjuna. *See* Bhagavad-Gita
Artistic creativity, 159–173
Artists, 169
Aryan culture, 147
Ayer, A. J., 153

Baptism, 39
Beginner's mind, 89
Bellah, Robert, 215
Bhagavad-Gita, 30–31
  on chaos, 66–67
  on duty, 76
  everyday world in, 179–180
Bisocial engineering, 185–186
Bodhisattva, 114
Brahman, 177
Brahmins, 81
Buber, Martin, 244
Buddha, depiction of, 163–164
Buddhism
  artistic creativity, 163–164
  dhamma, 113–114, 131–132
  ethics in, 131–132
  logic in, 149
  Pure Land, 29, 37
  Zen, 84, 96
Bunyan, John, 28
Butler, Joseph, 148

Castes, 75–77
Catholic High Mass, 111
Chaos, 66–67
Chinese art, 168
Choice and dialogue, 245–247
Christ
  depiction of, 161, 162
  El Greco's portrayal, 163
  from historical perspective, 224
Christian nurture, 112
Christianity
  pastoral care, 112–113
  reason in, 148–149
  social gospel movement, 77–78, 129
Civil religion, 215
Civil rights movement, 136–137
Codrington, Robert H., 197
Coexistence of religious forms, 201–202
Comparative studies, 222–234
Comptuer-generated speech mechanism, 184
Conditionedness, 8
Conflict
  dialogue and, 245–247
  reactions to, 256–257

Confucian Canon, 66, 74, 81, 113, 147, 177–178
Confucianism
  on cosmic order, 177
  jen, 78–79, 260
  learning of, 63–64
  li, 74, 80
  Tao in, 69–71, 73–75
  virtues in, 125
Consciousness of meaning, 259
Contemporary religious processes, 254–256
Content of book, 22–23
Copernicus, Nicolaus, 180
Cosmic Law, 67–73
  characteristics of, 68–69
  figure illustration, 65
  harmony with, 63–83
  spiritual discipline distinguished, 88
Cosmologies, 174–189
Creation, 176–177
Creative process, 170
Cross-cultural study, 9–10
Cultural anthropology, 216–218
Cultural dimension, 5–7
  examination of religion in, 10
  intention and, 14
Cultural reductionism, 252
Cultural situations, 229–232
Cynics, 130

Dance, 164
Darwin, Charles, 182
Dead, worship of, 199
Declaration of the Rights of Man, 133
Definitions
  extension of, 255–256
  functions of, 143–145
  power of, 142–143
Deism, 227–228
Descartes, Rene, 152–153
Devotional services, 111–113
Dhamma, 113–114, 131–132
Dharma, 71–72
  personal expression and, 79
  social expression and, 80
  ultimate transformation and, 75–77
Dialogue, religious, 11, 235–249
Diderot, 151, 152
Disharmony, 66–67
Divided self, 115–116
Divine will, 127–130
Drama, 164
Durkheim, Emile, 198, 214, 218
Dynamics of religion, 250–251
Dynamism, 227

Eckhart, Meister, 97–98
Education, 155
Effective power, 2–3
Egocentricity, 79
Egyptian Gods and Goddesses, 162
Einstein, Albert, 181, 182
El Greco, 163

Eliade, Mircea, 201–202, 228
Empathic view, 253–254
Empirical data, 12
Enlightenment, 98
  rationality and, 152–153
Esalen, 119
Essences, 144
Eternal ideas, 178–179
Eternal reality, 38
Eternal rhythm, 177–178
Eternal self (*atman*), 91
Ethical culture movement, 72–73
Ethics
  and being human, 125–127
  and divine will, 127–130
  and human relationships, 113–114
  interreligious dialogue, 239–241
  natural good and, 130–132
Eucharist, 50–51
Evans-Prichard, E. E., 203
Everyday world, 178–180
Evidence for religion, 194–195
Evil, 261–262
Evolution theory, 182
Exclusivistic view, 242
Existential psychology, 212
Expectations and reality, 110

Faith, 35, 36–37, 230
  affirmations of, 241–244
  dialogue and, 241–244
  ethics expressed through, 128–130
  Martin Luther on, 146
Fate, 259–260
Feminist movement, 137
Ferkiss, V. C., 185–186
Ferre, Nels, 36
Filial piety, 74
Frazer, James G., 199–200
Freedom, 84–103
French Revolution, 132–133
Freud, Sigmund, 208, 209–210, 218
Friendship, 34
Fuller, R. Buckminster, 185
Fundamental ideas, 152–153
Funeral ritual, 75
Fung Yu-lan, 70, 75

Galileo Gallilei, 180
Gandhi, Mahatma, 134
Ganesh, 160–161, 163
Genetic engineering, 184, 185–186
Gestalt therapy, 119–120
God
  concept of, 143
  ethics and, 125
  Spinoza's use of word, 153
  world as creation of, 176–177
  see also Holy Presence
God's play, 179
Great Doubt, 262
Greeks
  moral philosophy of, 130–131
  Mueller on religion of, 196
  mythical expression, 72
Group therapy, 118–120
Guiding care, 112

Halal al Din Rumi, 33–34
Hanuman, 161
Hick, John, 240–241
High being, 200–201
Hinduism
    artistic creativity, 161, 162–163
    castes, 75–77
    dharma, see Dharma
    ecstatic fervor, 35
    God's play, 179–180
    standards of, 147–148
    as way of life, 63
Historical method of comparative
    religion, 223–225
Hofstadter, Albert, 170
Holy Communion, 50–51
Holy Presence, 22, 25–42
    alienation from, 27–29
    characteristics of, 29
    illustration of personal
        apprehension of, 27
    reality and, 26
    social expression of, 38–40
    ultimate reality/transformation,
        29–34
    visual images, 39–40
    see also God
Homosexuality, 146–147
Hopi Indians, 43
    dances of, 164
    kivas, 59
Human-heart (jen), 78–79, 260
Human relationships, 109–123
Humanism, 106–107
    psychology and, 211–213
Huxley, Aldous, 186
Huxley, Julian, 107, 155

Ideal and reality, 110
Illumination, 98
Images, 11
Imagination and art, 166–168
Industrial Revolution, 133–134
Initiation rites, 56–57
Insights, 254–255
Integral yoga, 84–85
Intention of religion, 14, 226
Interpretations, 142
Interreligious dialogue, 235–249
Irrational behavior, 150–151
Isaiah, 30, 38, 129
Islam
    obligatory prayer, 30
    revelation, 149
    social actions, 78
    standards, 147

Jainism, 94, 99
James, Edwin O., 202, 210
James, William, 208–209
Japanese art, 168–169
Jen, 78–79, 260
Jesus Christ. See Christ
Jones, Rufus, 35–36
Judaism
    ethics in, 128–129
    ritual celebration, 50
    social actions, 77–78

Jung, Carl, 208, 211

Kachinas, 164, 165
Karma, 76
Kluckhohn, Clyde, 210
Knowledge, 148–149
Koans, 96
Koran. See Qur'an
Krishna, depiction of, 162–163
Kroeber, Alfred L., 217

Language, power of, 53–55
Lao Tzu, 89–90
Legal rights, 125
Legislation, 135–136
Levy-Brühl, Lucien, 198–199
Levi-Strauss, Claude, 200, 217–218
Li actions, 74, 80
Liberation movements, 136–137
Liturgical art, 160–164
Logical analysis, 151–154
Logical positivism, 153–154
Luckmann, Thomas, 214
Luther, Martin, 37, 129, 146, 223

Magic, 199–200
Mahayana Buddhists, 95, 113–114
Malinowski, Bronislaw, 200
Mana, 77, 197
Mantras, 54
Marrett, Robert R., 197
Marx, Karl, 133, 134, 218
Masai initiation rites, 56–57
Maslow, Abraham, 117
May, Rollo, 212
Means to ultimate transformation,
    2–3, 21–22, 23–24
    see also Ultimate
        reality/transformation
Mencius, 74
Methodological assumptions, 15, 16
Micah, 113
Miki, 26
Mind steadiness, 93
Monotheism, 195
Mowrer, O. H., 117, 122
Mueller, F. Max, 195–196, 222
Muhammad, 38
Multiple religious forms, 201–202
Music, 164–165, 167
Muslims. See Islam
Muzzey, D. S., 72
Mystical experience, 99, 243
Myth, 43–44
    in Greek religion, 72
    ultimate transformation and,
        49–53

Nagarjuna, 149
Native American purification, 51–52
Nielsen, Kai, 105, 106
Nishitani, Keiji, 261–262
Nonattachment, 93–96
Northrop, F. S. C., 155
Novitiates, 113

Objectivity in commitment, 256–257
Obligations, 125–126

Oglala Sioux, 58
Oklahoma Creek Indians, 52
Organic whole, 68
Organization of book, 23–24
Original mind, 89
Origins of religious life, 193–206
Otto, Rudolf, 226–227

Panikkar, Raimundo, 242–243
Passover, 49–50
Pastoral care, 111–113
Pattern of meaning, 4–5
Pentecostal churches, 39
Perennial philosophy, 238–239
Perls, Fritz, 119–120
Personal apprehension of the Holy
    Presence, 22, 25–42
Personal expression, 3–5, 135–136
    artistic creativity and, 169–170
    Cosmic Law and, 78–79
    defined, 24
    ethical orientation and, 136–137
    genetic control and, 186
    Holy Presence and, 32–34
    human relationships and, 120–121
    rationality and, 154–155
    sacred symbols and, 44, 55–56
    spiritual discipline and, 97–99
Personhood, reality of, 244–245
Pettazzoni, Raffaele, 201
Peyote ceremony, 111
Phenomenology, 223, 226–229
Philosophy, 155
Physical existence, 174–189
Plato, 130–131, 178–179
Poetry, 168
Political freedom, 134
Polytheism, 195
Prayer, 25, 30, 36
Prehistoric religion, 202
Priests, 57–58, 111–113
Primal energy, 177–178
Primitive mentality, 198–199
Principle of uncertainity
    (Heisenberg), 183
Process of change, 2, 11
Profane world, 45–46
Protestant Reformation, 146
Protestantism
    ethical imperatives, 129
    and slavery, 134
Psychological bondage, 88–90
Psychological functions, 207–221
Psychotherapy, 117–120
Puberty rites, 56–57
Pure consciousness, 90–92
Pure heart, 128
Pure-impure notion, 46
Purification rituals, 51–52, 94

Qur'an, 53
    God's recitation in, 147

Radhakrishnan, Sarvapali, 63, 239
Rational-ethical humanist dialogue,
    239–241

Rationality, 141–158
  as grace, 151
  history of, 152–154
  interreligious dialogue, 239–241
  and knowledge, 148–149
  religious standards and, 146–148
  in traditional religion, 145–149
  ultimate transformation and,
    149–154
Reductionist view, 252–253
Reinterpretation of religion, 253
Religion
  defined, 1–3
  dimensions of, 3–9
  focus of, 231
  origins of, 193–206
  study of, 9–15
Religious pluralism, 251–254
Revelation, 8, 145–146
Rig Veda, 32, 81
Right action, 78
Righteousness, 126
Rituals, 178
  anthropological study of, 216–217
  of civil religion, 215
  funeral ritual, 75
  psychology of, 210
  puberty and initiation, 56–57
  ultimate transformation and,
    49–53
Robotics, 185
Rogers, Carl, 117–118, 119
Russian Revolution, 134

Sacred, awareness of, 228
Sacred people, 57–58
Sacred places, 58–59
Sacred realm, 46–48
Sacred ritual, 49–53
Sacred symbols, 43–62
Sacred time, 59
St. Sebastian, 160, 161
St. Theresa, 25
Salat, 55
Samskaras, 51
Savior, 34
Schmidt, Wilhelm, 200–201
Scientific world view, 180–186
Secularization, 215–216
Self-affirmation, 212
Self-awareness, 10–11, 261
Self-fulfillment, 208
Sentiment, 211
Shankara, 97–98
Shibayama, Abbot Zenkei, 81, 84,
  223
Shinto, 177
Shiva, 58–59
Smart, Ninian, 231
Smith, Huston, 239

Smith, Joseph, 25, 39, 142
Smith, Wilfred C., 229, 230, 242
Social expression, 24
  Cosmic Law and, 80–81
  creativity and, 169
  ethics and, 136–137
  genetic engineering and, 185–186
  and Holy Presence, 38–40
  human relationships and, 120–121
  insight and, 99–101
  rationality and, 155
  sacred symbols and, 44, 56–59
  spiritual discipline and, 99–101
Social functions, 207–221
Social gospel movement, 77–78, 129
Social identity, 198
Social justice, 134
Social order, 128
Social-political revolution, 132–138
Social responsibility, 124–140
Socialism, 134
Sociology, 213–216
Socrates, 130–131
Spinoza, 153
Spiritual adept, 100
Spiritual discipline, 84–103
Spiritual reunion, 97–98
Sri Aurobindo, 84–85, 93, 99
Sri Ramakrishna, 25–26
Structuralism, 217
Studying religion, 9–15
Subconscious, 210
Subjectivity in commitment, 256–257
Sunni Islam, 128
Supreme God, 198
Sutras, 147
Symbolic transformation, 64
Symbols
  sacred, 43–62
  of unity, 259

Tabus, 77
T'ang, Chün-i, 63–64, 259–261
Tao, 69–71, 73–75
Tao Te Ching, 89–90, 91, 96
Taoism, 85, 96
Technology, 182–186
Thanksgiving, 36
Therapeutic techniques, 117–120
Tillich, Paul, 148, 149, 258–259
Time, 59, 176–179
Totemism, 198, 199–200
Traditional religion
  ethics in, 128–130
  human relationships in, 111–114
  interreligious dialogue and, 241
  rationality in, 145–149
Transformation, processes of
  charts of, 4, 27, 45, 65, 87, 115,
    135, 151, 167, 184

  see also Means to ultimate
    transformation
Transhumanism, 107
Truth, 150–151
Tylor, Edward Burnett, 196–197

Ultimate dimension, 3, 7–9
Ultimate reality/transformation, 2, 3,
  23–24
  chart of process, 4
  Cosmic Law and, 67–78
  culture and, 6
  defined, 23
  dynamics of, 106
  Holy Presence and, 29–34
  human relationships and, 114–120
  as integrated self, 116
  interreligious dialogue and,
    237–244
  myth and, 49–53
  reason and, 149–154
  sacred realm and, 46–48
  sacred symbols and, 44, 45, 48–55
  science and, 182–186
  social-political revolution to,
    132–138
  spiritual discipline and, 90–96
Ultimate values, 8, 11
Union, 97–98
Unity of all meaning, 259
Universal dimension, 10
Universal moral nature, 72–73
Upanāyana, 51
Upanishads, 91–92

Values
  dialogue and, 244–245
  ultimate value, 8, 11
van der Leeuw, Gerardus, 226,
  227–228
Vedic religion, 58
Visions, 25–26
Visual images, 39–40

Wach, Joachim, 214–215, 229–230
Weber, Max, 214
Wesley, John, 35, 129
Whitehead, Alfred N., 152, 240
Wisdom, 84–85, 91–92
Witnessing, 38–39
Words, 53–55, 142–145
Worship, 35–36

Yin/yang, 70
Yoga, 84–85
  eternal self, 99
  spiritual discipline and, 92–93

Zaehner, Robert C., 243–244